BUILDINGS OF ALASKA

SOCIETY OF ARCHITECTURAL HISTORIANS

BUILDINGS OF THE UNITED STATES

Buildings of

ALASKA

ALISON K. HOAGLAND

New York   Oxford
OXFORD UNIVERSITY PRESS
1993

Buildings of the United States is a series of books on American
architecture complied and written on a state-by-state basis. The primary objective
of the series is to identify and celebrate the rich cultural, economic, and geographical diversity
of the United States as it is reflected in the architecture of each state. The series has been commissioned
by the Society of Architectural Historians, an organization devoted to the study, interpretation,
and preservation of the built environment throughout the world.

OXFORD UNIVERSITY PRESS

Oxford   New York
Athens   Auckland   Bangkok   Bombay
Calcutta   Cape Town   Dar es Salaam   Delhi
Florence   Hong Kong   Istanbul   Karachi
Kuala Lumpur   Madras   Madrid   Melbourne
Mexico City   Nairobi   Paris   Singapore
Taipei   Tokyo   Toronto
and associated companies in
Berlin   Ibadan

First published in 1993 by Oxford University Press, Inc.,
200 Madison Avenue, New York, New York 10016

First issued as an Oxford University Press paperback, 1994

Oxford is a registered trademark of Oxford University Press

Buildings of Alaska has been supported, in part, by grants from
the National Endowment for the Humanities, an independent federal agency,
and the Graham Foundation for Advanced Studies in the Fine Arts.

LIBRARY OF CONGRESS CATALOGING-IN-PUBLICATION DATA
Hoagland, Alison K., 1951–
Buildings of Alaska / Alison K. Hoagland.
p.   cm.—(Buildings of the United States)
At head of title: Society of Architectural Historians
Includes bibliographical references and index.
ISBN 0-19-507363-0
ISBN 0-19-509380-1 (PBK.)
1. Architecture—Alaska—Themes, motives. I. Society of
Architectural Historians. II. Title. III. Series.
NA730.A4H63   1993
720'.9798—dc20   92-46463

10 9 8 7 6 5 4 3 2 1

Printed in the United States of America
on acid-free paper

Foreword

It is with pride and pleasure that the Society of Architectural Historians presents this volume to the public. It is among the first in the monumental series, Buildings of the United States, undertaken by the Society.

Buildings of the United States is a nationwide effort, indeed a national one. Heretofore, the United States was the only major country of the Western world that had not produced a publication project dealing with its architectural heritage on a national scale. In overall concept, Buildings of the United States is to a degree modeled on and inspired by The Buildings of England, the series of forty-six volumes conceived and carried out on a county-by-county basis by the eminent English architectural historian Nikolaus Pevsner, first published between 1951 and 1974. It was Pevsner himself who—years ago, but again and again—urged his American colleagues in the Society of Architectural Historians to do the same for this country. In method and approach, of course, that challenge was to be as different from The Buildings of England as American architecture is different from English. Here we are dealing with a vast land of immense regional, geographic, climatic, and ethnic diversity, with an architectural history—wide-ranging, exciting, sometimes dramatic, as it is—essentially compressed into three hundred years; Pevsner, on the other hand, was confronted by a coherent culture on a relatively small island with an architectural history that spans over two thousand years. In contrast to the national integrity of English architecture, therefore, American architecture is marked by a dynamic heterogeneity, a heterogeneity woven of a thousand strands of originality, or, actually, a unity woven of a thousand strands of heterogeneity. It is this quality that Buildings of the United States will reflect and record.

Unity born of heterogeneity was a condition of American architecture from the beginning. Not only did the buildings of the Russian, English, Spanish, French, and Dutch colonies differ according to national origin, in the transformation process they also assumed a special scale and character, qualities that were largely determined by the aspirations and traditions of a people struggling to fashion a new world in a demanding but abundant land. Diversity even marked the English colonies of the Eastern Seaboard, though they shared a common architectural heritage. The brick mutations of the English prototypes in the Virginia Colony were very different from the wooden architecture of the Massachusetts Bay Colony: they were different because Virginia was a plantation society dominated by the Anglican church, while Massachusetts was a communal society nurtured entirely by Puritanism. As the colonies became a nation and developed westward, similar radical contrasts became the way of America's growth. The infinite variety of physical environment, together with the complex origins and motivations of the settlers, made it inevitable that each new state would have a character uniquely its own.

This dynamic diversity is the foundation of Buildings of the United States. The primary objective of each volume will be to record, to analyze, and to evaluate the architecture of the state. All of the authors are trained architectural historians who are thoroughly informed in the local aspects of their subjects. In developing the narrative, those special conditions that shaped the state, together with the building types necessary to meet those conditions, will be identified and discussed: barns, silos, mining buildings, factories, warehouses, bridges, and transportation buildings will take their place with the familiar building types conventional to the nation as a whole—churches, courthouses, city halls, and the infinite variety of domestic architecture. Although the great national and international masters of American architecture will receive proper attention, especially in those volumes for the states in which they did their greatest work, outstanding local architects, as well as the buildings of skilled but often anonymous carpenter-builders, will also be brought prominently into the picture. Each volume will thus be a detailed and precise portrait of the architecture of the state that it represents. At the same time, however, all of these local issues will be examined as they relate to the architectural developments in the country at large. When completed, therefore, the series will be a comprehensive history of the architecture of the United States.

The series was long in the planning. Indeed, the idea was conceived by Turpin Bannister, the first president of the Society of Architectural Historians (1940–1942). It was thirty years, however, before the society had grown sufficiently in strength to consider such a project. This happened when Alan Gowans, during his presidency (1972–1974), drew up a proposal and made the first of several unsuccessful attempts to raise the funds. The issue was raised again during the presidency of Marian C. Donnelly, when William H. Jordy and William H. Pierson, Jr., suggested to the board of directors that such a project should be the society's contribution to the nation's bicentennial celebration. It was not until 1986, however, after several failed attempts, that a substantial grant from the National Endowment for the Humanities, which was matched by grants from the Pew Charitable Trusts and the Graham Foundation, made the dream a reality. The activities that led to final success took place under the successive presidencies of Adolf K. Placzek (1978–1980), David Gebhard (1980–1982), Damie Stillman (1982–1984), and Carol Krinsky (1984–1986). Development and production of the first books has continued under those of Osmund Overby (1986–1988), Richard Betts (1988–1990), and Elisabeth Blair MacDougall (1990–1993). And all the while, there was David Bahlman, executive director of the SAH at the headquarters of the society in Philadelphia. In New York were Barbara Chernow and George A. Vallasi of Chernow Editorial Services, Inc., who were valuable resources during the initial stages of the project. A fine board of editors was established, with representatives from the

American Institute of Architects, the Historic American Buildings Survey, and the Library of Congress. These first volumes have now been seen through production thanks to the very able work of the managing editor, Susan M. Denny, who joined the project in 1991. Buildings of the United States is now part of the official mission of the Society of Architectural Historians, incorporated into its bylaws.

In the development of this project, we have incurred a number of obligations. We are deeply indebted, both for financial support and for confidence in our efforts, to the National Endowment for the Humanities and the Graham Foundation for Advanced Studies in the Fine Arts. We would also like to express our gratitude to a number of individuals. First among these is Dorothy Wartenberg, formerly of the Interpretive Research Program of the NEH, who was particularly helpful at the beginning, and our current program officer, David Wise. For the conceptual and practical development of the project, profound thanks go to the current members of the editorial board, listed earlier in this volume, and the following former members: the late Sally Kress Tompkins, the late Alex Cochran, Catherine W. Bishir, S. Allen Chambers, Jr., John Freeman, Alan Gowans, Robert Kapsch, and Tom Martinson. Next are our present and former project assistants—Preston Thayer, Marc Vincent, and Robert Wojtowicz. And there are the two previous executive directors of the society, the late Rosann Berry and Paulette Olson Jorgensen. The Dean of the College of Arts and Science at the University of Missouri–Columbia supported the work of a graduate research assistant. The maps in this volume were prepared by the computer cartographers at the Geographic Resources Center in the Department of Geography at the University of Missouri–Columbia, thanks to the effort and ability of Christopher Salter, director of GRC, Timothy Haithcoat, program director, and Karen Stange Westin and Pamela Huebner, project coordinators. Finally, thanks are due to our loyal colleagues in this enterprise at Oxford University Press in New York, especially Ed Barry, Claude Conyers, Marion Osmun, Stephen Chasteen, and Leslie Phillips.

The volumes, state by state, will continue to appear until every state in the Union has its own and the overview and inventory of American architecture is completed. The volumes will vary in length, and some states will require two volumes, but no state will be left out!

It must be said, regretfully, that not every building of merit can be included. Practical considerations have dictated some difficult choices in the buildings that are represented. There had to be some omissions from the abundance of structures built across the land, the thousands of modest but lovely edifices, often rising out of a sea of ugliness, or the vernacular attempts that merit a second look but that by their very multitude cannot be included in even the thickest volume. On the other hand, it must be emphasized that these volumes deal with more than the highlights and the high points. They deal with the very fabric of American architecture, with the context in time and in place of each specific building, with the entirety of urban and rural America, with the whole architectural patrimony. This fabric of course includes modern architecture, as, on the other end of the scale, it includes pre-Columbian and Native American remains.

As to architectural style, it was our most earnest intent to establish as much as possible a consistent terminology of architectural history: the name of J. A. Chewning, mastermind of our glossaries, must be gratefully mentioned here. The *Art and Architecture Thesaurus*, a comprehensive publication and database compiled by The Getty Art History Information Program and published by Oxford University Press, has also become an invaluable resource.

Finally, it must also be stated in the strongest possible terms that omission of a building from this or any volume of the series does not constitute an invitation to the bulldozers and the wrecking ball. In every community there will be structures not included in Buildings of the United States that are clearly deserving of being preserved. Indeed, it is hoped that the publication of this series will help to stop at least the worst destruction of architecture across the land by fostering a deeper appreciation of its beauty and richness and of its historic and associative importance.

The volumes of Buildings of the United States are intended as guidebooks as well as reference books and are designed to facilitate such use: they can and should be used on the spot, indeed should lead the user to the spot. But they are also meant to be tools of serious research in the study of American architecture. It is our earnest hope that they will not only be on the shelves of every major library under "U.S." but that they will also be in many a glove compartment and perhaps even in many a rucksack.

ADOLF K. PLACZEK
WILLIAM H. PIERSON, JR.
OSMUND OVERBY

Acknowledgments

I first went to Alaska in my capacity as a historian for the Historic American Buildings Survey in 1982, and my first debt of gratitude goes to those who arranged and enabled that trip: Robert L. Spude, Leslie Starr Hart, and Robert J. Kapsch. In subsequent years I always enjoyed working with the National Park Service staff members in the Anchorage office, in the parks, and on Alaskan HABS/HAER teams and am privileged to regard some of them as my friends.

Particularly helpful in this current endeavor were Steven Peterson and Russell Sackett, who provided a stream of suggestions and insights. The state's preservation office opened its files and offered ideas; I am grateful to Judy Bittner, Joan Antonson, and Donna Lane. I taxed the patience of more librarians and archivists than I can mention here, but I appreciate their suggestions and assistance. For ideas on contemporary architecture, I interviewed a number of architects, including Edwin B. Crittenden, Wayne Jensen, Bryce Klug, Thomas Livingston, Kenneth Maynard, Paul Voelckers, and Jeffery Wilson. Alaska Airlines provided some relief from the air fares.

Back in Washington, my thanks go to Bob Kapsch for letting me out of my job for a year and to Sara Leach, Gray Fitzsimons, and Kim Wallace for filling in behind me. During the fieldwork I was happy to be accompanied briefly by some knowledgeable newcomers to Alaska; I want to thank Gray Fitzsimons and Lynne Monroe for bringing an aura of wonder and for reminding me what was different about the place. Many people were kind enough to read drafts of all or part of this manuscript. I am particularly indebted to S. Allen Chambers for encouragement in the beginning and Catherine Bishir for some late-inning enthusiasm. Other readers to whom I owe thanks include Jo Antonson, Katherine Arndt, Donna Lane, Georgeanne Reynolds, Russ Sackett, Barbara Smith, and Bob Spude. William H. Pierson, Robert Winter, and Osmund Overby were some of the few who made it through the entire manuscript; I am grateful for their reading. I especially appreciate Ozzie for his fresh approach to the fieldwork and for his cogent suggestions at all levels of the production and Susan Denny for her persistent cheerfulness while editing multiple drafts.

Special thanks to two more people, whose skill in the field is exceeded only by their geniality: Jet Lowe, HABS/HAER photographer, whose appreciation for Alaska is reflected in these photographs, and Jean Swearingen, who endured me as a houseguest far longer than she should have and whose enthusiasm is contagious and unending.

The inclusion or exclusion of specific buildings may be a matter of some debate, but their appearance in this volume is not meant to confer honorific status. Rather, they were selected for specific points of architectural history that they illustrate, for their accessibility to and likelihood of being visited by the reader, and for the author's ability to visit them, which sometimes depended on a quirk of fate. The foundation for these entries, both their selection and interpretation, lies in surveys and nominations undertaken or supervised by the state historic preservation office and the National Park Service. This initial list was supplemented by determined searches, casual conversations, and documentary research. Although based on surveys, this guidebook is not a survey itself, and selections are intended to be representative rather than all-inclusive.

While it is impossible to see much of the state in any one visit, the very size of the place should not be discouraging. Alaska is at least six states in one, each an equally rewarding discovery. The architecture stands as signposts along the way, pointing to the people who built the place, their cultural influences and aspirations, and how they lived in a majestic and awe-inspiring land.

Although I had previously spent several seasons in Alaska, traveling 20,000 miles in the state in the summer of 1990 was an unforgettable experience. I was impressed not only by the natural splendors and variety of architecture but also by the people I met, whose great pride in their place is revealed in their hospitality. My deepest thanks and respect go to those who build, inhabit, and appreciate the buildings of Alaska.

ALISON K. HOAGLAND

Contents

List of Maps

Guide for Users of This Volume

Buildings of Alaska is arranged in two parts. The first section is an introduction to the history of the area and the way its built structures relate to the people who lived in the region. The second part of the book is a guidebook.

Readers who are traveling to Alaska will probably need additional guidebooks that explain the logistics of getting to places, available accommodations, and hours and fees of sites open to the public. Particularly valuable in this regard are two guidebooks published annually by Alaska Northwest Books, *The Milepost* (for settlements on the road and ferry systems) and *The Alaska Wilderness Milepost* (for more remote villages). For information on additional historic buildings, many towns distribute a walking tour guide, usually available at the visitor information center. Sites open to the public also provide maps and other specific information. For additional information, see the bibliography of sources consulted (page 307).

This guidebook is organized geographically and divided into six regions. Within some of the regions, a spiral arrangement was more logical than a linear one; South-Central, Interior, and Northern are arranged this way. Thus, South-Central begins with Anchorage, in the center of town, and works out; then considers the Kenai Peninsula, Matanuska-Susitna Valleys, and Copper River and West. Interior begins with Fairbanks, working from the center of town out to nearby communities both east and west; then communities farther afield, south, west, east, and north. The Northern region is also arranged circularly, beginning with Barrow, moving southwest to Point Hope, east to Anaktuvuk Pass, and north to Prudhoe Bay. The remaining regions are organized more linearly. Southeast is arranged north to south; Western also north to south; and Southwest northeast to southwest.

Each entry begins with an identifying code, which is a two-letter abbreviation of the region and the number of the property within the region. Next are listed the date it was built, the architect, if one is known, and dates of major additions or alterations to the property. The address or specific location follows.

Detailed maps of each region and the major cities and towns are provided so that anyone with this book, *The Milepost,* and a little patience can locate the properties. The maps identify locations of specific structures by entry number, but without the regional code.

Almost all of the properties described in this book are visible from public roads or public land, or in some cases from the water. If they are not, "not visible" is noted at the end of the heading. Buildings that are open to the public are so noted at the end of the appropriate entries. Of course, we know that the readers of this book will always respect the property rights and privacy of others as they view the buildings.

BUILDINGS OF ALASKA

Introduction

ALASKA'S NATURAL SPLENDORS ARE OVERWHELMING. From the snow-covered peak of Mount McKinley to the volcanic islands of the Aleutian chain, from the expansive treeless tundra of the North Slope to the tall spruce and deep fjords of Southeast, the nature of Alaska is wild, vast, and magnificent. Humans are diminutive by comparison, and their architecture equally so.

Isolated constructions of indigenous materials in the wilderness, wood-frame bungalows in orderly small towns, or glass and metal high-rises in the cities, the buildings portray attempts to harmonize with, ignore, or tame this remote northern land. As illustrations of ways of living, the buildings reveal personal attitudes and cultural precepts, reflecting the variety of people who built them.

The history of Alaska's architecture involves three major cultural groups—Natives, Russians, and Americans. Each of these groups includes different factions, yet a basic imperative unites each of them. The Natives constructed dwellings that were most responsive to the climate, and entirely of indigenous materials. The Russians brought their horizontal log, blocklike dwellings to America; that building form was suitable for much of the area they inhabited. The Americans were possessed by the idea of the frontier even as they pretended to ignore it by building houses in forms familiar back home.

Since the earliest structures that can be documented in Alaska were built by its Native population, this introduction begins with a discussion of Eskimo, Aleut, Athapaskan Indian, and Northwest Coast Indian traditional architecture, in turn, bringing the story up to the present by discussing the evolution and disappearance of traditional dwellings in the years since contact with whites. Next, Russian settlement and architecture are described. In addition to a handful of buildings that survive from Russian times, Russian Orthodox churches continue to be built in traditional forms, and an examination of their architecture brings the Russian period to the present. The last section, on the American period, begins by describing general patterns of American building and then treats the history and architecture chronologically.

Native Alaskan Architecture

Occupying Alaska for thousands of years before Russians and Americans arrived, the Natives[1] constructed dwellings as fascinating for their similarities and differences as for their complexity. Although almost none of these structures survives, they are an important aspect of the culture of each of the Native groups. Eskimos, Aleuts, Athapaskan Indians, and Northwest Coast Indians each had a readily identifiable architecture. After the arrival of whites in Alaska, Natives were subject to many influences, which their architecture reflected: technological innovations, such as glass windows; spiritual instruction, which resulted in the construction of Russian Orthodox churches; moral inculcation by American missionaries, who insisted that Natives abandon communal habitations for single-family dwellings; and general shifts in style and fashion, which heightened the popularity of new-style dwellings. Yet there are many features of traditional dwellings that render this architecture important in the context of Alaskan history, among them the use of indigenous construction materials, their responsiveness to the climate, and their accommodation of Native culture and society.

The Eskimos, who inhabited the north and west coasts of Alaska and several hundred miles inland, constructed semisubterranean dwellings out of sod, driftwood, and whalebone—not snow—and added long entrance tunnels to trap cold air. The Aleuts, occupying the volcanic Aleutian Chain, built large semi-subterranean dwellings that were entered through a hole in the roof. The Athapaskan Indians, living the highly mobile life of hunters and fishermen in the Interior, built moss- or bark-covered structures or portable willow-frame, skin-covered tents, while the Northwest Coast groups, fishermen in the resource-rich Southeast, constructed highly sophisticated plank dwellings ornamented with carvings and paintings. These identifiable forms varied, however, influenced by different climates, available materials, and neighboring groups. The following discussion of Native architecture is much simplified; determinants of building form, such as patterns of subsistence and cultural traditions, are only alluded to here. Although presented here as static, pre-contact architecture changed over time, just as it did after contact with whites.

The first people arrived in Alaska some time before 10,000 B.P.[2] Migrating from Siberia either on sea ice in winter or by boat, these people spread throughout North America. In Alaska, they developed, slowly, into four major groups: Eskimos, Aleuts, Athapaskan Indians, and Northwest Coast Indians.

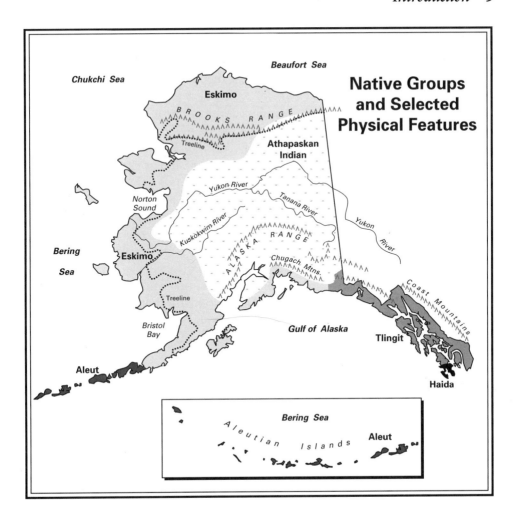

Native Groups and Selected Physical Features

Within these groups there are further divisions, usually determined by language.

ESKIMOS

The igloo, a domical structure made of snow blocks and strongly identified with the Eskimo, does not exist in Alaska and never has, except as a temporary, emergency structure. Central Eskimos, residing in Canada, lay claim to this snow structure. *Igloo* is, however, a general Eskimo term for house, and of these Alaskan Eskimos have a wide variety. The basic form is a semisubterranean structure, framed with driftwood or whalebones and covered with sod, with a tunnel entrance.

Culturally, Eskimos are usually categorized by their language, which falls into two branches: Inupiaq and Yupik. Inupiaq is spoken by North Alaskan Eskimos, and Yupik by three groups south of Norton Sound: Bering Sea, Siberian (of which Saint Lawrence Islanders are the only Alaskan example), and Pacific Eskimos.[3] The latter are closely aligned with the Aleut culture and will be considered in the next section.

Climatically, the Eskimos are strongly identified with the Arctic, a region narrowly defined as north of the Arctic Circle. A more appropriate identification would be with the region beyond the tree line. This provides a visual demarcation that coincides with most—but not all—of the area that the Eskimos inhabit. Although treeless, the area is served by rivers originating in timbered regions, which bring driftwood with them. The climate is cold, with very cold winters and cool summers. Along the Arctic coast, nearly three months of full daylight in the summer are complemented by nearly three months of full darkness in the winter. The land is mostly a coastal plain composed of tundra, moisture-retaining soils in which mosses, lichens, and grasses grow. Frozen nine to ten months of the year in the north, the tundra turns to bog in the summer; the underlying permafrost permits no drainage. The tundra in summer is nearly impassable, but in winter, with the help of sleds and snowshoes, it is more easily traversed. The Eskimos domesticated the indigenous malamute dog for assistance in pulling sleds.

For the most part, Eskimos settled on the coast, on rivers, and in the foothills on the north slope of the Brooks Range. They sought high ground, which would give them protection from flooding and ice and also provide an opportunity to spot game and invaders. Villages were usually arranged informally, either clustered around the men's house or in family groupings.

Most of the Eskimos had a central base and traveled seasonally searching for game and fish. This pattern ranged from caribou hunters of inland North Alaska, who moved several times a year, to whalers on the North Alaskan coast, who had large, permanent villages. Bering Sea hunters and fishermen were more nomadic than the whalers but less so than the caribou hunters. Although difficult to determine, the size of the base villages reflected the permanence: some villages of the North Alaskan coastal Eskimos might have had five hundred occupants, while those of the caribou hunters were usually less than one hundred.[4]

Coastal North Alaskan Eskimos built semisubterranean dwellings with long entrance passages. Walls were constructed of vertical driftwood planks or whalebones and covered with sod, mounded to conceal the shape of the framework; plank-covered floors were several feet below ground level. The gable roof had a ridgepole; the front of the roof had an opening covered with seal gut to provide light. The dwelling, which measured about 10 feet by 14 feet on the interior, was entered through the long tunnel, 4 or 4 1/2 feet high, which served as a cold trap. On either side of the underground tunnel were separate areas for cooking and storage. The tunnel surfaced in the house, where

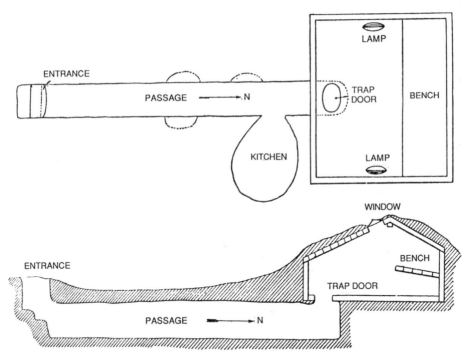

Plan and section of an Eskimo dwelling, as found by John Murdoch at Point Barrow in 1887–1888. The tunnel entrance traps cold air, and sod covers the dwelling, insulating it.

a wide bench along the rear wall provided space for sleeping or sitting. The interior was heated with a soapstone or pottery lamp that burned seal oil; body heat also contributed a significant amount of warmth.[5] In fact, the dwellings were so warm that the inhabitants usually removed most of their clothes while inside. This basic structure could vary in a number of ways—size, existence of a fireplace, roof framing, depth of the tunnel, and bench position.

For most Alaskan Eskimos, the household was the basic economic unit. Composed of an extended family of several generations or of two related families, it ranged in size from eight to twelve people among the North Alaskans to slightly more among the Bering Sea Eskimos. Accordingly, Bering Sea Eskimo dwellings were larger, measuring about 15 feet square. Primarily because of the availability of fuel for heat and the less extreme temperatures as well as household size, dwellings toward the south tended to be larger.[6]

The dwellings of the North Alaskan Eskimos around Kotzebue Sound had fireplaces, as did most dwellings to the south; the bleak environment of the north coast provided little firewood and precluded this luxury. A stone-lined fireplace occupied the center of the living area and was vented through a hole in the roof. In 1866, Frederick Whymper, an artist with the Western Union Telegraph Expedition, visited a village on the lower Yukon, and noted:

In summer, the dwellings resemble grassy mounds. Whalebones lie in the foreground and ships sit on the water beyond in this photograph taken at Barrow in 1923.

> The fire was built on the floor in the centre of the chamber, and when it burned low the embers and sticks were always thrown out of the smoke-hole in the roof by the natives inside, and it was then covered with a skin. This process effectually shut in all the warmth, but with it a good deal of smoke and carbonic acid gas. The entrance-hole was also usually covered with a deer-skin, and the mixture of close smells inside the house, arising from more or less stale fish, meat, old skin clothes, young dogs, dirt, and smoke, was very sickening. The dogs scrambling and fighting on the roof above, sometimes tumbled through the smoke-hole on the fire below, upsetting all the cooking arrangements, and adding a new smell to those above mentioned—that of singed hair! It need not be said that they retreated with great alacrity, yelping and snarling as they went.[7]

In contrast to the gable roofs of the North Alaskan Eskimos, Eskimos in the Kotzebue Sound area placed four posts near the center of the structure to support stringers. They set four corner posts to support additional stringers and laid planks from one to the other.[8] The Bering Sea Eskimos also used this roof design, as well as one that was cribbed.

The location of benches was affected by tunnels and fireplaces. Benches stood several feet above the floor if the tunnels were not deep, or if there were no fireplace. Bering Sea Eskimo houses had low benches on the side walls and sometimes on the rear wall, a short shallow tunnel, and a fireplace.[9] The dwellings of the Kotzebue Sound North Alaskan Eskimos had a plan distinctive among Alaskan Eskimos: the main living area adjoined one to three sleeping alcoves.[10]

The interior of the dwelling pictured on p. 7, looking toward the entrance, which is a hole in the floor. Above it is a membrane-covered skylight.

Inland North Alaskan Eskimos, who subsisted on caribou, had less permanent settlements. Not only did they move from summer to winter quarters and back again, but the nature of their subsistence required a larger move every decade or so. As a result, they did not excavate their winter dwellings. They built dwellings with four center posts and short, flat-roofed entryways,[11] and they used several different plans. Two families might share a dwelling, in which case there would be two apartments reached from a common tunnel, or separate tunnels leading to adjoining apartments.[12] For temporary structures, inland North Alaskan Eskimos built large, dome-shaped tents, whereas the coastal North Alaskan Eskimos erected small, conical tents.

The most important structure in any Eskimo village was the kashim, or men's house. The presence of a kashim denoted a village, and larger villages had more than one. There, the men of the village congregated to make decisions, repair their boats, take baths, and, in some societies, to eat and sleep. They were also used for dances and ceremonies, and visitors were usually feasted and housed there. Frederick Whymper described some of the many uses:

> In the village at Unalachleet, as in most others of the coast, there are buildings set apart for dances and gatherings of the people; at other times, indeed, they are used for occupations requiring space, as the manufacture of sledges or snow-shoes. These buildings may be regarded as the natives' town-hall; orations are made, festivals and feasts are held in them, and the passing stranger is sometimes accommodated in them, as in an Eastern *caravansary.*[13]

Among the coastal North Alaskan Eskimos, the kashim was occupied by whaling crews during the whaling season.[14] In the permanent villages of the Bering Sea Eskimos, men and boys lived in the kashim, being served their meals by the women, who lived in the family houses. In its construction, a kashim was similar to a family dwelling, only larger, ranging from 12 feet to 25 feet square.

Another structure found in most Eskimo villages was the storehouse. Along the northern coast, there were storage alcoves in the tunnel of the house, a meat cellar nearby, and a storage rack in back of the house. South of Norton Sound, however, the storehouses were often elevated wooden structures, known throughout Alaska today as caches. Four posts stuck in the ground elevated the 10-foot or 12-foot square structure about 5 feet; the flooring projected beyond the walls, providing an outdoor platform for storage of sleds and kayaks; the enclosed portion served as storage for food and perishables. More elaborate examples, constructed where wood was plentiful, were higher (6 feet to 8 feet tall), had vertical wood plank walls on front and rear, horizontal planks on the sides, and a gable roof.[15] In addition, most villages had storage racks to elevate sleds and kayaks, keeping the rawhide covers and lashings out of reach of the dogs.

Culturally and linguistically, the Natives of Saint Lawrence Island belong to the Siberian Eskimo group; their architecture reflects that heritage. For reasons not yet clear, their dwellings changed form drastically during the nineteenth century. Early in the century, Saint Lawrence Islanders lived in semisubterranean, sod-covered dwellings, often framed with whalebones, and reached through a passageway. By the twentieth century, these dwellings had been replaced by

By 1898 on Saint Lawrence Island, Eskimos were building large, skin-covered, plank-walled dwellings unlike any others in Alaska.

Eskimos on Little Diomede Island used available materials to build some of the few stone-covered dwellings in Alaska.

Photographed in 1913, the dwellings of the King Island Eskimos were supported by poles to accommodate the steep terrain.

a distinctively Siberian, skin-covered structure of driftwood slabs stood on end and chinked to form a wall. The plan was an "oblong octagon,"[16] and the roof had a ridgepole supported by two posts, four center posts (for larger structures), or no ridgepole at all (for smaller ones). The rafters were tied to the ridgepole or clustered together and covered with tightly stretched walrus hides, weighed down by stones, driftwood, and bones. The interior measured 7 feet to 8 feet wide by 10 feet to 18 feet long.[17]

The Natives of the Diomede Islands belong to the North Alaskan Eskimo grouping and to two countries; Big Diomede Island is today in Russia. Little Diomede Island is covered with boulders, which were used in the construction of the houses. The roof was framed by four corner posts supporting beams; the floor and walls were driftwood planks. The dwelling was insulated by a layer of sod, which was then covered with stones. Access to the dwelling was through an underground passage that was lined with stones and braced by timbers.[18]

The Natives of King Island are also North Alaskan Eskimos with distinctive building forms. Their winter dwellings were covered with stones in a manner similar to those on Little Diomede Island, but their summer dwellings were built on poles, set on the steep cliffs of the island. Poles that were 10 feet to 20 feet long supported a platform, the rear of which rested on shorter poles or on the sharply sloping ground. On this platform was a walrus-skin tent. Generally square in shape, with a flat roof, the dwelling had two rooms, a storeroom measuring 16 feet by 10 feet in front of a living room measuring 7 feet by 8 feet, which was plank lined. An insulating layer of moss was placed between the plank interior and the walrus-skin exterior.[19]

ALEUTS

The barabara, a semisubterranean dwelling with entrance through the roof, is the creation of the Aleuts, who inhabit the Aleutian Chain. Severe depletion of their numbers, disruption of their society, and relocation of their villages by Russian traders in the eighteenth century make the Aleut pre-contact culture difficult to interpret. Some Pacific Eskimos also identify themselves as Aleut. Of the Pacific Eskimos, most is known about the Koniag, who inhabited the island of Kodiak and the Alaska Peninsula, and the Chugach, of Prince William Sound.

The Aleutian Chain, Alaska Peninsula, and much of Kodiak Island are beyond the tree line, an extremely rugged, volcanic land, whereas the land abutting Cook Inlet and Prince William Sound is forested. The Aleuts and Pacific Eskimos tended to inhabit coastal lands, or occasionally sites on rivers. They derived most, if not all, of their subsistence from the water. Accordingly, they settled near good landings, such as gravel beaches. The Koniag had some of the largest settlements in the region, of up to five hundred people.

Reached through a hole in the roof, the Aleut barabara housed several families. This barabara was drawn in 1778 by John Webber, who was traveling with the British explorer Capt. James Cook.

Resembling a grassy mound from the exterior, the Aleuts' barabara was one of the largest dwellings among Alaska Natives, ranging from 70 feet to over 200 feet in length and over 30 feet wide.[20] In an oblong or rectangular shape, the barabara had a rough post-and-beam construction, which was then covered with sod. The dwelling was excavated 3 feet or 4 feet, and access was through a hole in the roof, then down a notched pole serving as a ladder. The center of the barabara was a communal space, as several related families occupied the dwelling; along the sides, cubicles housed individual families. Stone seal oil lamps were used for heat and light. Fires for cooking were outside.

The Koniag constructed similar dwellings, but with a side entrance. Two to four rooms housed individual families, substituting for the cubicles.[21] There was a fireplace in the common area, and sometimes in the smaller rooms as well. The Chugach constructed plank houses, similar to the Northwest Coast Indians, who were their neighbors to the east, but divided them as the Koniag did, with a central common room and private compartments.[22]

Like other Eskimos, the Koniag built kashims, or larger ceremonial houses. The Aleuts used their large barabaras for ceremonial gatherings. Summer dwellings were makeshift structures.[23]

ATHAPASKAN INDIANS

Linguistically related to the Navajos and Apaches of the American Southwest, the Northern Athapaskans occupy much of the Interior Region of Alaska and western Canada. In Alaska today there are eleven linguistic groups. Only one of the Alaskan Athapaskan groups lived along the coast at the time of European contact—the Tanaina of Cook Inlet. The others were based inland, in a hilly and mountainous land of coniferous forests, laced with rivers and interspersed with wide-open tundra; it is also an area of extreme temperatures. Athapaskans subsisted on caribou and salmon. Highly mobile because of their hunter-gatherer nature, the Athapaskans built simple structures with forms often influenced by their neighbors. Among the Athapaskans, the more sedentary the group, the more complex its architecture.

The Han Indians, based along the upper Yukon, built a moss-covered dwelling for their permanent house, which they occupied during the salmon run in late summer and for much of the winter. About 25 feet square, the dwelling was excavated 1 1/2 feet. Posts and beams supported a gable roof. The Han constructed walls of vertical split poles, 6 inches to 8 inches in diameter, and laid moss on the exterior of this wall, as well as on the roof. The interior contained a fireplace vented through smoke holes on either side of the ridgepole, brush for bedding, and willow mats.[24] The Tanana of the upper Tanana River and the Ahtna of the Copper River, likewise fishermen, built similar dwellings, sometimes covering them with bark.[25]

As a semipermanent or temporary shelter used for hunting in the winter, the Han Indians built an oblong hemispherical skin-covered dwelling, similar to the temporary dwelling of the inland North Alaskan Eskimo. Placed on ground where the snow had been scraped away, this dwelling was framed by spruce poles, bent toward the middle, strengthened by cross poles, and covered with caribou skins. An opening in the center of the roof emitted smoke, and there was an entrance through an opening in one end. These dwellings ranged in size from about 7 feet by 10 feet to 12 feet by 18 feet and housed two nuclear families.[26] The Kutchin and the upper Tanana, primarily hunters of large game, built similar dwellings.[27]

Neighboring Eskimo groups influenced the building forms of the Koyukon of the middle Yukon, the Ingalik of the lower Yukon and the middle Kuskokwim, and the Tanaina of Cook Inlet. In contrast to the Athapaskans, all three groups had relatively sedentary settlements, as the Koyukon and Ingalik fished and the Tanaina hunted sea mammals. Their dwellings were semisubterranean, excavated 3 feet to 4 feet, generally with entrance tunnels and fireplaces.[28]

The Athapaskans built a variety of outbuildings. The Han, Tanana, Ahtna, and Ingalik all had platform caches, similar to those of the Bering Sea Eskimos. The Ingalik also built smokehouses, similar in construction to their summer dwellings, for preserving large quantities of salmon. These smokehouses were deliberately porous to allow the salmon to dry as much as to smoke it. The smoke gathered near the rafters, where the salmon was hung, and at ground level the smokehouse was almost habitable, yet smoky enough to deter mosquitoes.[29] The Tanana had separate, domical sweathouses, constructed in much the same way as their skin- or bark-covered dwellings.[30]

NORTHWEST COAST INDIANS

The northernmost of the Northwest Coast peoples (which refers to the Northwest Coast of North America, not Alaska), the Tlingit lived in resource-rich Southeast Alaska, a heavily forested seacoast setting. The Southeast Region receives over 50 inches of precipitation annually (and in some places over 100 inches), the climate is temperate, the coastal waters remain open all winter, and there is relatively little snowfall. Five kinds of Pacific salmon spawn in the streams, providing the main subsistence. Other fish and sea mammals are abundant. A variety of fur-bearing and edible animals inhabit the woods. The Tlingit, who put up the stiffest resistance to Russian invaders, were also adept traders, valuing steel tools, Hudson's Bay blankets, and crafts of other Native groups.[31] The ease of life, compared to the more extreme climates that faced other Native groups in Alaska, allowed the Tlingit to form a highly sophisticated society that developed a complex architecture in terms of construction and carved ornamentation.

The importance of status to the Tlingit was reflected in their villages and buildings. Tlingit society—and each village—was divided into halves, the Ravens and the Wolves or Eagles. Within each half were clans; each of these was composed of several lineages or local divisions; and each of these was com-

Broad gable fronts of plank houses line the shore in the deserted Tlingit village of Cape Fox, photographed by Edward S. Curtis in 1899.

posed of several large communal households. Within the household, location in the rear of the house indicated high status, with status diminishing nearer the door.[32]

Tlingit villages were oriented toward the water, composed of a single or double row of houses, clustered by clan. Villages ranged in size from a few houses to sixty; households contained twenty-five to fifty related people.

The Tlingit constructed plank houses without pegs or nails and with roof supports largely independent of walls. Stout construction was essential to a house's role as a fortification, for the Tlingit were frequently under threat of attack. They used spruce logs for the primary supporting posts, while they split the more easily worked hemlock into thinner planks for the walls. Red cedar, which had to be imported from the Queen Charlotte Islands, might be used as a finish material by a particularly wealthy household.

Some of the best-documented examples of the plank house were those constructed by the Chilkat Tlingit, who inhabited the area at the head of Lynn Canal. The Whale House viewed by George T. Emmons in 1885 was constructed by 1835, while a similar house, drawn in detail by Louis and Florence Shotridge, was not clearly identified.[33] In both cases, the structure that supported the gable roof was almost entirely separate from the structure supporting the walls and was located within it. Four large vertical planks, set in the ground in a square about 40 feet on a side, supported two principal purlins—round logs about 2 feet in diameter. Resting on these, planks ran crosswise and supported smaller round logs, which were placed closer together and served as minor purlins. Again, these purlins supported beams, which supported the ridgepole. Rafters supported the roofing material, which consisted of planks and split shingles.

To form the walls, four heavy vertical planks were placed at corners to form a 50-foot square, and three more at the midpoints of the side and rear walls. The front wall in the gable end was composed of vertical planks, while the side and rear walls were horizontal planks.[34] The ends of the horizontal planks were tenoned, fitting into grooves that ran the length of corner and midpoint planks. The sill plate along the front wall was likewise grooved to receive the tenon at the end of each vertical plank.

The only opening in the walls was the doorway, set in the front gable facade, which faced the water. The low doorway was set several steps above the ground, forcing visitors to enter singly, in a crouching position. Often there was a platform or porch across the front. The ridgepole was discontinuous, leaving room for a smoke hole, usually covered by an adjustable windscreen.

Inside, the house had two or sometimes three stepped levels, each 2 feet or 3 feet apart. The lowest, center level was excavated 3 feet or 4 feet and contained the fire pit; except for this space, all of the floors were planked. The upper and outer level was the sleeping level, partitioned into distinct areas. Located toward the front of the house, under the platform, was a steam bath,

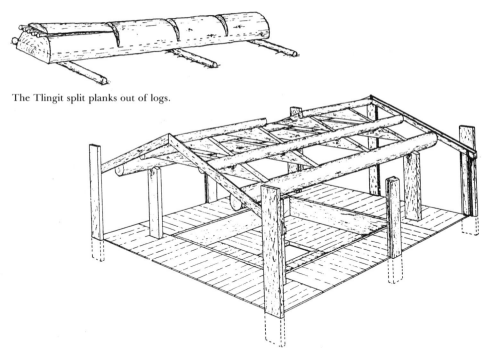

The Tlingit split planks out of logs.

An axonometric view of a Tlingit plank house showing the framing system, in which interior posts support the principal purlins. Exterior vertical planks are grooved to receive the ends of horizontal planks.

although alternatively this might be located in a separate structure. Toward the rear of the house, a screen ran between the two interior planks that supported the roof, designating the space of the chief and his immediate family.

Several parts of the house were heavily decorated with carved ornamentation in the Northwest Coast style, which featured creatures outlined and joined by form lines, covering the entire designed area. The Chilkat decorated the interiors of their houses, as seen in the Whale House at Klukwan, which Emmons called "the most widely known and elaborately ornamented house . . . in Alaska." The screen at the rear of the house was carved in low relief and painted to represent the rain spirit. A great central figure with outstretched arms, through whose belly was the entrance to the chief's apartment, was flanked by crouching figures. The planks supporting the roof were carved in high relief, each post relating a hero story about the clan or lineage.[35]

Ornamentation on the exterior of the house was not practiced much by the Chilkat but was more common among Tlingit groups farther south. The corner planks at the front of the house, which projected above the roofline, were often ornamented, and sometimes the entire front facade was decorated.[36] Totem poles, freestanding posts carved to relate legends or family history or to commemorate someone, were rare among the Chilkat and northern groups but were found more frequently among the Tlingit to the south. Unlike the neigh-

In 1895 Winter and Pond photographed the Whale House in Klukwan described by George T. Emmons. Northern Tlingit groups such as the Chilkat did not decorate the exterior of their houses, nor did they erect totem poles.

The interior of the same house displays a wealth of ornamentation, not only carved on the screen at the back of the house but also woven in the Chilkat blankets spread out for the photographer.

boring Haida, who integrated totem poles into their dwellings, the Tlingit poles were set in front of the house, to the side of the entrance.

Construction of a house was an important social event, the occasion of the naming of the chief of the new house while memorializing the dead of the old one. The house owner contracted with his opposite moiety to construct the building, whom he would then reward with a potlatch upon completion, distributing gifts in the knowledge that he would be repaid in the future, and thus solidifying social relationships. Beyond immediate social and status concerns, however, the house also reflected the cosmology of the Tlingit. The house symbolized the world, with the careful attention to status within the dwelling symbolizing the occupants' place in the world order. The square plan was akin to the planet, which was considered square; the floor represented the earth, the roof embodied the heavens, and at the center of the house, the fire pit symbolized the center of the universe. The animistic nature of Tlingit beliefs is reflected in the carved ornament, which was almost always of creatures. Entering the house, or the chief's quarters, through the belly of a carved animal symbolized rebirth.

The Chilkat house described above was the general form used by all Tlingit.[37] Most houses other than those of the chiefs were smaller, measuring about 30 feet on a side. Outbuildings included a smokehouse, important in a fishing village, which was built in the same general form as the house. The smokehouses contained two or three fireplaces, with horizontal boards suspended above to spread the smoke throughout the structure; the fish were hung to dry, as much as to smoke.[38]

The Tlingit moved to temporary fish camps in the summer. In contrast to the care they lavished on the permanent dwellings, here they built flimsy structures constructed of boards or bark, with gable roofs.[39]

Closely related to Tlingit architecture is that of the Haida, another Northwest Coast Indian group. Located primarily in the Queen Charlotte Islands of British Columbia, the Haida also occupied Prince of Wales Island in Alaska. There they built dwellings similar to the Tlingit, with gable roofs supported by interior posts, mostly independent of the wall structure. The Haida produced highly carved and painted ornamentation on their dwellings. The central totem pole in the front facade, the corner posts, and the ends of the purlins were carved and painted, although facades were rarely painted. Inside, the screen at the rear of the house and the planks that lined the interior excavation were also ornamented.[40]

A third Northwest Coast Indian group found in Alaska is the Tsimshian. They built no traditional dwellings here; they immigrated en masse from British Columbia in 1887 and built the missionary-influenced town of Metlakatla.

CHANGING ARCHITECTURAL FORMS

The near-total disappearance of traditional dwellings vividly illustrates the dramatic change that whites inflicted on Alaska.[41] As the Russians and Americans seized political control of Alaska, their cultures prevailed. While the newcomers had differing motivations, which will be discussed in the later sections of this introduction, their impact on Native architecture will be briefly examined here.

Native culture underwent fundamental transformation after contact with whites. Subsistence patterns, settlement patterns, and house forms all changed. While this was not necessarily a progression—new house types had actually appeared before any shift in subsistence—it does cover three important areas of western influence.

Some subsistence patterns changed without white influence. The Bering Strait Eskimos witnessed the disappearance of caribou from the Seward Peninsula, which might be attributed to the introduction of firearms but might also be due to natural shifts in the range of the caribou population.[42] Inland North Alaskan Eskimos, confronted with the problem of declining caribou herds, migrated to the coast, where they adopted different subsistence patterns, and later to permanent settlement in Anaktuvuk Pass, which is today the only community of these inland Eskimos.[43] Nonetheless, the trading opportunities provided by whites had a profound effect on Native subsistence throughout Alaska. The market for furs and whale products effectively removed the Natives from a strictly subsistence economy.

The Kutchin Athapaskans illustrate this shift. The fur trade in the mid-nineteenth century resulted in the establishment of trap lines, altering the Kutchins' attitudes about the land. Whereas previously the Kutchin had been highly mobile, hunting and gathering without permanent settlements, the trap lines—a set path through land that was "owned" through continuous use—necessitated a more sedentary existence. Dog teams were introduced, enabling a trapper to reach a greater area from a base camp. Gradually, trading posts developed into villages, which became permanent, winter-long habitations when schools were established. No longer would a family spend the winter out on a trap line; instead a man made shorter trips to them without his family. Larger dog teams, and finally snowmobiles, have been used to cover greater distance in shorter trips.[44]

The neighboring Han Indians, who had lived on salmon before the arrival of whites in the area, turned to hunting to provide meat and trapping to provide furs for the growing non-Native population. The Han entered the market economy and, after the 1897 Klondike gold rush to their territory, their diet shifted to one of store-bought food.[45]

Today, rural Natives depend on both subsistence—food won from the natural environment—and cash. They obtain cash from seasonal wage labor, social security, and welfare, for steady, year-round jobs are rare in rural villages.

The plank houses in the Indian village of Sitka, photographed in 1882, show little evidence of architectural change.

By 1886, new clapboarded fronts with windows and doors ornament the traditional houses in Sitka. The smoke hole covered by a wind screen indicates that traditional living patterns continue inside.

By the 1890s, new two-story clapboarded houses had replaced the traditional dwellings in Sitka.

As the subsistence pattern changed, so did the settlement pattern. Trading posts and canneries acted as magnets in the nineteenth century, and villages developed around them. In the late nineteenth and twentieth centuries, missions and schools likewise created villages. In fact, American missionaries often deliberately located missions away from Native villages to avoid intervillage rivalries and to force Natives to move and build anew.[46] The search for year-round work and higher education has drawn increasing numbers of Natives to the cities so that nearly 20 percent live in Anchorage and Fairbanks today.

Other changes in settlement patterns were responses to natural disasters. The eruption of the Katmai volcano in 1912 eradicated some villages and forced relocation of survivors, as did the 1964 earthquake.[47] On a smaller scale, the erosion of a riverbank necessitated moving a village, sometimes only several hundred yards. The village of Minto on the Tanana River was moved back from the bank several times until 1971, when the people moved to a new site 25 miles away.[48]

The dwellings changed as well. The Aleuts put windows and doors into the walls of their barabaras in the early nineteenth century.[49] They acquired Russian-type stoves for heating and cooking. As household size shrank—in part due to Russian oppression and disease—structures likewise were built smaller. A visitor to Unalaska in the late 1830s described the barabaras as being 14 feet by 21 feet with an entrance hall/storeroom and living quarters, housing one or two families,[50] whereas previously they had been 30 feet by 70 feet, housing several families. With these changes, though, the barabara survived well into the twentieth century.[51]

In the Southeast Region, the Tlingit seized upon American house forms. An 1882 photograph of the segregated Indian village of Sitka shows a village of plank houses, some with their original round openings. By 1886, the fronts of these buildings were clapboarded and had windows and doors. And just eight years later, most of these buildings had been replaced with American two-and-a-half-story buildings.

Like Sitka, the Chilkat Tlingit village of Yindastuki evolved by 1904 from plank houses to transitional dwellings to American framed houses. But until World War II, the dwellings were communally owned, were noticeably larger than American dwellings, and housed multiple families. Although two stories tall, these houses were not divided on the interior. The first floor was a large living space and the second floor an open sleeping space.[52] In Angoon, a Tlingit village bombarded by the U.S. Navy in 1882 in a tragic incident, the new houses were American in style, one and a half stories with a gable front. The plan, however, was one undivided space, and some still had central smoke holes.[53]

The introduction of the sheet-iron stove at the turn of the twentieth century transformed Eskimos' traditional dwellings: tunnel length was reduced, the cold trap eliminated, and the kitchen brought into the main room.[54] When the Eskimos adopted an American style of housing, they adapted the new forms to the climate. At Point Hope the Natives built wood-framed houses but, finding them difficult to heat, covered them with sod blocks, so they resembled the Eskimos' original dwellings.[55] On the Nushagak River, near Bristol Bay, the Eskimos put windows and doors in their traditional dwellings and later built log cabins.[56]

The "pernicious practice" of building American-style dwellings had adverse consequences, particularly in the harsher climates.[57] While the traditional semisubterranean dwellings were criticized by non-Natives for being damp, dark, and, above all, smoky, the newer houses were cold and drafty. No longer could a house be heated by one seal-oil lamp, as the traditional Eskimo dwellings had been. Available driftwood, increasingly used to heat these new houses, disappeared rapidly. Because fuel had to be imported, the Eskimo could no longer live a purely subsistence existence.

Single-family houses brought an even more profound change than the materials of the dwelling itself. Although the extended family is still important and cooperation among families on specific projects is common, the nuclear family is increasingly responsible for its own economic welfare. To some extent this was the result of a change in the subsistence pattern; the introduction of rifles and other conveniences made the subsistence life more secure but at the same time required less cooperation among kin groups.[58] Whereas previously the members of a village had to cooperate to round up a herd of caribou, now a solo hunter with a rifle can shoot all of the caribou his family requires.

Federal and state housing programs in the mid-twentieth century encouraged the shift to single-family households and wood-framed houses. In 1949, Congress funded a Remote Dwelling Program for Alaska with the explicit aim of replacing Natives' semisubterranean dwellings. The program provided $500

A group of Native carvers repairing a totem pole at the U.S. Forest Service's shop at Saxman in 1941, signifying a new interest in traditional crafts.

loans to Natives to purchase building materials for a frame dwelling measuring 10 feet by 12 feet or 14 feet by 18 feet. In its three-year life, the program made about seven hundred loans to thirty villages. Other government efforts included log cabins built by the Alaska Rural Development Board in Beaver in 1958–1959[59] and rammed earth houses built by VISTA volunteers in Kotzebue and Mountain Village in 1968.[60]

Stores, schools, and churches provide a counterpoint to the collection of small houses in a village. The 1976 resolution of the Molly Hootch case, a suit brought by a Native who demanded secondary-level education in her village, required the state to make a high school education available in every village that had an elementary school. As a result, scores of schools have been constructed in villages in the last fifteen years. The schools usually contain a gymnasium, library, and other facilities available to the community and have become major, important structures in the villages. Distinctive in the townscape, too, is the church, usually Russian Orthodox in areas the Russians had occupied.

Today, extensive housing constructed by government agencies such as the U.S. Department of Housing and Urban Development and the Bureau of Indian Affairs has transformed most Native villages. Manufactured housing, arranged in regular rows, characterizes the Native village today. Traditional housing is beginning to be recognized as an object of historical and cultural interest. Just as Native organizations are reviving language and crafts, they are reconstructing traditional dwellings as outdoor museums.[61] Admired for their energy efficiency, use of indigenous materials, and craftsmanship, the traditional dwellings are visible expressions of Alaska's Native cultures.

Russian Alaskan Architecture

After Vitus Bering discovered Alaska for Russia in 1741, independent fur traders (promyshlenniki) colonized the southwest coasts. Receiving only sporadic support and attention from the Russian tsars, the acquisition of Alaska was a commercial venture, not an attempt to build an empire. In the first half-century, the promyshlenniki imposed their will on the Natives, enslaving and mistreating them in their quest for sea otter and fur seal pelts. When Tsar Paul I chartered the Russian-American Company in 1799, granting it a hunting and trading monopoly in the new land, Russian settlement began in earnest. Although the Russians developed sixty settlements in their 126-year occupation, the Russian population in America was never more than about eight hundred and never penetrated very far into the Interior, leaving vast stretches of Alaska unknown.[62]

Faced with difficulties protecting such a large and distant territory and with the rapid depletion of the sea-mammal resources, Russia sold Alaska to the United States in 1867. The few buildings that survive from the period of Rus-

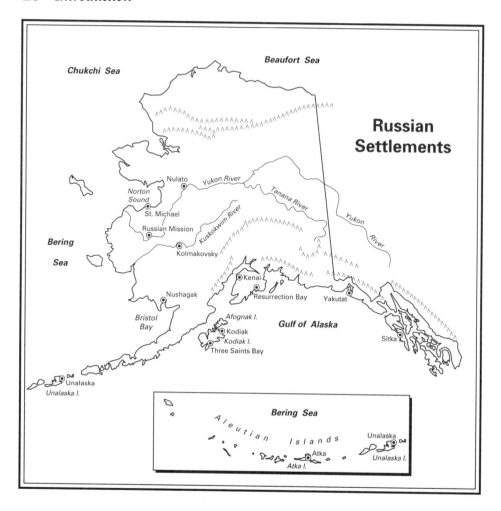

sian occupation are built of horizontal logs and are probably typical Russian-American construction. Despite repeated entreaties from Russian officials to build imposing and orderly settlements, the colony maintained a pragmatic appearance. The greatest architectural legacy is in the Russian Orthodox churches that continue to be built today. By imposing their religion on the Natives, the Russians also bestowed their architecture, so that churches with onion domes and three-part plans dot the landscape today, an unmistakable reminder of the period of Russian dominance.

RUSSIAN SETTLEMENT

For the first fifty years after Bering discovered Alaska, Russian exploration was sporadic, and settlement even more so. Although British, Spanish, French, and, later, American ships made exploratory journeys to Alaska, Russia managed to claim the land as its own. Rather than controlling the colony militarily, however, Russia left it to the promyshlenniki to enforce its claim. The promyshlenniki, however, were less interested in scientific knowledge or political empires than in furs. Originating as hunters and traders of the sable in Siberia, the promyshlenniki saw the potential of sea otter furs from the North Pacific, for which they found a ready market in China. They traded Alaskan furs for Chinese tea, a Russian obsession. Not adept at hunting sea otter, however, the promyshlenniki obtained the furs from Aleuts, who were well practiced and who had vessels ideally suited to the task in the form of kayaks, or baidarkas. The Aleuts' cooperation was not voluntary, however. The Russians forced them to hunt by demanding tribute and taking hostages. This mistreatment, added to the spread of disease and warfare, nearly annihilated the Aleuts, reducing their population by 80 percent.[63]

Although the independent promyshlenniki spurned permanent settlements, a small village at Unalaska, extant from the 1770s, did serve as a way station. Here they built barabaras, in a form adapted from the Aleuts. Russian barabaras were above ground and were entered from a doorway placed in the wall, rather than through the roof. In the same treeless environment that the Aleuts experienced, Russians pragmatically copied their sod-covered, arched-roof dwelling.[64] The Russians in turn influenced Aleut barabaras, for the Natives began to shift the entrance from the top to the wall and to include windows and stoves.

The Russians at Unalaska also built log houses—small, hip-roofed buildings of driftwood logs. Modest log houses were, in fact, typical in Russian America throughout its existence. Like the Russian izba, or cottage, they were blocklike in form, square or rectangular in plan, constructed of horizontal logs, either round or hewn.[65] Borrowing Native traditions, however, the Russians covered the roofs with earth or grass.

Grigorii Ivanovich Shelikhov, a trader whose company was to gain exclusive control over the fur trade in Alaska, first visited the territory in 1784. In partnership with Ivan Golikov, Shelikhov established a permanent settlement at Three Saints Bay on Kodiak Island. By 1790 this settlement consisted of five buildings described at the time as being "after the Russian fashion"—probably of log construction. The barracks were "laid out in different apartments, somewhat like boxes at a coffeehouse, on either side, with different offices."[66] The small settlement, on a treeless harbor site like Unalaska, had a mixture of driftwood-log buildings and barabaras, arranged in an informal plan.

This was but one of Shelikhov's settlements in Russian America; in distributing some 160 of his fellow countrymen, Shelikhov sent only 40 to Three Saints. The others were spread over six different sites around South-Central Alaska, mostly in small settlements ranging from 10 to 40 people. Shelikhov also established forts at Afognak Island, Cook Inlet, and Prince William Sound.[67]

In instructing his manager, K. A. Samoilov, as to the construction of the posts, Shelikhov had an eye to comfort and practicality: "Build the harbors and forts I planned on Afognak Island and at Kenai, strong and substantial. Build sheds for baidaras and baidarkas and back of the fortification warm and comfortable barracks for Aleuts, with partitions, and a bathhouse for native employees and for the hostages."[68] Shelikhov also left instructions for a house for Vasilii Petrov Merkul'ev, who apparently performed the duties of a quartermaster:

> Build for Merkul'ev where he chooses, at the harbor or where the artel [work crew] barracks are, a good house, well ventilated, where his wife can keep merchandise, with double walls and plenty of windows, so I or someone else can stay there too. The walls, floors and ceilings should be smoothly finished, and left to dry for a year, first without artificial heat and without nailing them down. Later, after they are dried with stoves, they should be nailed and must be made tight so that the sand cannot sift down from above.[69]

The reference to double walls suggests a plank or board covering on the outside of the log walls, which, like the floors and ceiling, was nailed in place. Sand was used as insulation between floors.

In 1790 Shelikhov hired the merchant Aleksandr Andreevich Baranov to manage his settlements on Kodiak Island. In his nearly thirty years in Alaska,

Shelikhov's settlement at Three Saints Bay, in a drawing by Martin Sauer published in 1802 but drawn c. 1790–1792, had a mix of Aleut and Russian forms. The illustration was keyed as follows: 1, portable church; 2, observatory tent; and 3, galiot.

Baranov was to wield tremendous power, establishing Russia's sovereignty in the face of Native resistance and meeting the competition from other world powers. One of Baranov's first actions was to move the settlement from Three Saints Bay to Pavlovsk Harbor, the present-day town of Kodiak. Located farther north on the island of Kodiak, where there were trees and a better harbor, the town was much more substantial and fortified than that at Three Saints Bay.

As was typical in Russian America under Baranov's reign, Kodiak was set on a promontory, a site that was more militarily advantageous than those of earlier settlements. The Natives posed the greatest threat to Russian control, but well-fortified settlements also sent a message to European powers that Russia's interest in Alaska was sincere. The impressive buildings at Kodiak included a semicircular, two-story, hewn-log fort and numerous other log buildings with grass-covered roofs. The Russians divided the upper floors of the multistoried buildings into three rooms, which were used as living quarters. They covered windows with seal intestines and heated the houses with stoves.[70]

The traditional Russian log construction is illustrated by the one building that survives from this period, which the Russian-American Company built as a warehouse some time between 1805 and 1808 (see entry SW001, p. 284).[71] The thick hewn logs are laid horizontally and notched at the corners. Each is

View of Kodiak from the Sarichef atlas, published in 1826. The J-shaped fort is crowned with a flag, and the church has an octagonal cupola.

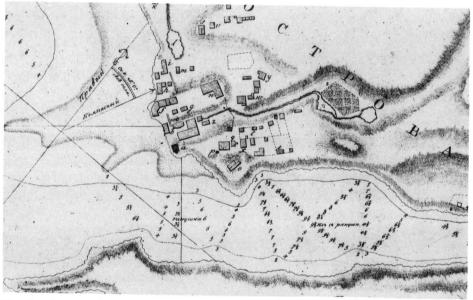

The plan of Kodiak, also from the Sarichef atlas. The key to the map includes a, the church; and f, the fort.

gently grooved on the bottom to fit tightly over the one below. Although the size of buildings was usually limited to the length of the timbers, here the logs are lapped and interlocked at midpoint, to create the 66-foot-long walls. The roof was probably originally hipped but was changed to gable with a central pediment, probably in the mid-nineteenth century. After the building's conversion to a residence at the turn of the twentieth century, a bay window and porch were added, but the building remains a fine example of early Russian construction. It is the oldest building in Alaska.

The plan of Kodiak was undistinguished, with hardly a straight street or right-angle placement of buildings, and the town soon fell into disrepair; when

Russian Orthodox missionary Father Gideon visited in 1804, he found that a third of the fort "has already collapsed with age" and that "all these buildings are dilapidated."[72]

Wood was a natural material for construction, not only because of its ready availability in the territory on the Gulf of Alaska but also because it was traditionally used in eastern Russia. The spruce forests of Pacific Alaska provided the raw materials for ships as well as for buildings, and later even the sawdust was used to pack ice for export, during a brief attempt to diversify the economy. Wood was also used as fuel. Brick, needed to build hearths and chimneys, was being made in Kodiak as early as 1795, although not easily, according to Archimandrite Ioasaph: "It is extremely difficult to make bricks even for local needs: they bring the clay from a small island, they dry, crush and sift it, and then use it for making bricks; both the Russians and the domestic servants are occupied [in this work]."[73] Soon, however, the Russians were producing from three thousand to six thousand bricks per year on Kodiak Island and would have made more, except for the shortage of lime.[74] Lack of skilled builders prevented the use of stone as a construction material. Baranov complained: "It would do no harm to send a couple of men skilled in erecting buildings. We were going to build a stone powder magazine, but the lack of experienced people prevented us last year (1802), and now there are still fewer."[75]

In 1805, Russian-American Company representative N. P. Rezanov proposed constructing half-timbered buildings. Although there is no evidence that any such buildings were actually constructed, the Russian-American Company's efforts to civilize Alaska are crystallized in Rezanov's vision of Alaskan settlements as European villages:

> To save labor and speed the construction I have ordered that buildings be made out of *fachwerk*. Foundations are to be built out of cobble stones, and instead of log walls, a light frame is to be erected, poles put between upright, and the space between filled with stones mixed with clay and chopped grass. These walls will be covered inside and outside with lime. The floors will be covered with sawdust with clay on top, and in every room will be a fireplace for ventilation. I ordered the roofs made out of grass, filling it with clay till smooth and finishing with a mixture of clay and lime. The buildings will look as if they were built of bricks. The roofs being light will not require heavy timbers to support them and will be safe from fire. The fireplaces will dry up the walls and floor very quickly. The construction will be easy, because the young trees grow right there on the beach; stones obstructing the roads can be used to good purpose and the place will be cleared. Excellent lime is obtained here from sea shells. According to my plans heavier lumber is required only for the ceilings.[76]

Churches were another sign of stability and civilization, and the Russians built the first church in Alaska in Kodiak. The first priest did not arrive in Alaska until 1790, although many Aleuts were converted by the promyshlenniki, who as church members were empowered to baptize in the absence of a priest. Priest Vasilii Sifsof, traveling with the Billings-Sarychev expedition (a Russian government-sponsored scientific expedition led by an Englishman), brought a tent to serve as a portable church; it was erected shortly after their arrival. But the first serious attempt at bringing Christianity to the colony was undertaken by Shelikhov, who wished to gain favor with Empress Catherine II. In 1794, Shelikhov brought ten missionaries to Kodiak from the monastery of Valaam, near the Russian-Finnish border. Led by Archimandrite Ioasaph, they were promised that a church had already been erected. When they arrived, however, they did not have even a portable church. The following spring, Ioasaph complained to Shelikhov:

> We do not have a travelling church even now. I asked the clerks and Aleksandr Andreevich [Baranov] to give us canvas for a tent but did not get it. Aleksandr Andreevich volunteered to build a small church here and construction began on November 21st. It was to be four sazhen [28 feet] square, with an addition of 1–1/2 sazhen [10 feet] for the altar, but the log walls are still not ready, so I have nothing to report to the Most Reverend Metropolitan.[77]

The Church of the Holy Resurrection was completed by 1796,[78] and in illustrations it appears to have been a complex structure with two cupolas and an irregular plan, far grander than most of the chapels, or first churches, at other Russian-American settlements.

Baranov soon came into conflict with the missionaries, who found his men profane and their own living conditions abominable. The missionaries objected to the Russians' treatment of the Natives, particularly their brutality toward the men and their loose morals with the women. On the other side, the company men found the missionaries worthless, as they did no labor in a seriously undermanned colony. In the face of threats by Baranov, the missionaries were afraid to come to church and were rendered ineffective.[79] Two exceptions were Hieromonks Makarii and Iuvenalii, who traveled widely and reported they had baptized five thousand Natives. The others stayed close to home except for Father Herman, who secluded himself on Spruce Island, where he worked with the Natives. Missionary activity in Russian America was essentially dormant from 1796 to 1816.[80]

In 1793, Shelikhov petitioned Empress Catherine II for assistance in establishing a settlement on the mainland of Alaska, near Cape Saint Elias. In the return order, written in the name of the tsarina by Lieutenant-General Ivan Peel of Irkutsk, Shelikhov was granted permission but also was instructed to lay out his town with some eye to aesthetics:

> The houses with all additional buildings must be comfortable and attractive, properly removed from each other for fire safety. The streets must be straight, wide and divided into blocks with vacant plazas left in convenient places for future public buildings. In a word, knowing the local conditions, order this first settlement in America to be built as a standard city. Any disfiguring of

it with crooked, narrow, impassable lanes and bypaths must not be permitted, so that in the future this first settlement may become the beautiful abode of a multitude of people, and the glory and renown of Russian art and taste may not be impaired![81]

Shelikhov dutifully passed these instructions on to Baranov, emphasizing first the public relations value:

> It remains now, after finding a good location on the mainland, to build a well planned settlement, one that will look like a town instead of a village, even at the start. In case it cannot be avoided and some foreign ship comes, let them see that the Russians live in a well organized way. Don't give them a reason to think that Russians live in America in the same abominable way as in Okhotsk.

He next addressed location and site planning:

> Please, dear friend, for your own pleasure and satisfaction, plan the new settlement to be beautiful and pleasant to live in. Have public squares for meetings and gatherings. The streets must not be very long but wide, and must radiate from the squares. If you choose a place in the woods, leave the trees on the streets in front of the houses and in garden. The houses should be well separated, which will make the settlement look bigger.

Specific architectural advice was brief:

> The houses must be of uniform type and size. . . . The public buildings such as the church, monastery, office of clerical affairs, guardhouse, warehouses, store, etc., must be planned and constructed, and their sites chosen in the style of big cities.

Designing the buildings was left up to the priests, two of whom had been trained as engineers:

> Send us a journal, plans, and your report about the opening of this new settlement. . . . Write on the plans the names of the buildings and the purposes they are to serve. You would do well to enclose sketches showing the profiles of the buildings. Fathers Juvenal and Stefan will do that for you. After you have the sketches made, you can construct the buildings according to them.[82]

As ethnographer Svetlana Fedorova has pointed out, Shelikhov also suggested dwellings similar to the Siberian connected farmhouse:

> . . . well built white cottages, with a passage to an adjoining pantry and cold room, or storeroom. Out-buildings such as barns, cattle-sheds and cellars should be placed in wings, taking care that they appear clean and attractive from the streets.[83]

Baranov had neither the manpower nor the equipment to build any such city; at the time, fewer than three hundred Russians were under his command.[84] What resulted, in 1796, was a paltry settlement at Yakutat, where Baranov had hoped for agricultural development to feed the rest of the colony. The site was poorly suited, the settlement was never a success, and it was finally destroyed by Tlingit Indians in 1805.

Shipbuilding was a more substantial accomplishment of Shelikhov's company. In 1791 Shelikhov sent shipbuilding materials to Baranov, who selected a heavily wooded site on the Kenai Peninsula called Resurrection Bay (present-day Seward). With a British shipbuilder in charge, the first ship was completed in 1794, and two more the next year, indicating some degree of craftsmanship and expertise. The Russians built at least twenty more ships at various shipyards in Alaska and California before 1867.[85]

Shelikhov died in 1795, but his company prospered, led at first by his widow, Nataliia, and then by his son-in-law, N. P. Rezanov. The politically well-connected Rezanov formed the Russian-American Company out of Shelikhov's holdings and in 1799 was able to obtain exclusive rights to trade in Alaska for a period of twenty years, renewed twice. With its future secured, the Russian-American Company had reason to develop substantial settlements, and Baranov, elevated to general manager in 1802, was prepared to lead the way.

The Russian-American Company turned its attention to the east and south, due to the diminishing sea otter population of the Aleutian Chain and Alaska Peninsula. As a result of overhunting, the sea otters rapidly declined in numbers, and the Russians were forced to go farther to find them. A similar situation was developing in the Pribilof Islands, home of the fur seals. Discovered by the Russians in 1786, the Pribilofs were exploited for more than a million furs, until Rezanov, told that the fur seal population had declined by 90 percent, was forced to institute conservation measures in 1805.[86]

Under the direction of Baranov, the Russian-American Company built a fortification on Sitka (now Baranof) Island, in Southeast Alaska, in 1799. The Tlingit Indians resisted the Russians. In 1802 they destroyed the fortification, massacring nearly all of the Russians and Aleut laborers there. In 1804, Baranov returned, destroying the nearby Tlingit village and building a new fort on its site. Named Novo-Arkhangelsk, or New Archangel, it became the capital of Russian America in 1808 and evolved into the present-day town of Sitka. Situated on a rock outcropping and surrounded by a palisade, the fort loomed over the harbor.

Again, Baranov received instructions regarding the appearance of the town. After visiting Alaska in 1805, Rezanov wrote, "The buildings should be constructed in straight lines according to the plans, in order to attract the people by their good appearance and to provide comfort for the Company's employees."[87] Faced with the necessity of running a fur-trading enterprise, not an empire, Baranov again disregarded architectural advice. Although some straight lines are apparent from the plan, Sitka was only slightly more organized than Kodiak.

Capt. Vasilii Mikhailovich Golovnin, a naval officer sent to inspect the colony in 1810, could say only this about Sitka: "In the fort we could see nothing

The governor's house at Sitka was built on a rock outcropping and heavily fortified, as depicted in an 1827 drawing by von Kittlitz.

remarkable. It consisted of strong wooden bastions and palisades. The houses, barrack magazines, and manager's residence were built of exceedingly thick logs."[88] One effect of the repeated directives to put forth a good appearance was that many of the buildings were oriented parallel to the street and shore-line, presenting their broadest face. Like Kodiak, Sitka consisted of log struc-tures with hip roofs; like the surviving warehouse in Kodiak, the company store in Sitka was a low, one-and-a-half-story structure of thick round logs, hip-roofed with a pediment.

The visiting naval officer Golovnin objected generally to the appearance of the settlements in Russian America, thinking they gave the wrong impression: "Foreigners visiting the colonies and finding nothing resembling provinces or fortified places belonging to the Russian crown, that is, nothing like a regular garrison, may quickly conclude that these places are nothing more than tem-porary defensive fortifications built by hunters to protect themselves against the natives, and consequently may have no respect for them."[89] This conflict between naval officer Golovnin's concern for the empire and merchant-manager's Baranov's concern for the bottom line caused the navy to assume a larger role in the Russian-American Company.

Under Baranov, the colony continued to prosper. By 1815, Kodiak had eighty-seven buildings and Sitka, forty-five.[90] Baranov built a church at Sitka, and once again Russian Orthodox missionaries were welcomed. Priest Alexis Soko-lov, in reporting to the company's board of directors, had nothing but praise for Baranov:

> Arriving September 7, 1816, to the fort Novo-Arkhangelsk on Baranov Is-
> land, I was pleased to find a newly built, large and artistically finished two-

The blocklike quality of these log buildings is emphasized in this 1827 drawing by von Kittlitz. The two-story octagonal church was built in 1816.

> story chapel, which was soon fitted for services as the temple of the Lord;
> adorned with becoming ornaments; provided with gilded silver vessels and
> other fixtures. March 18 of the same year it was consecrated with suitable
> rites to the name of St. Archangel Michael, thanks to the earnest coopera-
> tion of . . . Baranov.[91]

Contemporary illustrations of this church depict an octagonal log building, two
stories in height, topped by an octagonal cupola. Gabled seams along the conical roof emphasized the verticality of the structure.

In 1820, paint was provided for buildings in Sitka, probably to retard the
rapid deterioration of the wood and to preserve the metal of the roofs. The
manager was instructed by the home office in 1822, "Please note that flat roofs,
covered by iron, seem better for Sitkha buildings than steep roofs, liable to
destruction from the strong gales you often have there."[92] The standard colors
were red for roofs and yellow ocher for the buildings.

Candles or oil lit the houses, and Russian stoves heated them. These stoves,
more akin to fireplaces than to the present-day notion of stoves, were described
by scientist William H. Dall in 1870:

> Here they are built of fragments of basalt, the prevalent rock, and smeared
> inside and out with a mortar made of clay. A damper in the chimney is so
> arranged as to shut off all draught, and is taken out when the fire is made.
> After the whole has been thoroughly heated by a wood fire the coals are

removed. The damper is put in, thus preventing the escape of hot air by the chimney, and without further fire this stove will warm the room for twenty-four hours. It is admirably suited to the climate and the country, and its only objectionable point is the amount of room it occupies.[93]

Turning even farther south, the Russian-American Company developed another settlement—this time in California. Founded in 1812, Fort Ross was intended to serve as a southern outpost for the fur trade, as well as an agricultural settlement to feed the rest of the colony. Neither aspect was very successful—the numbers of sea otters were dwindling in northern California and the Aleuts and promyshlenniki made poor farmers. Although Fort Ross expanded foreign trading opportunities, the settlement was abandoned in 1841.

During the Russian-American Company's second charter, which extended from 1821 to 1841, the company turned its attention north and inland. The board of directors even considered moving the capital back to Kodiak.[94] Baranov had been replaced as general manager in 1818 and as a result of a corporate reorganization, a succession of naval officers administered the colony. The Russian government's first concern during the second charter was to establish boundaries of Russian America through negotiations with the United States and Great Britain. By two agreements, in 1824 with the United States and in 1825 with Great Britain, Russian America's southern boundary was established at 54°40' north latitude. American and British ships were given permission to fish and trade in Russian American waters.[95]

In the 1820s, the Russian Orthodox church gained a permanent foothold in Russian America. A provision in the second charter instructed the company to maintain the missionaries, paying their salaries and providing adequate churches and priests' houses. As a result, the church sent a priest named Ioann Veniaminov to Unalaska in 1824, and an Alaskan creole priest, Iakov Netsvetov, to Atka in 1828.[96] Both of these men translated the Bible into appropriate dialects of the Aleut language. Veniaminov produced ethnographic studies of the Aleuts, took a strong interest in science and medicine, and was an accomplished carpenter, designing and building the first Church of the Holy Ascension at Unalaska.

In 1834, Veniaminov went to Sitka. Elevated to bishop and given a new name, Innocent, in 1840, he remained in Sitka until 1858 when he was recalled to Russia. While in Sitka, he designed and built Saint Michael's Cathedral. The large log structure, cruciform in plan, had three altars. Low gable roofs were crowned at their crossing by a large dome, 28 feet in diameter, while a square bell tower in the front rose three stories. Surely the most magnificent building in Russian America when it was completed in 1848, the cathedral was destroyed by fire in 1966 but has since been reconstructed (SE040, p. 185).

During its second charter, the Russian-American Company looked north and began establishing posts on the lower Yukon and Kuskokwim rivers. The Russians began their explorations of the land north of the Alaska Peninsula in

The military outpost of Saint Michael on Norton Sound had a small collection of buildings protected by a palisade. The octagonal church stood outside the walls, in the foreground. Henry Wood Elliott made this 1870 drawing from a sketch by scientist William Henry Dall.

1819, when they established a redoubt, or small fortification, called Novo-Aleksandrovsk (New Alexander), at the mouth of the Nushagak River. In the 1830s, they established posts on the Kuskokwim River (Kolmakovsky), on Norton Sound (Michaelovsk, or Saint Michael), and on the Yukon River (Nulato). When outfitted as redoubts, these outposts gained a military appearance, emphasizing palisades and corner towers, but they were poorly manned and presented no real military threat. Frederick Whymper described the post at Saint Michael in 1866:

> The station is built on the model of a Hudson's Bay Company's fort, with enclosure of pickets, and with bastions flanking it. Inside are the store-houses and dwellings of the employes, including the "casine" (*caserne*), or general barrack, bath and cook-houses. These painted yellow, and surmounted by red roofs, gave it a rather gay appearance.[97]

Lieutenant Zagoskin, traveling among the northern posts in the early 1840s, had a more cynical view of these settlements:

> A Russian is everywhere the same. Whatever the spot he chooses, whether it be on the Arctic Circle or in a blessed California valley, he establishes his characteristic Russian-type cabin, his cooking-place, his bath, and he provides himself with a housekeeper. But since some of the people who enter the colonial service come from simple backgrounds, when they are kept under semi-martial conditions, they call the area where they live, surrounded

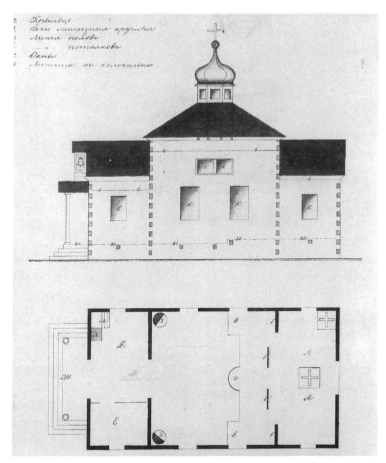

Plans and side elevation of a church to be built at Kvikhpak (now Russian Mission), sent there in 1849. The plan is a standard Russian Orthodox layout, with (left to right) porch, narthex, nave, and sanctuary. The iconostas, separating the nave and sanctuary, is pierced by several doors.

> by a stout fence, a "fort," the cabin the "barracks," the smoke opening a "window," the kitchen the "mess" and even the housekeeper has a different name.[98]

The list of tools and materials required for building a church at Kvikhpak (present-day Russian Mission) in 1849 hints at the simplicity of construction. The entire list was, "2 large ripsaws, 4 carpenter axes, 5 chisels, 6 gimlets, 1 small anvil, 1 hammer, 1 grinding stone, 1000 nails, 100 spikes, 10 sheets of iron, 200 bricks, 4 pr. door hinges, 10 pr. shutter hinges, 100 window panes 13–1/3″ x 12″, paints, wallpaper and cloth."[99]

Bishop Innocent sent Father Iakov Netsvetov to Kvikhpak, where he built the church in two years with the aid of four Aleut carpenters. Kvikhpak's wooded site was remote, hundreds of miles from the nearest sawmill. The log construction was typical of Russian building at similar sites throughout Alaska. The men used the ripsaws to make planks for the floor, doors, and shutters. They used sheet metal to cover the roof and the bricks to form a Russian stove. They laid up walls of horizontal logs, spiked at intermediate points and notched at the corners. The instructions for building included drawings, which showed a square nave with a pyramidal roof topped by an onion dome. The sanctuary and vestibule had gable roofs. The vestibule roof projected slightly to protect the bells, which hung above the gable-roofed porch.[100] The simple list of tools was intended to produce quite a complex building.

The church was the primary mission between the Russian posts of Saint Michael and Kolmakovsky; the three missions covered the area from Norton Sound to Bristol Bay. There was also a church at New Alexander (present-day Nushagak). Through these missions and attendant chapels, Innocent expanded the church's presence in Alaska from four churches and priests in 1840 to nine churches and thirty-five chapels less than twenty years later.[101]

More importantly, Innocent prescribed an attitude toward the Natives that was gentle and respectful. His instructions to a missionary in 1853 included the following:

> Ancient customs, so long as they are not contrary to Christianity, need not be too abruptly broken up; but it should be explained to converts that they are merely tolerated. . . .
>
> On no account show open contempt for their manner of living, customs, etc., however these may appear deserving of it, for nothing insults and irritates these savages so much as showing them open contempt and making fun of them and anything belonging to them. . . .
>
> In giving instruction and talking with natives generally, be gentle, pleasant, simple, and in no way assume an overbearing, didactic manner, for by so doing thou canst seriously jeopardize the success of thy labors. . . .
>
> Those who show no wish to receive holy baptism, even after repeated persuasion, should not in any way be vexed, nor, especially, coerced.[102]

By the time of the company's third charter, which extended from 1841 to 1861, the populations of sea otters and fur seals had declined and the bureaucracy had grown so that the company was hard put to make a profit. Early in the nineteenth century, manager Baranov had warned, "The company cannot exist by hunting alone . . . the amount of furs is diminishing every year."[103] Various ventures were undertaken. Both coal and ice were exported from Alaska to San Francisco in the 1850s. The company, frustrated at watching Americans corner the whaling trade, encouraged whaling among Russians and Aleuts. But all attempts at diversification were unsuccessful.

Despite the decline of the Russian-American Company's profits, however, the 1840s and 1850s were the period of greatest architectural sophistication. Captain 1st Rank Adolph Etholen, from Finland, the chief manager in Sitka from 1840 to 1845, oversaw considerable construction. Etholen brought other Finns, accomplished shipbuilders, who probably also applied their craftsmanship to buildings. P. A. Tikhmenev, the historian of the Russian-American Company, listed the projects during Etholen's tenure:

> [A] new pier at New Archangel, on a stone foundation, and armed with twelve cannons, constituting the lower battery of the port; a stock warehouse; a building for the library; a depot for charts and astronomical instruments and for magnetic observations; living quarters for the observatory personnel; a Lutheran church; a social club; barracks for married soldiers; a powder magazine; a laundry; a new church on Kad'iak Island; and a sawmill and flour and water mill.[104]

Some of the more impressive structures in Sitka rose in the 1840s, including Saint Michael's Cathedral, mentioned above, and the Bishop's House, one of the few Russian-era buildings still standing in Alaska (SE041, p. 187). The Russian-American Company built the two-story, hip-roofed Bishop's House of hewn logs. The symmetrical fenestration and dramatic metal-clad roof created an imposing exterior, while the wallpapered and carpeted interior provided comfortable surroundings. A seminary occupied the first floor, and the second floor housed Bishop Innocent's chapel, living quarters and library.

One building in Sitka survives from the early 1850s, the Russian-American Company's Building No. 29 (SE049, p. 193). This modest structure has been much altered over the years, but the original section was log construction, three bays wide, two stories tall. Like the Bishop's House, a layer of sand between floors insulated the building, and a bay at one end accommodated the stairway.

Architectural elaboration increased rapidly in the late 1850s, when the sawmill in Sitka was converted to steam power. At that time, the sawmill included "a planer, and machines for making blocks, cornices, window frames, and shingles. Patterns for the foundry are also made here and machines for the foundry, sheet metal shop, and blacksmith shop."[105] The most ornate example of Russian architectural craftsmanship was an Italianate company office building. Constructed in 1857, the building, which measured 80 feet by 40 feet, was constructed of logs and had a gable roof and five-bay front, dramatized by a peaked center bay. The log walls were covered with planks, laid flush to give a flat surface, ornamented by pairs of round-arch windows, a bold modillioned cornice, and wooden quoins at the corners. This full-blown example of the Italianate style in the Russian settlement partook of popular trends throughout the United States, seen in government-built customhouses and commercial buildings in frontier towns as well as in long-settled cities.

Despite this one model of modernity, Sitka's overall dilapidation struck visitors. Artist Frederick Whymper remembered the bright colors and old buildings when he visited Sitka in 1865:

> The houses yellow, with sheet-iron roofs painted red; the bright green spire and dome of the Greek [Russian Orthodox] Church, and the old battered hulks, roofed in and used as magazines, lying propped up on the rocks at

The log customhouse in Sitka, built in 1857, was architecturally the most elaborate building in the Russian colony, with modillions, dentils, quoins, and paired, round-arch windows. Eadweard Maybridge photographed it in 1868.

the water's edge, with the antiquated buildings of the Russian Fur Company,
gave Sitka an original, foreign, and fossilized kind of appearance.[106]

William Healy Dall visited Sitka at the same time as Whymper and was slightly more critical, "Much of it was more primitive than many western towns where the shingles are yet bright from the sawmill; yet the place was eighty years old."[107]

Meanwhile, Kodiak had been experiencing changing fortunes. While somewhat neglected in the first years of Sitka's prominence, Kodiak was revitalized in the 1820s with the proposal to return the capital there. At that time, the chief manager of the company sent a book of facades of various buildings so that the Kodiak manager could select some; the appearance of these buildings was paramount.[108] When the capital did not return, Kodiak sank into another period of neglect. In the 1840s, chief manager Etholen undertook two ventures that affected Kodiak Island. The first was to consolidate the Native settlements, as had been done on Atka and Unalaska. On Kodiak and neighboring islands he consolidated sixty-five Native settlements into seven; much depleted by a smallpox epidemic in the late 1830s, the Native population on Kodiak was 1,365.[109] Secondly, in the town of Kodiak, Etholen constructed a new church, one with three altars.[110] In 1861 Captain-Lieutenant Pavel Nikolaevich Golovin described the settlers' houses in Kodiak (population 360): "They have large light homes with outbuildings, stockpens, gardens, et cetera. The interior walls in many homes are papered or are covered with sailcloth that has been decorated."[111] Etholen's building program was so great that in 1851 the company's board of directors cautioned the next administrator against new construction:

> The colonial authorities must . . . exercise the greatest discrimination in designing new buildings. . . . you are therefore requested to keep in view that every extravagance in buildings for the mere purpose of affording spacious and luxurious lodgings for the employees and servants, being a direct burden, without adequate return to the Company, must be studiously avoided.[112]

In the face of declining revenues, the company retrenched. An architectural impact was no longer desired. Instead, Russia began to look for ways to rid itself of a colony that had become a burden.

THE RUSSIAN ORTHODOX CHURCH

Often at odds with the Russian-American Company, the Russian Orthodox church endeavored to tend to the spiritual needs of the Russians in America and to carry out missionary work among the Natives. By 1860 there were nine Russian Orthodox churches (those served by resident priests) and thirty-five chapels (with visiting priests) operating in Alaska. After the departure of the Russian government, the church continued its involvement in Alaska; it prospered among the Natives, who today support eighty churches and chapels and count twenty thousand members throughout the state.[113]

These church and chapel buildings constitute the most visible influence that the Russians have had on present-day Alaska. Other lasting cultural influences include associations with the Russian language: the language was spoken in some Native communities well into the twentieth century; Russian words have found their way into the language; and Russian names are in evidence throughout the state.[114] The steam bath is another custom that may have been passed from the Russians to the Natives. Although the Native baths were part of the social structure before contact with the Russians, they were fire baths, or dry air, as opposed to the Russian-introduced steam bath, where water was splashed on hot stones.[115] But the persistence of the religion ranks as the most indelible trait of Russian governance, and the church buildings as tangible illustrations.[116] While not one church building remains in Alaska from Russian times, forms typical of the Russian era are even now being built.

Architecturally, buildings of the Russian Orthodox church in Alaska are characterized by three-part plans, axial symmetry, an east-west orientation, wooden construction, and onion domes. While each of these elements has its origin in Russia, its characteristic incorporation into the Alaskan churches results in a style that is distinctly Alaskan.

In typical Alaskan Russian Orthodox churches, the basic elements are the sanctuary, which contains the altar; the nave, which holds the worshippers; and the narthex or vestibule. The nave and sanctuary are separated by the iconostas. This screen, which runs across the width of the building, is ornamented with icons and carvings and pierced by several doors. The doors in the center, the royal doors, are opened and closed during the service, alternately disclosing and concealing the altar; only the priest and deacon are allowed to walk through these doors. Flanking doors provide access for auxiliary clergy, altar boys, and laymen. Icons, painted representations of religious figures, are arranged on the iconostas in a prescribed order. Besides the visual feast of the icons, Russian Orthodoxy appeals to other senses as well: an a cappella choir accompanies most services, bells outside the church ring at designated times during the service, and incense permeates the air.

The sanctuary, located at the east end of the building, is accessible only to the priest and his lay assistants during the service, and only to men at other times; women are not permitted within. In the nave, the congregation usually stands throughout the service—men on the right and women on the left— although benches are provided for the elderly. The churches also have some sort of vestibule or narthex, closed off from the nave, to protect the nave from cold outside air. Each of these rooms—sanctuary, nave, and vestibule—is often expressed on the exterior through a different building shape or roof form, thus providing the articulation of the three-part plan.

Although the way in which these elements are arranged in Alaskan churches is standard—sanctuary, iconostas, nave, and vestibule, running from east to west on axis—particular plans vary dramatically. When the sanctuary is a separate element, it can be rectangular or polygonal in plan; when it is incorporated into the same mass as the nave, it occasionally retains a polygonal plan. The vestibule or narthex is rectangular, ranging from a small enclosed porch to a space the width of the nave. The greatest variety of plans is found in the nave, which can be a simple rectangle, an octagon, a square, or a cross.

The rectangular plan derives from the standard Russian dwelling, the izba, a blocklike square or rectangle with a gable roof. This was simply transferred to a church; the sanctuary could be added in an additional block in the east end and the vestibule on the west.[117] The 1936 church in Lower Kalskag (WE022, p. 276) and the 1905–1906 church in Saint Paul (SW018, p. 297) are examples. While the sanctuary, nave, and vestibule have different dimensions, they are united by the similar slopes to their gable roofs.

The octagon is most likely a remnant of the tent-roof churches of Russia, known as the shater. These shater, which may have derived from fortification watch towers, had tall, dramatic tent roofs and octagonal plans. Favored by a dissenting sect of the Russian Orthodox, these church forms were banned in the seventeenth century. The octagonal plan, with a more modest roof, survived and in Alaska was a common form for the first church building on a site.

In this lithograph by Louis Choris, c. 1820, the octagonal church built at Unalaska in 1808 is on the left. The buildings to the right are a mix of mounded barabaras and hip-roof Russian structures. In the foreground, Aleuts in traditional headwear paddle a kayak.

The chapel built in Unalaska in 1808, for instance, was in this form, incorporating the sanctuary within the octagon. Another example of the octagon was at the outpost of Saint Michael, while the first church in Sitka was a two-story variation. The only surviving example is the church in Juneau, constructed in 1893–1894 as the first Russian Orthodox church in that town (SE021.1, p. 175).

The third Alaskan church form is the square, or nearly square, plan with a hip roof, which was often crowned by an onion dome.[118] Often similar in dimensions to the rectangular plan, the buildings are distinguished by their roof forms; the hipped roof of the square plan emphasizes its squareness, while the gable roof of the rectangular plan expresses its linearity. Examples of the square form include the 1821 church at Saint Paul, with the sanctuary, narthex, and bell tower forming separate elements.

The fourth plan is the cruciform, a form found only rarely in Alaska. Saint Michael's Cathedral in Sitka, constructed under the supervision of Bishop Innocent in 1844–1848, is the best example of this type, with gable-roofed arms intersecting the gabled nave, crowned by a large dome on an octagonal drum (SE040, p. 185). The cathedral has three altars. The Church of the Holy Resurrection in Kodiak, constructed in 1874, and its replacement built in 1946 (SW002, p. 284), were also cruciform in plan, as was the church at Ninilchik, erected in 1901 (SC068, p. 123). A variation and combination of the square and cruciform plans appears in the Church of the Holy Ascension, constructed in Unalaska in 1894 (SW014, p. 291), also with three altars. Here, the tall nave, almost square in plan, is crowned by a hip roof, but the wings, also hip roofed, give the church a cruciform plan.

The church at Saint Paul in the Pribilof Islands, built of driftwood in 1821, has a standard arrangement of sanctuary, nave, and narthex (left to right).

Built after the Russians had sold Alaska to the United States, this architecturally sophisticated church in Saint Paul was supported by the Aleut congregation, which paid $15,000 for its construction in 1873–1875. The church was demolished in about 1906 when the present church was built.

The use of these four forms was not a chronological progression; all of them were in use at one time. One of the earliest forms used, and simplest to construct, is the gable-roofed rectangular plan, which is the most frequently used in the twentieth century.

Other architectural elements found in various combinations—the bell tower, onion dome, and interior dome—enliven these basic plans. The bell tower, which in Russia stood apart from the church, in Alaska was attached—either rising from the roof of the narthex or rising directly from the ground—and was always centered on the facade to preserve the symmetry. Onion domes, the most distinctive element of Russian Orthodox churches, usually crowned the bell tower and nave. Beside the bold onion domes atop the churches, there were interior domes as well, usually set on octagonal drums. They rose over the nave, like that at Saint Michael's Cathedral. Located just in front of the iconostas, these domes were often lit by windows in the drum, shedding light on the iconostas and the priest who stood in front of it to speak. Interior domes were also constructed without windows, appearing as a recess in the ceiling.

Despite the variety of forms, the materials remained constant: wood was invariably the structural material. While the earlier churches were constructed of horizontal logs, the church forms adapted well to light wood framing. Coverings of horizontal wood siding were common on both log and wood-framed structures. Today sidings include aluminum and cement asbestos shingle.[119]

Color enlivened the churches, both inside and out. On the interior, brilliant colors drew all eyes to the iconostas and altar, and gilding and lighting made the icons and altar sparkle and glow. The exteriors of most of the existing churches are painted white, often with blue and sometimes green trim, but they were traditionally much more colorful. In 1879, the Unalaska church had "a bright blue, onion-shaped dome that rests on a bright green tower. The frame structure of the church is a vivid yellow."[120]

The churches were often situated a little apart from the village, preferably on a small hill. This emphasized their separateness—clearly this was not a house, either in shape or size—and displayed their unusual forms, dominating the village.

All of these elements combined to produce buildings with lively profiles. The sanctuary, nave, and vestibule were easily identified on the exterior, each defined by a different form; when joined by additional exterior elements such as bell tower, dome, and onion domes, the effect was dazzling and unmistakable—a uniquely Alaskan Russian Orthodox church.[121]

Eastern Orthodox churches are found today scattered over many parts of the Lower 48. Though they represent several ethnic groups from different parts of Europe, they share, along with the Alaskan Orthodox, a common Byzantine religious source, and all cling faithfully to their architectural tradition. This results in unmistakable common features in their churches, such as the domes on the exteriors, the hierarchical organization of the interiors, and the

The interior of the church in the preceding photograph. The mahogany iconostas is ornamented with handsome icons imported from Russia.

icon screens, even though the historical background of the Orthodox church in Alaska is very different from that in the Lower 48, where it is essentially the result of twentieth-century immigration from eastern Europe. And even as the native carriers of the tradition are unique to Alaska, so is the remote but moving landscape in which their churches were found.

Other traditions of Russian architecture were not carried through to the American period. Although Americans built log cabins, they were derived from western America and rarely featured squared logs or hip roofs. In boomtowns of the American gold rush period, sawmills were established, so wood-frame construction, which was fast and inexpensive, was prevalent. The sturdy, block-like Russian dwellings disappeared from the Alaskan landscape, except in a few settlements that were predominantly Russian and creole. Russian influences on domestic architecture were forgotten when Americans started pouring into Alaska in search of instant riches.

American Alaskan Architecture

When the Stars and Stripes was raised over Sitka on 18 October 1867, the first wave of American opportunists was already populating the town. Although few stayed for very long, they set a pattern that has characterized Alaska for more than a century. Alaska attracts newcomers in search of opportunity: to get rich quick panning for gold, to spread religion among heathens, to test themselves against the elements, to settle in a young state that values abilities over patrimony. Most of these Americans brought to this challenging new world familiar elements from home: language, clothing, food, and architecture.

If false-fronted commercial buildings along a boardwalk characterized towns in the goldfields of California, then that is what the new settlers would build in Alaska. If Queen Anne cottages populated the neighborhoods of Seattle, then they too would be built here. If Cape Cod cottages expressed the suburban ideal, then they would be built here. But Alaska is not a carbon copy of the Lower 48; the architecture differs markedly. First, the buildings are by and large less stylish, although the basic forms can be linked to popular styles. Second, indigenous construction materials are limited to wood and concrete. Consequently, structures of wood or concrete and prefabricated buildings characterize the construction scene. Finally, the climate—to an extent found in no other state—shapes architecture in a variety of ways.

The plainness of Alaskan buildings, like many frontier dwellings, reflects the expedient nature of their construction. For the first or even second building on a site, an immediate need for shelter was the primary concern. As a result, the buildings were constructed with an eye to practicality, not fashion. Log cabins, requiring few tools and little fabrication, were usually the first buildings to replace tents at a given site and remain today the preferred form for wilderness sites and do-it-yourself builders. To the extent that the wood-framed buildings reflect prevailing styles, they do so more by form than ornament. Queen Anne cottages were built in the Lower 48 cities as one-story buildings, often L-shaped, featuring bay windows and front porches with gingerbread trim. In Alaska, these cottages were built, but without the stylistically identifying ornament. Bungalows, too, were plainer, as simple front-gabled, one-story buildings with front-gabled porches but without the art glass, wide eaves, and battered porch posts that would clearly identify them as bungalows. Yet the form of these small buildings recalls their more fashionable cousins.

Construction materials posed a special challenge in Alaska. In the part of the state that is forested, wood was the chosen frontier building material, as in the settlement of the rest of the United States. Whether log cabins or wood-framed houses, the architecture used wood freely and without artifice. This reliance on wood has continued to the present, with consciously rustic buildings employing exposed wood trusses and log (or branch) ornament. Even though today most commercial lumber is imported, wood continues to be a popular material. Not so brick and stone. Alaskan clay does not lend itself to satisfactory construction brick, and all brick is imported. While the state has some fine stone, including marble, the rugged Alaskan topography renders its transportation too expensive for widespread use. Concrete, on the other hand, has been used extensively as a construction material since the 1920s. Mixed in Alaska, poured in place, and fireproof, it has been an ideal material for public and commercial buildings. In the last two decades, architects and contractors have experimented with colored and textured concrete, increasing its viability as a decorative as well as functional material. Also currently popular for commercial buildings are enameled, metal panels. Colorful and durable, they are well suited to the climate.

The high cost of imported materials and labor in addition to the short building season create a situation in which prefabricated buildings are extremely practical. The canvas tent of the gold stampeders was one of the first prefabricated shelters, and it began a long tradition. Galvanized iron buildings were brought to gold-rush towns such as Nome and Circle. Ready-cut buildings, buildings whose lumber was prepared to specification and shipped in to be assembled on site, were also used. Other buildings were designed to be mobile. The wanigan, a one-room, wood-framed dwelling, was built on skids (sledlike runners) so that it could be moved in the wintertime.

World War II sparked development of several forms of prefabricated dwellings. The quonset hut, Loxtave buildings (horizontal plank walls with a locking system at the corners), and Harman houses (a prefabricated steel design) appeared in Alaska in the 1940s. A modern wanigan, likewise favored for remote working conditions, is the ATCO trailer popularized during pipeline construction—a bland box of four rooms, each with an exterior entrance. (ATCO was founded in Calgary as the Alberta Trailer Company but is today known just as ATCO.) With the automobile, tents became campers, towed on a trailer. Mobile homes were a larger, more permanent version. Without the wheels, these buildings are known as manufactured houses—two long prefabricated sections put together to form a "double-wide" house. Although this housing form's uniformity, bland design, and lack of cultural identity are seen as the scourge of the Alaskan landscape today, it continues a long tradition of prefabricated construction.

Strong regional differences in climate were reflected in Alaska's traditional Native architecture. The architecture of the last century, while maintaining some regional variations, is far more uniform, responding to cultural imperatives. The most visible cold-weather adaptations in American Alaskan architecture include orientation of the building, small size, and vestibules, or arctic entries, added to everything from log cabins to quonset huts. Permafrost, which underlies about 60 percent of Alaska, melts when the insulating tundra layer is removed or when heat from a building is transferred to the ground, causing a building to settle unevenly, or even to cave in. Where possible, building sites on permafrost are avoided. But where necessary, buildings can be built on piling and the building leveled as the piles sink unevenly; on thermopiles, which dissipate heat around the piles; or on a thick layer of gravel.

The climate affects design most noticeably in northern and western areas, where severe temperatures combine with strong winds. Architects and builders have invented a number of high-tech solutions to cope with severe cold, strong winds, and drifting snow, particularly for the North Slope and other arctic regions. Roofs are designed for minimum wind resistance, and structures are set on raised piers so that snow blows under them. Water and sewer pipes are placed in insulated conduits called utilidors. Prefabrication is especially favored, due to construction costs that include labor at over $100 an hour on the North Slope.

Aside from climate and materials, Alaska's architecture is explained by its history—how Americans influenced Native architecture to the point of extinction of traditional forms, how the exploitation of Alaska's natural resources influenced settlement and development, how official neglect discouraged permanent building, and later, how government intervention spurred development. Even beyond Alaska's unique heritage framed by Natives and Russians, Alaska's history as an American district, territory, and state is like no other.

FROM THE PURCHASE TO THE GOLD RUSH

After the expansion-minded United States acquired Alaska in 1867 for $7.2 million, this nation largely ignored its new holding. In its first thirty years as a U.S. possession, Alaska saw only sporadic and unenthusiastic official interest. Two major exports in the late nineteenth century, salmon and gold, attracted Americans. Although most of the profits of these industries went to San Francisco or New York, some of the workers stayed. By 1897, on the brink of the Klondike gold rush, the American influence in Alaska was evident in its more than five thousand U.S. residents, in the growing influence of the Protestant missions, and in the boomtown architecture.

The fur trade, which had been the Russians' primary source of income, diminished toward the end of the nineteenth century. The Pribilof Islands produced an average of $2.5 million worth of fur seal skins annually from 1870 to 1890 for the Alaska Commercial Company, which had obtained a monopoly from the U.S. government. After 1890 the fur seal population fell off dramatically, and conservation measures were taken. The San Francisco-based Alaska Commercial Company also traded in the western part of the territory for beaver, marten, and other furs trapped by Natives. A half-dozen fur companies challenged the Alaska Commercial Company's dominance.

Aided by new canning technology, the salmon-packing industry rose to prominence in Alaska's economy after its introduction in 1878. The Russians

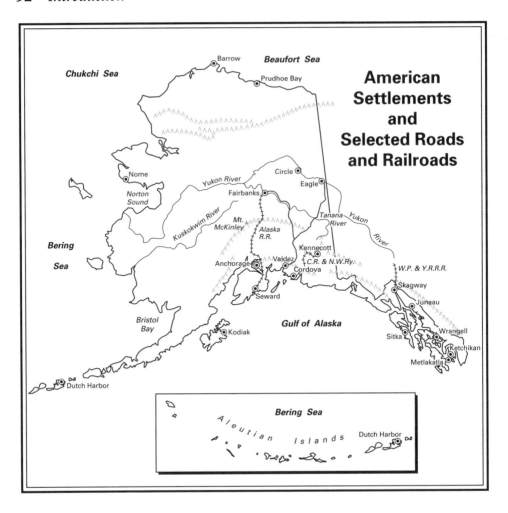

American
Settlements
and
Selected Roads
and Railroads

had salted salmon, mostly for local consumption. At first, the Americans continued to salt and dry salmon but had difficulties finding markets for the products. The canning industry began in 1878 when the Cutting Packing Company built a cannery at Old Sitka, 6 miles north of Sitka, and Sisson, Waters and Company built another at Klawock on Prince of Wales Island. These canneries, the first of many financed by San Francisco capital and using machinery to top and solder the cans, produced about thirteen thousand cases per year. In 1882, a cannery built on the Karluk River on Kodiak Island doubled total output.[122] Salmon canning continued to increase geometrically as new canneries were constructed and new areas were fished. By the turn of the century, there were fifty-five canneries producing over $2 million worth of canned salmon per year.

Architecturally, canneries were distinctive because of their proximity to water, large size, wood-frame construction, and gable roofs. To accommodate drastic tides (varying 30 feet in Cook Inlet, for example) and to facilitate disposal of waste, canneries were often built on piling out over the water. The industry was mechanized incrementally. Mechanical filling machines were developed in 1884, and machines to remove heads, fins, and guts became available in 1903. New machines required larger buildings, stretching for 100 feet or even 200 feet in length. These wood-framed buildings, often covered with vertical-plank siding, contained the cannery machinery and supplies. Other buildings at cannery sites included the machine shop, mess hall, and lodging for the workers. The canneries were typically used only a month or two out of the year. After depleting a fishery area, cannery operators closed plants and moved machinery to new locations, leaving the buildings to deteriorate.

As with any resource-based industry, the proliferation of canneries was a mixed blessing for Alaska. They tended to be owned by non-Alaskan companies, to employ nonresidents, and to be used only seasonally. In 1901, the industry employed 4,584 whites, who were probably both seasonal and permanent residents; 2,388 Natives, who were obviously permanent residents; and 4,664 Chinese, members of labor gangs, who were imported only for the short salmon season and then returned to San Francisco or Seattle.[123] The companies owning the canneries became larger and larger; when the industry overproduced in 1891, driving the price down, the Alaska Packers Association formed to regulate output.[124] By 1901, the association and one other corporation controlled forty of the fifty-five canneries.[125] The intense harvesting of salmon was devastating to many Natives. By setting a trap at the mouth of a river, the canneries often blocked the salmon run so effectively that Natives fishing upstream were unable to catch enough salmon to survive. Effective legislation to protect the salmon run was not enacted until 1906.

Gold was the resource that would put Alaska on the map, and gold brought Americans to Alaska long before the Klondike gold rush of 1897–1898. As early as 1861, prospectors stampeded to the Cassiar District in British Columbia. Reached by the Stikine River, whose mouth was close to Fort Wrangel (present-day Wrangell) in Alaska, the Cassiar District had attracted more than a thousand miners by 1875.[126] A number of them wintered in Fort Wrangel, and others searched the coast for strikes.

The most significant early gold strike in Alaska was at present-day Juneau, where Richard T. Harris and Joe Juneau struck gold in 1880. The two men staked claims, organized the Harris Mining District, named for Richard, and laid out a grid-plan townsite, eventually named for Joe. By the next year, over one hundred men had followed, most of them mining placer gold. Placer mining, requiring only a washing process to separate gold from gravel, could be undertaken with few men and little equipment.

But Juneau's real wealth lay in lode deposits. John Treadwell, a California contractor and mining engineer, developed the first lode gold mine in 1882. On Douglas Island, across the Gastineau Channel from Juneau, the Glory Hole,

The Presbyterians' boarding school for Native boys in Sitka was housed in the building on the left. Under construction when this photograph was taken c. 1883 is the building for the girls, who had previously been educated in Wrangell.

an open pit mine, covered 13 acres on the surface and was excavated to a depth of 2,000 feet by 1917. To separate the gold from the hard rock in which it was lodged, Treadwell built a 5-stamp mill in 1882; by 1888, he had 360 stamps, to form one of the nation's largest gold plants. (A stamp mill was a giant iron hammer that pulverized the chunks of ore so that the gold could be separated out.) Large timber-framed structures sheltered these mills, while additional wood-framed buildings housed administrative offices, workers, and mess halls. The Treadwell operation required a large capital investment but remained profitable until a disastrous cave-in and flood in 1917. The four Treadwell mines had turned the ground into a honeycomb of drifts and shafts. The cave-in flooded three of the mines; the fourth operated only until 1922.[127]

By the late 1880s, prospectors had penetrated the interior of Alaska, finding an occasional strike. The first rush followed the 1886 discovery of gold on the Fortymile River. A larger strike at Birch Creek in 1893 helped create the Yukon River town of Circle City (named for its supposed location on the Arctic Circle; actually, it was 75 miles south). Claiming to be both the "greatest log cabin town in the world"[128] and the largest town on the Yukon before the Klondike gold rush,[129] Circle's population soared from about 500 in 1895 to 1,200 in 1896, and lots sold for $2,000. In 1896, the nearby diggings produced over $1 million worth of gold.[130] Judge James Wickersham, who held court there in 1900, described Circle City in its heyday:

> Every building was constructed of round spruce logs cut in the nearby forest. The Grand Opera House was of the spread-eagle type of architecture, the only double-decker in the city. The saloons, the stores, the church, and

the sanctum of the *Yukon Press*, the dance halls, and the Indian rancheries, miners' cabins and dog houses were all one-story and squat, with every flat pole roof covered a foot deep with sod.[131]

But with news of discovery of gold on a tributary of the Klondike River on 17 August 1896, Circle's population shrank, and by 1900, Wickersham recorded that the town was "almost abandoned."[132]

Just as Russian promyshlenniki were complemented by Russian Orthodox missionaries, American fishermen and miners were accompanied by American Protestant missionaries, the most notable of whom was Rev. Sheldon Jackson. In 1877, Jackson accompanied the first Presbyterian missionaries to Alaska, who established a mission in Wrangell. Even though he had only reluctant support from the national church, Jackson, like other American missionaries through the history of the United States, saw an expansive role for Presbyterianism in converting and educating the Natives. Unlike the Russian Orthodox missionary Veniaminov, Jackson advocated the eradication of Native culture in favor of a complete adoption of an American way of life. In 1882, he rebuilt the Sitka Mission, then called the Industrial Home for Boys. This boarding school for the most promising Natives instructed them in vocational skills and the four R's (reading, 'riting, 'rithmetic, and religion) and introduced them to American

Native graduates of the Presbyterians' school were encouraged to build these single-family cottages in which to set up American-style housekeeping.

dress and behavior. In theory, these "educated" Natives would return to their villages and influence their neighbors.

The situation of the Natives in Sitka provided one of the more formidable tasks for the missionaries. The Sitka Tlingits, segregated by the Russians into a village of traditional plank houses on the west side of town, had long lived in the shadow of the white town and depended economically on the whites for trade. The Presbyterians deliberately built the Sitka Mission apart from the Indian village, on the east side of town, to separate the students from the evil environment from which they came. The first building expressly built for the school, Austin Hall, was constructed in 1882, reusing materials from the abandoned cannery 6 miles away. The two-story building, measuring 100 feet by 50 feet, had a jerkinhead gable roof.[133] Two years later the boys' dormitory was joined by one for girls. These early buildings do not survive, but the school has evolved into Sheldon Jackson College, still operating in Sitka (SE045, p. 190).

The Presbyterians also established a revolving loan fund so that recent graduates of the school, married to one another, could set up housekeeping in appropriate American-style single-family dwellings. The houses were 24 feet square, one and a half stories, with a living room, kitchen, pantry, and wood closet on the first floor and two bedrooms and a closet on the second.[134] The loans were for $350, payable in five annual installments. That sum paid for building materials; the construction was undertaken by the graduates, who had been trained in the building arts. By 1898, eight houses had been constructed and five of the loans had been paid off.[135] The houses were clustered near the school, away from the Indian village.[136]

At the same time, the missionaries encouraged the Natives in the Indian village to replace their communal dwellings with single-family housing. The missionaries repeatedly expressed concern for sanitation to combat disease, particularly tuberculosis. But more important was their goal of civilizing the Native. American-style housing was equated with the American way of living, most explicitly in several annual governor's reports. Gov. Alfred P. Swineford described the Aleuts in 1886, "That they are well advanced in civilization is evidenced by the fact that they live in comfortable houses."[137] Two years later, Swineford described the Indians in Sitka, "With their dawning civilization has come a desire for better things, and as fast as they can accumulate the means they employ them in the building of new houses of modern style."[138] By 1902, James G. Brady, governor and former missionary, boasted that not one traditional dwelling remained in Sitka.[139]

Another approach to missionary work was undertaken by Rev. William Duncan at Metlakatla. Duncan, a Church of England lay missionary who first settled among the Tsimshian Indians near Port Simpson, British Columbia, developed a community of loyal followers. Arriving in Canada in 1857, Duncan attracted nearly a thousand Tsimshians to a close-knit, self-sufficient community. Demanding that the Natives give up their old ways, Duncan housed them in wood-framed, single-family dwellings, introduced them to capitalism and the Bible, and instituted a form of limited self-government.

After a quarrel with his church in 1887, Duncan moved the entire community to New Metlakatla (present-day Metlakatla) on Annette Island in Southeast Alaska, where they established a new village. Within three years, they had built ninety-one houses. Most were square, wood-framed, two-story structures, many with a Victorian irregularity of plan and ornament. Unusual buildings included a twelve-sided, twelve-gabled church, which became the town hall when a new church was built in 1896. The new church, measuring 70 feet by 100 feet, was a twin-towered Gothic creation, with two-stage buttresses, constructed of wood. To aid in self-sufficiency, Metlakatlans built a sawmill and a cannery and purchased their own ship. In 1891, Annette Island was declared an Indian reservation by the U.S. government, the first in Alaska. The success of Duncan's community depended on excluding the world at large (the Tsimshian police force was particularly harsh with anyone caught furnishing liquor to the residents). Duncan's exceedingly paternalistic society ultimately disintegrated when its members demanded more power than Duncan saw fit to give them.[140]

Duncan's isolationist approach contrasted with Jackson's strategy of selectively training and then mainstreaming Natives, and the latter view was adopted by most other missionary groups in Alaska. Because his resources were limited and the land so vast, Jackson called a meeting in 1880 with representatives of other Protestant denominations to invite them to open missions around Alaska. Representatives chose to focus their attentions on the various regions of the state. The Methodists at the meeting selected the Aleutian Islands; Baptists, Kodiak Island and Cook Inlet; and Episcopalians, the Yukon River.[141] The Presbyterians had a clear claim to Southeast, and they also took Point Barrow. Other denominations, among them the Roman Catholics, also began missionary activity in Alaska at about this time.

The Episcopalians, continuing the Church of England's work on the Yukon River, arrived in the Interior about the same time as American gold seekers. At remote sites such as Nenana and Anvik, they opened stations that had a church, a school, and often a hospital. The educational and medical services attracted area Natives, who were encouraged to build a new settlement with log or wood-framed dwellings in the shadow of the mission. Most of the mission buildings were modest in size, plain in appearance, and usually log in construction. The church might be distinguished by a bell tower, and the school might have more windows than other buildings, but generally they were little different architecturally than other American Alaskan buildings. One exception was Saint Peter's-by-the-Sea Church, the seat of the bishop, which was located in the capital, Sitka. Saint Peter's timber frame was filled with stone and the front featured a round arch in the gable end (SE044, p. 189). This picturesque church, constructed in 1899, was equalled in aesthetic achievement by the mission church at Tanana, which also featured a round arch in the gable

The Episcopalians' mission churches were usually small log buildings, marked by a modest cupola. This is Saint Stephen's in Fort Yukon, photographed in 1909.

end, but was constructed of logs and frame and sided with shingles (IN031, p. 235).

The Roman Catholic Mission at Holy Cross on the Yukon had some of the largest and most elaborate buildings on the river. The church, not unlike a late eighteenth-century New England church, was built in 1886. The large, wood-framed building had a square bell tower topped by a Baroque belfry; round-arch windows punctuated walls that were sided horizontally. Inside, the ceiling was barrel-arched, spaces were separated by columns, and the walls were ornamented with carving and painting. Nearby, a two-and-a-half-story frame building with prominent dormer windows served as the boarding school. Several dozen log cabins, the common domestic form for Americans in the Alaskan Interior, housed a Native population.

Extending his influence far beyond the church, the pioneer Presbyterian missionary Sheldon Jackson arranged to be appointed Alaska's first general agent for education in 1885. A sharp politician who spent most of each year in Washington, D.C., even while general agent for education, Jackson took this appointment as a mandate to continue his civilizing of the Natives. Faced with woefully inadequate funds to educate a widespread population, he used the missions to accomplish his goals. He employed mission teachers as government teachers and transferred four Presbyterian schools (at Hoonah, Wrangell, Haines, and Howkan) to the government. At the end of his twenty years as general agent, there were forty schools around Alaska with an enrollment of two thousand.[142]

Jackson was also active as a self-appointed Alaska lobbyist to Congress. When acquired in 1867, Alaska fell under jurisdiction of the War Department. After ten years, the army withdrew, leaving the U.S. Customs Service in charge. The 1884 Organic Act established the first civil government for Alaska and became as notable for what it did not do as for what it did. This Organic Act provided for a governor, with no real power, and a district court judge. Instead of granting territorial status, the act declared Alaska a district to be governed directly by Congress in the same way as the District of Columbia. Furthermore, the Organic Act did not extend any land laws to the district, thereby discouraging settlement and development.

As it was impossible to homestead or to acquire property through any other means, residents had no incentive to build substantial houses. Houses could be built, but their ownership was not guaranteed. In Sitka, Americans occupied the buildings left by the Russians, who had nearly all departed by 1870. The government, too, occupied Russian buildings. Where Americans did build extensively, such as at Juneau, they constructed plain houses of light wood framing, supplied by new sawmills that increasingly provided lumber for local needs. By 1901, there were twelve sawmills operating in Southeast.[143]

Americans' interest in Alaska was hesitant at first. Although attracted by the natural resources, they migrated there in fits and starts. Many came with no intention to settle permanently and may also have been discouraged by the lack of economic stability and law and order. The government did not put money

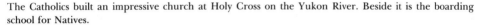

The Catholics built an impressive church at Holy Cross on the Yukon River. Beside it is the boarding school for Natives.

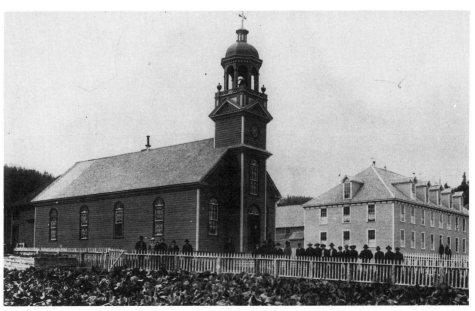

into construction or public works, and as a result, neither did private interests. At the beginning of the gold rush, Alaska's white settlement was concentrated mostly in port towns, housed in old Russian buildings or in wood-framed boomtown buildings.

FROM THE GOLD RUSH TO THE FIRST WORLD WAR

Alaska's somnolent state changed abruptly when, late in 1896, gold was discovered in Canada's Klondike region. Although it was not until the next summer that word of the strike reached "Outside" (that is, beyond Alaska), by 1898 thousands of people were pouring into the Klondike to find their fortunes. Their hopes were justified; the Klondike would yield over $200 million in gold, as it became North America's largest placer goldfield outside of California. The romance of the gold, especially in a depression-ridden United States, attracted the adventurers as never before.

An estimated 100,000 people started for the goldfields, although only about a third ever got there.[144] Perhaps 2,000 of them attempted the all-Canada routes, but most came by way of Alaska. From northern Southeast Alaska, the prospectors climbed the Chilkoot Trail, which was too steep for packhorses or sleds so that all supplies had to be carried on one's back. Another, even longer and higher route from northern Southeast Alaska was the White Pass; an even longer route was the Chilkat Trail. Other courses included going up the Yukon River by steamboat, a circuitous but less taxing route, or over the Valdez Glacier, the most dangerous course. The profitable areas in the Klondike were soon claimed, and would-be miners spread out throughout the Yukon and Interior Alaska.

Subsequent strikes in Alaska caused this mobile population to rush to each emerging scene—to the Koyukuk in 1898, to Nome in 1899, to Fairbanks in 1902, and, for the next decade, to a host of lesser camps. As a truly equal-opportunity endeavor, gold mining probably reached its height in Nome, where gold lay only 1 foot to 4 feet below the beach sands. The gold was also easily separated from the sand by the simple technique of placing the sand in a rocker with water and rocking until the sand shook out and only the gold remained. A judge ruled that no claims could be staked on the beach. This opened the way for over 2,000 men and women to crowd together on Nome's beaches where they retrieved over $2 million in gold in a single year.[145]

In most places, placer mining was more effective when undertaken with a team of two or three. Miners shoveled the gravel into a long sluice box and mixed it with water until the heavier gold separated out. To uncover old streambeds where gold-rich gravel was likely to be, miners used high-pressure water in a technique called hydraulic mining. An elevated water source fed into smaller and smaller hoses to produce the pressure. The need for water, however, prevented hydraulic mining in the winter. When the placer gold ran deep below ground, miners sank a shaft and hoisted the gravel to the surface. (When the underground diggings ran parallel to the ground's surface, they were called drifts, and the process, drift mining.) Permafrost both helped and hindered the operation. Because the ground was constantly frozen, the shafts needed little timber shoring; but to loosen the gravel, the ground had to be melted with steam points. Steam required boilers, brought in by sled in the winter, and vast quantities of wood to fire them.

Placer gold could be obtained through drift mining, a two-person procedure.

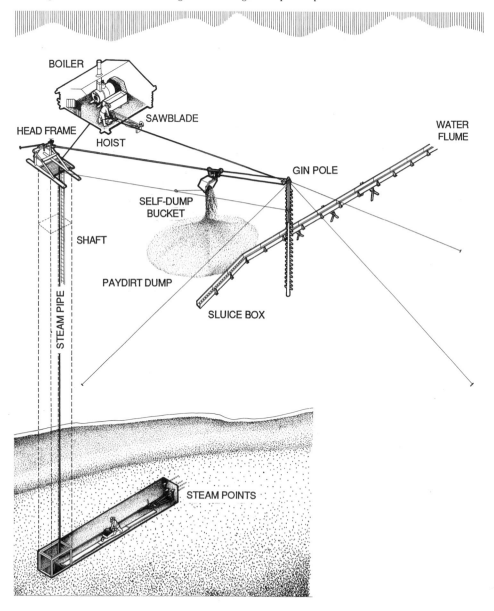

Population of Alaska[148]

YEAR	TOTAL POPULATION	NATIVE	NON-NATIVE
1880	33,426	32,996	430
1890	32,052	25,354	6,698
1900	63,592	29,542	34,050
1910	64,356	25,331	39,025
1920	55,036	26,558	28,478
1930	59,278	29,983	29,295
1940	72,524	32,458	40,066
1950	128,643	33,863	94,780
1960	226,167	43,081	183,086
1970	300,382	50,554	249,828
1980	401,851	64,103	337,748
1990	550,043	85,698	464,345

Although some placer mining sites were worked for several decades, most were quickly exhausted and the miners moved on, abandoning their log cabins. Where they had drift mined, they left behind a shaft as well as the underground workings, while hydraulic mining rearranged streambeds. Neither left the mark in the landscape that the later dredges would.

In contrast to these simple, individual gold-mining operations, the discovery of an exceptionally rich copper deposit in Alaska resulted in a large corporate undertaking. Located on the Kennicott River in the Wrangell Mountains, the copper required an extensive mining operation to extract it and a means of transporting it to market. The large capital investment that was required was provided by the Alaska Syndicate, formed by the Guggenheim and J. P. Morgan interests, who bought the claims and invested $25 million in the largest, most costly, and most complex mine in Alaska. At Kennecott (the mining operation went by a misspelling of the glacier and river), large, wood-framed, gable-roofed buildings sheltered the operation, which consisted of crushing the ore, separating out the copper, and processing lower-grade ore on site (SC119, p. 148).[146]

Alaska's rapid population growth, from less than 5,000 whites in 1890 to more than 30,000 in 1900,[147] was only the first of many booms that Alaska would experience over the next century. The census figures reveal these surges. The new population demanded new public works. Coastal shipping was greatly aided by the construction of a dozen lighthouses between 1902 and 1906. They were the first built by the U.S. government in Alaska and maintained by the U.S. Lighthouse Service.[149] Set on a rocky island, the lighthouse tower was often attached to the keeper's dwelling, sometimes rising out of the roof. The first was the lighthouse on Sentinel Island, constructed in 1902; it had a jerkinhead gable roof and a square tower on the center of its facade. Although most of the lighthouses were replaced with concrete, functional structures in the

The first lighthouse to help guide ships through the Southeast Passage was the one on Sentinel Island. Like most of the dozen lighthouses built at this time, the tower bearing the light was incorporated into the lightkeeper's dwelling.

Nenana was a construction camp built by the Alaska Engineering Commission. From right to left in this 1917 photograph are the general offices, bachelor quarters, mess house, hospital, and cottages. Only the latter remain.

1930s, the light at Eldred Rock maintains its original 1906 appearance: a two-story octagonal concrete-and-wood building with a tower rising from the peak of its roof (SE015, p. 168).

Water was the most efficient transportation system both for traffic entering Alaska and for traffic within Alaska. Nearly all communities were located on the coast or on rivers. The first steamboat appeared on the Yukon River in 1869, and in 1898 and 1899, more than one hundred steamboats worked the Yukon. Besides bringing people and goods into the region, steamboats also facilitated contacts between the villages on the river, creating a linear community. In the winter, the smooth surface of iced-over rivers made the best trails. Dogs, harnessed together in a team to pull sleds of freight and mail along the frozen rivers, served as the most practical form of transportation for about six months of the year.

The construction of major public roads began in 1900 with the Trans-Alaska Military Road, more a trail than an actual road, from Fort Liscum near the port of Valdez to Fort Egbert near the border town of Eagle in the Interior. In 1905, a reapportionment of money from Alaskan business license fees resulted in the creation of the Alaska Road Commission, a three-man board under jurisdiction of the War Department, charged with constructing roads.[150] By 1920, the board had constructed nearly 5,000 miles of unpaved roads and trails, over 1,000 of which were suitable for wagons.[151] Most travel was by sled dogs or packhorses and took place in the winter.

To serve travelers, a number of roadhouses opened along the routes to provide meals and lodging. Privately constructed, roadhouses were located about 20 miles apart, a good day's haul by dog sled. Due to their remote locations, roadhouses were usually simply constructed of round logs, although larger than their single-family counterparts. When a party of New Yorkers tried to drive the Valdez-Fairbanks trail in 1910 and failed, they ended up hiking a portion of the trail. One of them described the accommodations:

> The Alaskan road house is a distinct institution of pronounced characteristics. Downstairs: one living room containing a large drum stove and racks on the rafters above for the drying of wet garments, a miscellaneous assortment of home-made "easy" chairs; and sometimes a rocker or two; one card table, and a trough for two tin wash basins. These are the essentials. There are variations, the favorite being a small bar in one corner. The dining-room is usually lacking in superfluous embellishment, but contains in their sublimated form all the important elements, namely, tables and benches.
>
> Upstairs are two divisions: one contains double tiers of wooden bunks well supplied with heavy woolen blankets; the other is more or less subdivided by low partitions, which may enclose spring mattressed cots. This is called "the ladies' half," for women often travel the Valdez trail. Your male sourdough, as a rule, scorns the affectation of this superfluous privacy and ease, and foregathers with his fellows. The price for "a bed" is the same, and you will sleep in blankets in either case.[152]

Often landmarks in the wilderness, roadhouses served an important social function, being a place to exchange information about people, gold, and trail conditions.

When the federal government began construction of the 470-mile Alaska

Railroad in 1915, there were several privately constructed railroads already in existence. In 1898, construction began on the White Pass and Yukon, a 101-mile line (only 22 of which were in Alaska) that took gold seekers from Skagway to Whitehorse on the Yukon River, in Canada. The Copper River and Northwestern Railway, the Alaska Syndicate's 196-mile line from Cordova to the copper mines at Kennecott, was under construction from 1906 to 1911. The Alaska Northern led from Seward northward. Begun in 1902, it was foundering financially and had penetrated only 72 miles when the Alaska Railroad took it over. The Alaska Railroad also acquired a 45-mile narrow-gauge line in the Tanana Valley, serving the goldfields around Fairbanks. Another railroad, the Solomon and Council City, was constructed in the goldfields near Nome.

Running from Seward north to Fairbanks, the Alaska Railroad, completed in 1923, achieved its purpose of opening the territory for settlement. Besides construction of the line itself, the Alaska Engineering Commission (AEC), the construction arm of the railroad, built temporary construction camps and laid out townsites.[153] One of the more successful towns was Anchorage, which the AEC established as the northernmost port along the line. They laid out the town on an unrelieved grid plan, built housing for their employees, and sold lots to the public. The AEC's interest in Anchorage continued: it managed the city for the first five years, from 1915 to 1920, and moved its headquarters there in 1917. Up and down the line, the AEC built bungalows of various appealing designs for its managers, while construction camps were often log buildings. Section houses—permanent bunkhouses for maintenance crews along the lines—were of utilitarian design. Depots, on the other hand, were an advertisement for the railroad. In the Craftsman style, they were long, low hip-roofed structures, with overhanging eaves. In general, the AEC buildings reflected prevailing styles and methods of construction in the U.S. at the time.

The same pattern prevailed in much of the commercial and domestic architecture of Alaska, depending on the proximity of a sawmill. Where a sawmill operated, usually in established towns such as Juneau or in industrial boom-towns such as Kennecott, wood-frame construction covered with horizontal siding proliferated. Such houses were often in the form of Queen Anne cottages, sparsely ornamented. Because of heating costs the houses were small, and such forms as the bungalow or cottage were the most practical and comfortable. Often built without basements, these small wood-framed buildings were easily moved, responding to the mobile population and to the value of building materials. Frequent additions intensified the dynamic nature of the building. The interiors, filled with wallpaper, carpets, lamps, and furniture imported from the Lower 48, reflected popular trends and personal taste.

A remarkably well-documented example of the construction of a wood-framed cottage appears in the journal of Judge James Wickersham, kept when he built a house in Fairbanks in one week in 1904 (IN010.1, p. 220). Wickersham designed the house himself and helped build it. His first task was to clear the site and build a fence; "the first picket fence in the Tanana Valley—real planed pickets and will paint them."[154] He started construction on 23 May, carrying the lumber from the sawmill on his back as "there is not *yet* a *wagon* in the Tanana country—except one made by nailing lumber together for wheels."[155] He hired a carpenter and laborers but found them expensive and so did much of the work himself. By 28 May he reported the house completed, except for doors and windows. On 11 June he drew a plan in his journal, which showed the T-shaped house, with two rooms, 14 feet by 16 feet and 12 feet by 14 feet. He commented: "Have been particular to make the house tight and warm. Have it beautifully papered. Have good carpet of Japanese matting. . . . Two very comfortable rooms and good spring bed." Two years later, he expanded the house to six rooms.

Commercial buildings were also wood-framed, with the false fronts popular in American frontier towns. Skagway, an archetypal boomtown, grew from a homestead to a population of 8,000 within two years of the Klondike gold strike. Boardwalks lined the unpaved commercial streets. The grid plan of the town oriented lots toward the major streets; commercial buildings had expensive, and therefore narrow, frontages. Generally taller than they were wide, these commercial fronts were placed directly on the building line. False fronts rose above the gables, making the building appear more substantial and providing space for signs and advertising. Customers entered through a central, recessed doorway, or sometimes via a canted corner. Soon the transfer point of most transportation into the Klondike, Skagway's excellent access to Seattle markets encouraged importation of plate glass and pressed metal ornament to enrich the thriving commercial district.[156]

By contrast, in remote areas, or in towns before the sawmills got there, log cabins were the rule. Although some log cabins were hardy, permanent structures, others, erected in haste, were meant only to serve for a winter or two. In 1914 Rev. Hudson Stuck described the fluidity of the population, one of the factors contributing to the impermanent nature of some log cabins.

> The prospectors and miners, who constitute the bulk of the white population, are not often very long in one place. Many of them might rightly be classed as permanent, but very few as settled inhabitants. It is the commonest thing to meet men a thousand miles away from the place where one met them last. A new "strike" will draw men from every mining camp in Alaska. A big strike will shift the centre of gravity of the whole white population in a few months. Indeed, a certain restless belief in the superior opportunities of some other spot is one of the characteristics of the prospector.[157]

For whatever its intended duration, the log cabin could be quickly erected by one or two men. In the Interior, where trees were smaller than in Southeast, the cabins tended to be of round logs and were thus unlike the hewn-log structures of the Russians. The corners were most frequently saddle notched. Foundations were dispensed with; sill logs were laid directly on the ground. Most

Fairbanks in the early twentieth century had a mix of log and frame buildings. The house in the center of the photograph is a hip-roof, wood-framed cottage, while left of it is a log cabin. The log building on the right is the George C. Thomas Library (IN001.1).

commonly, a cabin had one room with a door in the gable end. The gable roof was formed of poles, running perpendicular to the ridgepole and purlins, on which were piled moss and earth for insulation. Sometimes settlers flattened fuel cans or butter tins to be used as roof shingles. One or two windows provided the only light; a sheet-metal stove, brought in by river, furnished heat. An arctic entry, or unheated vestibule, was often added to the entrance. Settlers might reuse planks from one building to the next, and stoves and stovepipes traveled with their owners to new cabins.

One prospector described the process of constructing his cabin on Alder Creek, near Seventy Mile, in July 1910:

> There we put up a tent, got a small sheet iron stove to cook on and started to build a cabin. Cut and hauled in the logs, gathered moss to chink and cover the roof after first splitting six to eight inch sticks with a whip-saw covering the rafter logs. Then shoveled a foot of dirt on top of that. We whip-sawed lumber for the floor and door, window frames were handmade during the winter and the glass put in them. Put a six inch ventilator in one end. Cabin, when finished, was 14 by 18 feet inside and very comfortable.[158]

Another miner described the process of whipsawing the required timbers.

> Now whip sawing lumber in the middle of summer is not what it is cracked up to be between the heat and mosquitoes and it does get hot in the Yukon Country in July and the mosquitoes it is terrible, especially when you happen to get a snarly twisty log and the timber on the banks of Forty Mile is

Miners cut planks manually from logs by whipsawing, a two-person task.

unusually so, well Jack and Sid did the sawing and the language they used was equal to the greatest expert on profane words in the world. The boys would saw awhile, sit down and wipe the perspiration off their faces and the saw dust out of their eyes and when they would saw, they would have to use both hands and keep the saw straight on the lines and then a mosquito or several of them would find a tender place they would have to stop and knock that mosquito off.[159]

The interior furnishings were handmade and basic, as a description of this cabin in Circle City in 1896 attested:

At the back—generally—were the bunks, usually two high, with poles for "springs," with hemlock or spruce boughs on them on which were put the robes or blankets. This made a good bed until the boughs shed their needles when they were like so many sticks and far from comfortable until renewed; which they sometimes were and sometimes not![160]

Yet the cabins could be appealing and comfortable. Four years before building his house in Fairbanks, Judge Wickersham had built a log cabin in Eagle and described it in reassuring terms in a letter to his mother in 1900 (IN042, p. 241):

Our new cabin in Eagle is 17 by 22 feet square, with a kitchen 10 by 17 feet and an outhouse at the kitchen door for wood, etc. It has a fine floor, and I am lining it with canvas and then putting on wall paper; it is first chinked with oakum and then with moss, and the roof is covered with sawed poles from the comb to the eaves; over the poles I put heavy oiled sail cloth, and over that a layer of three inches of dry moss, and then covered it all with four inches of sand. The house will be banked up high with dirt, and good storm doors made, plenty of wood will be piled inside—then let the storms blow as they will, we'll be warm and comfortable still.[161]

Miners, particularly those who stayed in the country for a while, needed additional buildings to accommodate tasks other than prospecting. In the winter, trapping afforded a reasonable income; dog teams aided this endeavor but required doghouses. Dogs needed to be fed, and although salmon was readily available, it had to be caught during the runs in summer and preserved by drying or smoking, necessitating smokehouses. In order to store a year's supply of food out of the reach of dogs and wild animals, trappers built caches, or elevated storage sheds. Vegetables from greenhouses provided variety to the diet, and, of course, there were outhouses.

The first public and commercial buildings in remote areas tended to take the form and materials of the log cabins. The U.S. Commissioner's Court in Chisana, for instance, resembled any standard log cabin. Probably constructed in 1913–1914 during a gold stampede, the courthouse is a 15-foot-square, one-story cabin of round logs, with a gable roof and a shed-roofed addition (SC121.1, p. 153). Roadhouses and store buildings outgrew houses, but they also used log construction. The two-story Northern Commercial Company Store in Wiseman, constructed about 1910, overshadowed the one-story cabins in the town (IN052, p. 249). Corrugated, galvanized iron, easily transported into the Interior by river, was a convenient, cheap, and fireproof material. Mostly used on warehouses, it appeared in Circle and Eagle before 1900 and also covered a large addition, since demolished, to the store in Wiseman.

The influx of Americans into Alaska at the turn of the century resulted in new attention from Washington, D.C., and, eventually, self-government. A valueless homestead act, enacted in 1898, was replaced with an effective one in 1903.[162] A criminal code was enacted in 1899 and a civil code in 1900. The latter provided for three judicial districts (one of which was established by Judge Wickersham in Eagle and then moved to Fairbanks in 1904) and also moved the seat of government from Sitka to the thriving gold-mining town of Juneau. In 1906, Alaska elected a delegate to Congress, and finally, in 1912, received full territorial status.[163]

Reflecting this new federal attention, the Governor's Mansion, designed by Supervising Architect of the Treasury James Knox Taylor, was constructed in Juneau in 1912. This Colonial Revival building, domestic in style, originally had a small portico and steep gable dormers; it was considerably altered in 1936 (SE016, p. 170).

The thousands of gold seekers pouring into Alaska also raised concerns about law and order. The army, which had left Alaska in 1877, returned, contribut-

The order of Fort Seward in the foreground contrasts with the random development of Haines in this photograph by Winter and Pond.

ing not only a military presence but also mounting several exploratory expeditions and, by 1904, setting up a communications system that linked Alaska with the rest of the United States. The army established posts at Saint Michael on Norton Sound, Fort Egbert near Eagle, Fort Gibbon on the Yukon, Fort Davis near Nome, Fort Liscum near Valdez, and Fort Seward near Haines. Each of these posts had simple wood-framed buildings, notable for their large size and formal arrangement. The two- and three-story buildings, particularly the larger ones such as the barracks, were a stark contrast to the small one-room log cabins of the other Americans. In each post's careful arrangement around an open parade ground, the fort was a contrast to the towns that had a grid plan, if any, and no planned open space.

FROM THE FIRST WORLD WAR TO STATEHOOD

Although completion of the Alaska Railroad in 1923 promised new economic growth, in fact the decade of the 1920s was not a prosperous one in Alaska. The white population had dropped from about 36,000 in 1910 to 28,000 in 1920, while the Native population stayed relatively constant, ranging between 25,000 and 30,000 from 1900 to 1930. Many whites, lured Outside during World War I, either to enter the army or to take high-paying industrial jobs, did not return to Alaska after the war. The prosperity in the rest of the United

States was too promising. In fact, Alaska's economy did not pick up until the late 1930s, and then, during and after World War II, it experienced unprecedented growth.

After the First World War, there were no dramatic gold strikes attracting the individual prospector. Gold production continued, but as placer gold became more difficult to reach, gold mining required dredges and other equipment that demanded significant capital. By 1929, 71 percent of Alaska's placer gold was extracted by dredges—large, flat-roofed structures that floated in ponds they created by dredging. On board, gold was separated from gravel, which was then discarded. Mineral output declined steadily, from $23 million in 1920 to $10 million in 1933, the lowest yield since 1904.[164] When Franklin D. Roosevelt raised the price of gold from $20.67 per ounce to $35 in 1934, gold production increased again. Annual production rose to nearly $24 million in the late 1930s.[165] Copper production, which had soared during the First World War, dropped in the 1920s, and the mighty Kennecott Mines closed in 1938.

By 1940, forty-eight dredges operated around Alaska, compared with twenty-eight in 1930.[166] On Coal Creek, a tributary of the Yukon River between Eagle and Circle named for its deposits of coal that were never profitably mined, individuals had been placer mining since the turn of the century. In 1934 the claims were consolidated and bought up by a company called Gold Placers Inc., the vice president of which was Ernest Patty, formerly the head of the University of Alaska mining school. Gold Placers' dredge could process low-content gravel profitably, but it transformed the Coal Creek valley, churning up 5 1/2 miles of the streambed. The men who worked the mine were housed in simple frame buildings (IN050, p. 247). On a larger scale, the Fairbanks Exploration Company, organized in 1924, operated eight dredges in the Fairbanks area.

For years, Alaska's agricultural potential had been heralded and frequently discussed, but never realized.[167] In the 1930s, however, Alaska farming made headlines. In 1935, 202 families were brought to Alaska through a resettlement project of the Federal Emergency Relief Administration (soon to become the Works Progress Administration). The colonists, mostly farmers from the northern United States, received plots of land in the Matanuska Valley northeast of Anchorage, loans to pay for them, and aid in clearing the land and building their homes.

Houses were built according to one of five floor plans provided by government architect David R. Williams and constructed of either wood frame or logs sawn flat on three sides. Four of the plans were for one-and-a-half-story houses, with bedrooms in the half story; four of them had a combined living room and kitchen; and none had a separate dining room. The houses had side-gable roofs and were either L-shaped or had some element, such as a vestibule, projecting from the mass of the building. Owners could make minor variations. The barn designs were standard, a 32-foot-square gambrel-roofed structure, often constructed with logs on the lower portion and frame above.[168]

Two hundred farms such as this were built in the 1930s in the Matanuska Valley through the sponsorship of the Federal Emergency Relief Administration.

The Matanuska colony received extensive publicity, both across the country and in Alaska. Although the project was not entirely successful—disgruntled colonists left because of bureaucratic inefficiencies—the attention it brought to Alaska was significant.

The airplane transformed transportation in Alaska. Anchorage built its first airport in 1923,[169] and air mail service was inaugurated by Ben Eielson in 1924, with a flight from Fairbanks to McGrath.[170] As air travel became increasingly common through the 1930s, remote villages were suddenly easily accessible. Roads continued to be improved. Settlements, previously oriented to waterways and railroad lines, developed at crossroads and along the highways.

Domestic architecture followed patterns established by the 1910s. Log cabins were constructed in remote areas. In the 1920s, when buildings were first constructed at the new Mount McKinley National Park (now Denali National Park), they were designed in the Rustic style, typical of U.S. park construction in the 1920s and 1930s. These log structures, designed to be compatible with the landscape, were also typical of contemporary construction in the Interior; here log cabins constituted a viable architecture, not a nostalgic reference to the past.

Alaskan cities increasingly resembled developed areas in the rest of the United States. Mostly conservative in their appropriation of popular styles, small wood-framed houses adapted Colonial Revival vocabularies, as the construction of symmetrical one- and one-and-a-half-story dwellings spread out from the town cores. Occasionally a gambrel roof hinted at Dutch Colonial influence, or a steep and swooping gabled entrance indicated Tudor Revival longings.

Commercial architecture began to lose its boomtown character as wooden structures were replaced by Moderne or Art Deco buildings. Concrete, which was mixed locally and fireproof, was particularly suited for these sleek styles. Some of the most flamboyant applications of the Art Deco were movie theaters erected by Cap Lathrop, who had a chain across the state. The Fourth Avenue Theatre in Anchorage, designed in 1941 but not completed until after the war, featured a concrete facade with a curving "4th Avenue" sign in Art Deco lettering and a highly polished interior with Alaskan murals (SC004, p. 84). At its opening, the *Daily Times* called the theater "a landmark in the transition of Anchorage from a frontier community to a city of permanence."[171]

Taking advantage of Public Works Administration money available in the late 1930s, a number of combined post offices and courthouses were built around the territory. Executed in concrete, the style was generally Moderne: smooth, unornamented designs that featured a rectilinear flatness. Classical references were stylized, such as piers resembling columns or geometric grooves replacing capitals. The U.S. Post Office and Courthouse in Anchorage (Gilbert Stanley Underwood, 1939–1940) (SC003, p. 84) is a two-story, twelve-bay rectangle punctuated at each end by a three-story, recessed block. The pier-and-spandrel design of the main block heightened the sleekness and spareness of the design. In Fairbanks, the U.S. Post Office and Courthouse (George Ray, 1932–1933) was also concrete but in the Art Deco style, with extensive aluminum decoration (IN002, p. 216).

The territorial government received its most important piece of architecture with the Federal and Territorial Building in Juneau (James A. Wetmore, 1929–1931) (SE017, p. 172). The concrete structure was clad with stone and brick; the conservative design resembling a standard office building boasts a dazzling portico of large columns of Alaskan marble, and the lavish use of local marble continues in the lobby and hallways.

But by far the greatest impact of the federal government in this period was through its military presence. In the 1920s, the army had abandoned all of its posts in Alaska save one, Chilkoot Barracks (Fort Seward) near Haines. In 1939, perceiving a military threat from Japan, the government started construction of naval and air bases at Sitka and Kodiak, followed in 1940 by Ladd Field in Fairbanks and a naval base at Dutch Harbor, and in 1941 by Fort Richardson and Elmendorf Field in Anchorage.[172] In the next four years, the government spent more than $1.25 billion on military construction projects in Alaska.[173]

For the most part, the military used standard designs employed elsewhere in the United States. Office buildings were concrete, often in a Moderne or utilitarian style. Two of the most distinctive military building forms on the Alaskan landscape were housing for airplanes and people. Hangars, in requiring vast open plans, utilized various truss systems; several peacetime designs called for steel trusses. With material shortages during the war, however, bowstring timber truss systems were employed, such as those in the Birchwood and Kodiak, or T hangars, producing an arched roof.[174] Arches were also used in housing, in the form of the familiar quonset hut. In Alaska, however, the popularity of the quonset hut was surpassed by that of the Pacific hut, which employed the same design but was constructed of wood. Easily obtainable from the Pacific Northwest, wood obviated the use of corrugated steel, a critical wartime material.[175]

Besides massive construction projects, military activity had two other important effects in Alaska. One was the shift in population. Not only did military personnel inhabit the cities but the related construction work also attracted laborers from throughout the territory. Anchorage, which had a population of less than 4,000 in 1939, had 40,000 people by 1952.[176]

Secondly, 300,000 military men were stationed in Alaska during the war,[177] and many of them returned afterward. The major towns, which had grown from the military presence and spin-off development, attracted most of the postwar immigrants. After the war, Alaska's location continued to be strategic; the Cold War with the Soviet Union demanded a continued military presence. In 1960, nearly 33,000 servicemen lived in Alaska, constituting one-third of all employed workers. Including civilian workers, the number of military employees amounted to nearly half of the work force.[178] With the need for the military firmly established by a growing cold war, the population booming, and new economic activity promised by discoveries of oil in Cook Inlet, Alaska was finally granted statehood in 1959.

FROM STATEHOOD TO THE PRESENT

Since statehood, Alaska has become identified in the public's mind with oil. The Atlantic Richfield Company (ARCO) discovered a huge oil field at Prudhoe Bay in 1968, bringing unprecedented wealth to the state. The oil boom has produced new construction, attracted thousands of people, defined land ownership through settlement of land claims, redistributed the population, and effectively brought parts of the state into the modern era.

The Prudhoe Bay oil field, the largest in North America, was estimated to have 9.6 billion barrels of oil and impressive quantities of natural gas. ARCO and BP Exploration have developed facilities at Prudhoe Bay and neighboring fields, with potential fields still to be developed. In 1977 the first oil flowed through the Trans-Alaska Pipeline, connecting Prudhoe Bay to the rest of the world. Since 1979, Alaska has produced over 500 million barrels of oil annually.[179]

The North Slope facilities required the development of new technologies and innovative strategies to cope with the terrain and climate. All of the wells, roads, and buildings are located on gravel pads, which serve as an insulating layer between the structures and the permafrost. The oil fields have self-contained operations centers, providing space for work, recreation, eating, and sleeping. The 100-foot-by-122-foot modular units, fabricated in the Lower 48, were barged to Prudhoe Bay, then "crawled," or transported on tanklike tracks, for assembly on the site.

Oil production required an 800-mile pipeline to the ice-free port of Valdez. Construction began in 1974 and was completed in 1977 by Alyeska Pipeline Service Company, a consortium of oil companies. The 4-foot-diameter pipeline runs underground for about half of its length and extends above ground where there is permafrost.[180] Above ground, the pipeline is mounted on platforms 50 feet to 70 feet apart; supports have heat-disseminating refrigeration pipes. The pipeline is laid in a zigzag pattern to reduce stress during earthquakes and is occasionally elevated or buried to allow migrating animals to pass.[181] The $8 billion Trans-Alaska Pipeline claims to be the largest private construction project in history (SC101, p. 141).[182]

The oil boom brought unprecedented growth of the major cities. After modest expansion in the 1960s, Anchorage burgeoned in population from 48,000 in 1970 to 174,000 in 1980. Half of the population of Alaska lives in the Anchorage area. In the same decade, Fairbanks grew from 15,000 to 23,000, and Juneau, from 6,000 to 20,000.[183] Increasingly, the domestic architecture resembles that of the Lower 48, as prefabricated housing has become popular with Alaskans. War-surplus quonset and Pacific huts were readily adopted after the war, until an ordinance passed in Anchorage in 1969 limited the construction and repair of such housing and signaled the end of their acceptability.[184] By 1955, there were twenty-five trailer courts in the city, and between 1960 and 1965, over 2,000 mobile homes were sold in Anchorage alone.[185] With the encouragement of the U.S. Department of Housing and Urban Development, manufactured housing (similar to mobile homes but built without wheels) was developed in 1969 to fill the need for inexpensive (and therefore mass-produced) housing. On average 24 feet by 42 feet or 44 feet, with three bedrooms, this type of housing was readily accepted throughout Alaska.

A devastating earthquake in 1964, centered near Prince William Sound, caused major destruction in the region. Valdez was completely destroyed, and survivors decided to move the town. More than 300 miles away, Kodiak was hit by a tidal wave and suffered significant damage. Much of downtown Anchorage was destroyed due to subsidence. Studies of surviving buildings, in areas where there was no subsidence, determined that tall, slender buildings, buildings with a high ratio of window to wall, and buildings with monolithic masonry finishes were most likely to be damaged.[186] Anchorage has been rebuilt in a more modern idiom, with a handful of pre-statehood high-rise buildings now mingling with a large number of more recent skyscrapers, some found crowded together downtown, others on spacious, suburban parcels. Construction has sprawled

After World War II, private owners acquired quonset huts to ease the housing shortage. This one was photographed in Anchorage in 1956.

outward as well as upward, however, as seen in shopping malls, which, particularly suited to an environmentally hostile climate, are located in and around the major cities. Although Anchorage and Fairbanks have been slow to adopt skywalks or underground connections—linkages that one might think natural in a northern climate—some have recently been built.

One state proposal that foundered was a new state capital. Juneau, accessible only by ship or airplane, is not centrally located. Voters approved a capital move initiative in 1974, and two years later they selected a site for the new government at Willow, located 35 miles north of Anchorage, for the new government center. The Capital Site Selection Committee, advised by architect Kevin Lynch, held a competition to design the new capital city. After preliminary screening, five firms were selected to develop presentations; their designs ranged from villages to megastructures. The winner, Bull Field Volkmann Stockwell, architects, and Sedway-Cooke, planners, both from San Francisco, presented a linear layout, with a strong downtown centered on a grand commons—a glass-enclosed landscaped area. The size of the city, intended to have a population of 37,000, was kept small to encourage pedestrian rather than motorized transportation. Arcades at street level attempted to appeal to pedestrians; private automobiles were to be prohibited from the main street. A very different approach was proposed by Lane-Knorr-Plunkett with EDAW, Inc., and William Pereira Associates. Their high-tech megastructure consisted of an intense urban core 1 mile in diameter. From it, four arms radiated, with housing and secondary shopping at the ends of the arms; between the arms was an in-town wilderness. The $4.4 billion price tag of the BFVS scheme frightened voters, however; and they have refused to approve a bond issue to finance the move.[187]

Rich from oil revenues, the state government has spread that wealth around through its capital improvement fund. Communities across the state have received schools and firehouses, buildings not usually funded by state government. Through Percent for Art programs, these capital improvements projects are richly decorated with artwork. In 1975, the state enacted legislation requiring that one percent of construction costs of public buildings be allocated to artwork for that building (one half of one percent in the case of rural schools). In 1978, Anchorage also adopted a One Percent for Art program. Together, these programs have commissioned more than three hundred pieces of art, costing nearly $8 million. Alaskans profited handsomely from timely passage of the legislation that coincided with a boom in public construction.

Anchorage received four major public buildings in the 1980s: the Z. J. Loussac Public Library (designed by Environmental Concern, Inc.) (SC025, p. 96), the Alaska Center for the Performing Arts (Hardy, Holzman, Pfeiffer) (SC006, p. 85), the George M. Sullivan Sports Arena (Harold Wirum) (SC022, p. 94), and the William A. Egan Civic and Convention Center (CCC/HOK) (SC007, p. 87). In addition, the city funded a major expansion to the Anchorage Museum of History and Fine Arts (Mitchell/Giurgola) (SC019, p. 92). These new buildings brought a maturity and sophistication to architecture that Anchorage had not seen before. Divergent in style, the buildings range from the ice-cold, glass-lobbied convention center, to the highly ornamented, textural performing arts center across the street, to the elegant and restrained buff-brick museum.

Several of these major buildings were designed by Outside architects in association with local firms, a situation annoying to local architects who believe that Alaskan architects are as capable as any. Because there is no architectural school in the state, all architects are educated Outside, although there is a special arctic-engineering requirement for state registration. The architectural profession has become established only since World War II, rising with the state's population. Although architects had appeared in such gold-rush towns as Skagway and Nome at the turn of the century, they apparently did not stay long. N. Lester Troast and William A. Manley, among others, practiced in Juneau in the 1930s, designing largely in the Colonial Revival style. After his move to Anchorage in 1937, however, Manley adopted the Moderne style, providing some of Anchorage's best examples, and later the International style.

Edwin B. Crittenden's career is emblematic of the rise of the postwar architectural profession. Crittenden came to Alaska in the Coast Guard during the war and returned afterward to work for the Territorial Housing Authority. In 1950, he started his own firm, which gained and lost partners until in the 1980s CCC Architects and Planners emerged as the largest architectural firm in the state. With a practice beginning with a log cabin visitor information center in Anchorage (SC001, p. 83) and including schools, hospitals, churches, and libraries across the state, CCC was influential not only in the number and quality of buildings but also in the number of architects who apprenticed in the firm and went on to establish their own Alaskan practices. Hit by the dip in oil prices and subsequent economic recession in Alaska, CCC went out of business in 1986.

Another architectural firm that grew with the state was that founded by Linn A. Forrest in Juneau. Forrest, an aptly named architect with the U.S. Forest

Service, worked on Rustic masterpieces such as Oregon's Timberline Lodge before coming to Alaska in the 1930s. As regional architect for the U.S. Forest Service, Forrest headed the totem pole reconstruction project, which also involved the reconstruction of three traditional plank houses in Southeast. In 1952 Forrest started his own firm and developed a wide-ranging practice throughout Alaska. Although Forrest died in 1987, his firm continues under the name of Minch Ritter Voelckers.

The federal government also constructed new buildings during the 1970s and 1980s, using both local and Outside architects. Federal housing programs have changed the face of rural villages, as manufactured houses bring an unfortunate uniformity to the architecture. The federal government has also built for itself, such as the Federal Building in Anchorage, designed in the 1970s by CCC/HOK in partnership with John Graham of Seattle. Although the building occupies two city blocks, its mass is broken, lessening the impact of its size. Entrance is at one corner, which is chopped off and set back; the central hallway runs diagonally through an atrium in the building (SC018, p. 92).

Across the street from the Federal Building, the subterranean federal annex, with a park on its roof, reflects the energy-consciousness of the 1970s. With energy-efficient construction a national concern, it was natural that Alaskans examine energy use carefully. Some argued that the traditional log cabins were the most energy-efficient houses around, claiming that heat-retaining log walls have a higher R-value than most wood-framed and insulated walls.[188] Most modern construction incorporates energy conservation measures—thicker insulation, vapor barriers, and triple-pane windows, for instance—not readily visible in the design.

The feverish construction pace of the previous two decades slowed in the late 1980s when oil prices dropped and the Prudhoe Bay field passed the halfway production point. The state's population decreased. While recent architecture is far more sophisticated than that built previously in Alaska, it has lost some of its distinctive character.

Progressive Alaskans may resent being associated with log cabins, but log cabins remain a clear expression of what is Alaskan. At the same time, the constructed landscape of the state includes many other building forms, such as Russian Orthodox churches, false-front boomtown commercial buildings, small bungalows and cottages, log roadhouses, and concrete Moderne public buildings. Whether using local materials to build immediate shelter or importing stylistic trends from the Lower 48, immigrant Alaskans demonstrate their ambiguous relationship with the frontier. Alaska's rich architectural imagery may be overshadowed by the dramatic natural beauty of the state, but it forms the substance of a tangible history of humans reckoning with nature.

South-Central Region (SC)

SOUTH-CENTRAL ALASKA, WHERE MORE THAN HALF OF THE state's population resides, stretches along the Gulf of Alaska from Icy Cape to the west side of Cook Inlet and encompasses the land north to the Alaska Range. This area includes the Saint Elias, Chugach, and Kenai mountain ranges, which have extensive glacier systems and are largely uninhabited. The region also has broad plateaus between river systems, including the agricultural heartland of the Matanuska and Susitna valleys. Cook Inlet and Prince William Sound account for a significant portion of Alaska's tidal shoreline. The climate is primarily maritime, although in the mountains temperatures can range sharply. Anchorage, in a bowl protected by the Chugach and Kenai mountains, gets only 15 inches of precipitation annually, while Whittier, on Prince William Sound, receives 174 inches.

Although the South-Central Region was inhabited by Natives, Russians, and Americans, evidence of the converging cultures is much less noticeable than in other regions. Creeping urbanization has swallowed up Native villages so that they survive distinctly only in the remote areas. No buildings of the Russian era are extant in this region, although the Russian Orthodox churches illustrate the Russians' cultural influence on the Natives. The building fabric of the region today dates from the American period.

Pacific Eskimos inhabited the coastal areas, and Athapaskans dominated the inland parts. In the late eighteenth and early nineteenth centuries, both groups traded with the Russians, who established several settlements in the South-Central Region, not all of them successful. Aleksandr Redoubt (English Bay) dates from about 1790, and within a few years the Russians founded a boat-building enterprise on Resurrection Bay (Seward). By 1803, the Russians supported three forts on Cook Inlet, two on Prince William Sound, one at Cape Saint Elias, and

79

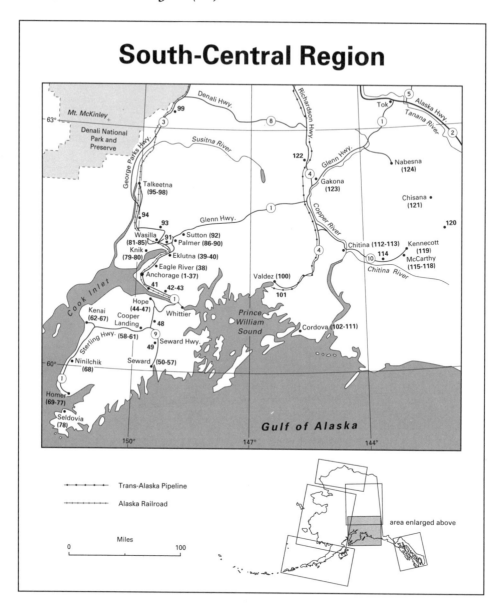

South-Central Region

Trans-Alaska Pipeline

Alaska Railroad

Miles
0   100

area enlarged above

two on Yakutat Bay. The Russian-American Company continued to build out-posts in the nineteenth century, although none of them developed into major posts, and no buildings remain today.

The Americans' first interests in the region lay in salmon and gold. A can-nery was established in Cook Inlet as early as 1880. The existence of gold was known, even by the Russians, but the first gold rushes did not occur until the late 1890s, in both the Willow Creek region, north of Cook Inlet, and on the Kenai Peninsula. These gold strikes, as well as known deposits of copper in the Wrangell Mountains and the potential for coal mining, stimulated railroad construction. Two private railroads were built, the Copper River and Northwestern, which began at Cordova and followed the Copper River north to the Kennecott copper mines, and the Alaska Central, which was reconstituted as the Alaska Northern and finally bought by the Alaska Railroad.

It was the Alaska Railroad in 1915 that opened up the region and accounted for the founding of Anchorage and several other towns along its route. From the port of Seward in the south, the 470-mile line crossed the Kenai Peninsula, passed through Anchorage, and continued across the agricultural lands of the Matanuska Valley and the Willow Creek mining district on its way to Fairbanks. Because one of the avowed purposes of the government-run railroad was to facilitate the development of Alaska, townsites were marketed heavily and private enterprises were encouraged to mine coal and gold.

Several other government endeavors helped attract the concentration of population that exists today. In the 1930s, a New Deal program to provide new farms to farmers and to attract new settlers to Alaska brought midwestern farmers to the Matanuska Valley, amid national attention. A heavy buildup of Fort Richardson (now Elmendorf Air Force Base) during World War II and continued military investment in the region after the war brought thousands of soldiers, as well as contractors, to the government.

By the time oil was discovered in Prudhoe Bay in 1968, Anchorage was the largest city in the state, and oil companies naturally located their regional headquarters there. Anchorage quadrupled in size during the oil boom, dominating the region, if not the rest of the state. Some major public buildings in Anchorage have brought a new sophistication to the architecture of the region, but not without diluting its vernacular appeal.

Anchorage Area

Anchorage

Anchorage is a place of jarring contradictions, a discontinuous modern highrise city growing out of a frontier settlement with almost no points of transition. A grid-plan railroad town, Anchorage might have been an average American city were it not for its attractive location and its continued boomtown growth. Located at the head of Cook Inlet, on a peninsula separating Knik and Turnagain arms, Anchorage is sheltered on the east by the Chugach and Kenai mountains and on the north by the Talkeetna Mountains and the Alaska Range. Set between these jagged, snow-covered mountains and a sea with 35-foot tides, Anchorage in 1940 was a small city in a splendid location. Unprecedented growth during World War II and the oil boom of the 1970s have resulted in an expansive city of 226,000 people in 1990, half of the state's population.

As the northernmost point on the proposed Alaska Railroad that could also be reached by sea, Anchorage started as a supply point for railroad construction in 1914. A tent city immediately appeared in the Ship Creek valley. In 1915, a townsite on the bluff south of Ship Creek was laid out by the Alaska Engineering Commission, the construction arm of the Alaska Railroad. The plan consisted of 121 square blocks, each 300 feet on a side. Each square was bisected by a 20-foot-wide alley and divided into twelve lots, 50 feet by 140 feet. Every street was 60 feet wide.

Several blocks were withheld for public purposes. These Federal and Municipal Reserves are today occupied by federal and city buildings constructed in the 1930s. The School Reserve, once occupied by Pioneer School (SC020), is now the home of the Alaska Center for the Performing Arts (SC006). Two adjacent blocks withdrawn as a Park Reserve are occupied by the Anchorage Museum of History and Art (SC019) and the Public Safety Building. The Park Strip (officially Delaney Park) is the swath of blocks just south of the original townsite. Originally meant to be developed, it was withdrawn as a firebreak and park area and served briefly as an airstrip in the 1920s. Other parks were established as the development of the city moved south and east.

On 10 July 1915, the lots were auctioned off, and the development of Anchorage began. For the first five years the Alaska Engineering Commission administered the townsite, but in 1920 the city of Anchorage was incorporated with a population of 1,856.

The first generation of Anchorage's buildings—some of which remain—was characteristically wood frame, one and two stories, with a minimum of ornamentation. Housing built by the Alaska Engineering Commission for its employees often had elements of the bungalow, with front porches, prominent roofs, and front gables repeated in porches or vestibules. Commercial buildings, which clustered on Fourth Avenue from the start, were on the same scale as the residential but had false fronts and storefront windows.

The appearance of a new construction material—reinforced concrete, which was used for commercial and public building in the late 1930s—brought a stylistic maturity to the architecture of the town. The city hall (SC002), U.S. Post Office and Courthouse (SC003), and Alaska Railroad Depot (SC013) were constructed of this material in styles that ranged from Classical Revival (city hall) to Moderne (post office). The exuberantly Art Deco Fourth Avenue Theatre (SC004) was also of this period. At the same time, housing continued to be modest, with gable-roofed Cape Cod styles growing in popularity. The city burst beyond the bounds of the original townsite and into the area south of the city.

The construction of Fort Richardson (now Elmendorf Air Force Base) (SC036) on the bluff north of Ship Creek and continued military building after the war resulted in a population boom; Anchorage grew from a little more than 4,000 in 1940 to 44,000 in 1960. The first annexation of a suburban area—South Addition—occurred in 1945, and the first zoning ordinance was enacted in 1946. The first high-rises, the McKinley Apartment Building (now McKay

Building) and the Inlet Towers (SC021), were built in 1951. The residential city continued to spread south and east.

On 27 March 1964, Anchorage was rocked by an earthquake that caused some parts of downtown to drop 30 feet. The north side of Fourth Avenue was particularly hard hit and has been rebuilt with low commercial buildings. Downtown became a checkerboard of one-story bungalows next to twenty-story office buildings. The discovery of oil at Prudhoe Bay in 1968 resulted in another boom for Anchorage, which became regional headquarters to the oil companies. Between 1970 and 1980, the city of Anchorage consolidated with its surrounding borough, and the population grew from 48,000 to 174,000. In the next decade it gained another 50,000.

Such rapid growth has been disastrous for the rational development of the city. Traffic jams are ironic in a state of such incredible space. Tokens of a honky-tonk town—such as the portable, electric signs found in front of every bar and liquor store—have recently been banned, and developers are now required to landscape the public space surrounding their developments. Slowly, Anchorage is maturing as a city.

Anchorage has embarked on Project 80s, an effort to improve public facilities. An 11-mile coastal trail, winding around the city, was one non-architectural result of these expenditures. Several important public buildings were constructed—Sullivan Arena (SC022), Egan Convention Center (SC007), Loussac Library (SC025), Anchorage Museum of History and Art (SC019), and the Alaska Center for the Performing Arts (SC006). Ranging from the glass modernism of the Egan Convention Center to the multigabled, multitextured Postmodernism of the Performing Arts Center, they have added interest and sophistication to the architectural scene.

SC001 Visitor Information Center

1954, Edwin B. Crittenden. Fourth and F streets

The Visitor Information Center is a most atypical log cabin. Anchorage was never strictly a log cabin town, but the log cabin stands here as a symbol of the perceived frontier character of the town. Unlike most log cabins, this one was designed by an architect, Edwin B. Crittenden. Built in Homer in 1954 and moved to Anchorage, the cabin has round logs, saddle notched at the corners. The gable roof of sod on poles is typical, but the stone fireplace and chimney are not. Also atypical is its northern orientation.

SC002 Anchorage City Hall

1936, E. Ellsworth Sedille. 524 West Fourth Ave.

In 1936, City Hall was constructed on the site designated as a Municipal Reserve. The two-story, reinforced-concrete building in a Beaux-Arts Classical design has a rusticated first floor and round-arch opening with exaggerated voussoirs. Above a belt course, the second floor is finished smooth, crowned by a modillioned cornice and a pedimented parapet. The center section, three bays wide, projects. A one-story, flat-roofed wing to the west, although disrupting the symmetry of the building, was original; it is now two stories, with a one-story addition.

The design is attributed to E. Ellsworth Sedille, a local architect. The Gastineau Construction Company constructed the building for $75,000, nearly half of which was funded by the Public Works Administration. The building contained the mayor's office, city council, all municipal offices, the library, three jail cells, and firemen's quarters. After 1979,

SC001 Visitor Information Center

when the municipal offices moved to the Hill Building, the building was renovated as a bank and offices.

SC003 U.S. Post Office and Courthouse

1939–1940; 1940–1941, west wing; Gilbert Stanley Underwood. 605 West Fourth Ave.

With flat surfaces, sparse ornament, and sculptural shapes, the U.S. Post Office and Courthouse was the most modern building that Anchorage had seen in 1940. U-shaped in plan, the two-story main block is twelve bays long, each with a metal spandrel between the first- and second-floor windows. At each end, a three-story block containing an entrance is set back. With flat roofs and sharp edges, the three-dimensional blockiness of the reinforced-concrete building is its distinguishing feature. Ornament is limited to a thin line defining the window bays and horizontal lines at the top of the chimneys.

Gilbert Stanley Underwood, a Los Angeles-based architect who also designed the post offices at Sitka and Nome, designed the building. The McCarthy Brothers Construction Company of Saint Louis, Missouri, began construction in 1939, but before it was completed, the government decided to add a wing. Stretching 116 feet along G Street, the two-story wing is similar to the original building. In fact, the building was designed with additions in mind so that eventually the complex would form a quadrangle, enclosing the square.

Costing $546,000 to construct, it was located on the Federal Reserve, replacing some one-story, wood-framed buildings that had housed government offices. Unlike the city hall diagonally opposite, which was built in the center of its square, leaving ample grounds around it, the U.S. Post Office and Courthouse was built on the front of the square, defining the streetscape for its 255-foot front.

The longitudinal hallway in the 60-foot-wide main block has a ceramic tile wainscot. At the west end is the Federal District courtroom, which has a WPA mural depicting a mountainous Alaskan landscape by Richard Haines of Iowa and Arthur Kerrick of Minnesota.

Although most of the federal offices have moved out of the building, the Public Lands Information Center is located here, making the building a destination point for out-of-town visitors.

SC004 Fourth Avenue Theatre

1941–1947, B. Marcus Priteca and Augustine A. Porreca; interior, Anthony B. Heinsbergen and Frank Bouman. 630 West Fourth Ave.

The Fourth Avenue Theatre is a true movie palace, creating surroundings of fantasy and delight. When built, the theater, measuring 62 feet by 130 feet, seated 960 and was embellished by a rose, chartreuse, and light blue color scheme. Silver and gold bas-relief murals on the walls and the Big Dipper on the ceiling remain to enchant the audience. In the lobby, where 200 people can wait in inclement weather, a gold-leaf mural of Mount McKinley is the focus of attention. (The murals are canvas, with the bas-relief in carved Masonite, finished with silver and gold leaf.) Curving elements in the lobby and theater and fluted walnut woodwork throughout add further elegance. The refreshment stands are a later addition, as the original owner, Cap Lathrop, felt refreshments were inappropriate in his palace.

On the outside, the 87-foot-by-130-foot reinforced concrete building is three stories

SC004a Fourth Avenue Theatre (lobby)

SC004b Fourth Avenue Theatre (auditorium)

tall; the first floor is finished with travertine marble. At the third floor, sets of banded windows flank the slightly taller, projecting center bay, which is bisected by a swirling "4th Avenue" sign, written vertically in Art Deco lettering, on a 40-foot pylon. A marquee extends across the front of the building.

Cap Lathrop, a prominent Alaskan industrialist and millionaire, developed this building as one of a string of movie theaters. Designed by B. Marcus Priteca, a prominent Seattle theater architect, assisted by Augustine A. Porreca, also of Seattle, the building was constructed by C. William Hufeisen. Anthony B. Heinsbergen and Frank Bouman from Los Angeles executed the interior decoration, including the murals. Ground was broken in 1941, but all construction activity ceased because of the war. Begun again in 1946, construction was finally completed in 1947. By that time, the style was slightly out of date, but nonetheless fantastic.

Formally named the Lathrop Building, the building contains more than theater. The basement, second, and third floors on the west side of the building housed Lathrop's radio and television stations and offices (and are still occupied by a television station), while in the same space of the first floor, there is a restaurant. A penthouse apartment on the roof was constructed in 1959–1960.

The theater underwent some alterations when it served briefly as a repertory theater in the 1980s. The murals and original lights remain; the seats have been recovered so the original color scheme is not so evident. Fine woodwork decorates the theater and lobby, however, and all of the original spaces are intact. Currently vacant, the Fourth Avenue Theater awaits the next reel.

SC005 Holy Family Cathedral

mid-1940s–1952, Augustine A. Porreca. Fifth Ave. and H St.

Seattle architect Augustine A. Porreca designed a small church in the same style that he used for theaters—Art Deco. Begun in the mid-1940s, construction proceeded slowly, as funds became available; the interior was not completed until 1952. The one-story church, ornamented with geometric lines, has a two-story, square bell tower at the front corner. Entrance was originally on the side, through the base of the bell tower. When Anchorage was elevated to the status of archdiocese, the church became a cathedral, necessitating a more formal entrance. A stylized portico was added to the front, and two pairs of doors with oversized transom windows replaced a large window with concrete mullions. The renovation was designed by the architectural firm of McEntire and Pendergast. In 1970 the exterior, which had always been a natural gray color, was painted off-white.

SC006 Alaska Center for the Performing Arts

1985, Hardy Holzman Pfeiffer Associates, in association with Livingston Slone, Inc. 621 West Sixth Ave.

The $71 million Alaska Center for the Performing Arts is a controversial exercise in Postmodernism. Most of the drawbacks concern its site, which is more than a city block in the original townsite. Its achievements include a lively, many-textured exterior and three fine theaters inside, and it stands as both the symbolic and active center of culture for the city. Designed by Hardy Holzman Pfeiffer Associates of New York, in association with Livingston Slone, Inc., of Anchorage, this beneficiary of the capital improvement fund was begun in 1985; the first theater opened in 1988.

The center includes three theaters on a confined site. The massing is arranged with the extremely tall flies of each theater set in the center of the building, with steep hip roofs falling away. The pitch of the metal-clad roofs is interrupted by snow fence constructions, which were part of the original plans, not an afterthought, as is widely believed. Although F Street was closed and its right-of-way incorporated into the building site, access is a problem, as there is no drop-off for automobiles, and the entrances are on the wrong sides of one-way streets. There is no parking within the building; although a second-level connection to an adjacent parking building was planned, it was not built.

To break up the mass as much as possible, the architects used a variety of textures, several gabled entrances, porticos, and arcades. The first floor is clad with a small, textured brick, the second with a larger concrete block, and the upper stories with stucco scored in an even larger pattern. The whole is toned in shades of brown and rose that lighten from bottom to top. The tall and narrow gabled pavilions, which denote the lobby areas on three sides, also provide strong vertical elements. These are countered by the blue hor-

Anchorage (SC23–SC25, SC32–SC34, SC37). See map, p. 95, for SC1–SC22; see map, p. 97, for SC26–SC31; see map, p. 103, for SC35; see map, p. 105, for SC36.

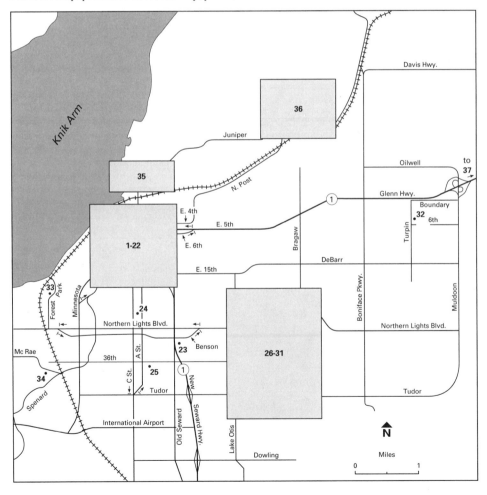

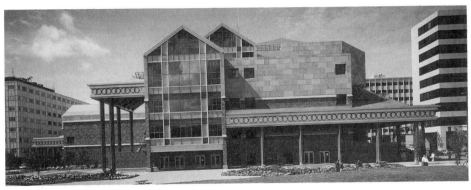

SC006 Alaska Center for the Performing Arts

izontal stringcourse and computer-programmed neon fascia that encircle the building and add a stabilizing horizontal thrust.

On the interior, the lobby areas are well lit by multistoried windows and decorated by work from Alaskan artists, including stylized masks on the walls, marble mazes in the windows, and the carpet on the floor, all funded by the city's One Percent for Art program. Each theater is separated from the lobbies and exterior walls by a circulation ring, insulating it from outside noise. The largest theater is the Evangeline Atwood Concert Hall, seating 2,146. The acoustics of this U-shaped theater with two balconies are particularly fine. The baffling on the ceiling, an acoustic shell of gypsum wallboard on metal studs, is known as the aurora borealis; it also conceals the lights. The Discovery Theater—so named because the oil companies donated funds for it—seats 777 and occupies the round element at the southwest corner of the building. The 372-seat Sydney Laurence Theater is constructed within the walls of the theater of the same name that previously stood on the site. Its asymmetry—so that the audience is not evenly balanced in front of the stage—indicates a more informal space. Rehearsal halls await the final $3 million in funds. A fourth theater, a "black box" experimental theater, is planned for eventual construction on the northwest corner of the site.

The PAC has become a lightning rod for public opinion about Postmodern architecture in Anchorage. Although resented more for its cost than for its design, the building's critics also point out the inconvenience caused by limited access. Yet the building has made many people who were previously apathetic to architectural design take note, and it provides Anchorage with performing arts facilities that would be the envy of many cities twice its size in the Lower 48.

SC007 William A. Egan Civic and Convention Center

1983, CCC Architects and Planners. 555 West Fifth Ave.

Constructed in 1983, the convention center—named for Alaska's first governor—is a modern design, unrelated to its surroundings. A glass-enclosed lobby that extends along the Fifth Avenue front, concealing the windowless block that is most of the building, is an interesting solution to an intriguing design problem of a convention center. Convention centers are essentially collections of empty rooms with no need for windows. Here, CCC Architects and Planners enlivened the facade with a two-story, round-arch, glass-covered lobby. That arch is repeated in the glass canopy extending over the sidewalk. The light-filled lobby, decorated in mauves, with a pink granite floor, contains public art, including a dramatic work of glass beads.

There are two levels of windowless meeting rooms in the main block. On the first floor, the 20,000-square foot Explorers Hall has a 22-foot ceiling height and can be divided into three rooms. On the lower level, the Summit Hall has a 12-foot ceiling height and can be divided into fourteen rooms. A partial mezzanine level at the east end contains administrative offices.

CCC was founded by architect Edwin B. Crittenden. Through three decades of practice during which the firm's name changed several times, it remained one of the largest and most influential architectural firms in Alaska. In the 1960s Crittenden formed a partnership with Cassetta, Wirum, and Cannon, that was known as CCW&C. After Wirum left in 1969, the firm formed an association with the San Francisco office of Hellmuth, Obata, Kassebaum and was known as CCC/HOK. In 1980 that association was dissolved and the firm worked under the name CCC Architects and Planners. In the midst of a building recession in 1986, CCC Architects folded but left a legacy of architecture and planning throughout the state.

SC008 **Anchorage Hotel**

1936, E. Ellsworth Sedille. Fourth Ave. and E St.

The Anchorage Hotel is a simple Moderne building with vague Gothic evocations. Reportedly designed by E. Ellsworth Sedille, architect of the city hall across the street, the wood-framed building with stucco finish was constructed in 1936 as an annex to a hotel on the corner of Third Avenue and E Street. The pointed, vertical piers delineating the bays give the Anchorage Hotel a distinctive appearance, but the sign over the first floor introduces a horizontal element it did not originally have.

SC009 **Kimball Building**

1915. 500–504 West Fifth Ave.

Although plain to the point of homeliness, Kimball's store is a fine example of an early commercial building. The wood-framed, bevel-sided building has two commercial storefronts spanning the front facade, with a blank false front above them. The building is two stories on the E Street side, sloping to one story, but the false front on Fifth Avenue keeps an even cornice. Built in 1915, it originally measured approximately 40 feet by 60 feet.

Irving and Della Kimball sold general merchandise in a store that occupied the width of the first floor, with storage space above; they lived in the rear of the building. Irving Kimball died in 1921, but his widow continued the business. After her death in 1958, the store was divided in half and the east portion rented out; Kimball's continued in the west half. The only visible changes to the structure have been the covering of the transom windows with signs and additions made to the rear in the 1940s.

SC010 **Fifth Avenue Mall**

1987, Kober/Sclater Associates. Fifth Ave. and C St.

With four retail levels, the $67 million Fifth Avenue Mall is essentially vertical, unlike spread-out suburban malls. A saucer-shaped skylight at the northeast corner lights the food court on the fourth level and the courts at each of the several levels below. The mall connects directly to an existing J. C. Penney's store and with skybridges to an adjacent Nordstrom's. A third-level skybridge off the northeast corner also joins the mall to a twelve-hundred-car parking garage, built by the city at a cost of $27 million.

Designed by Kober/Sclater Associates of Seattle, the mall has a busy exterior. Because malls need few windows—in fact they are incompatible with an interior focus—the vast walls of a downtown mall provide an interesting design problem. Here, the architects decided on a trompe l'oeil effect, with large, small-paned glass windows, which are, in fact, blind. The rose-colored brick of the exterior is ornamented at the top with a double row of darker colored squares, also resembling windows. Beneath this running pattern and between the large blind windows are dark vertical piers. At ground level, there are actual show windows that are hooded by canopies. The interior is finished with tiles, neon, and stainless steel for a hip, jazzy effect.

Because of a severe dip in the economy just as this building was nearing completion, it opened to a landlord's nightmare, with only 10 of the 110 stories occupied. It still has not been fully leased.

SC011 **Loussac and Loussac-Sogn Buildings**

1941 and 1946–1947, William A. Manley. 411 and 425 D St.

Two three-story buildings in the Moderne style were built side by side in the 1940s for Z. J. Loussac. Loussac opened a drugstore in Anchorage in 1916 and became wealthy through that and other investments. After the Second World War, he turned to philanthropy and politics, serving two terms as mayor beginning in 1947. He arranged that his philanthropic foundation receive his share of the income from the Loussac-Sogn Building.

The Loussac Building, an apartment and office building measuring 70 feet by 40 feet, was constructed in 1941. The reinforced-concrete structure has a strong horizontal emphasis, with single and double windows in a band, connected by fluted panels. The rough-finished walls are unornamented, and the flat roof has no cornice. The original storefronts survive; they are asymmetrical, with panes of glass meeting at the corners without mullions.

The Loussac-Sogn Building was constructed after the war, in 1946–1947. Like the Loussac Building, the 100-foot-by-140-foot Loussac-Sogn Building, built around an interior courtyard, has a strong horizontal emphasis, with double windows in a band separated by fluted panels. The two-story entrance adds a vertical counterthrust. The walls are smooth finished, and the flat roof has no cornice.

William A. Manley designed the Loussac-Sogn Building; judging by similarities to the Loussac Building, he may have designed that too. Manley, who came to Anchorage in 1937, had a flourishing architectural practice until 1976 (in partnership with Francis B. Mayer, 1948–1972). Manley also designed the Central Building at Third and G in 1946 in the same style as these. He was an accomplished designer in the Moderne style, a style that characterizes downtown Anchorage. The Moderne style, simple and austere, was well suited for Alaska, where architectural ornamentation was seen as an unnecessary frill.

SC012 Wendler Building (Club 25)

feet, originally had a canted entrance under the turret, with one wide store window across the front and a smaller one on the side.

In 1915, A. J. Wendler and R. C. Larson operated a grocery store on the first floor, with Wendler and his family living on the second. Although Larson soon left the business, members of the Wendler family owned the building until 1983. In the mid-1930s, the building was converted to apartments, necessitating the removal of the store windows and corner entrance. In 1948, Wendler's daughter, Myrtle Stalnaker, opened the Club 25 restaurant in the building.

Besides the changes to the fenestration at the first-floor level, additions include a shingled pent roof below the modillioned cornice and a wide band of cut-out ornament below the second-floor windows. Perhaps the latter inspired the neon ornament on the Performing Arts Center; the similarity is striking. The building originally stood at the corner of Fourth and I streets. In 1983, facing demolition, the building was moved to its present site, where it could maintain the same orientation to the intersection. A three-story brick building was constructed to wrap around it but is so different as to appear unconnected.

SC012 **Wendler Building (Club 25)**

1915. 1930s, remodeling. 400 D St.

Featuring a corner turret, the Wendler Building was built in 1915. Although turrets are frequently found on commercial buildings in slightly earlier commercial buildings in other cities, this was the only one built in Anchorage. The two-story, wood-framed building, which measures approximately 26 feet by 62

SC013 **Alaska Railroad Depot**

1942. 411 First Ave.

Separated from downtown by landscaped open space and located at the bottom of a hill, the depot is a highly visible monument to the railroad that built Anchorage. Constructed in

SC013 Alaska Railroad Depot

1942, the original structure, of reinforced concrete with a stucco finish, was limited to the three-story section measuring 218 feet by 45 feet. The flatness of the facade, flat roof, and lack of a cornice point to the Moderne style, yet conventions such as the belt course separating the first and second stories and three-bay pavilion at the entrance are references to the Beaux-Arts Classical. Bands of fluting between the bays in the center pavilion allude to pilasters, while the vertical lines in the spandrels between the second- and third-floor windows are a modern convention.

The waiting room is an airy space, well lit from windows on the front and back. The window surrounds are light maple woodwork, with reeding and Greek key ornament. Quarry tile flooring and ceramic tile wainscoting are original features. The waiting room occupies the east end of the first floor; the central entrance leads to the offices upstairs, and baggage and freight rooms occupy the remainder of the first floor.

The architect of this building is not known, although William A. Manley is a likely candidate; newspapers note only that it was "designed locally." Working drawings were produced by Alaska Railroad staff, and the building was constructed by the J. B. Warrack Company for $261,000. In 1948, coinciding with postwar modernization of the line, two-story wings were added to each end.

SC014 **Leopold David House**

1917. 605 West Second Ave.

The well-preserved bungalow at 605 West Second Ave. was built for Anchorage's first mayor, Leopold David. The one-and-a-half-story building, which measures 25 feet by 40 feet, has a wood frame covered with clapboards. Above a new concrete foundation, the lower walls are flared, covered with wood shingles, and painted a darker color. Tucked inside the front gable and asymmetrically placed to the right is a gabled porch with paired box columns. To the left of it is a semihexagonal bay window. The roof has exposed rafter ends, brackets in the gables, including on the gable dormer, and jigsawn ornament at the ends of the bargeboards. The only alterations have been an unfortunate square window in the front gable and the introduction of an office in the basement.

Leopold David, a Jew born in Germany in 1881, was an American immigrant success story. Moving with his parents to Brooklyn, New York, as a child, David entered the army after the death of his parents. After being stationed at Fort Egbert, Alaska, he moved to Seward in 1905, where he operated a pharmacy. He married Anna Karasek and in 1910

SC014 Leopold David House

was appointed U.S. commissioner in Knik; David also studied law, and after arriving in Anchorage in 1915, he worked as a lawyer. He was also active in community affairs. When Anchorage was incorporated in 1920, he was elected mayor, serving three terms. He died of a heart attack in 1924.

SC015 Alaska Engineering Commission Cottages

1916–1917. Second and Third avenues

After the Alaska Railroad decided to move its headquarters to Anchorage, the Alaska Engineering Commission—the construction arm of the federally owned railroad—erected nineteen dwellings to rent to its employees. Most were built on three blocks on the north side of the original townsite, just down the hill from the growing commercial district. The houses were simple buildings, one or one and a half stories, wood framed, in a variety of plans, some of which were reused. They are cottagelike in size, with some elements of the bungalow. Many have been converted to offices, reflecting their location on the edge of downtown, but the area maintains its residential scale.

SC015.1 Cottage 23

1916–1917. 618 Christensen Dr.

This one-story house is wood-framed with novelty siding. The side-gable roof extends to cover the front porch, which originally had exposed rafter ends. A large shed dormer has been added to the front. The original occupant of the house was Walter DeLong, the AEC general storekeeper.

SC015.2 Cottage 21

1916–1917. 542 West Second Ave.

Andrew Christensen, head of the AEC's Land and Industrial Department, originally occupied this house. In charge of the disposition of the public lands, Christensen was known for his glowing oratory, which apparently spurred buyers to bid more than they had intended at the public auctions. The one-story, hip-roofed cottage had exposed rafter ends at the eaves and a gabled porch.

SC015.3 Cottage 25

1916–1917. 645 West Third Ave.

The best example of a design that was used at least four times in this residential development, this one-and-a-half-story house has a side-gable roof, the center portion of which originally extended in the center to cover the porch as a shed roof. In this example, still owned by the U.S. government, the entrance has been changed to a gable-roofed vestibule and the roofline has been raised in the rear, but the beveled siding and exposed rafter ends are original elements. Other examples of this design are Cottage 26 at 637 West Third Avenue, now displaying Tudor Revival characteristics; Cottage 27 at 627 West Third Avenue, wood shingled with a gable entry; and Cottage 20 at 534 West Second Avenue.

SC016 Oscar Anderson House

c. 1915. 420 M St.

One of the first houses built after the sale of townsite lots in 1915, the Oscar Anderson house is now operating as a house museum. The simplicity of the dwelling is representative of the first houses; this one is a rectangular, 20-foot-by-40-foot, wood-framed building with beveled siding. Bungalow details include brackets and shingles in the front gable, exposed rafter ends at the cornice, the one-story, hip-roofed porch across the front (now enclosed), and the shed-roofed dormer on the west side. The plan is simple: living room, dining room, and kitchen on the first floor, with a small shed-roofed addition at the rear. There is a wainscoting of narrow beaded boards and simple, dark-stained woodwork.

SC016a Oscar Anderson House (living room)

SC016b Oscar Anderson House (kitchen)

On the second floor, there are bedrooms front and rear; in the middle, lit by the large dormer, is an additional bedroom that doubles as a hallway.

Swedish-born Oscar Anderson arrived in Anchorage in 1915 when it was still a tent city named Ship Creek. He went into business as a butcher and meat packer and later was president and general manager of the Evan Jones Coal Company. Two carpenters, Aaron Wicklund and Gerhard "Stucco" Johnson, built the house; Johnson also built houses in Seward. Anderson lived in the house for nearly sixty years. After his death in 1974, his third wife, Elizabeth, donated the house to the city. When the house was moved from its original site on top of the bluff to its present site at the foot, the brick fireplace was rebuilt and enlarged. The house is furnished and open to the public, providing an excellent illustration of a vernacular dwelling.

SC017 Hotel Captain Cook

1964–1965, first tower, Edwin B. Crittenden and Associates. 1970s, second tower, Maynard and Wirum. Fifth Ave. and K St.

Hotel Captain Cook rose out of the wreckage of the 1964 earthquake, symbolizing the viability of the city. Construction on the first tower, designed by Edwin B. Crittenden and Associates, began in June 1964. Construction continued through the winter—the first major Anchorage building where this was done—and the 125-room hotel opened in July 1965. Built to the seismic requirements of the Uniform Building Code, this nine-story building had squarish windows set in a grid of porcelain enamel panels. The second tower—fifteen stories—was designed in the early 1970s

by Maynard and Wirum in much the same style, and a third eighteen-story tower was added later. All are connected by a one-story portion that includes the public spaces. The unusual mustard color of this assemblage of buildings adds to its distinctiveness on the Anchorage skyline.

SC018 Federal Building / U.S. Courthouse

1976–1979; 1979–1980, annex; Associated Architects of Alaska and John Graham Company. 701 C St.

Although occupying two city blocks, the mass of the Federal Building is broken in such a way that the building does not seem huge. The steel-framed building, faced with precast concrete and reflective glass, is arranged in six modules, ranging from two to six stories in height, connected by an atrium that runs diagonally through the building. The strong horizontal emphasis, created by banded, smoky-glass windows, is interrupted by the division of the building into modules. Courtrooms occupy the west end of the structure, and offices the east. The $64 million building was designed by Associated Architects of Alaska, a consortium assembled for this project, including representatives of CCC, an Anchorage firm, and HOK's San Francisco office, in association with the John Graham Company of Seattle.

Using money left over from construction of that building, the government built an annex soon after. Occupying one whole block to the south, the one-story building is set partially underground, with a park on its roof. Entry is through a glass-enclosed, above-ground portion along the north, to a long ramp that takes the visitor underground. The building is further lit by lightwells along the sides. The $7.5 million building was designed by CCC/HOK and John Graham and was completed in 1980.

SC019 Anchorage Museum of History and Art

1966–1968, Kirk, Wallace and McKinley, in association with Schultz/Maynard. 1973–1974, west addition, Kenneth Maynard Associates. 1984–1986, Seventh Ave. addition, Mitchell/Giurgola Architects, in association with Maynard and Partch. 121 West Seventh Ave.

One of the most handsome buildings in the city, the Anchorage Museum of History and

SC019 Anchorage Museum of History and Art

Art is actually an addition to an older structure. The museum tripled in size when it added a two-story section on its Seventh Avenue side in 1984–1986. Designed by Mitchell/Giurgola Architects of New York, in association with Maynard and Partch of Anchorage, the new museum is a model of restraint and elegance.

Along the Seventh Avenue front, the mass of the building is stepped back, in four planes. The planes are pierced by two-story openings reminiscent of porticos and a one-story arcade. The buff brick wall is ornamented with brownstone trim in vertical lines and topped by a row of square medallions, a decorative effect borrowed by the Fifth Avenue Mall. Here, the facade is interesting but not busy.

The original museum, constructed in 1966–1968, can be seen on the Sixth Avenue side. Designed by Kirk, Wallace and McKinley of Seattle in association with Schultz/Maynard of Anchorage, the virtually windowless building has blank brick walls ornamented with a broad frieze of derivative Native design, executed by sculptor Alex Duff Combs. The building was expanded to the west in 1973–1974, with Kenneth Maynard Associates replicating the original design.

In the new building, the warm oak interior is arranged around an atrium, illuminated by a glass drum above the roof and glass-block windows at the rear. The large atrium, with a green slate and marble trim floor, has a dramatic, seemingly unsupported stairway over a shallow pool. In addition to the galleries surrounding the atrium, the first floor contains an auditorium, museum shop, and space for exhibit storage. On the second floor

are the galleries of the permanent historical and anthropological exhibit, as well as offices and library. In the basement is a parking garage.

The old building is incorporated into the new one, and visitors pass from one to the other without being aware of the difference. The old building is one story, however, and at the rear of the second level of the atrium, a portion of the old frieze that marks the space of the older building can be seen up close.

SC020 **Pioneer School**

1915. Third and Eagle streets

The Pioneer School, the first school in Anchorage and the only remaining early public building, was constructed by the Alaska Engineering Commission in 1915. As an arm of the U.S. government, the AEC did not intend to get into the education business, but because Anchorage was not empowered to govern or tax itself, it was left to the AEC to provide a school as part of its mission to make the townsites appealing places to settle. The two-story, hip-roofed structure measures 58 feet by 30 feet and was designed to house ninety pupils in two classrooms per floor. The original entrance was in the middle of the long side, opening into a hall and stairway. The $5,000 contract was given to builders Parsons and Russell.

The burgeoning population of Anchorage rendered the school inadequate almost immediately. In addition, the school had no running water and did not meet the town's own standards for sanitation. By the fall of 1917, enrollment stood at two hundred, and a new school was built for $12,000.

The first school, which had originally stood on the School Reserve, the block bounded by Fifth and Sixth avenues and F and G streets, was moved across the street to the corner of Sixth Avenue and E Street. After installation of two new entrances—one at the end and the other a diagonal one in the opposite end—and new windows, it served as the social hall of the Pioneers of Alaska, Igloo 15, until 1964.

After the 1964 earthquake, the school was moved to its present site in Crawford Park. Set on a steep slope, the building now has a basement level, visible at the rear. An additional stairway was constructed on the inte-

SC023 BP Exploration Building

SC024 CIRI Building

rior, and the walls, floors, and ceilings have new coverings. The original room arrangement—essentially three equal spaces per floor (hallway flanked by classrooms)—has long been lost. The building serves as a public meeting hall.

SC021 **Inlet Towers**

1951–1952, Earl W. Morrison in association with Donald MacDonald. 1200 L St.

Inlet Towers was one of two apartment buildings constructed in 1951–1952 to alleviate the severe housing shortage that Anchorage was experiencing. The other was the McKinley Apartment Building (now McKay Building) at Fourth and Denali on the other side of downtown. The two fourteen-story buildings—the first high-rises in Anchorage—

shared a similar design: corner windows and strong vertical elements emphasized by a two-tone paint scheme. Both were badly damaged in the 1964 earthquake.

Although the original owners had different corporate names, the use of the same architect and the fact that the building permits were issued on the same day indicate that the same developers were behind them. Each cost more than $1 million to build.

SC022 **George M. Sullivan Arena**

1983, Harold Wirum and Associates. Sixteenth St. and Seward Hwy.

One of the Project 80s buildings that changed the face of Anchorage, the sports arena is named after the mayor who initiated these projects, George Sullivan. The concrete stanchions that carry the inner seats are exposed on the exterior as vigorous verticals, strongly capped by the wide horizontal fascia of the roof. Entrances are at the corners sheltered by projecting rounded upper stories surfaced with glazed tile. The Brutalist design was by Harold Wirum and Associates. Completed in 1983, the building was the first of the major capital improvement projects to be erected. Used for concerts and special events, as well as for sports, the arena seats nearly nine thousand people.

SC023 BP Exploration Building

1982–1985, HOK. Seward Hwy. and Benson Blvd.

BP's Alaskan headquarters building is the most elegant of the oil-era Anchorage office build-ings. Opened in 1985, it stands on a 36-acre site that accommodates parking in an attractive landscaped setting. The thirteen-story building has facets on the north and south and a stepped roofline. The building is faced with a combination of pink granite and pre-cast concrete, the granite located mostly on the diagonals of the facade, while the concrete is used on the orthogonal planes. The two materials work well together, and the impression of the building's color varies from pink to gray, depending on weather and lighting.

Designed by HOK's San Francisco office, the building has a two-story section attached to the high-rise by a three-story, glass-covered atrium. Interior furnishings are rich, including cherry paneling in the lobby and thir-

Anchorage (SC1–SC22)

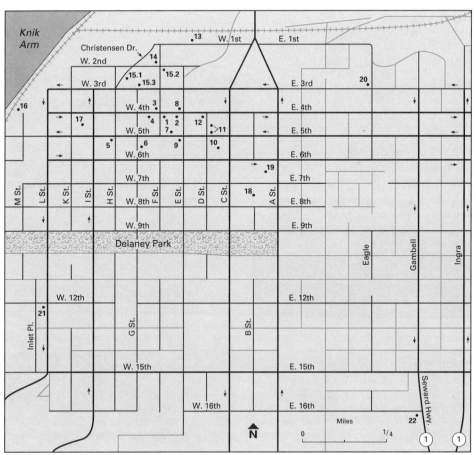

teenth floor. Eighteen major pieces of art, most by Alaskan artists, were commissioned for the building, both indoors and out, and contribute to the plush surroundings.

SC024 CIRI Building

1976–1977, Maynard NBBJ. 2525 C St.

The CIRI Building has been heralded as one of the first office buildings in Anchorage to break out of the box mold. The Cook Inlet Region, Inc., one of a dozen Native corporations set up under the 1971 Alaska Native Claims Settlement Act to manage money and land distributed by the federal government, wanted a distinctive headquarters building. The ten-story building with a reflective glass and spandrelite curtain wall has chamfered and cantilevered corners, which belie its essentially rectangular shape. Along the north wall is a plant-filled atrium, into which stairways open. The IRMA roof—inverted roof membrane assembly—is a flat roof frequently used on major commercial buildings in Anchorage. Rigid foam on the outside is held down with loosely laid concrete pavers; water runs down through the insulation to the composite roof deck. Despite its glassy appearance, the CIRI Building exceeded industry standards for energy conservation.

SC025 Z. J. Loussac Public Library

1982–1986, Environmental Concern, Inc. 3600 Denali St.

Z. J. Loussac Library defines its important spaces with massive cylinders. The building consists of three of these linked together and with a square block at one end. Faced in light brown brick with concrete trim, the building has a glass-roofed entrance at the second level. What could have been an attractive and functional building was severely harmed by cost-cutting measures taken to keep to the $41 million budget of this capital improvement fund project.

Environmental Concern, Inc. (ECI), of Spokane won a two-phase design competition. The firm originally designed the building with a parking garage to have second-level access to the library. When the garage was eliminated in order to cut costs, the architects proposed a raised parking lot so that entrance would still be at the second level. That too was abandoned, and as a result the library has no obvious entrance except an exterior stairway to the second-level entrance that is hazardous in winter.

On the first floor, the Anchorage Assembly Chambers occupy one of the cylinders, and a public auditorium another; each is two stories tall. Entrance is underneath the stairway, off a service road. Between the three cylinders, the second and third floors of the library are open, appealing spaces, with part of the third overlooking the second, while the fourth is mostly restricted to staff. At the third level, the Alaska Room is reached by a skybridge that is wide enough to accommodate a lounge. Occupying the third cylinder, the Alaska Room profits from controlled access. The third floor consists of a balcony; the reference section of the Alaska Room is on the second floor, while the first, mostly underground, is restricted to staff.

Although the library has a spacious site, it turns its back on the road in order to face south, toward the parking lot. Not easily reached by pedestrians, the library is often resented by taxpayers who feel that too much money was spent on the building and not enough on books to put in it. A welcoming entrance might have elicited a more positive response.

SC026 Saint Mary's Episcopal Church

1955, Edwin B. Crittenden and Associates. 4502 Cassin Dr., corner of Lake Otis and Tudor roads

Construction began in 1955 on this unusual, asymmetrical A-frame church, set on a sloping site. On the downhill side, the large wooden beams of the A-frame meet the ground more vertically; a concrete basement level is tucked under the church. On the uphill side, the beams are more parallel to the ground, extending beyond the church building. Ap-

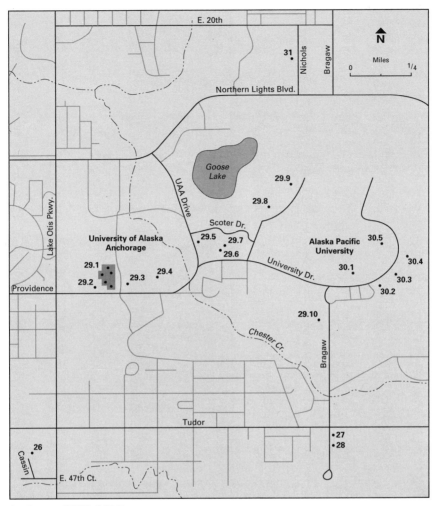

Anchorage (SC26–SC31)

proached up an easy flight of stairs on this side, a flat-roofed portico is supported by extended beams. Wooden shingles cover the ample roof, while the walls of the church—visible only on the uphill side and on the gable ends—are covered with vertical wood siding.

On the uphill side, there is a narrow band of windows close to the eaves, while on the downhill side, the band of windows in the steep roof is larger, yielding a spectacular view of the Chugach Mountains. At the altar end of the church, the window, with panes of colored glass, is nearly the full height of the roof. On the interior, the light wood pews contrast with the dark wood of the ceiling. With such a tall ceiling, there is a sense of space and openness.

Located at the busy intersection of Lake Otis and Tudor roads, the church is on a wooded bluff, set back from the streets. A stylized concrete campanile is located beyond

SC026 Saint Mary's Episcopal Church

SC027 Anchorage Police Department Building

SC028 Animal Control Center

the portico at the edge of the bluff. Also in the complex are a two-story parish hall and a rectory, both of complementary design. The buildings are arranged in a naturalistic setting, taking advantage of the hilly, wooded site and the spectacular view.

SC027 Anchorage Police Department Building

1986, GDM and Associates. 4501 S. Bragaw

Interesting for its use of concrete, the Anchorage Police Department Headquarters was designed by GDM and Associates of Fairbanks and completed in 1986. The two-story building is entered through its gable end, with a one-story section off to one side. The walls are clad in gray concrete, scored to resemble square tiles, and liberally trimmed with a smooth pinkish concrete. In the 1980s, colored concrete emerged as a popular material among Alaskan architects, and this building is a good example of its versatility.

SC028 Animal Control Center

1986–1987, Livingston Slone, Inc. 4711 S. Bragaw

The Animal Control Center is a lively building, endeavoring to make visitors—viewed as potential adopters—feel warm and happy about the place, while serving its primary function of animal storage. The one-story building has a two-story, gabled pavilion marking the entrance; the primary colors of its open framework contrast with the gray paint of the vertical-board walls. The pavilion is the entrance to a translucent-roofed transverse hallway, which retains the colorful framework. This strong axis also defines the

functions; to the left are rooms pertaining to people, while on the right are dog and cat kennels. The reception desk is located at the far end of the hall, so visitors must walk past potential adoptees in their cages. The building was designed by Livingston Slone, Inc., of Anchorage.

SC029 University of Alaska Anchorage

UAA and Providence drives

Comprising thirty-six buildings constructed since 1970, the University of Alaska's Anchorage campus provides a fascinating catalog of recent architectural work in the area. Most of the buildings are long and low, a distinct contrast to the mountainous backdrop. The campus, bounded on one side by Providence Drive and on the other by Goose Lake Park, has a linear plan, leading east into the foothills of the Chugach Mountains. The earlier buildings tended to have concrete exteriors, but by the mid-1970s metal sandwich panels, with different colored enamels, and tinted and reflective glass were favored. The bright colors were intended to enliven Anchorage's long dark winters. Within these parameters, the hands of different architects can be readily discerned.

SC029.1 Buildings A–F

1970, Buildings A–E, McEntire and Pendergast. 1970–1972, Building F, W. J. Wellenstein

These earliest buildings on the campus, A–F, were constructed for the Anchorage Community College, which was founded in 1954 and merged into the university in the 1980s. They are at the west end of the campus and have a unified design: one and two stories, with concrete and pebbled exteriors.

SC029.2 Williamson Auditorium

1974–1975, Bloomfield/Farr/McClure/Nixon

Located in the southwest corner of the campus, the auditorium has a monolithic concrete exterior, somewhat relieved by an irregular plan.

SC029.3 Health Sciences Building

1982–1983, TRA/Farr

Like so many other buildings on the campus, the Health Sciences Building is finished in concrete, but it has ribbon windows and a decidedly horizontal emphasis.

SC029.4 Campus Center, Sports Center, and Bookstore

1977, Lane-Knorr-Plunkett (Campus Center). 1977, CCC/HOK (Sports Center). 1983, Harold Wirum and Associates (Bookstore)

Designed by Anchorage firms, these three buildings are grouped together and linked to form what is intended to be the core of a quite elongated campus. The Sports Center is finished with beige enamel panels, while the Bookstore is a heavily bermed building with reddish glass.

SC029.5 Engineering and Science Buildings

1977, McClure/Nixon/Farr (Science Building). 1981, TRA/Farr (Engineering Building)

Linked by a second-level spine to the Campus Center, Sports Center, and Bookstore, the Engineering and Science buildings are extremely similar—two stories, ribbon windows, little ornament, flat roof—but their colors set them apart. The Science Building is clad with beige enamel panels and a slightly purplish glass, while the Engineering Building has purple enamel panels, bronze windows, and a thin orange line at the cornice.

SC029.6 College of Arts and Sciences

1974, Lane-Knorr-Elliot

Departing from the horizontal trend, this building has two large sections covered with dark glass, separated by a slightly taller concrete section. The college is connected to the Consortium Library.

SC029.7 Consortium Library

1973, CCC/HOK

The library, shared with Alaska Pacific University, has ribbon windows of dark glass alternating with horizontal strips of bronze-colored panels.

SC029.8 Administration Building

1983, Wellenstein/BOORA

More recent work includes the two buildings at the east end of the campus, one of which is the Administration Building. Gray enameled panels and ribbon windows of reflective glass are arranged in a quirky design. The V-shaped building has an open center, an arcade at the first level, and windows that increase in size near the center of the V. The building is trimmed with thin orange lines.

SC029.9 Arts Building

1986, CCC Architects

Another of the more recent structures on the campus, the Arts Building opened in 1986. The silver-gray panels are accented with red trim, contrasting with the smoky black glass of the ribbon windows. The theater, on the right, is evident by the fly, and the building has an appropriately broad and public entrance in the center. The V-shaped building faces a mountainous landscape against which its low, prismatic high-tech form is eloquently juxtaposed.

SC029.10 Student Housing

1985, William A. King Associates

The student housing complex departs from the linear plan of the campus and from the general horizontal thrust of the buildings. Constructed on Bragaw Street, a short distance away from the Arts Building, the three-story buildings have a number of gabled pavilions. Their clapboard coverings and vertical emphasis contribute to a woodsy, residential appearance.

SC030 Alaska Pacific University (Alaska Methodist University)

University Drive

Set in wooded hills on the east side of Anchorage, Alaska Methodist University opened in 1960; in 1978, the university changed its name to Alaska Pacific University. Located just east of the University of Alaska, the campus is spread out on winding roads; few buildings are visible from each other.

SC030.1 Grant Hall

1959–1960, Manley and Mayer

The oldest building on the campus, and the one seen first when arriving from the west, is Grant Hall. The best Alaskan example of the International style of the postwar years, it was designed by an Anchorage firm. The two-story building has a mixture of wall materials: rough stone, glass and aluminum, and vertical wood siding on a circular element that contains a theater. A mural of the earth on a blank front wall was added much later. Originally, administrative offices were in the cantilevered portion to the left, while the main block of the building contained classrooms and the library. Today the building holds administrative offices and classrooms.

SC030.2 Gould Hall

1960, Manley and Mayer

Diagonally opposite Grant Hall is a dormitory with horizontal emphasis that is interrupted by squarish windows and vertical piers.

SC030.3 Grace Hall

1989, CCC Architects

Next to Gould Hall is the newest building on the campus, a three-story building faced with silver enamel panels, bright green trim, and dark glass in ribbon windows.

SC030.4 Moseley Sports Center

1980s

Moseley Sports Center is a windowless concrete block set next to an all-glass entrance. The sculpted garden wall adorning the exterior is part of the frieze from the original building of the Anchorage Museum of History and Art.

SC030.5 Atwood Center (Campus Center)

1966, Edward Durell Stone, in association with Manley and Mayer

The Campus Center, which was renamed the Atwood Center in 1983, is an arrangement of symmetrical rectilinear boxes. The internationally known architect, Edward Durell Stone, designed it in association with local architects Manley and Mayer. The crisp lines of the flat roofs and square buildings have an astonishing appearance when seen in their natural setting. The complex is composed of three buildings, set in a U-plan, connected only by the podium on which all three sit and by the flat roof that covers them all. Each of the buildings is 25 feet tall, with precast concrete panels alternating with window bays of bronze-colored glass in bronze-colored frames.

The center building, which was constructed as the Student Union, is a two-story building 113 feet on each side. The podium extends 10 feet on the sides and 30 feet in the front and rear; the roof is just 1 1/2 feet smaller. Six square columns across the front and rear support the flat roof. The first floor contains the post office, lounge, radio station, and various offices, while the second floor is the dining room, entirely open around the central kitchen.

Offset from the front corners of the Student Union are the two residential buildings. Each of these is 73 feet square, three stories. Again, the podium extends 20 feet in front and rear and 10 feet on the sides, and the roof is 1 1/2 feet smaller. Four square col-

SC030.5 Atwood Center (Campus Center)

umns on front and rear support the roof. The building to the south (left) is a dormitory, and the one to the north, apartments, but in both cases the rooms are arranged around the perimeter walls. A lounge on the second floor is open up to the third floor and lit by skylights.

Stone envisioned a formally laid out campus, of which this would be the centerpiece building. According to his plans, the hill behind the building would be taken down, opening up a view across the city and making the back of this building the front. Additional buildings would be constructed in a right-angled U-plan and would incorporate Grant Hall (which would receive a new facade). The buildings would be built at the same elevation and would be connected.

Although the rest of Stone's plans were never realized, the campus center exhibits an architectural sophistication that few Anchorage buildings of the period shared. Stone's modern architecture had little regard for setting, however, illustrated not only by the geometric regularity of the building but also by his proposal to re-landscape the mountain.

SC031 **Helen S. Whaley Center**

1972, Maynard and Wirum. 1990, rear addition, Charles Bettisworth and Company. 2220 Nichols St.

This one-story school building employs colored concrete in a tapestry effect. The 4-inch-high concrete blocks were mixed in three colors of red and drab and laid randomly. Beige concrete serves as an accent, comprising the splayed lintels, sills, and jambs of the windows, as well as the covering of a porch across the front. The windows are set very low to the ground, as the school was originally

designed for handicapped children. A large addition in the rear is built of concrete blocks of the same colors but in an 8-inch height, so that the polychromy is more emphasized. The colorful and bricklike qualities of the concrete illustrate its flexibility as a finish material.

SC032 **Saint Innocent Orthodox Christian Church**

1970–present, Services Unlimited and Associates. 6724 East Fourth Ave.

Saint Innocent's was founded in 1967 as a mission that administered to the transient Orthodox who found their way to Anchorage. Ground was broken for this church in 1970, and construction—proceeding as finances allow—is still under way.

Unlike other Russian Orthodox churches in Alaska, Saint Innocent's has a multifaceted plan and multidomed profile. Most Orthodox Alaskan churches have simple lines, with an occasional polygonal sanctuary or as many as five onion domes. Saint Innocent's tall, hip-roofed nave is surrounded by a number of adjacent rooms, chapels, towers, and hallways, all projecting from the core and all with similar hip roofs. A high, concrete-block basement gives way to vertical wood siding and a blue asphalt roof covering.

SC033 **KENI Radio Building**

1947–1948, Augustine A. Porreca. 1777 Forest Park Dr.

The two-story, reinforced-concrete building housing KENI radio is an Art Deco gem. Flat-roofed and flat-surfaced, ornament is limited to 1-inch grooves in angular designs. A three-

SC033 KENI Radio Building

story tower at the entrance and beveled corners provide further interest. The wood-trimmed interior contained three apartments, as well as the control room for the radio station.

Cap Lathrop owned KENI, the second radio station in Anchorage, which went on the air in 1948 with the completion of this building. For the design, Lathrop hired one of the architects who had worked on his Fourth Avenue Theater, Augustine A. Porreca, from Seattle.

SC034 **Garden of Eatin**

1940s. 2502 McRae Rd.

Quonset huts were widely used in postwar Anchorage, which experienced a severe housing shortage. Declared surplus by the military, they were relocated to residential areas of the city. This quonset hut was erected on this site in 1948 or 1949 for Hans and Jerry Kirchner, who had a farm here. In 1951, they converted it to a restaurant. The present owner acquired it in 1970, adding the large lounge and banquet facilities building in 1978.

In the Garden of Eatin, the essential form of the quonset hut is readily apparent, despite small wooden additions at each end, one of which is a connection to the large facility. The rounded building has a corrugated metal exterior, with three shed-roofed windows on a side. On the interior, the ceiling has been dropped in the center, so that it is flat rather than rounded, but the sense of space survives.

SC035 **Government Hill**

Government Hill is aptly named, as the Alaska Railroad, a federal agency, withdrew this neighborhood from general development in 1915, reserving it for housing for government workers. After an initial building spurt, the hill remained largely undeveloped until the 1940s, when the government—the Army Corps of Engineers as well as the Alaska Railroad—again built housing. The housing on Government Hill forms a fascinating textbook of standard-plan and prefabricated housing, most of which is now privately owned.

With high labor costs, short building season, and lack of indigenous construction materials, prefabricated housing was a practical solution to the city's housing shortages. Manufactured housing, so popular today, is part of a long succession of prefabricated construction types, some of which are illustrated on Government Hill.

SC035.1 **AEC Cottages**

1915. 223 West Harvard, 255 West Harvard, 349 West Harvard, 335 West Harvard, 313 West Harvard, 239 West Harvard

In 1915, the Alaska Engineering Commission built thirteen cottages for its employees on Government Hill, across the basin from the townsite. Only six of these cottages are recognizable, although others may exist under many layers of alterations. The identical three-room cottages were one-and-a-half stories, measuring 23 feet by 34 feet. Steeply pitched gable roofs were echoed in the pitch of gable-roofed porches in the gable fronts. The simply ornamented houses also had exposed rafter ends.

The best example is the cottage at 223 West Harvard, which retains its four-over-four-light windows, and the front porch enclosed with large four-light windows. It has been covered, however, with fake-brick asphalt siding. The cottage at 255 West Harvard retains its original form and is covered with clapboards. The window sash and the porch have been altered, however.

SC035.2 **Quonset Huts**

late 1940s. 100 1/2 West Cook, and 208 1/2, 224 1/2, and 240 1/2 East Cook

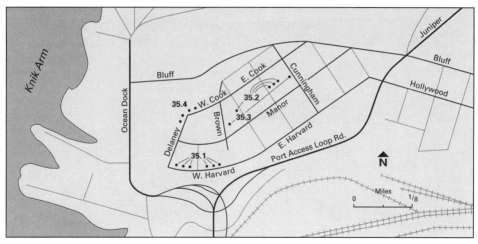

Anchorage (SC35)

After the Second World War, two types of prefabricated houses that were declared surplus by the government were moved to Government Hill. The quonset hut, a corrugated-metal building widely used during the war, was one of these. The Alaska Railroad moved quonset huts onto the rear of lots, intending that they serve as temporary housing while more conventional houses were constructed on the front of the lots. More than 120 quonset huts were moved into this neighborhood. At least six survive today, and four are still used as houses. All have vestibules added on the front, and some have additions in the rear.

SC035.3 **Loxtave Houses**

late 1940s. 821 Brown, 240 1/2 Cunningham

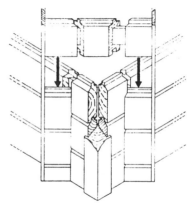

SC035.3b Detail of Loxtave corner construction

A second type of prefabricated construction declared surplus by the government was the Loxtave house. Designed by the U.S. Navy, these horizontal plank structures are assembled with a locking system at the corners. More than a dozen were erected on Government Hill, and two survive. The house at 821 Brown is in the best condition, with a vestibule added to the end but no other obvious alterations. The other, at 240 1/2 Cunningham, has gable-roofed entries on the side and front.

SC035.4 **Harman Houses**

late 1940s. 928 Delaney, 944 Delaney, 243 West Cook, 255 West Cook

Yet another prefabricated building type is the

Harman house, a metal building. Built by the Alaska Railroad, it is a simple one-story, gable-roofed building. Harman houses were constructed of thin sheet steel fastened to steel wall studs and roof trusses. Partition walls had steel studs covered with wallboard. Windows were metal-framed. The exterior finish was a special paint, resembling stucco. Despite an initial order of 4,200 houses, the Philadelphia-based Harman Corporation filed for bankruptcy in 1948, after less than two years' existence. Only 400 houses had been shipped.

The four Harman houses constructed on Government Hill have new exterior sidings, and all but the house at 928 Delaney have had large additions. The house at 944 Delaney retains an original casement window. The house at 243 West Cook was the only one of the four built as a split-level.

SC036 **Elmendorf Air Force Base** (Fort Richardson)

In 1940, the U.S. Army began construction on a permanent air base just north of Anchorage, where there was access to the railroad and proximity to the port. Named Fort Richardson, it included Elmendorf Field. The Eleventh Air Force was organized here in 1942, and after the war was renamed the Alaskan Air Command and transferred back here from Adak in 1947. Three years later, the army moved to the eastern part of the base and named it Fort Richardson; the original site is known as Elmendorf Air Force Base.

In June 1940 the quartermaster general's office began construction of an airfield and housing for 7,000 men. The constructing quartermaster designed the base in a generally semicircular plan, set in the right angle of intersecting runways. In January 1941 the Corps of Engineers assumed control of all army construction. Housing and support facilities for an additional 7,500 men at Fort Richardson were authorized in December 1941, and the base continued to expand.

Now composed of hundreds of buildings, most of them undistinguished, the base has a few buildings of interest, dating from its first decade.

SC036.1 **Col. Everett S. Davis Building**
1947–1948

The Davis Building is headquarters to the Alaskan Command—an organization of army, navy, and air force commanders—and the Alaskan Air Command. The reinforced-concrete building has the blockiness of the Moderne style and the ornament of the Art Deco.

A central three-story block is flanked by tall, two-story windows in end bays. Originally those windows were all glass block, and they remain partially of that material. Set back from the front are two-story blocks on each side, and set back from that, two-story lateral wings. The flat roof is accented by zigzag ornament at the cornice. The interior has been remodeled, and little original detail remains. In 1977, the building was named for the first commander at Elmendorf and father of the Alaskan Air Command.

SC036.2 **Maj. Darrel C. Pyle Building**
1942

Set close to the intersection of the runways, this building sat at the head of a parade ground. Now the headquarters of the tactical fighter wing, the Pyle Building was built of concrete with horizontal lines. The hip-roofed building has hip-roofed dormers, giving it a domestic, Colonial Revival feel. The two-story entrance bay has stylized pilasters.

SC036.3 **Hangars**
early 1940s

Radiating from this building are three hangars. The steel arches of the roofs are anchored in concrete walls. The end walls are wooden, and there have been office additions on the sides and ends.

SC036.4 **Quarters 1**
1942

Quarters 1, the home of the commanding officer, is a duplex converted to a single-family home. With vinyl siding and a large glass vestibule on the front, the house is undistinguished.

Most of the housing for field-grade officers is two-story, hip-roofed duplexes, five bays wide, with hip-roofed entries. All of them have new siding, which is a dramatic change on a plain building.

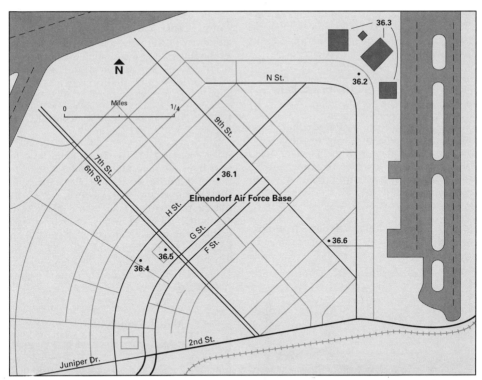

Anchorage (SC36)

SC036.5 Alaska Chateau

1942

The Alaska Chateau is a five-unit building for visiting officers. With a hip roof and vinyl siding, like its neighbors, it has three hip-roofed entries into the five townhouse units.

SC036.6 Kashim Club

1941–1942

One complete anomaly on the base is the Kashim Club, built as an enlisted men's club (and named after the traditional Eskimo ceremonial dwelling). Probably to emphasize the informality of the club, the building is constructed of logs, sawn flat on three sides. A stone chimney on an end wall adds to the rustic nature.

SC037 Alaska Army National Guard Armory

1990, Charles Bettisworth and Company. Fort Richardson, visible at mile 9, Glenn Hwy.

An unusual curved building, the National Guard Armory is also exceptionally large, measuring 900 feet by 100 feet. Accommodating the curve of Glenn Highway, the building comprises a quarter circle, presenting a long, bowed face to the highway and the mountains beyond. The first floor is faced with polychromatic concrete blocks, while the second has a metal covering.

Anchorage Vicinity

SC038 Hiland Mountain Correction Center

1974, CCC/HOK. Hiland Road, Eagle River

Built in a wooded setting, the Hiland Mountain Correctional Center is a campuslike collection of buildings. Receiving favorable recognition in the national architectural press when they were constructed, the one-story buildings have vertical wood siding and extensive glass, giving them an open, pastoral appearance. The plan is irregular, so that it does not have the look of an institution. Only the 6-foot chain-link fence indicates that this complex is not as open as the architecture would make it appear.

SC039 Eklutna Village Historical Park

Eklutna

Within the Greater Anchorage Area Borough, but 25 miles northeast of the city in a rural setting, is the site of the Tanaina village of Eklutna. Two Russian Orthodox churches form the core attraction of Eklutna Village Historical Park.

SC039.1 Saint Nicholas Russian Orthodox Church

1897

This simple log building was erected at this site in 1897, when a group of Tanaina moved here from Knik. One of only a handful of nineteenth-century Russian Orthodox churches in Alaska, Saint Nicholas's retains the traditional elements and forms.

The church is a small, 19-foot-by-30-foot hewn-log structure with a gable roof. At the west end, the shed-roofed vestibule, open in front, supports a bell tower. The walls, which have lap joints in the middle of the long sides, have diamond notches at the corners (or, perhaps, an untrimmed dovetail). During restoration in 1976–1977, the vestibule and bell tower were replaced and new concrete block footings were installed.

The interior is simply furnished, with plywood wainscoting and cloth tacked on the walls and ceiling. Two-thirds of the building is devoted to the nave, which is separated from the sanctuary by the iconostas. Extending to the ceiling, the iconostas has sophisti-

cated wooden moldings and several oil-on-canvas icons thought to be quite old. The simplicity of the structure and the spareness of the furnishings contrasting to the splendor of the icons are characteristic features of Alaskan Russian Orthodox churches.

SC039.2 New Saint Nicholas Church

1954–1962

Mike Alex, a Tanaina Indian chief, and his sons built the new Saint Nicholas Church to the south of the old church. The church has the same size and general form as the old one: a rectangular main block, gable roof, vestibule, and bell tower. The gable-roofed vestibule and tower support a belfry and onion dome. On the inside, the church has some icons from the abandoned Aleutian village of Unga, as well as nineteenth-century processional banners.

SC039.3 Eklutna Cemetery

The brightly painted spirit houses in the cemetery are neither an Athapaskan nor a Russian Orthodox tradition but seem to be an original product of the collision of two belief systems. Traditionally, the Tanaina would cremate their dead and put the ashes in a spirit house. The Russian Orthodox encouraged burial, and somehow, by the twentieth century, the spirit house was widely used to cover graves.

Today, the dead are buried and the grave covered with a blanket—whose colors often denote clan associations—for forty days. Then the small gable-roofed structure known as a spirit house is erected. The color scheme is selected by the family and often is consistent within a family grouping; color and shape of the ridge ornament are particular to the individual. The fences around the graves are a Russian influence, as are the Orthodox crosses at the foot of the grave and the tradition of graves facing east.

SC039.4 **Visitors' Center**

1920s. 1990, moved and renovated

The building serving as a visitors' center is the Alaska Railroad section house, which was moved from Girdwood, 40 miles southeast of Anchorage, to its present site and renovated in 1990. A one-story, wood-framed structure, the building is covered with novelty siding. Its sweeping hip roof is its most notable feature. Other elements, such as the fenestration and the plan, have been drastically altered. Originally, the interior would have contained a large dining room and kitchen, bunk room, and separate rooms for the section foreman and his family. Today it is one open space.

SC040 **Mike Alex Cabin**

mid-1920s. Eklutna

The house built by the Tanaina Indian chief Mike Alex illustrates the pervasiveness of the log cabin, which by that time had infiltrated Native culture. The 17-foot-by-20-foot gable-roofed structure was built of hewn logs, 8 inches to 10 inches high, dovetailed at the corners. In the 1930s, in order to enlarge the cabin for his growing family (he eventually had thirteen children), Alex removed the front wall and added a room, which was 17 feet square and the same height as the rest of building. The addition was of 6-inch logs, sawn flat on three sides, lapped at the corners. There is a gable-roofed vestibule, as well as a small addition in the rear. Although the building was originally set directly on the ground, a concrete foundation has been added.

Mike Alex (1907–1977), one of the last Native chiefs, witnessed great changes during his lifetime. In the summers, he fished at Fire Island in Cook Inlet, and in the winters, hunted and trapped from Eklutna, as was traditional among his people. Alex also worked for the Alaska Railroad, however, becoming a section foreman. He was a devout Russian Orthodox, building a new church and encouraging the preservation of the old one. In his later years, he helped compile Tanaina

place names and legends to ensure the preservation of his language and culture. His position as village chief was replaced by a village council, as the traditional tribal structure gave way to incorporation as Eklutna, Inc.

SC041 **Potter Section House**

1929. Mile 115.3 of Seward Hwy., mile 100.6 of Alaska Railroad

Within the Greater Anchorage Area Borough, but 11.7 miles south of the city in a rural setting along Turnagain Arm in Chugach State Park, is the Potter Section House. The plain, one-and-a-half-story house at Potter's Marsh was constructed as a railroad section house, or home to a crew of men charged with maintaining a section of the track. Potter was the site of a construction camp, beginning in 1916, and once the railroad was completed, a section house was located there. This one was built in 1929 according to standard plans that were used at least four times; this is the only building of that design still standing.

The building, which measures 28 feet by 36 feet, has gable-roofed, enclosed entrances in each gable end. Covered with novelty siding, the wood-framed building has exposed rafter ends at the eaves. On the first floor, a large dining room and kitchen, 14 feet by 27 feet, served the crew of six to eight men, who lived on the second floor. The first floor also contained quarters for the foreman and his family, as well as a bathroom, through which were the stairs to the second floor.

The house served its original function until 1978, when it was moved less than a mile to its present site. In 1986, it opened as the visitors' center for Chugach State Park and as a railroad museum. Located between the highway and the railroad tracks, it is accompanied by an outhouse, coal shed, meat cache, and vegetable garden, giving a sense of the place.

Girdwood Vicinity

SC042 **The Bird House**

c. 1903. Mile 100.5, Seward Hwy., Girdwood

Perhaps of more immediate interest to bar-hoppers than to architectural historians, the quaintness and dubious charm of the Bird House derive from its architecture and bawdy interior decor. The one-story, gable-roofed building was apparently built in three sections. The oldest is constructed of round logs square notched at the corners. Built on boggy ground, it has sunk so far into the ground that the sill of the window is now below ground. An addition was constructed of round logs, saddle notched at the corners, and another addition of vertical half logs. The sloping floors and slanting walls of the semisubterranean building contribute to its rustic quality.

A Bird Creek prospector probably constructed this building as a base for his trap line operation in about 1903. During construction of the Alaska Railroad near here, other buildings were erected at the site. In the 1920s, after the railroad was completed, Gus Bystedt homesteaded the site and eventually joined the original building with one from the railroad era. In 1963 a new owner, Cliff Brandt, opened the Bird House and began the eccentric collection of calling cards and memorabilia that is freely stapled to the walls. Thirsty architectural historians will easily justify a trip to the site.

SC043 **Crow Creek Consolidated Mining Company**

1898–1906. Crow Creek Rd., Girdwood

Eight buildings remain at this site from a gold mine that operated between 1898 and 1906. The Crow Creek Consolidated Mining Company ran the most productive gold mine of the Turnagain-Knik region in the early twentieth century. Here, placer gold was uncovered through hydraulic mining, which required a strong stream of water to expose old streambeds, violently altering the landscape. The hydraulic giant, or nozzle and hose, carved out a gorge 250 feet deep. The gravel was then washed through sluice boxes that were 200 feet long, in which the gold would settle.

The buildings up on the bluff, away from the workings on the creek, depict a mining camp that served twenty or thirty miners. Surviving from the early period are the commissary, blacksmith shop, original manager's house, four-man bunkhouse, ice house, tool shed, and smokehouse. All of them are small in scale, constructed of a rough wood frame with board-and-batten siding, as in the case of the mess hall, bunkhouse, and commissary, or round logs, as in the blacksmith shop. The ice house, by the pond, has double plank walls, with a layer of sawdust between. The buildings are functional; additional buildings were also constructed to serve specific purposes.

Ownership changed several times after 1906, but the mining continued to be profitable. In 1915 a sawmill was constructed, creating a diversion flume to reroute Crow Creek and to permit the previous creek bed to be mined. In the 1920s the existing mess hall burned down. The manager's house was expanded into a new mess hall, and a new manager's house was built.

In 1967, as an Alaska Purchase Centennial project, the mine was opened to the public. Numerous artifacts found on the site are used as decoration, but they are informative nonetheless. Visitors are permitted to try their hands at panning for gold.

Kenai Peninsula

Hope

Hope is an inviting town of log cabins and frame cottages, rooted in the gold rush. Located on Turnagain Arm at the mouth of Resurrection Creek, Hope served as a supply point for gold miners on the Kenai Peninsula. Although gold mining on the Kenai was never as successful as at other places in Alaska, it was one of the first areas where gold was known to be found and had been identified by the Russians by 1850. The rush to the Kenai began in 1896, and when prospectors on a steamer from Seattle disembarked at Resurrection Creek, they named the place after the youngest member of their party, Percy Hope.

Hope experienced the boom and bust of most gold-rush towns. That winter, about 80 people stayed in Hope, and by 1899, there were 200 men and 3 women. A post office was established there in 1897, the Alaska Commercial Company opened a store in 1898, and the first school and a community hall were built in 1902. Hope also had four saloons, three stores, two hotels, and a sawmill for local use.

By 1910 the boom was over; 35 to 40 people wintered in Hope that year. By 1930 it was down to 15, but up to 71 in 1939. The 1964 earthquake caused about half of the townsite to subside, but about two dozen buildings from Hope's heyday remain.

The grid plan is still evident, defined by unpaved roads and fenced yards. Most of the houses are small, one story, with gable fronts and metal roofs. The structures are both log and wood frame. Not all of them date from the turn of the century; a square hip-roofed bungalow, constructed of logs, was built in 1924. Houses built in the last two decades tend to be larger, but remarkably compatible with the earlier architectural character.

SC044 **General Store**

1900. Near the end of Main Street (since the earthquake)

One of the oldest buildings in town, the general store is also the most prominent, although its size would be viewed as modest in

Hope

any other context. The one-and-a-half-story, wood-framed building is covered with beveled siding. The first owner was George Roll, who operated it until his death in about 1940. The next owner, Norwegian-born Iver Nearhouse (Naerhus), operated it for about fifteen years.

SC045 Social Hall

1902. Main St.

The large Social Hall is one story high and constructed of logs, square notched at the corners. Rounded on the exterior and chinked with cement, the logs have been hewn flat on the interior. The gable front has a shed-roofed porch.

SC046 Methodist Church

c. 1940. Corner of Second and A streets

The Methodist church is an L-plan, log building with a concrete foundation. Residential in appearance, its logs are square notched at the corners and the gable roof has exposed rafter ends.

SC047 School

1937–1938. Corner of Second and A streets

Across the street from the Methodist church is a one-and-a-half-story, wood-framed school. Covered with clapboards, the building has a side-gable roof with cornice returns on the gables, features of the Colonial Revival style. Double and triple windows mark this as a schoolhouse.

Moose Pass Vicinity

SC048 Summit Lake Lodge

1988, gift shop. Mile 45 Seward Hwy.

A collection of three buildings, the romanticized log cabin is at its most characteristic here. The restaurant and motel are earlier and are like many other commercial log cabins. The gift shop, built in 1988 by the Wood Weavers, is a virtuoso piece of modern log cabin construction. It is made of large, closely fitted logs with saddle notched, overlapped corners. The gable roof is carried on massive log trusses carrying log purlins. The gable

ends are largely glazed, dramatically opening the building to the outside.

SC049 Alaska Nellie's Homestead

1920s. Mile 23 Seward Hwy.

One of Alaska's larger-than-life characters, Nellie Neal arrived in Seward in 1915 and ran several roadhouses for the Alaska Railroad during its construction. In 1923 she married Billie Lawing and moved to the site of a roadhouse at mile 23, then called Roosevelt. With the completion of the railroad, the need for roadhouses was ebbing, but Nellie foresaw that this site on Kenai Lake would be a good tourist spot and an excellent location for a restaurant.

The Lawings converted the roadhouse to a restaurant and room for Nellie's big-game hunting trophies, which included three glacier bears. Trains stopped for ten minutes to hear Nellie's lectures on Alaskan wildlife, and famous people came to visit her. In 1924 a post office was established at Roosevelt, with Nellie as postmistress; the name chosen for the post office was Lawing.

Although the original roadhouse no longer stands, Nellie's store does, a two-story structure constructed of round logs, saddle notched at the corners. In her autobiography, *Alaska Nellie*, she vividly describes how she and her husband moved the building to this site from its original location across the lake. Because of the dismantling and reconstruction necessary in moving a log building, this passage describes the construction of a large building, as much as moving one.

We anchored the boat on the bay, near where the building stood. He began by taking off the roofing paper, while I took out the doors and windows. The lumber from the roof was then taken off, which gave me the job of removing the nails.

Billie carefully marked each log, to make it easier when rebuilding. The logs were rolled into the lake, making a raft on which we loaded the doors, windows, and lumber; then the raft was towed by the boat to a small bay at Lawing, near where we had cleared the lot on which to build. With the hoist, I pulled the logs from the water, while Billie did the rigging.

. . . We began by putting in the stringers for the foundation; the first logs and the floor were then put down. I pulled the logs with the hoist, while Billie placed them where they belonged, and put in the drift bolts to hold them.

Small logs were used as stringers for the second floor. The heavy lift came when the last two rounds of logs were put on. We had to work from a scaffold when putting up the rafters. After the roofing lumber was put on, we cut and prepared the roofing paper, which was put on over the lumber.

I heated the tar used in sealing the seams of the paper, then carried it up the ladder, where Billie did the work of sealing and nailing down. The windows and doors were then put in place. We were several weeks tearing down, hauling and rebuilding this two-story loghouse, which added a much needed building to our tourist resort. They said "it couldn't be done," but we did it. (pp. 92–93)

Also at the site is her house, a one-story, wood-frame building with an irregular plan, evidence of several additions over the years. Clad with vertical boards, with battens in places, the house has a Yukon stove in the living room and oilcloth on the walls.

Seward

Nestled at the foot of 3,000-foot Mount Marathon, Seward is set on Resurrection Bay, a scenic harbor on the southern side of the Kenai Peninsula. Seward's fortunes involved the transportation industry, beginning with a Russian boat-building enterprise established in Resurrection Harbor in 1793. Nothing remains of this site, and the settlement did not survive. The railroad was the industry that ensured the success of Seward, founded in 1903.

In 1902 a group of Seattle investors headed by John E. Ballaine surveyed a course for a railroad to interior Alaska. Resurrection Bay, cherished as the northernmost ice-free port, was selected as the terminus. Although his partners never thought that the site would be more than a temporary construction camp, Ballaine saw its potential as a permanent city. In 1903, his agents negotiated with Mary Lowell, a Native who was the only resident of the projected townsite. She filed a homestead claim and then Ballaine bought her property, securing title to the townsite. He laid out the new town in a grid plan and named it Seward.

Construction began on the Alaska Central Railroad, but by the time the road had reached 20 miles north, Ballaine sold his interest in the railroad, keeping his investment in the town. By 1907 the investors ran out of money and construction was halted at mile 51.

In 1909, armed with fresh capital and a new name, the Alaska Northern Railroad continued construction, this time reaching mile 72 before running out of money. After intense lobbying, the U.S. government bought the railroad as it existed in 1915 to use as the first 72 miles of the Alaska Railroad. The Alaska Railroad initially located its headquarters in Seward but moved to Anchorage two years later. The railroad reached Fairbanks, 470 miles from Seward, in 1923.

In the first decades of the twentieth century, Seward was also the terminus of the Iditarod Trail, an overland route to the goldfields of the Iditarod. Besides having a healthy fishing industry, Seward still serves as a major transportation point, being a stop on the state ferry system and the terminus of the Alaska Railroad.

As platted by civil engineer C. M. Anderson, Seward had wide streets and

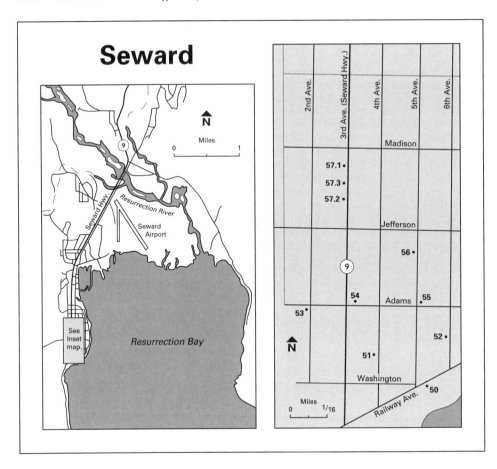

narrow lots. Jefferson Street was 100 feet wide, with all other east-west streets 66 feet wide, and north-south streets 80 feet wide. The lots were 30 feet by 100 feet, which perhaps dictated the small size of the houses. Development began on the south side of town, initially concentrating south of Jefferson Street. With the railroad terminal on the southeast edge of town, the heart of the city was in those first few blocks. In addition, Lowell Creek ran down Jefferson Street, impeding circulation. The U.S. Army Corps of Engineers' first project in Alaska was a 400-foot-long diversion dam, constructed in 1939–1940 to divert this creek from the streets of Seward. During the 1964 earthquake, Seward's waterfront, and the docks and railroad yards vital to the town's economy, were destroyed. The railroad terminal and small-boat harbor were rebuilt farther north, and the town began expanding in that direction. Unstable lands beyond Sixth and Railroad avenues, on the edge of the water, are used as parklands.

Seward's buildings are small and mostly wood framed. New commercial buildings in the older section of town tend to be large but not tall. The houses, which are also located in the old part of town, favor the bungalow form, or even smaller cottages; plain, one-story, gable-fronted buildings are also common. Particular to Seward is the popularity of stucco covering. Applied to older buildings in the 1910s or 1920s, or covering then-new buildings, stucco appears to be the historic cladding of choice.

SC050 Alaska Railroad Depot

1917. 501 Railway Ave.

The handsome, hip-roofed railroad station in Seward was constructed for the Alaska Railroad. The construction arm of the railroad, the Alaska Engineering Commission, built eight stations along the 470-mile route using a standard design in a style popular for railroad depots across the United States. Three of the Alaskan depots survive.

The one-story building measures 98 feet by 24 feet, with a waiting room on the west end, a ticket office in the center, on the track (now water) side, and a baggage and freight room on the east end. The broad hipped roof with hipped dormer, the deep eaves carried on brackets, and the shingled walls contrasting with clapboarded water table are Craftsman-style details. There is a temporary construction at the west end, which was originally open under the roof. The interior has been renovated, but rooms are still used for their original purposes.

In 1928, after the Alaska Railroad had built new dock facilities at the foot of Fifth Avenue, the depot was moved there from its original site at Adams Street. After the 1964 earthquake, the railroad moved its terminus farther north, and the depot became the passenger office for the Alaska Marine Highway system.

SC051 Brown and Hawkins Store

1904-c. 1915. 205–209 Fourth Ave.

The Brown and Hawkins Store was built by accretion and today reveals its growth from its founding in the earliest days of Seward. The store was established in 1903 on this site in a previous one-story building; the first part of this store was constructed in 1904. Theodore William Hawkins and Charles E. Brown had met in Valdez, where they opened a general merchandise store together. In 1903, they moved to the new town of Seward. Furnishing goods to miners, fishermen, and rail-

road people, Brown and Hawkins also founded the Bank of Seward, originally located in their store. Brown was part owner in a steamship company, and Hawkins was president of the Independence Mine north of Anchorage. Brown moved to Anchorage and opened a store there in 1915; it closed in 1926. Hawkins operated the Seward store until his death in 1946, and it has remained in the family since.

The building constructed in 1904 was a two-story, wood-framed structure with large display windows flanking a central, recessed entrance. Brown and Hawkins acquired a one-story building next door (north, right) and in 1909 had a second floor added with a single false front across the two buildings. It also had a balcony, supported by thin columns, that extended over the sidewalk.

Some time between 1911 and 1915 Brown and Hawkins acquired the one-story building on the other side for use as a hardware department. A few modifications were made to that building, including the installation of a balcony.

The building has been severely altered, but even in its evolved form, it is the best evidence of Seward's original commercial strip.

SC052 Cable Office

1905. 219 Sixth Ave.

The one-and-a-half-story, wood-framed bungalow at 219 Sixth Avenue was constructed in 1905 as the cable office. The Washington Alaska Military Cable and Telegraph System (WAMCATS) used both underwater and overland cables to connect military posts in Alaska to the United States. Seward was connected to Valdez in 1905, and in 1924, when the cable was replaced, Seward became the northern terminus for the underwater cable, rather than Valdez. In 1931, the cable was abandoned in favor of radio communications.

John E. Ballaine donated a 30-foot-by-100-foot lot for this building, but when Maj. W. A. Glassford requested an additional lot for a 30-foot-square feet house, Ballaine refused. The government finally leased two lots.

The first floor of this building served as the cable office, with space for the operator, the public, and equipment. The second floor contained quarters for the operators. The gable-fronted building has cornice returns on the gable and is three bays wide with a center door. The hip-roofed porch across the front has chamfered box columns and a balustrade; on its roof is a balustraded porch. The building has been covered with stucco and has a concrete foundation.

SC053 Saint Peter's Episcopal Church

1905–1906, W. J. Stone. 1917, rectory. 239 Second Ave., corner Adams St.

Saint Peter's Church is a small parish church with a steeply pitched gable roof. Covered on the outside with wood shingles, the church has pointed-arch windows and doors. In the plan of a Latin cross, the building has two-stage buttresses and a parapeted gable. There is a gable-roofed vestibule on the front, echoing the pitch of the gable roof over the nave. The rather plain interior has a dramatic mural as its focal point, on the reredos. Installed in 1925, the painting by Jan van Emple, a Dutch artist, depicts the Resurrection of Christ, using Seward as the setting and Alaskans as the observers.

W. J. Stone, an architect who also supervised construction, designed the church. Stone also formed a general construction company and served as agent for the Miracle Pressed Stone Company. He designed the concrete-block Bank of Seward (since demolished), apparently using his "pressed stone" as the building material. In 1908, Stone was arrested for embezzlement in Santa Cruz, California.

In 1917, a bungalow-style rectory was built adjacent to the church. The low gable roof is echoed in the entrance porch, which has battered box columns. The one-story, wood-framed building is finished with wood shingles and rests on a concrete foundation.

SC054 Van Gilder Hotel

1916. 307 Adams St.

The three-story, reinforced-concrete Van Gilder Hotel was built as an office block in 1916. E. L. Van Gilder intended that it be a two-story building but was persuaded to add a third story for fraternal lodge rooms. Upon completion, Van Gilder was forced to sell it at a loss and leave Seward. The new owner, Charles E. Brown of Brown and Hawkins, sold it within a year to M. A. Arnold of Seattle, who succeeded in renting out the building as offices, apartments, and lodge rooms. In 1921, however, it was converted to a hotel, the finest in Seward.

The building, which measures 34 feet by 85 feet, had all the modern conveniences in 1916. Each office suite on the first and second floors had hot and cold running water, central heat, and frosted glass partitions. The exterior has remained virtually unchanged, with a central round-arch entrance, paired windows, and a decorative cornice. The interior retains much of the original plan, a central corridor with rooms on each side.

SC055 Ray Building

1916. 500 Adams St.

A substantial building, the reinforced-concrete Ray Building was constructed in 1916 as a bank. The Harriman National Bank of Alaska opened in Seward in 1915, constructed this building the next year, and closed in 1922. The building also housed the high school from 1916 to 1928 and apartments and offices over the years. In 1933, Lee Vincent Ray (1877–1946), a prominent politician who had served as mayor of Seward and president of the first territorial legislature, bought the building.

The two-story building constructed in the Beaux-Arts Classical style, the traditional language of banks, has two-story pilasters dividing the front into three bays and the side into six. The large proportion of window to wall gives the building a modern appearance, making it more an office building than a temple of finance.

SC056 Swetmann House

1916. 325 Fifth Ave.

This stucco-covered house with fanciful Flemish gables is an unusual bit of whimsy. The house was built in 1916 by Gerhard "Stucco" Johnson, an accomplished builder known for his expertise with stucco. Probably soon after his marriage in 1921, Elwyn Swetmann bought the building and moved it to its present site. Swetmann owned the Seward Drug Company and in 1946 bought the Bank of Seward. Members of the Swetmann family lived here until the 1970s.

The one-and-a-half-story house is not large, measuring approximately 17 feet by 25 feet. Its most distinguishing feature is its stepped gable ends, creating a curlicued and angled profile. A shed dormer also adorns the roof. Entrance is through a shed-roofed porch, which has been partially enclosed, into a living room that extends the width of the building. The dining room has a semi-hexagonal bay window, and the kitchen is behind it.

The Swetmann family left the building to the local library, which opened the building for several years as a house museum. Now the building is back in private hands.

SC057 400 Block of Third Avenue

Known as Millionaire's Row, these houses have a modest bearing, compared to the houses in the Lower 48, that belies their nickname. Nonetheless, these were the houses—all built in 1905—for the prominent citizens in town. For example, the house at 413 was built for George Winter, a treasurer of the Alaska Central Railroad; number 417, for the head of the commissary of the railroad, Murray B. Holland; and number 429 for Eugene Hale, brother of an owner of the Bank of Seward. The houses are one-story cottages with porches and bay windows.

SC057.1 Ballaine House

1905. 437 Third Ave.

The largest of the lot was built for investor John E. Ballaine's brother Frank, who was the on-site manager of John's investment. The one-and-a-half-story house is a cross between a farmhouse and a bungalow. The house has a steep gable roof with gabled dormers but has been severely compromised by the addition of aluminum siding. Originally, narrow clapboard siding contrasted with wood shingles in the gables and on the roof; the foundation was cobblestone.

SC057.2 Stewart House

1905. 411 Third Ave.

At the other end of the row from the Ballaine house is the Stewart house. Built for F. H. Stewart, who was treasurer of the Alaska Central Railroad until 1907, the one-story, hip-roofed house was originally shingled. Hinting at Richardsonian solidity, a handsome round tower rises just above the wide overhanging eaves. The gable-roofed front porch has been enclosed, and the building was stuccoed. A large ell has been added to the south. At the time of its construction, the newspaper noted, "It is designed to be one of the handsomest dwellings in town."

SC057.3 Cameron House

1905. 423 Third Ave.

The best preserved of the row is the Cameron house. Built for the construction engineer of the Alaska Central Railroad, the wood-frame building has clapboard walls and shingled gables. Curved walls and hoods at the gable windows enliven the one-and-a-half-story, L-shaped house.

Cooper Landing

Four buildings built between 1905 and 1927 mark the historic town of Cooper Landing, founded as a trading post on the Kenai River in the 1880s by Joseph Cooper. Although a wave of gold miners populated the town in about 1898, no buildings remain from that period. By about 1905, trappers who also earned their livings as guides and temporary laborers were attracted to this site on the Kenai River.

SC058 Dunc Little Cabin

1905

Duncan McGregor Little was a Nova Scotian who had joined several gold rushes. When he settled at Cooper Landing, he trapped and prospected and occasionally worked as a camp cook. The house, now in a deteriorated state, is a log building with saddle-notched corners. One story and one room, it was clearly built by and for one man.

SC059 Charles and Beryl Lean House

c. 1910

The Lean house was built out of bridge timbers by Frank Towle, a prospector. The 4-inch-by-12-inch timbers were laid horizontally and covered on the exterior with vertical boards. The front door originally faced the river; it was closed off before 1925, although a front porch was added about 1930. In 1919 Frank Towle's wife, Grace, sold the house to Charles Lean, who that year married a woman named Beryl. Charles worked as a guide, trapper, and woodcutter, and obtained seasonal work from the Bureau of Public Roads. The Leans also ran a roadhouse and resort, using the schoolhouse in the off-season for sleeping quarters.

SC060 Riddiford School

1925

Charles Lean built the first room of the Riddiford School in 1925. At that time the post office was named Riddiford for the man who had donated the land. The territorial school board sent the first teacher to Cooper Landing in 1929, and the building functioned as a school until 1938. The one-story, gable-roofed building is constructed of logs, saddle notched at the corners. A second room, in the same style as the first, was built onto one end, a year or two after the first.

SC061 Cooper Landing Post Office

1920

Jack Lean, Charles's brother, built the Post Office around 1920. The front-gabled, steeply pitched portion was the original section. Jack Lean was a dog musher, carrying the mail on the Iditarod Trail, and was also part owner of some roadhouses in Rainy Pass. When he settled in Cooper Landing, he worked as a trapper and guide and carried the winter mail to Kenai. In the late 1930s he opened a store at Cooper Landing, probably adding the gable-roofed portion perpendicular to the original at that time. That section now serves as the post office, with the mail room located in an incompatible addition to the rear. Both of the original sections are of horizontal logs. The first has saddle-notched corners and a gable roof that extends in front to cover the porch, with bracing in the gable. The second section is constructed of logs sawn flat on three sides and placed on a concrete foundation.

Kenai

Set on a bluff overlooking Cook Inlet, on the west side of the Kenai Peninsula, Kenai and its surrounding area were home to the Kenaitze Indians for centuries before the Russians discovered it in 1791. One of several fur-trading enterprises, the Lebedev-Lastochin Company established Fort Saint Nicholas (Nikolaevskii Redoubt) at this site. Further reinforced by the Russian-American Company, Saint Nicholas was the principal Russian community on the Kenai Peninsula by 1867.

After the United States acquired Alaska in 1867, it sent a U.S. Army contingent to Fort Saint Nicholas, which was renamed Fort Kenay. One hundred and four soldiers occupied the eleven log buildings for only seventeen months, leaving in September 1870. In the 1880s, the first of several canneries was established on the Kenai River, the beginnings of a still-active industry.

The discovery of oil in 1957 brought a new prosperity to Kenai. Although the oil drilling took place elsewhere, at sites north of Kenai and out in Cook Inlet, the town boomed. New development oriented to the automobile swamped Kenai, producing what one historian has called "a bland hodge-podge of architectures and ways of life."

The old section of town, near Main, Cook, and Mission streets, has several log cabins with both round and hewn logs. Dating from the early twentieth century, most of them have dovetailed notching at the corners. Exhibiting a characteristic peculiar to Kenai and Ninilchik, the logs are not equal in each dimension but are hewn to a thickness of about 4 inches. As such they resemble thick planks rather than logs, but the corner dovetailing is a log-building convention.

SC062 **Fort Kenay Museum**

1967. Mission and Overland streets

The museum is located on the second floor of the two-story log building on the site of a Russian school. Behind it, in a fenced enclosure, is a collection of log buildings moved there from various sites around town. The buildings are still in the process of restoration, and little documentation of their histories or previous locations exists. Still, the buildings exhibit a variety of construction techniques.

SC062.1 **Cache**

Closest to the museum building is a cache, raised about 10 feet off the ground. The hewn-log building has dovetailed corners and a gable roof.

SC062.2 **Building 1**

1928

Next to the cache is a log building with a side-gable roof. The logs are taller than they are wide, and, in fact, are 4-inch thick planks. The cabin was constructed by a Finn named Emil Ness in about 1928; Ness was said to have constructed four other such buildings around town. A man named Lindel was the first owner of this 17-foot-square building, which had several owners over the years and was added onto and expanded. When the building was donated by Jim and Peggy Arness, the additions were removed before the cabin was moved to the museum.

SC062.3 **Building 2**

early twentieth century

Kenai

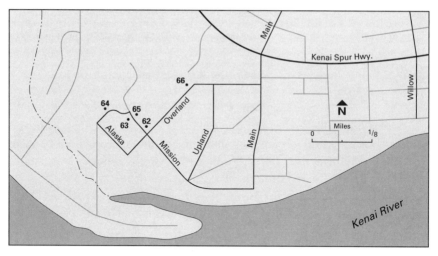

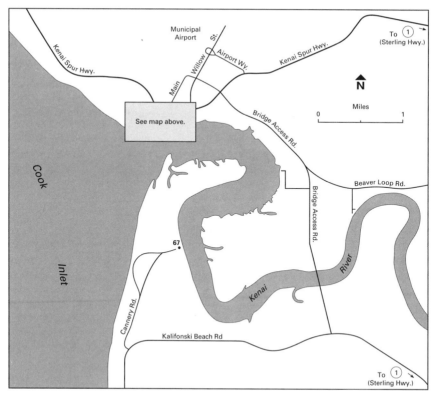

Building 2, next to Building 1, has a gable front. The hewn-log walls are lap jointed and nailed.

SC062.4 **Building 3**

c. 1910

Moving clockwise around the compound, the next building was also built by Emil Ness; the dovetailed corners have a distinct similarity to Building 1. Said to have been built about 1910 in Kasilof, the building was subsequently moved by George Miller, who donated it to the city.

SC062.5 **Building 4**

early twentieth century

Building 4, closest to Overland Street, is constructed of hewn logs, square notched at the corners, but extended beyond the notching.

SC063 **Holy Assumption Russian Orthodox Church**

1894–1895; 1900, bell tower. Mission and Overland streets

The Church of the Holy Assumption is a dramatic and well-proportioned building, adeptly using standard exterior forms to create interesting spaces on the interior. The priest, Father Alexander Yaroshevich, may have been the designer, although the core of Holy Assumption is similar in form to the Holy Ascension Cathedral in Unalaska, which was built at the same time.

Like most Russian Orthodox churches in Alaska, the exterior of this church reveals the use of the spaces within. The square nave is the taller portion; on the interior, the ceiling of this space is octagonal, reaching a height of 15 feet. The gable-roofed section to the west, now an extension of the nave, was originally walled off into two rooms. Today it opens into the nave, separated only by two columns. Entry is through the first floor of the bell tower, 15 feet 6 inches square. Above the second story is a pyramidal roof, out of which rises the octagonal belfry, with a tent roof that supports an onion dome.

On the east end of the church, the sanctuary has two roof forms, a gable roof to match the one on the west and a polygonal roof to cover the polygonal end of the sanc-

tuary. Both the sanctuary and nave have cupolas topped with onion domes.

The church is constructed of logs, hewn to a 6-inch width and dovetailed at the corners. It was covered with beveled siding soon after construction. The iconostas has icons dating from the construction of the church, while others are even older, including one painted on wood, dating from the eighteenth century. A picket fence sets the church off from the town, but its distinctive form and three onion domes are enough to isolate it from its domestic surroundings.

SC064 **Saint Nicholas Russian Orthodox Chapel**

1906. Near Mission St.

Never finished, the simple chapel to Saint Nicholas has a pure form that is charming. The chapel was constructed over the graves of Igumen (Abbot) Nicholas, the first Russian Orthodox missionary in Kenai, his assistant Makarii Ivanov, and an unidentified monk. It is thus near the site of the first church, as these clergy would have originally been buried in the churchyard. It is also near the site of Saint Nicholas Redoubt, the Russians' outpost at Kenai.

The 19 foot 10 inch square chapel is constructed of 5-inch-thick logs, hewn flat on two sides and grooved on the bottom to fit snugly over the one below. The logs were dovetailed at the corners and braced on the interior. The pyramidal roof has four cross gables and is topped by a cupola and onion dome. There is a low double door on the west side, and two windows on two sides.

In the late 1980s, the building was further braced; bolts were driven through the logs, marring the exterior appearance and damaging the historic fabric.

SC065 **Russian Orthodox Rectory**

1881–1894, Mooser and Pissis. Mission St.

In an effort to improve the living conditions of the Russian Orthodox clergy, Bishop Nestor contracted with the Alaska Commercial Company for four new priests' houses in 1880. Architects Mooser and Pissis of San Francisco drew up the plans, and the building at Kenai was constructed in 1881, although not completely finished and occupied until 1894. The

SC063a Holy Assumption Russian Orthodox Church (iconostas)

SC063b Holy Assumption Russian Orthodox Church (top, section; bottom, floor plan)

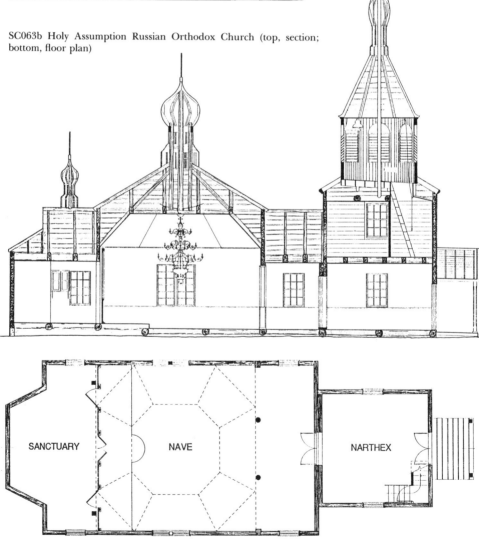

SANCTUARY   NAVE   NARTHEX

120

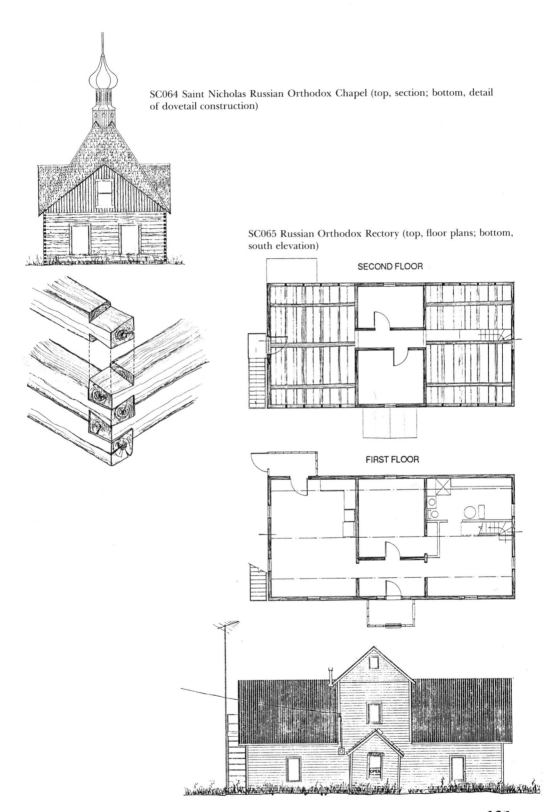

SC064 Saint Nicholas Russian Orthodox Chapel (top, section; bottom, detail of dovetail construction)

SC065 Russian Orthodox Rectory (top, floor plans; bottom, south elevation)

SECOND FLOOR

FIRST FLOOR

Bishop's House at Unalaska (SW015, p. 293) was constructed as part of this building program; the other two, at Kodiak and Nushagak, no longer stand.

The house is a simple rectangle in plan, 40 feet by 21 feet. The center section rises two stories, with two bedrooms on the second floor, while the rest of the building—two rooms on a side—is one story. The building is covered with a cross-gable roof. The walls are constructed of hewn logs, about 6 inches wide, covered with wood shingles. The original window sash has been replaced with single sash.

SC066 Agricultural Experiment Station

early twentieth century. Overland St.

A group of wood-framed, white-painted buildings occupies the site of an agricultural experiment station, operated by the U.S. government from 1899 to 1908. Beginning in 1899, in an attempt to test the feasibility of agriculture in Alaska, the U.S. Department of Agriculture established a number of experiment stations, where land was cultivated and crops carefully analyzed. Kenai's was not a success; it closed after only nine years.

The original buildings on the site included a one-and-a-half-story log cottage for the superintendent, a barn measuring 64 feet by 24 feet built from lumber salvaged from a cannery, and an implement shed covered with tin salvaged from another cannery. The property has remained in government hands and has been occupied by a variety of government agencies. The extant buildings, which appear to have been built by one of the later occupants, include a one-and-a-half-story house with a side-gable roof and a gable-roofed vestibule in the center of the front; an eleven-bay garage, built in two sections, and proba-

bly originally a barn; and another building, with several additions in the front, and a quonset hut added to the rear. All of the buildings are clad with novelty siding.

SC067 Wards Cove Packing Company Cannery

c. 1914. Cannery Rd.

Built about 1914 for Libby McNeil and Libby, the Wards Cove cannery at Kenai is still operating. Most of the machinery is fairly new, but the plant has been updated piece by piece, so the machinery still defines individual tasks.

The buildings are large, plain, and gable-roofed, most of them with gable ends toward the water. Most of the work takes place in the cannery building. Fish are brought in either by conveyor or forklift from the boats, which dock just outside. Inside, the fish are moved by conveyor belts, with different processes being accomplished by machine, aided by hands. The fish are gutted, deslimed, loaded into cans, cooked, and taken outside to cool. Neighboring buildings include the can warehouse, where cans were once manufactured (although they are now purchased ready-made); the egg house, where fish roe is canned; the ice house; the freezer plant (much of the business is now frozen fish); and the power plant.

Additional buildings house workers and administration. The company provides beds for a work force of about two hundred, a unionized group of college students and Japanese. Bunkhouses and the mess hall accommodate these workers. This cannery, like most, is an agglomeration of old and new buildings, most covered with corrugated metal. They comprise an easily identifiable, distinctive form on the landscape.

Ninilchik

The village of Ninilchik was founded in 1846 as a colony for Russian pensioners, most of whom had married Native women and wished to remain in Alaska when their tours of duty with the Russian-American Company were over. Fifty years later, the priest who visited the village as part of the circuit around his parish noted that Ninilchik "resembles our Russian villages." Located on the lowlands near the mouth of the Ninilchik River, the village is surrounded by high bluffs. The houses in the village, arranged in a seemingly random plan, include about a dozen log structures with either flat or round logs, all neatly dovetailed at the corners. As in Kenai, most of the logs are much narrower than they are tall, having been hewn to about a 4-inch thickness. Most of the houses are one cell, but some have additions.

One possible source for the similarity of these structures is a master carpenter named John "Peg Leg" Astragin, who lived here at the turn of the century. One example of his work is a one-and-a-half-story house, now painted red. The side-gable roof has an unusual gable-roofed dormer, which projects so that it is supported by columns. The walls are logs, carefully dovetailed. The house was built around the turn of the century and may have served as the rectory. With its second-story gabled projection, it bears a passing resemblance to the rectory in Kenai.

SC068 Holy Transfiguration of Our Lord Russian Orthodox Church

1901

Occupying a spectacular setting on top of a high bluff overlooking the village, the Holy Transfiguration of Our Lord Church is one of only four Alaskan Russian Orthodox churches built in a cruciform plan. Elaborate by Alaskan standards, such a grand church is unexpected here; when this church was built in 1901 the village had a population of only about one hundred. The church was probably designed by Father Alexi Andreev Oskolkoff, then the resident priest. Today, the congregation is served by a visiting priest from Kenai.

The log church with carefully dovetailed corners is covered with beveled siding. At the crossing of the gable roofs of the nave and transept, there is an octagonal cupola topped by an onion dome, one of five onion domes on the church. The square bell tower on the west end is two stories high; its pyramidal roof supports a square belfry, which is also topped by an onion dome.

On the interior, the low ceilings of the nave and transepts rise to an octagonal dome in the center, crowned by the cupola that sheds light into the nave. The church has a sur-

SC068 Holy Transfiguration of Our Lord Russian Orthodox Church

prisingly intimate feel on the inside; the nave is only 24 feet long, and the transepts are only 10 feet wide. The nine-bay iconostas is ornamented with four large oil-on-canvas icons.

The front of the vestibule, under the porch, has been faced with an unsightly varnished wood, but the church otherwise remains remarkably unchanged. The beveled siding was applied some time after 1916. A wider bell tower replaced the original, which had round-arch openings in the belfry; the ends of the original are visible in the interior of the vestibule. The churchyard and cemetery are neatly fenced. The location of the church, high above the village, leaves no doubt as to its intended supremacy in villagers' lives.

Homer

Homer is an appealing seaside town, remarkable for its 5-mile-long sand spit extending into Kachemak Bay. From 1899 to 1902, a company town flourished briefly at the end of Homer Spit, which was higher and wider before the 1964 earthquake. Coal was mined just west of present Homer, but the town grew up on the end of the spit, where the docking facilities were. A 7 1/2-mile railroad connected the two sites. None of the buildings from this early town remains.

The town of Homer, on the mainland, grew slowly. A herring industry and fox-farming enterprises flourished in the 1920s but collapsed in the 1930s. Fishing has remained the mainstay of the economy.

Homer strikes the visitor as a relatively new town; while a couple of buildings predate 1930, most were built in the thirties and forties. The size and form of these early buildings, though, evoke the pioneer life; the houses are small and simple, without frills. The building materials are either log or wood frame. Many of the houses have been moved around town.

SC069 Post Office

1927. 528 East Pioneer Ave.

This building served as a post office for only nine years. One room and one story, the building is constructed of horizontal round logs, square notched at the corners. The gable roof is covered with wood shingles, as is the front gable. The building was moved to its present site in the mid-1950s.

SC070 Harrington Cabin

c. 1935–1936. 581 East Pioneer Ave.

The Harrington cabin, across the street from the post office, is also simple. Charlie Erickson built the 14-foot-by-18-foot cabin for Stanton Shafer on the Harrington homestead; it was moved to its present site in 1975. The horizontal round logs are square notched at the corners and covered with corner boards. The side-gable roof is covered with wood shingles, and there is a shed-roofed porch and boardwalk.

SC071 Jones House

1930s. 178 East Pioneer Ave.

The Jones house measures 18 feet by 30 feet and is a wood-frame structure covered with beveled siding on the front and wood shingles on the sides. It has a gable front with a shed-roofed porch. There are splayed lintels over the openings and exposed rafter ends at the eaves. The structure was moved to the present site from Halibut Cove, then rebuilt and re-sided.

SC072 Kranich House

1944–1945; 1947, porch. 111 West Pioneer Ave.

Almost a bungalow in appearance, the Kranich house has a gable roof with dramatic shed-roofed dormers. The wood-framed building, covered with cement asbestos shingles, was designed by Arleen Kranich and constructed in 1944–1945 for her and her husband, Bob. The enclosed hip-roofed porch across the front was added in 1947.

SC073 **Pratt House**

1939. 304 West Pioneer Ave.

One of the largest houses in town, the Pratt house has been made even larger by a two-story addition on one side. Originally four bays wide, the building had a side-gable roof and a gable dormer. Sam Pratt designed the building, which was built in 1939, for him and his wife, Vega.

SC074 **DaSylva House**

1946. Corner of Pioneer Ave. and the Sterling By-Pass

Another of the modest houses of Homer, this simple wood-framed, side-gable house has beveled siding. It is one and a half stories tall and has a three-bay front with a porch.

SC075 **Putnam House**

1936 or 1937. 3682 Main St.

William and Agnes Putnam had this one-story, wood-framed building constructed. The side-gable roof is covered with wood shingles, and the wood-framed structure with clapboards. Stones are embedded in the concrete foundation.

SC076 **Inlet Trading Post**

1937. Corner Main St. and Bunnell Ave.

The Inlet Trading Post is a two-story, decidedly commercial building. With a flat roof and no cornice, the wood-framed building has a storefront with recessed entry at the first level. The walls are covered with beveled siding on the front and asphalt brick on the sides. There is a hip-roofed porch across the front and additions to one side. Built as "Berry's," the building houses a grocery store on the first floor and a hotel on the second. Beginning in 1944, it was called the Inlet Trading Post.

SC077 **Salty Dawg Saloon**

post-1964. End of Homer Spit

At the end of the spit, the Salty Dawg Saloon incorporates several log buildings into one chaotic structure, assembled into their present arrangement after the 1964 earthquake. The corners of the log buildings exhibit both dovetailing and nailing into corner boards. The striking three-story octagonal structure, covered with wood shingles, looks like a lighthouse but was built to house a water tank. One of the log buildings incorporated into the structure may be one of the earliest in town.

Seldovia

Seldovia, a pleasant fishing village at the mouth of Kachemak Bay, on Cook Inlet, has an unusual history as the crossroads of several Alaskan cultures. Aleuts, Eskimos, and Indians were all reported among the early population. Russians, too, knew of the area, and some settled here. A trading post was also established early by the Americans, but even so the village remained a Native town until the twentieth century. Fishing now dominates the economy; five canneries were located here in the 1950s.

The 1964 earthquake caused the town to drop almost 4 feet. The subsequent urban renewal project encompassed the area below a 32-foot elevation and called for a major reconstruction of the waterfront. Although planners Lutes and Anderson encouraged residents to retain some of Seldovia's more charming characteristics, such as steep slopes, piling foundations, and boardwalks, many of them were lost in favor of economic revitalization. A hill was leveled to provide a site for residential development in the heart of the city, and the boardwalk that had constituted the main street was replaced with asphalt. Yet some boardwalks remain to contribute to Seldovia's charm, which is also enhanced by the lovely setting.

SC078 Saint Nicholas Russian Orthodox Chapel

1891

Saint Nicholas Chapel is the oldest Russian Orthodox church on the Kenai peninsula. The gable-roofed building is rectangular in plan, with the sanctuary incorporated into the main block of the nave. A square cupola lights the nave from above. The square bell tower, which is two stories tall, supports an octagonal belfry, with bells dated 1894 and 1896. The western third of the nave was an addition. The wood-framed building is covered with wide novelty siding, except for the bell tower, which is clad with a narrower beveled siding.

On the interior, the seven-bay iconostas fills the east wall of the nave. The central octagonal dome has a painted border of crosses.

The building, which was restored in 1981, sits on a bluff overlooking the village, the preferred location for these churches.

Matanuska-Susitna Valleys

Knik

North of the Kenai Peninsula, on the other side of Anchorage, is the abandoned settlement of Knik. Located on the northwest side of Knik Arm, Knik was founded in the nineteenth century as an Athabaskan trading post. The most visible reminder of the Athapaskan population here is a Russian Orthodox cemetery, about 100 yards behind the Knik Hall. About two dozen graves are adorned with spirit houses, much like those at Eklutna, where most of the Knik Natives moved.

By 1898, with the discovery of gold in the Interior, Knik became an important transshipment point for supplies to the Interior. As the first port in South-Central Alaska, Knik was also the hub of several trails leading to the Interior and to the south. After gold strikes in the Iditarod region in 1908, Knik also became a stop on the Iditarod Trail; in 1911, the U.S. government established this trail as a mail route. By 1915, Knik had a population of about five hundred, with four general stores, four hotels, a movie house, a pool room, a post office, and a school.

In 1915, however, the Alaska Engineering Commission determined that the

Alaska Railroad would bypass Knik. Supplies to the Interior would be unloaded at Seward and brought by rail. Knik's decline was rapid; in 1916 the post office closed and in 1919 the mail to the Iditarod was unloaded at Wasilla, no longer passing through Knik. Today, two buildings remain in Knik.

SC079 **Knik Hall**

Between 1900 and 1914

Knik Hall is a two-story, wood-framed building with a gable roof. The horizontal boards covering the building are flush boards on the front and clapboards on the sides. Across the gable front is a one-story, shed-roofed enclosed porch, wood-framed with board-and-batten siding. Although little is known of its origin, the hall was apparently built some time between 1900 and 1914 and served as a roadhouse, store, and pool hall. It now houses the Knik Museum and the Dog Mushers Hall of Fame.

SC080 **Cabin**

early twentieth century

Little is known about the one-story log cabin near Knik Hall. The round logs are saddle notched at the corners. The gable roof is constructed of sawn planks, with plywood and asphalt on top. There is an enclosed, shed-roofed porch of horizontal half-logs across part of the gable front.

Wasilla

Knik was a small port on Knik Arm that served as a supply point for the Willow Creek District and much of interior Alaska until 1915, when the Alaska Railroad plotted a course 13 miles northeast of the town. The railroad established Wasilla just northeast of Knik as a construction camp, but in 1917 a townsite was platted and lots were sold. Knik residents moved their buildings to Wasilla, and the new town thrived as Knik became a ghost town.

Today, Wasilla is the largest town in the Matanuska-Susitna valleys and also serves as a bedroom community for Anchorage, 42 miles southwest. Recent development has not enhanced the urban quality of Wasilla; instead, shopping centers have been built in the heart of town, on the north side of the railroad tracks and Parks Highway. Only a handful of historic buildings remain on the townsite; efforts at historic preservation have been focused on moving isolated buildings to Wasilla's Frontier Village.

SC081 **Alaska Railroad Depot**

1917. Parks Hwy. and Knik Rd.

The Alaska Railroad Depot at Wasilla is one of only eight built at the time the railroad was constructed and is virtually unaltered, as seen in this photograph taken shortly after construction. The 52-foot-by-33-foot building has a low hip roof with broad eaves ornamented with exposed rafter ends. The roof is covered with shakes (originally asphalt), while the walls have vertical wood siding to

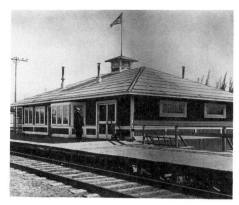

SC081 Alaska Railroad Depot

the height of the window sill and horizontal novelty siding above. A projecting bay window on the track side denotes the stationmaster's office. On one end was the waiting room, and on the other, the freight room. The side of the building away from the tracks was devoted to the agent's quarters. The most visible alteration to the 1917 building—the removal of a small square cupola in the center of the roof—is minor; the building remains a pristine example of Alaska railroad architecture.

SC082 **Dorothy Page Museum** (Wasilla Community Hall)

1930–1931. 323 Main St.

When a Swedish immigrant named Chris Stern died in 1927, he left his property to benefit the community of Wasilla, where he had homesteaded since the turn of the century. Using the funds he bequeathed, local residents built this community hall in 1930–1931, once again turning to the romanticized log cabin as the appropriate architectural expression. Remodeled in 1967 as a museum and visitors' information center, it was named the Dorothy G. Page Museum in 1989 and devoted to local history.

The one-story building measures 30 feet by 50 feet and is constructed of round logs, square notched at the corners. A one-story, gable-roofed porch across the front has rustic characteristics: vertical logs with small poles as braces support the roof; the gable is not enclosed, revealing two king-post trusses; and there is a half-wall of horizontal logs.

SC083 **Frontier Village**

Behind the Wasilla Museum is a collection of historic buildings moved from sites throughout the locality, now sitting in unnatural proximity to each other. Despite the loss of historical context, the buildings illustrate various construction methods.

There are four log buildings at the village, illustrating a variety of log construction techniques. None of the four illustrates the notching most commonly used in the wilderness, saddle notching. To some extent, the finish of the logs dictates the kind of notching. Thus, round logs are most easily saddle notched and are more likely found in expeditiously constructed buildings; hewn logs lend themselves to dovetailed notching, and both hewing and dovetailing require a higher level of axemanship. Variations such as diamond notching indicate a personal style, while lap jointing is the least secure joining technique.

The Walter Trensch cabin is constructed of round logs, diamond notched at the corners. The shed-roofed addition on one side is constructed of hewn logs, lap jointed. The Paddy Marion cabin is constructed of hewn logs, cut in half so that they are wide planks, rather than square logs. They are neatly dovetailed at the corners. The doors and windows of the building have been changed in size. Between these two cabins is a log barn, constructed of a combination of hewn and round logs, dovetailed at the corners. A shed-roofed addition on the rear is clapboarded, and there is a shed-roofed porch along the side. The newest building at the site is the Capital Site Cabin, constructed of logs sawn flat on three sides. Unlike the others, this cabin's roof is covered with sod.

In addition to the log cabins, the village has three wood-framed buildings—a school, a store, and a house. The last is a one-and-a-half-story building constructed in 1936. The village also has a selection of outbuildings, including a shed-roofed, log steam bath; a fiberglass greenhouse; a wood-framed smokehouse; and a sod-roofed, log cache.

SC083.1 **Wasilla Elementary School**

1917

A simple one-room schoolhouse, the Wasilla Elementary School was constructed in 1917, shortly after the townsite had been laid out.

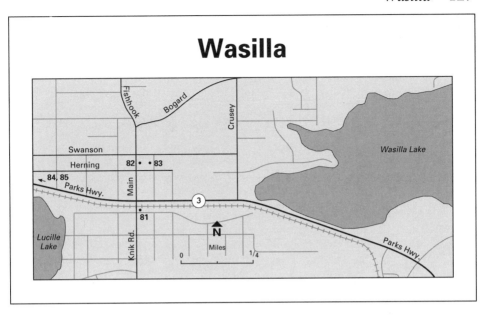

A larger school was built in 1934, but with the arrival of the Matanuska colonists, that new school was soon overflowing and the old school was pressed back into service. It also served as a community hall and temporary church.

The one-story, one-room schoolhouse measures approximately 22 feet by 36 feet and is wood-framed with beveled siding. On the interior, narrow, beaded boards are used for wainscoting, stained and placed vertically, and for wall coverings, painted white and placed horizontally. The tray ceiling is covered with the same material.

Originally located about three blocks away, the school was built on wood posts. A concrete foundation was added in the 1930s. The school was moved to its present site in 1979 and placed on a wood post foundation.

SC083.2 Teeland's

1905

Orville George Herning first opened the country store now known as Teeland's as a general supply store in Knik in 1905. When Knik was bypassed by the Alaska Railroad, Herning moved his small log store (no longer extant) to the townsite of Wasilla, adding a large wood-framed store building. The 23-foot-by-75-foot wood-framed building was covered with corrugated metal. Entrance was through a center door, between large windows. The second floor of the one-and-a-half-story structure was used for storage.

Walter Teeland bought the store in 1947 and operated it until 1972. Teeland changed the entrance from the front to an entryway on the side. The next owner, Julian Mead, added a liquor business in an attached shed. He donated the building to the Wasilla-Knik-Willow Creek Historical Society in 1987. When it was moved from its former site on the Parks Highway, about a block away, a new lower level was built, creating a basement story in the rear.

SC084 Birchwood Station

1916. Mile 50 Parks Hwy.

Now on its fourth site, the Birchwood Station has been removed from the railroad it used to serve. Built as the railroad station in Birchwood, near Anchorage, this building was moved to Willow in 1931 to serve as the station there. In the 1960s it was acquired by the State Highway Commission, which moved it about a mile to serve as a maintenance facility. In 1963, it was moved to its present site where it now houses a craft shop.

The hip-roofed building has an unusual second-story dormer, repeating the form of the bay window above which it sits. The hip roof has exposed rafter ends and brackets at its broad eaves. The wood-framed building is covered with novelty siding, placed vertically up to window-sill level, and horizontally above. The building has been doubled in size by an addition to the rear, and the porch across half of the front is not original, but the station retains its railroad-building appearance.

SC085 **Whitney Section House** (Museum of Alaska Transportation and Industry)

1917. Neuser Museum Drive, mile 46.7 Parks Hwy.

In 1917 the Alaska Railroad built this section house less than 5 miles north of Anchorage, on land that is now part of Elmendorf Air Force Base. Originally housing only the section foreman and his family, the building accommodated the entire crew after the adjacent bunkhouse burned in 1934. No longer used by the railroad, the section house was moved to the fairgrounds in Palmer in 1976 and to its present site in 1991. The one-story, wood-framed building is T-shaped, with exposed rafter ends at the eaves of the gable roof.

Palmer

Palmer was founded in 1916 as a stop on the Alaska Railroad's branch line to the coalfields of Chickaloon, but it was not developed until 1935, when it was selected as the site for the Federal Emergency Relief Administration's Matanuska Colony project. The U.S. government transported 202 families from the upper Midwest to homesteads in the Matanuska Valley in an effort to develop the farmlands of Alaska and to provide the families with a viable living. Palmer was selected as the headquarters for the organization running the project, the Alaska Rural Rehabilitation Corporation (ARRC).

Palmer initially consisted of a tent city to house temporary laborers and colonists until their houses were built. Administration offices and housing, churches, schools, and other buildings that make a community were soon under way. Today, many of the farms have given way to subdivisions, and Wasilla has become the biggest city in the Matanuska Valley. But Palmer continues to be headquarters for the Matanuska-Susitna Borough (named after the area's two major rivers), home to school and government offices. On the west side of the tracks is a modest commercial area, while on the east side are the Alaska Rural Rehabilitation Corporation buildings.

SC086 **Central School**

1935–1936. East Dahlia Ave. and South Denali St.

The old Central School, now the Borough Building, is a large two-story building occupying a pivotal site at the edge of an open space framed by ARRC buildings. Originally five bays wide, so that the entrance was in the center, the hip-roofed building received a two-story addition on one end. Changes in the window sash have also seriously altered the building, which is wood framed and covered with clapboard. The large building at-

tached to the north side was built as a community hall and also served as the school's gymnasium and auditorium.

On the north side of the school, on East Dahlia Avenue, are several one-story, gable-roofed buildings, built as administration buildings and the trading post. Beyond those are the cannery, creamery, and warehouse buildings related to the colony's dairy business. Most of these buildings are deteriorating but share the beveled siding, gable roofs, and diagonal boards in the gables that mark the ARRC buildings.

Palmer

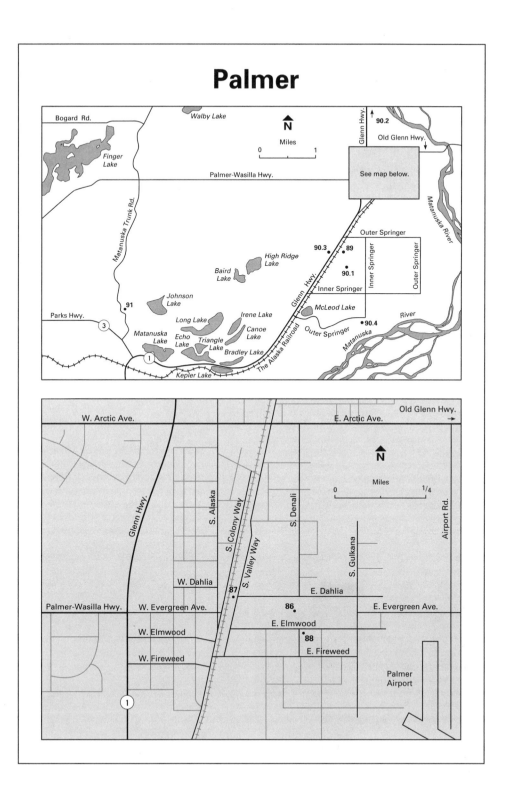

On the south side of the school is the housing area. The two-and-a-half-story, hip-roofed building on East Elmwood Avenue is the dormitory, now covered with aluminum siding. Houses for staff members varied in form, but most were one story with gable roofs.

SC087 **Alaska Railroad Depot**

1935. South Valley Way and East Dahlia Ave.

The Alaska Railroad built a branch line to the Chickaloon coal mines in 1916 with a stop in the town of Palmer. The railroad depot was not built until 1935, however, when hundreds of colonists were scheduled to descend on the Matanuska-Susitna valleys, disembarking at Palmer.

The original building was about 94 feet long, wood-framed and gable-roofed. The portion with the higher roofline was the warehouse, originally 28 feet long; it was extended to its full length of 84 feet in 1948. The shorter portion, about 66 feet long, housed the ticket office and waiting room on the track side and the agent's living quarters on the other side. At the end, an entrance half the width of the depot was also covered with a gable roof. It originally had open sides, but was enclosed in 1948. The building has a new metal roof and cornice and is covered with narrow clapboards.

SC088 **United Protestant Church (Presbyterian)**

1936–1937, Harry K. Wolfe. South Denali St. and East Elmwood Ave.

The ARRC donated land to three denominations to build churches, stipulating that they be constructed of logs. Although the buildings that it built for itself were not log, management of the ARRC apparently determined that log construction was appropriate for Alaska, whether practical or not. The Presbyterian congregation here used log with a vengeance, constructing a church that is the epitome of romanticized rustic architecture.

The United Protestant Church was constructed of logs in a manner more decorative than functional. Horizontal log walls give way to vertical logs at about the window-sill level, then revert to horizontal logs above the windows. The church has a low gable roof. Cruciform in plan, the lateral wings are near the front of the church, with the pastor's office on one side and meeting rooms on the other. The nave, which occupies the stem of the cross, is finished with exposed logs; log trusses are carried on posts, and there are log chandeliers. The nearby parsonage and garage are also built of logs, in the same pattern as the church.

The Presbyterian missionary Bert J. Bingle arrived at Palmer in 1935, one step ahead of the colonists. Although services were held immediately upon the arrival of the colonists, construction of the church did not begin until 1936. Harry K. Wolfe, assistant architect with the ARRC, designed the church as a volunteer. Volunteer workers were supervised by Leo B. Jacobs, an experienced construction foreman, and "the church of a thousand trees" was completed in the spring of 1937.

SC089 **Colony Village**

Alaska State Fairgrounds, Glenn Highway

Each of the 202 colonist families was provided with 40 acres, a house, barn, well, and outbuildings, and a loan of three thousand dollars to pay for them. The plans for these buildings came from Federal Emergency Relief Administration offices in Washington, where they were designed by an energetic Texan named David R. Williams—one of eighty-four agricultural communities he designed. The plans were standardized to expedite construction, which was carried out by temporary laborers, rather than the colonists themselves. The houses could be built of either logs or wood frame. Williams was a strong advocate of indigenous architecture, and although he did not visit Alaska until after construction had begun, it was probably his understanding that log architecture was indigenous to Alaska that caused it to appear in the Matanuska colony. In fact, log was still widely used in Alaska (and continues to be today), but in remote settings, where sawn lumber is not readily available. Standard-plan log houses strike a faintly artificial note.

Because the first colonists arrived in May 1935, only four months after the project was conceived, construction was chaotic, disorganized, and behind schedule. Many of the buildings remain, scattered around the Palmer countryside. Colony Village, another outdoor museum of the late 1970s, displays a sampling. Although the buildings are interesting in themselves, there has been no attempt to re-create a colony farm, either in the placement of the buildings or in their relation to one another.

SC089.1 **Wineck Barn**

1935

All of the colony barns were built to the same plan, 32 feet by 32 feet by 32 feet high, and the Wineck Barn is a good example. The lower portion of the walls is constructed of logs sawn flat on three sides, lapped and butted at the corners. Above that is a band of vertical boards to the cornice and horizontal boards in the gables. The gambrel roof is framed with scissor trusses. Despite its appealing form, the plan of the standard colony barn was widely criticized as being too small and inefficiently partitioned. In addition foundations were small pilings that soon deteriorated.

SC089.2 **MacNevin and Hesse-Smith Houses**

1935

The MacNevin and Hesse-Smith houses were built to the same house plan but of different materials. The MacNevin house is constructed of logs sawn flat on three sides, lapped at the corners. There is a side-gable roof and a center door. A large addition has been constructed on the rear. The Hesse-Smith house is identical, except that it is covered with beveled siding and has a gable-roofed vestibule. The post office operates out of the building during the state fair.

These houses represent one plan of the five from which colonists were allowed to

SC089.1 Wineck Barn

select. None had basements or even full foundations. As illustrated by these two houses, construction materials could be log or wood frame.

SC089.3 **Colony Church**

1936–1937

Although the ARRC demanded that the churches be built of logs, the Lutherans found available materials too valuable to ignore. They built a wood-framed church, using surplus materials from the government coal mine at Chickaloon. The shiplap siding on the exterior is rounded to resemble logs. The gable-fronted church has a two-story tower. It now serves as the entrance to an auditorium, which has been added in the rear.

SC089.4 **Evan Jones House**

1918

Not associated with the colony, this house was constructed in Anchorage in 1918 for Evan Jones, who developed the coal mine at Jonesville in the early 1920s. The one-story structure has a gable front.

Palmer Vicinity

SC090 **Colony Farms**

Many of the two hundred colony farms constructed in the 1930s in the vicinity of Palmer remain intact and can be viewed on a casual tour around the countryside. Particularly rich areas are the Farm Loop and Palmer-Fishhook roads; the Inner and Outer Springer Loop roads; and the Bodenburg Loop Road. Below is a sampling of colony farms.

SC090.1 Rebarchek Farm

1935 and later. Just east of the State Fairgrounds, on the south side of Rebarchek Rd.

Two of the few colonists still farming their original homesteads, the Rebarcheks claim to occupy the very first colony house completed. The continued use of the farmland has resulted in an accretion of farm buildings, all of which serve to illustrate the life of a colonist.

Construction began on Raymond Rebarchek's house in 1935, soon after he had chosen this tract through a drawing from a hat. Rebarchek, who was one of the crew building the house, was frustrated at the incompetence of his fellow workers; twice they took the partially built house down and started over. The third time, they used logs sawn flat on two sides, and then three sides, and the work proceeded more smoothly.

Although the Rebarchek house was apparently not one of the ARRC standard plans, it shares characteristics of size and form. The log house measures 33 feet by 25 feet and has one and a half stories with a low gable roof. In 1953 Rebarchek added a gable-roofed section on the front to provide a mud room entrance and a third bedroom on the second floor. At that time he also stuccoed the building. Shortly after construction he dug out a full basement.

The barn, 32 feet square, was constructed in 1936. Logs sawn flat on three sides were laid horizontally up to 8 feet high, then the walls and gambrel roof were wood framed. In 1950 Rebarchek added a concrete milking parlor and milk room in order to meet dairy standards. Although the original barn burned in 1980, it has been replaced with a colony barn moved from a nearby tract. The milking room burned more recently, but its walls are still standing.

Other outbuildings include the 12-foot-by-16-foot log well house-sauna, constructed by Rebarchek in 1935–1936; a vertical-log, shed-roofed chicken house, built in 1937; and a shed-roofed horizontal-log small barn, built in 1935.

SC090.2 Bailey-Estelle Farm

c. 1935. Southwest corner of Marsh Rd. and Glenn Hwy.

This farmstead has a standard colony barn and an atypical wood-framed house, with a gambrel roof and shed dormers.

SC090.3 Patten Farm

c. 1935. West side of Glenn Hwy. directly across from the Fairgrounds

The Patten farm has two colony barns, with log walls and gambrel roofs. The L-plan house is constructed of logs sawn flat on three sides.

SC090.4 Grover Farm

c. 1935. South side of the Outer Springer Loop Rd., about a half mile south of the Inner Springer Loop Rd.

In addition to the original barn and house, there is an octagonal silo at this farm.

SC090.2 Bailey-Estelle Farm

SC091 Agricultural Experiment Station

Matanuska Trunk Rd.

The U.S. government established seven agricultural experiment stations in Alaska between 1899 and 1917; this one was the last. The government played an important role in testing crops and livestock for profitable agricultural endeavors and promoted their findings to encourage settlement. Milton D. Snodgrass, a representative of the Alaska Railroad from 1930 to 1934 who ran this experiment station from 1923 to 1929, was instrumental in enticing farmers to this area.

The U.S. Department of Agriculture closed all of the Alaskan agricultural experiment stations in 1932. The Matanuska station is now operated by the University of Alaska Fairbanks. The cluster of buildings is surrounded by fields and pastures.

SC091.1 Central Cottage

1917

This bungalow is the residence of the station manager. The one-and-a-half-story house, wood-framed with beveled siding, has a gable roof with gable dormer. Entrance is through a corner porch recessed under the main roof, near the projecting bay window under the dormer. The 34-foot-by-42-foot house was painted a light tan with darker trim, while the interior woodwork was stained.

SC091.2 Kodiak Cottage

1917

The Kodiak cottage is another bungalow, moved from the station at Kalsin Bay, Kodiak, in 1923. The cottage was "ready-cut," referring to lumber cut to specification before shipment, and erected at Kalsin Bay in 1917. The six-room house is one and a half stories with a gable front. The gable-roofed porch is offset but shares the slope of one roof plane. The wood-framed building, covered with wood shingles, had a bathroom and a concrete foundation.

SC091.3 Bunkhouse

1928–1929

The two-story bunkhouse is a hip-roofed, foursquare building, measuring 34 feet by 44

SC091.2 Kodiak Cottage

feet, constructed for temporary laborers. The clapboard-covered wood-framed building had a mess hall, kitchen, reading room, bedroom, and washroom on the first floor, and five two-man bedrooms, washroom, and shower on the second.

SC091.4 Cottage

1929

In the summer of 1929 an additional bungalow was built south of Central Cottage. The 24-foot-by-34-foot building has a gable roof extending over a front porch and a gable dormer.

SC091.5 Laboratory

1984–1985, Selberg Associates

The two-story building has a stylized clerestory monitor roof and a rich series of shed roofs at lower levels. Corresponding to the dramatic profile are the dramatic interior corridor spaces. The exterior has stained wood siding. The laboratory is reminiscent of barn design but in a rich improvisation that seems appropriate both to its function and to its rural setting.

Sutton

SC092 Alpine Heritage and Cultural Center

Mile 61.5, Glenn Hwy.

The coalfields around Sutton were initially developed by the U.S. government, which hoped to find a source of coal for the navy. The Alaska Railroad was constructed with the intention of tapping the coalfields, and a spur line to Chickaloon was constructed in 1917. By 1922, however, the navy decided that the Alaska coal was of inferior quality and shut down its coal mine. Privately run coal mines in the area continued to provide coal for the government's use. The Evan Jones mine became the largest producer, employing as many as 250 men. In 1958 the underground workings were closed, but Evan Jones continued to strip-mine until 1967, when military bases in Anchorage switched to natural gas for fuel.

Although the landscape has been irrevocably altered, few buildings remain to remind visitors of the life that went on at these mines. The Alpine Heritage and Cultural Center is built around the enormous concrete foundations for the coal washing plant, built by the Alaska Engineering Commission and the Navy Alaskan Coal Commission in 1921–1922. The original buildings consisted of an 86-foot-by-132-foot washer and a 70-foot-by-80-foot power plant; they operated for only two weeks before the navy closed them down. Also at the center are several pieces of coal-mining equipment, including boilers, hoists. steam engines, tramcars, a washer, and a dryer. There are two one-room buildings at the center, both moved from other sites.

SC092.1 **Chickaloon Bunkhouse**

before 1918

Built as a coal mine bunkhouse, this building was dismantled and moved to Moose Creek in 1933; it was moved again in the 1950s. In 1984 the one-story, gable-roofed building was moved to its present site. Wood-framed, the building is covered with beveled siding and has a gable-roofed vestibule.

SC092.2 **U.S. Post Office**

1940s

The post office building is a small, one-story building originally constructed at Sutton. The wood-framed building has both beveled and flush sidings.

SC093 **Independence Mine**

1936–1941. Willow-Fishhook Rd.

Located on the barren east face of Granite Mountain in Talkeetna Range, well above the tree line, the buildings of Independence Mine cling to the rugged terrain in a vertical alignment that uses gravity to assist production. Now operated as a state park, Independence Mine is a fine example of a hard-rock gold

SC093 Independence Mine

mining operation. Most of the twenty-seven buildings constructed during the region's gold-producing peak around 1940 still stand. In best condition are the buildings associated with the life of the miners, and this aspect of the gold mine is well interpreted.

Placer gold was found in the Willow Creek district as early as 1897. The first hard-rock gold claim was filed in 1906, and by 1909, there was a minor stampede to the Willow Creek district. Of the thirty-eight hard-rock gold mines and prospects, fifteen produced gold. One of those is Independence.

In 1934 Alaska-Pacific Mines began to buy up claims, and in 1938, when its name was changed to Alaska-Pacific Consolidated Mining Company, the claims consisted of two primary holdings: the Independence Mine and the Alaska Free Gold Mine, both in the Fishhook Creek valley. Between 1937 and 1940 the company employed on average two hundred men and milled more than seventy thousand tons of ore here, averaging thirty-eight dollars of gold per ton. The mine was forced to close in 1943 by order of the War Production Board, and never regained its former productivity.

Active mining took place in the mountains, above the mill site. Aerial trams took equipment up to the mine, and brought ore down to the cluster of buildings below. Because of

the heavy snowfall, most of the buildings were connected by covered walkways. The buildings were simple in design, wood-framed with beveled siding, with corrugated-metal gable roofs. All of the buildings, save one, were painted silver with red trim.

Besides the buildings mentioned below, buildings still standing at the site include administrative offices; a warehouse-bunkhouse; plumbing, sheet metal, and electrical shops; an apartment house for the mine manager, mine foreman, mill foreman, and shop foreman; and various storage buildings. Miners with families were encouraged to build their own houses, which they did at a nearby site called "Boom Town." Although twenty-two houses were reported here in 1942, none has survived intact.

All of the surviving buildings at the mine site were constructed between 1936 and 1941. The heavy snowfall has taken its toll on the buildings; many of them are severely deteriorated and have caved in. Yet by their placement on the landscape and their general form, an understanding of this hard-rock gold mine can be gained.

SC093.1 Mill
1937

The mill, now deteriorated, was the heart of the operation and the destination of the aerial trams bringing ore down from the mountain. The trams took the ore to the upper bin on the uphill side of the structure. After sorting and crushing, the finer ore went to the lower bins. It was then transported by belts into the ball mills, just below, where the ore was fully crushed. Below the mills the concentrate tanks separated the gold from the ore. Off to one side was the clean up and assay room, for testing the product, added in 1938. Also in that year, a south wing was added for the powerhouse and machine shop. The diesel-powered generators provided electricity to all of the buildings at the mine complex. In 1939, the power plant was enlarged and a separate blacksmith shop was added.

SC093.2 Assay Office
1941

The one-and-a-half-story assay office, measuring 40 feet by 38 feet, was built to separate the assay function from the mill complex.

Different rooms on the first floor provided for drying and grinding, testing and weighing; the second floor was living space for the assayer.

SC093.3 **Bunkhouse**

1938, N. Lester Troast and William A. Manley

Designed by Anchorage architects, the first three-story bunkhouse was constructed in 1938. The stairway of the 24-foot-by-63-foot building is enclosed, with its own gable roof on the south end of the building. The first floor contained a bathroom, drying room, recreation room equipped with pool table and barber chair, library, nurses' station, and one bedroom. The second and third floors had double-loaded corridors with six two-man bedrooms on each side.

SC093.4 **Bunkhouse**

1940, Floyd A. Naramore and Clifton J. Brady

A second three-story bunkhouse was constructed in 1940, designed by Seattle architects. The 34-foot-by-78-foot building housed fifty men and also had a schoolroom/movie room with a seating capacity of eighty or ninety people, a first-aid room, hospital bedroom, and nurse's bedroom.

SC093.5 **Manager's House**

1939

The six-bedroom manager's house is a one-and-a-half-story building measuring 32 feet by 48 feet with an asymmetrical gable roof. The focus of the two-story living room is a rubble-stone fireplace. The wood-framed

building, deliberately painted a different color than the rest of the silver-painted mine buildings, was beige with a red roof.

SC093.6 **Mess Hall**

1941

Built to replace a mess hall that had become too small, the new mess hall is cross-shaped in plan, with a large, two-story section. The first floor contained the dining room, kitchen, bakery, butcher shop, and meat room, while the second floor had residential space. On the front a recessed porch sheltered entrances to the first floor and the stairway, while the second-floor loggia gave access to two apartments.

Willow Vicinity

SC094 **Sheep Creek Lodge**

1987. Mile 88 Parks Hwy.

The log cabin is thought to appeal to tourists, representing their preconceptions of Alaska. When this factor is combined with roadside architecture's traditional enlargement of scale to catch the eye of speeding motorists, something like the Sheep Creek Lodge results. Here, huge round logs with a glossy seal are saddle notched at the corners. The cross-gable roof projects to cover the front porch; in the gable is an exposed king-post truss. The building is raised 6 feet on a flagstone-faced concrete foundation. The huge building, fat logs, tall foundation, in fact, everything is larger than it should be, and more rustic than it has to be.

Talkeetna

Talkeetna was founded as a trading post for the Alaska Commercial Company in 1910; it was accessible by steamboat up the Susitna River from Knik. In 1912, however, the company moved its post and the young town faded until the Alaska Railroad established a construction camp at the site in 1915. The Alaska Engineering Commission sold lots here in 1918, and Talkeetna continued to be a supply point for the surrounding mining region. The community is still a prominent stop on the Alaska Railroad, serving as the main point of embarkation for climbers of Mount McKinley. Although located on a 14-mile spur off the Parks Highway, the town advertises its arts and crafts and attracts a fair number of tourists.

SC095 Ole and Annie Dahl Cabin

1920. South side of Main St., between C and D streets

Talkeetna has a mix of small wood-framed and log houses. One fine example of a log cabin is the Ole and Annie Dahl Cabin. Built the year they married, the house measures 21 feet by 27 feet and is constructed of round logs, chinked with cement and square notched and nailed at the corners. Notches cut out for the nail heads show particular attention to detail. The one-and-a-half-story building has a gable front; the shed-roofed porch, with its gable, is supported by saplings used as posts.

SC096 Fairview Inn

1920. Main and D streets

The most prominent building in town is the Fairview Inn, which was built by Ben Nauman; subsequent owners have maintained that use and name ever since. The building is a two-story, foursquare building with a hipped roof and exposed rafter ends at the eaves. The wood-framed, 36-foot-square building has beveled siding. Windows at the first-floor level are paired, and on the second single; all have one-over-one lights. A one-story wing has been added to the rear.

SC097 School

1936. D St.

Measuring 30 feet by 37 feet, the wood-framed building has clapboard siding. Entrance is through the gable end, which has cornice returns on the gable. Shed-roofed dormers lit the living space on the second story. The one-room schoolhouse is now a museum.

SC098 Section House and Depot

1930s, section house. c. 1934, depot

Behind the museum are two railroad-related buildings, the section house and the depot, moved to this site away from the tracks. The section house is a one-story, hip-roofed building. Next to it, also painted a mustard color with brown trim, is the depot, a small, one-story building with a hip roof and beveled siding. Built in 1920, the original depot burned in 1933. This one was built later, apparently to the same specifications.

Broad Pass

SC099 Leon Smith Igloo

1970s–1992. Mile 188.5 George Parks Hwy.

The closest thing to a traditional snow-block igloo in Alaska, this four-story hotel is the vision of one man, Leon Smith, who designed and built it, beginning in the early 1970s. It remains unfinished, with projected completion in 1992. Smith felt that it was "appropriate that Alaska have an igloo."

The circular-plan, wood-framed building contains 888 sheets of plywood, covered with urethane insulation on the outside, giving it its snowlike finish. The building has a four-story atrium, with forty-eight pie-shaped rooms opening onto interior balconies. On the first floor is the dining room (to seat ninety), kitchen, gift shop, and offices, as well as additional bedrooms. Though unusual in design and execution, the hotel conforms to building codes.

Such expressive buildings, known as "ducks," are rare along the highways of Alaska. The igloo—the residential form most associated with Alaska, correctly or not—makes a vivid advertisement to the passing automobiles.

Copper River and West
Valdez

Southeast of Anchorage, Prince William Sound has water deep enough for supertankers, surrounded by steep, jagged mountains. The effect is sublime. The largest settlement on the sound is Valdez, which served as a port of entry to the Alaska goldfields as early as 1897–1898. Its importance increased with the construction of the Valdez-Fairbanks Trail (Richardson Highway) just after 1900. In 1964, however, an earthquake measuring 8.4 on the Richter scale, whose epicenter was 50 miles west of Valdez, destroyed the city. The people of Valdez moved 3 1/2 miles west and rebuilt in three and a half years.

City Planning Associates of Mishawaka, Indiana, oriented the new city to the water, with the commercial district at the water's edge and the residential area behind. All of the residential streets end in a park strip, an open space that extends from the city hall to the mountains. The elementary school was built in the center of the park strip, on a site now occupied by Prince William Community College. The city, which had a population of eight hundred at the time of the quake, was planned to accommodate fifteen hundred; Valdez's population is now twice that. A new residential subdivision has been built to the west. In the portion laid out in 1964, the houses are a mixture of tract and manufactured housing with a few of the surviving buildings from old Valdez sprinkled among them. The municipal building, designed by Crittenden Cassetta Wirum and Jacobs, has a steeply pitched roof, reflecting the spectacular mountains that surround the sound. Most of the houses in the old town of Valdez had steep roofs—to shed the extreme snow load, as much as to respond to the terrain—but little of the new construction bears any relation to historic Valdez architecture.

Valdez experienced an enormous influx of people during construction of the Trans-Alaska Pipeline in the mid-1970s. The deep-water port facilities have rendered it an ideal location for the terminus of the pipeline. Alyeska's Marine Terminal has berths for four supertankers, enough tanks on land to hold the entire contents of the pipeline, the operations facility for the pipeline and pump stations, and facilities for treating ballast water. Valdez has a small fishing industry, but most of the city's economy depends on the oil pipeline.

SC100 **Valdez Civic Center**

1982, GDM and Associates, Inc. Clifton St.

Situated on top of a hill, with a lagoon at its base and the harbor beyond, the Valdez Civic Center is an exceptionally handsome building. The vertical flush wood siding is stained gray and devoid of ornament. A rounded element on the front denotes the stair tower. Entrance is on the side, through an extended angle of the building. The front of the building is occupied by the lobby, with windows giving views of the port, while the 486-seat theater and the auditorium, divisible into three smaller rooms, are behind. The gray wood walls lend the building a rustic appearance, suitable for its natural setting, but the clean lines and coherent plan give it a touch of elegance.

SC101 **Trans-Alaska Pipeline**

1974–1977

The terminus of the Trans-Alaska Pipeline is in Valdez, where the oil is loaded onto tankers at the Marine Terminal. Architecturally, the pipeline is of most interest as an illustration of construction techniques employed in the Alaskan terrain. The 800-mile pipeline runs above ground where there is permafrost—approximately half of its length—and underground where possible. Underground, the pipeline is laid on a gravel bedding 8 feet to 16 feet deep, and covered with gravel padding and dirt fill. Above ground, the insulated pipeline rests on Teflon-coated shoes on crossbeams that allow the pipe to move sideways 12 feet to accommodate natural expansion and contraction or movement due to earthquakes. The crossbeam supports are arranged in a zigzag pattern that converts longitudinal expansion into sideways movement. In places where the permafrost is just below the freezing point, and therefore most fragile, the supports are fitted with heat pipes containing a refrigerant. Heat is conducted up and into finlike radiators, which dispel the heat into the air.

In its 800-mile length, the pipeline rises over 5,000 feet, dropping again to sea level, and crosses eight hundred rivers and streams. Ten pump stations assist the oil in its journey from the North Slope. The pipeline is paralleled by the Dalton Highway from Prudhoe Bay to Livengood, the Elliott Highway from Livengood to Fairbanks, and the Richardson Highway from Fairbanks to Valdez, and is visible at many points along the way. Whether reviled as a blight on the landscape, or hailed as a Christo-like *Running Fence* that defines the landscape in human terms, the oil pipeline is a visual image that is increasingly identified with Alaska.

Cordova

Cordova is located in the foothills of Mount Eyak, on the east side of Prince William Sound, between Orca Inlet and Lake Eyak. At the turn of the twentieth century, an Eyak Indian village and some canneries were clustered at the west end of Lake Eyak. This proved to be a strategic location, however, for a railroad route to the interior of Alaska, aimed at providing access to copper mines and coalfields. Carving a path out of rocky mountainside and around glaciers, Michael J. Heney ensured the successful completion of the 196-mile Copper River and Northwestern Railway (CR&NWRy) in 1911.

The railroad yards were near the west end of Lake Eyak, where the CR&NWRy built shops and a roundhouse beginning in 1906. Obtaining a new townsite on Orca Inlet for the growing town, the CR&NWRy convinced the established businesses and residents to move to the new site. Platted in 1908, Cordova was a grid-plan town with four major streets parallel to the water, rising one above the other up the side of the steep hill. The railroad went through the middle of town, ending at a dock where the small boat harbor is now. By 1914 Cordova had a population of 870 and boasted three hotels, seven saloons, three churches, and a variety of businesses.

Cordova flourished as the terminus of the CR&NWRy, becoming the shipping point for all Kennecott copper as well as the receiving point for all goods headed for the mine and for the rest of Interior Alaska. By the time the Kennecott mines closed in 1938, 200 million tons of ore had been shipped out

Cordova

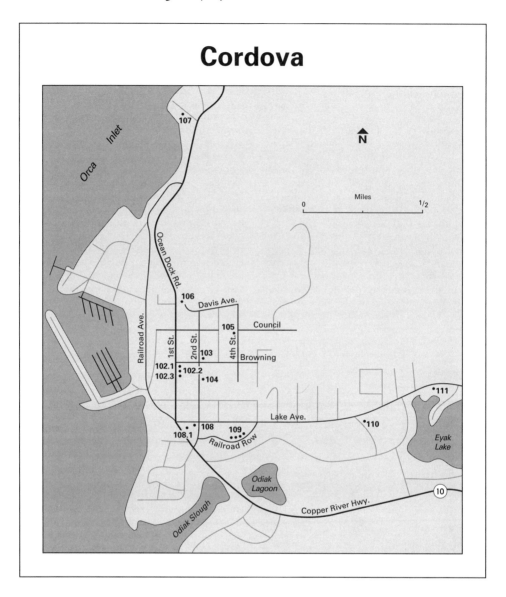

through Cordova. At the same time, Cordova developed its fishing industry, with new canneries appearing throughout the twentieth century; Cordova claims the title "razor clam capital of the world." The small boat harbor was built by the Corps of Engineers in 1938, and rebuilt after the 1964 earthquake.

Cordova remains today unconnected to the rest of the state by road. An attempt to convert the CR&NWRy to a highway ended in 1964, when the earthquake damaged the Million Dollar Bridge 40 miles northeast of Cordova. There have been sporadic attempts since then to resuscitate the highway, but Cordova remains a thriving fishing village, not entirely displeased with its isolation.

SC102 600 Block of First Street

Because of several fires, including a particularly devastating one in 1963, few early commercial buildings remain in Cordova. The utilitarian simplicity, expedient wooden construction, and lack of stylistic references, seen in the following buildings, characterize functional, frontier architecture.

SC102.1 Alaskan Hotel

1908; 1910, third story. 600 First St.

Although not an attractive building, the Alaskan Hotel is representative of early commercial buildings in Cordova. It was originally two stories; the third story was added in 1910. The building, 46 feet by 90 feet, is on a sloping site, so that the first story rapidly disappears. The flat-roofed wood-framed building has a bar on the first floor, reached through a canted entrance at the corner. The two upper floors, separated from each other and from the first floor by belt courses, have windows that are mostly paired. Above the third-floor lintels, a wide fascia is shingled, painted in a contrasting color; the deep cornice has simple modillions. The hotel had numerous owners and probably as many names; it is one of the oldest buildings in the commercial area. Its exterior ungainliness is somewhat compensated for by the handsome bar, imported from Katalla.

SC102.2 Cordova Hotel and Bar

1908; 1910, third story. 604 First St.

Cordova Hotel and Bar was built in the same idiom as the Alaskan. Constructed in 1908, with its third floor added in 1910, it has a plain clapboard facade and bracketed cornice.

SC102.3 614 First Street

1908. 614 First St.

The third 1908 building in this block is a two-story, flat-roofed one with a clapboard front and bracketed cornice. It originally housed a store on its first floor and rooming house above.

SC103 Reception Building

1908. Second St. and Browning Ave.

Built as the Reception Saloon in 1908, this two-story, wood-framed building has a clapboard exterior and modillioned cornice. The original storefront entrance was lost when the first floor was converted to apartments at the onset of Prohibition, but in the mid-1980s that storefront was restored. The building exhibits the plainness of Cordova's early commercial buildings.

SC104 U.S. Post Office and Courthouse

1923–1924, James A. Wetmore. Second St.

When a new post office building was first proposed for Cordova in 1912, 95 percent of all mail headed for Interior Alaska went through Cordova. By the time this building was constructed in 1923–1924, however, the Alaska Railroad had made Seward the primary port for the Interior.

Due to the slope of the site, this building is smaller than it appears. The L-shaped building, 49 feet by 84 feet, was constructed of reinforced concrete. The first floor was only 30 feet deep, however, containing the main entrance, a stairway, one room, and the boiler and equipment rooms. The second floor was the post office, and the third floor, the courtroom and jail.

The post office is exceedingly plain on the exterior; the doorway was marked by an entablature, which has been obscured by the recent addition of a marquee. The third-floor window sills are joined by a belt course; there is no cornice. A hip roof crowns the structure. On the interior, much of the original detail survives. James A. Wetmore, acting Supervising Architect of the Treasury, is credited with the design of the building, which was constructed by the J. B. Warrack Company of Seattle for $89,000. The post office and courthouse is the oldest federal building in Alaska still being used by the federal government.

SC105 Donohoe House

1919. 309 Council Ave.

One of a number of Craftsman-style houses in Cordova, the Donohoe house was built in about 1919 for an attorney. Merle K. "Mudhole" Smith, a pioneer aviator, was the second owner, acquiring it in 1945. The one-and-a-half-story house is wood-framed, covered with shingles. Its wide eaves are ornamented with exposed rafter ends and bracketed purlin ends in the gables.

SC106 Masonic Temple

1925. First St. and Davis Ave.

The Masonic Temple is unusual in Cordova for both its stucco covering and its Classical Revival design. The facade of the two-story building is crowned with a pediment supported by corner pilasters. The doorway has a broken pediment, again supported by pilasters. Built in 1925, the building houses club and lodge rooms on the second floor, with a kitchen and ballroom on the first.

SC107 Morpac Cannery

twentieth century. Ocean Dock Rd.

Built on piling, the Morpac Cannery incorporates several older buildings into a modern, working cannery. The one- and two-story, wood-framed buildings are covered with wood sheathing or corrugated metal and are well lit by small-paned windows. The complex includes processing buildings, equipment storage and workshop buildings, as well as offices, dormitories, and mess halls, to comprise one of the most picturesque canneries in Alaska.

SC108 Saint George's Episcopal Church

1918–1919. Lake Ave. between First and Second streets

Saint George's Episcopal Church is a small but well-designed picturesque country church. Measuring about 24 feet by 36 feet, the wood-framed church is covered with wood shingles.

SC107 Morpac Cannery

SC108 Saint George's Episcopal Church

Buttresses separate the window bays; the windows are round arched. A small belfry on the front of the gable roof is square, topped by a steeple. There is an enclosed vestibule on the front, also with a gable roof.

The church was designed by the congregation's talented minister, Rev. Eustace Paul Ziegler, who gained some fame as an artist. Local contractor Bartley Howard built the church for $4,000, a portion of which was donated by the Kennecott Copper Corporation. The church was Cordova's first—and still only—Episcopal church.

SC108.1 **Red Dragon Reading Room**

1908

Predating the church was Saint George's Mission, which soon acquired the name the Red Dragon, due to its color. The Copper River and Northwestern Railway donated the land and some money toward its construction, as well as the red paint that covered it. The second building in Cordova, it was intended as an alternative to the bars, offering a fireplace, easy chairs, books, and games. The building is simple: a one-and-a-half-story, gable-roofed structure, measuring 24 feet by 36 feet, of wood frame. Entrance is through a gable-roofed vestibule in the center of the long side. Originally one room, it was divided in 1946 to provide living quarters for the priest and a parish hall.

SC109 **Copper River and Northwestern Railway Houses**

1908–1918. Railroad Row

This row of cottages was built by the Copper River and Northwestern Railway for its employees. Although several types of buildings were constructed, including a two-story house for the superintendent at 314 Railroad Row, the basic type appears to have been a one-story, hip-roofed model. Although all of these cottages underwent changes after acquisition by private owners in the 1940s, their basic similarity identifies them as company built.

SC110 **Saint Michael the Archangel Russian Orthodox Church**

1925. Lake Ave.

Saint Michael the Archangel Church retains its simplicity and scale, despite changes to its vestibule and side walls. The gable-roofed church, measuring approximately 23 feet by 44 feet, incorporates the sanctuary within the main block of the nave. The vestibule, a separate element on the front, has changed in form over the years. In the early 1970s, the side walls of the nave and sanctuary were brought in about 2 feet, changing the original proportions of the church.

This small church is the third church for this congregation of self-described Aleuts. The Eyak Indians, now nearly extinct, originally occupied the Cordova area. In the twentieth century, Pacific Eskimos and Aleuts migrated here from nearby villages. Some of the migrations have been caused by natural disasters such as the 1964 earthquake, which obliterated whole villages in Prince William Sound. Other Natives have been attracted by Cordova's fishing industry and other opportunities.

Many of the icons came from the village of Nuchek in 1914–1915 and may have originated in Russia. The congregation, aided by members of the village of Chenega, built the church, using surplus lumber from the concrete forms of the U.S. Post Office and Courthouse in Cordova.

SC111 **Nirvana Park**

1930s. Lake Ave.

Alaska's climate is too harsh and the living too difficult to produce many follies, or idiosyncratic creations of visionaries. A rare example is found in Nirvana Park, developed in the 1930s by Henry C. Feldman, a Cordova businessman. Feldman carved statues, erected bridges and gazebos out of branches, and built a stone fountain in a style that goes beyond rustic into the bizarre. Winding paths and its wooded setting on Lake Eyak, which are all that remain, made Nirvana Park a popular retreat.

Chitina

Located in the Copper River valley beneath the towering heights of the Wrangell Mountains, Chitina lies at the point where the railroad to Kennecott diverged from what was to have been the main line north to Fairbanks or Eagle. It was thus a transportation hub. Although the townsite was laid out in 1906, the town did not boom until the Copper River and Northwestern Railway reached Chitina in 1910. Shortly after, the wagon road northwest to Tonsina was completed, connecting Chitina to the Valdez-Eagle and Valdez-Fairbanks trails, both important thoroughfares in turn-of-the-century Alaska. Because it became an access point to the Alaskan interior, Chitina managed to move beyond its limitations as a CR&NWRy company town.

Chitina once had five hotels and a bustling commercial area. The CR&NWRy never constructed the railroad line north to Fairbanks, however, and once the Alaska Railroad line was completed in 1923, transportation business shifted to the west. Chitina's fortunes rose and fell with the Kennecott Copper Company, which closed in 1938. In the 1940s, Chitina's population dropped to forty, and it proclaimed itself a ghost town. Today, only a few false-fronted buildings remain, but a mixture of frame and log houses survive, arranged in a vague grid plan.

SC112 **Copper River and Northwestern Railway Buildings**

1910

The Copper River and Northwestern Railway constructed a depot in Chitina, as well as maintenance shops. The only two remaining CR&NWRy buildings are located across the slough from the main part of town.

The cook house is a one-story, hip-roofed building of wood-framed construction painted in the standard Kennecott Company colors of red with white trim. The bunkhouse, of the same materials and color as the cook house, was built in two sections, as expressed by its gable roofs, one of which is slightly lower than the other. Both buildings were constructed in 1910 as part of the railroad's support facilities in Chitina.

SC113 **Chitina Tin Shop**

1912

One of the few restored buildings in town, the Chitina Tin Shop, a two-story, false-fronted structure, was constructed for Fred Schaupp (shown here as the middle building on the left, before restoration). The shop was used for metal fabrication, including the production of stoves and stovepipes and other sheet metal work, as well as repairs for guns, wagons, trains, and automobiles. A modest commercial building, measuring 17 feet by 33 feet, it is wood-framed, with beveled siding on the front and flush boards on the sides. Living quarters are on the second floor, and the shop, with its recessed center door and plate-glass windows, is on the first. The building was enlarged by the addition of a 15-foot-long section on the rear.

Chitina

Chitina Vicinity

SC114 **McCarthy Road**

1910–1911

Constructed from Chitina 60 miles east to its terminus at the Kennecott mines in the winter of 1910–1911, the CR&NWRy crossed two deep gorges. Over the Kuskulana River at mile 17, CR&NW engineer A.C. O'Neill designed a steel deck truss bridge 540 feet long, comprised of three Pratt truss spans. Over the Gilahina River at mile 28.5, CR&NW foreman Pat O'Brien designed an 800-foot-long wooden trestle, which was built in eight days. After a fire destroyed it in 1915, it was rebuilt in ten days. The rails were removed from the McCarthy Road in the 1940s, and the unpaved road is now open to vehicular traffic.

McCarthy

Founded in 1911 when the Copper River and Northwestern Railway arrived, McCarthy was the rough-and-tumble side of the carefully controlled environment at the Kennecott copper mine. Here, 4 miles down the road, liquor and women were readily available. In addition, the CR&NWRy constructed a depot and maintenance facilities here.

While it owed its existence to the Kennecott Copper Company, McCarthy boomed during the stampede to the goldfields of Chisana in 1913, when it served as a point of entry. Stampeders who arrived in Alaska by ship could take the train to McCarthy, before setting out on the overland trek to Chisana, deep in one of the most rugged regions of Alaska.

At its peak in 1916, McCarthy had a population of thirteen hundred (compared to Kennecott's four hundred), but its population diminished during World War I. In 1931 the territorial school was closed, as it had only two students. After the closing of the Kennecott Mines in 1938, McCarthy continued its decline until the late 1970s, when it had only a dozen residents. Today McCarthy has an appealing collection of small log and wood-framed buildings. A number of unused and deteriorating buildings hint at the town's former size.

SC115 McCarthy General Store

1914. Kennicott Ave. and Skola St.

The false-fronted McCarthy General Store contained a store on the ground floor and a rooming house above. The one-story portion, creating an L-plan, was added soon after construction. The entrance is in the corner, in a distinctively commercial arrangement. The principal developers and businessmen of McCarthy—J. B. O'Neill, Charles T. O'Neill, R. L. H. Marshall, and O. G. Watsjold—all owned the store at one time or another. Still visible is the sign painted on the front, "O.G. Watsjold, Groceries and Meat."

SC116 Johnson Hotel

1917. Kennicott Ave.

This two-story, false-fronted building was built for Mrs. Peter "Ma" Johnson. The hip-roofed porch with turned balusters has been added recently, in an attempt to identify it as a hotel; the original flat-fronted appearance was not so inviting. Paired one-over-one-light windows flank the central door; a secondary door on the front has been removed. The bedrooms were small, originally measuring 6 feet by 9 feet. A large two-story section has been added to the rear of the building.

SC117 Commissioner's Residence

1910s. Shushanna Ave. and McCarthy St.

Exhibiting slightly more style than most of the houses in McCarthy, the commissioner's residence boasts a gambrel roof. The walls are logs, square notched at the corners. The oriel in the gable is a recent addition, as is the stone foundation. Originally, the building had a shed-roofed porch across the front, with exposed rafter ends, and a six-over-six-light window at the second level. Little is known about the building, which was apparently constructed during McCarthy's first decade.

SC118 McCarthy Power Plant

1917. McCarthy St. and Shushanna Ave.

The power plant in McCarthy was built for the Mother Lode Coalition Mining Company, a small independent organization in the shadow of the Kennecott Copper Corporation. The Mother Lode Mine was the only rich claim on the west side of Bonanza Ridge. The ore was trammed down the mountain, then brought by sled or wagon into McCarthy, where it was shipped on the Copper River and Northwestern Railway.

The power plant was constructed to provide electricity to the tramway and the mine. Built in the townsite of McCarthy, close to the railroad that brought the necessary coal, the 40-foot-by-60-foot heavy timber-framed building was two and a half stories tall with a monitor roof supported by a Howe truss. Inside, a coal-fired boiler powered a steam turbine, and power lines conveyed the electricity the 12 miles to the mine.

In 1919 the tramway and power lines were destroyed by a snow slide, devastating the company, which sold out to Kennecott. The corporation removed the turbine to its plant but had no need for the building. Part of the building has been converted to an inn; the rest is used for storage.

Kennecott

SC119 Kennecott Copper Mines

1907–1925

One of the largest copper mines in the United States, the Kennecott Mines produced between $200 and $300 million worth of copper between 1910 and 1938. Located in the Wrangell Mountains, most of the buildings survive to illustrate the technology and work environment of this productive mine.

The site was staked in 1900 and soon acquired by Stephen Birch, a young mining engineer. Legal battles ensued and title was not cleared until 1905, when Birch's Alaska Copper and Coal Company was reorganized as the Kennecott Mines Company (a misspelling of the glacier). The Guggenheim family and J. P. Morgan provided the capital for development, investing $25 million before any copper had been produced. The investment included the mine and mill works, the 196-mile Copper River and Northwestern Railway running from the mine to Cordova, and a steamship line to connect the port of Cordova to the Guggenheims' smelter in Tacoma, Washington.

In 1911 the first load of copper, worth $250,000, was shipped. Four years later the

SC119 Kennecott Copper Mines

Kennecott Copper Corporation was formed out of the Kennecott Mines Company, the Copper River and Northwestern Railway, the Alaska Steamship Company, and the Beatson Copper Company—all in Alaska—and the new company began to branch out. By the 1930s, when the copper at Kennecott began to run out, the corporation had already invested in mines in southwestern United States.

The distinction of the Kennecott mine was not only in its size—it consistently ranked in the top ten of the nation's producers between 1915 and 1922—but also in the quality of the ore. Improvements in refining the ore prior to smelting were immediately implemented at this site to concentrate 2 percent or lower grade ore up to 50 to 80 percent before shipment to the smelter. Ammonia leaching, a process perfected by E. Tappan Stannard in 1915, was first employed on a commercial scale at Kennecott. Leaching involved using chemicals to dissolve the mineral and then precipitate it into a concentrate. Flotation, using oil or grease to separate mineral from ore through a bubbling action, was implemented in 1922–1923, as soon as the patent was cleared. Kennecott's ability to extract higher mineral values from low-grade ores accounted for its overwhelming profitability.

The mine complex is located at the foot of Bonanza Ridge, wedged between the steep mountainside and the moraine of the Kennicott Glacier. Forty-five buildings and about twenty-five outbuildings—all wood-framed, painted red with white trim—remain, all constructed between 1907 and 1925. Using grav-

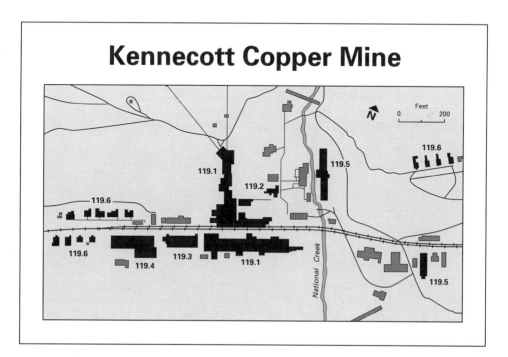

ity to advantage, the mill and related buildings cling to the mountainside in a linear arrangement perpendicular to the rail bed, which constituted the spine of the community.

Much of the work took place, however, up the mountainside, inside the earth. When the mine was abandoned in 1938, there were approximately 70 miles of tunnels in Bonanza Ridge. Ore was brought to the mill via trams. At the mine openings, bunkhouses, mine shops, and tramway stations were constructed; some of these remain. It is at the foot of the ridge, however, that the most impressive collection of buildings stands. Industrial buildings, residential housing, schoolhouses, a dairy barn, hospital, recreation hall, and store illustrate the self-sufficiency of the company town of Kennecott. Although most of the complex is in a ruinous condition, untended since its abandonment in 1938, it still evokes the grandeur and complexity of the copper mining industry. Located within the

boundaries of the Wrangell-Saint Elias National Park, the mine is privately owned and not open to the public. Some of the residential buildings have been sold to individual owners, who form a small community where once hundreds lived.

SC119.1 Mill

1910–1911 and later

The mill dominates the landscape, extending nearly 200 feet down the hillside. Two trams entered at the top, where ore was conveyed to the crushing department. Comprising about one third of the mill, the crushing department was built in 1910–1911. The middle third of the building was the gravity concentration department, also constructed in 1910–1911. Here the ore was separated in a purely mechanical operation, involving vibrating tables treating ever smaller ore. The bottom third of the building, below the railroad tracks, included the ammonia leaching plant, which

SC119.1 Concentration Mill/Leaching Plant

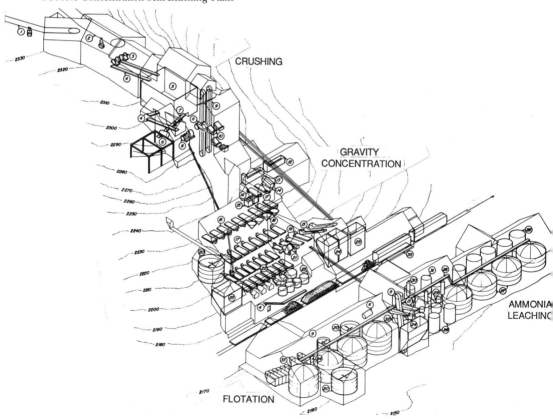

CRUSHING

GRAVITY
CONCENTRATION

AMMONIA
LEACHING

FLOTATION

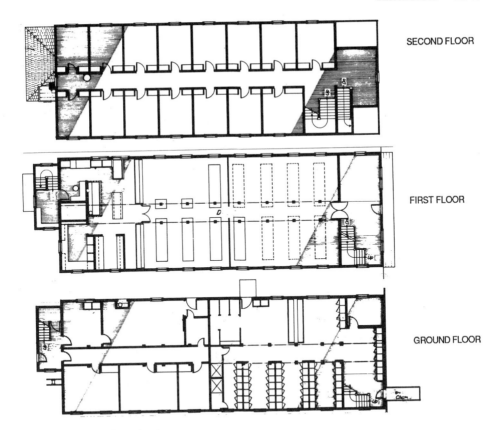

SECOND FLOOR

FIRST FLOOR

GROUND FLOOR

SC119.5 Bunkhouse (floor plans)

went into operation in 1916, and the flotation department, in 1923.

As originally built, the mill consisted of a series of shed-roofed sections stepping down the hill, each lit by a row of windows. As the mill expanded and adopted new processes, its original design became less clear; today it is a spectacular jumble of shed-roofed and cross-gabled sections. The mill has a heavy timber frame, amply cross-braced to provide resistance to the wind. It is finished with beveled siding painted red with white trim. The interior, however, is unfinished and purely functional, with the structure exposed. In a deteriorating state, the mill has lost most of its windows and part of its top story and roof, yet it is still an impressive structure.

SC119.2 **General Manager's Office**

1908 and later

Although the main work of the mine went through the mill, other buildings were re-quired to keep the mill running. The general manager's office, just northeast of the mill, is the oldest building on the site. The log structure, 17 feet by 21 feet, is the original portion; two wood-framed additions, and two small concrete ones, complete the structure. The concrete addition on the side of the building contained a safe for money, while the one on the end was used for drawing and plat storage. The interior is finished with beaded boards, vertical and unpainted on the wainscot, and horizontal and painted on the walls and ceiling. Here, too, most of the windows are broken out.

SC119.3 **Machine Shop**

1916

In a building next to the flotation department, machinery used in the mill was fabricated and repaired. The long, gable-roofed building has exceptionally large windows composed of four twelve-light sash.

SC119.4 **Power Plant**

1925 and later

Also distinctive is the power plant, with four tall smokestacks. The monitor-roofed building, constructed in three phases beginning in 1925, produced electricity and steam heat.

SC119.5 **Bunkhouses**

1908 and 1910, bunkhouses on National Creek; 1917, west bunkhouse

The people who worked at Kennecott also had to be provided for. Bunkhouses for the workers, who were all single men, were located near the heart of the operation, on National Creek, and on the McCarthy side of the complex. These were three-and-a-half-story buildings with shed-roofed dormers.

SC119.6 **Managers' Cottages**

c. 1915 and later

Cottages for managers, who had their families with them, were located on the periphery of the complex. One- and one-and-a-half-story buildings, they were small and simple, employing standard designs to cut costs.

Chisana Vicinity

SC120 **Solo Mountain Shelter Cabin**

c. 1913. 1926, rehabilitated. Goat Trail

With a gold strike in Chisana attracting some two thousand stampeders in the summer of 1913, several trails were used. Some miners attempted to travel by steamboat up the Tanana and White rivers from Dawson and Fairbanks, others overland from Whitehorse. Most,

SC120 Solo Mountain Shelter Cabin

however, set out on one of two routes from the head of rail service at McCarthy, both crossing 80 miles of extremely rugged country. The winter route was over the Nizina and Chisana glaciers on a trail flagged by George Hazelet, while the summer one was by the Goat Trail through the Skolai Pass and Chitistone Gorge.

Along these trails, private individuals operated roadhouses and the Alaska Road Commission built shelter cabins—essentially empty cabins for the convenience of travelers. The Solo Mountain Shelter Cabin was constructed about 15 miles south of Chisana on the Goat Trail, probably in 1913. The Alaska Road Commission hired Harry Boyden—who had the mail contract along this route—to rehabilitate or perhaps rebuild the cabin in 1926. The cabin, which measures 9 feet 8 inches by 11 feet 11 inches, is constructed of round logs, saddle notched at the corners. The gable roof has a split log sheathing, partially covered with corrugated metal. The isolation of the site and the simplicity of the small log cabin evoke the hardships of the journey.

Chisana

The site of a 1913 gold stampede, Chisana once had four hundred log buildings; today there are about twenty. Deep in the Wrangell Mountains, Chisana's location remains remote, not connected by road to anywhere else.

In May 1913, Billy James, his wife, Matilda James, and Nels P. "North Pole" Nelson discovered placer gold on Bonanza Creek. When Nelson went to Dawson for supplies, he spread word of the strike, and that summer 5,000 people headed for Chisana. One of the last stampedes in Alaska, Chisana attracted those who had lost out in Nome, Fairbanks, Dawson, and a host of smaller strikes. Although creeks were staked for 25 miles around Chisana, only Glacier and Bonanza creeks proved productive. By 1920, only 148 people lived in Chisana, and in 1939, the post office closed.

In the buildings that remain, the grid outlines of the original townsite are still evident. Most of the extant buildings are residential, but they share certain characteristics with the government buildings discussed below. All were constructed of round logs, chinked with sod or moss, saddle notched or V notched at the corners. Roofs were constructed of sod laid on poles or planks and often covered with metal in later years. On the interior, walls were covered with canvas. The foundations usually consisted of sill logs laid directly on the ground; on some cabins the earth is bermed around them.

Access to Chisana is by plane or packhorse, so new building materials are rarely introduced. The town is without electricity, telephone, sewer, or water.

SC121 U.S. Government Buildings

1913–1914

Although earlier gold miners in Alaska established their own self-governing mining districts, by the time of the Chisana strike the U.S. government had a clear role. A civil code adopted in 1900 provided that the U.S. district judges could appoint commissioners as needed. The commissioner, who served as justice of the peace, recorder, probate judge, and coroner, was assigned to a specific area, often in response to a gold rush and influx of population. Accordingly, U.S. District Judge Robert Jennings appointed Anthony J. Dimond as U.S. commissioner in Chisana in 1913. Dimond left Chisana the next summer but went on to a distinguished political career, including service as Alaska's delegate to Congress, 1933–1934.

Dimond and his successors built several log buildings in which to carry out their duties: a two-story courthouse, a residence, and men's and women's jails. The two-story courthouse does not survive, but the one-story log cabin known as the court may have dated from 1913–1914. The men's jail does not survive, but the women's does. This modest log cabin is a reminder that women were present in gold-rush towns and were not necessarily law abiding. The commissioner's residence is typical of other log cabins in Chisana; in fact, the three government buildings are hardly distinguishable from each other, despite their different purposes.

As buildings significant to this gold-rush town, the three were restored by the National Park Service in 1989–1990. Chisana is located within Wrangell-Saint Elias National Park, and is evidence that the parklands are not as pristine as they seem. At one time, five thousand eager prospectors were sifting the streambeds for gold.

SC121.1 U.S. Commissioner's Court

The U.S. Commissioner's Court is a log structure, domestic in scale. The round logs are saddle notched at the corners. The building is one room with a vestibule constructed of logs with a spline and corner posts. The roof, originally sod on split logs covered with a second roof of planks and tar paper, has been replaced by standard rafters, planks, and metal. A room added on the west in the 1960s was removed during restoration.

SC121.2 Commissioner's Residence

The commissioner's residence, a log cabin with saddle-notched corners, has several personal touches, seen in shelves and counters constructed around the windows. The doorway is flanked by windows, also an unusual touch.

SC121.3 Women's Jail

This building is a small structure, 11 feet by 15 feet; little distinguishes its use. The one-room building was constructed of logs, saddle notched at the corners. The sod-on-split-log gable roof has been replaced by rafters, planks, and metal. The men's jail does not survive.

SC122a Sourdough Roadhouse (exterior)

Sourdough

SC122 **Sourdough Roadhouse**

1906

Advertising itself as the oldest roadhouse still operating in its original building, Sourdough Roadhouse was built on the Valdez-Fairbanks trail in 1906. Known originally as Pollard's, from 1908 to 1922 Nellie Yeager operated it, calling it Sourdough Roadhouse and Trading Post. Constructed of round logs, saddle notched at the corners, the one-story building has a gable roof formed of sod on poles and covered with metal. Several additions have extended the roadhouse to the south. The living room and bar were located in the original section, with living quarters for the proprietor behind. Next to it was the dining room and store, and at the end, the kitchen.

SC122b Sourdough Roadhouse (interior)

These same uses prevail today, except that the proprietor's quarters have been replaced by a liquor store. Designated a National Historic Landmark, the roadhouse is important not only for its age and architecture but also for the road itself—a vital early connection.

Gakona

SC123 **Gakona Roadhouse**

1929

Arne Sundt built the two-story log roadhouse now serving as the Gakona Lodge and Trading Post. An earlier roadhouse, built in 1905, still stands, now used for storage.

Located between the Gakona and Copper rivers at the divergence of the Valdez-Fairbanks and Valdez-Eagle trails, Gakona was well situated for traffic. The U.S. Army built the Trans-Alaskan Military Road in 1900–1905 in order to join its post at Fort Liscum, near Valdez, with Fort Egbert, at Eagle. At the junction of the winter trail to

Fairbanks, the Valdez Transportation Company, which had the mail contract from Valdez to Fairbanks and Valdez to Eagle as well as a stage line to Fairbanks, built a roadhouse in 1905.

This first roadhouse, located on the banks of the Gakona River, is built of round logs, saddle notched at the corners. The original building measured approximately 20 feet by 30 feet, with a 15-foot-by-30-foot shed-roofed addition. On the interior, the ground floor was one open space, with a stove on one side. The second floor had two 5-foot-by-9-foot sleeping rooms partitioned with canvas on a light frame; the rest was one room.

The second roadhouse, also built of round logs, is L-shaped in plan, with several additions, and much larger than its predecessor. The corners of the gable-roofed building are square notched. Although patrons now sleep in private rooms, there is an air of shabby gentility and past grandeur to the lodge that adds to the roadhouse experience. There are more than a dozen buildings at the site, housing the bar, restaurant, and lodge. The location is still a prime one, and the roadhouse remains a popular stop.

Nabesna

SC124 Nabesna Gold Mine

1920s

The Nabesna Gold Mine, on the northern slopes of the Wrangell Mountains, was a profitable operation driven by one man, Carl F. Whitham. In 1925, after three years of prospecting on the mountain, Whitham found one of the richest gold veins ever reported in Alaska. Four years later, to raise capital, he organized the Nabesna Mining Corporation and sold stock.

The mill was modern in every respect, processing up to 50 tons of ore per day. Gold was recovered by shaker tables, flotation, and cyanide leaching. The mine itself was 2,000 feet up the mountain and eventually constituted 3 miles of underground workings. Ore was hand trammed to the portals, then lowered by aerial tram to the mill.

By the late 1930s, Nabesna employed sixty to seventy men. Whitham ran Nabesna with an iron hand, but he made it pay. All expenses were met from earnings, and the mine paid a dividend every year. By the fourth year, the dividend of $180,000 equalled the company's total capital investment. The mine was closed by government order during World War II, reopening only briefly afterward. Whitham died in 1947.

Most of the original buildings still stand today, although in a deteriorated condition. Many of the wood-framed buildings are clad in Celotex or tar paper, held with battens. The mill is built against the hillside, using gravity to assist the flow of materials. The top level contains the ore bin, and just below it the ball mill, which crushes the ore. Also at this level are the machine shop, flotation tanks, and cyanide leaching tanks. Below this level are the concentration tables. The buildings provide an excellent illustration of a small-scale hard-rock gold-mining operation.

Although the site is within the boundaries of Wrangell-Saint Elias National Park, the mine is privately owned and not open to the public.

Southeast Region (SE)

STRETCHING NEARLY 600 MILES SOUTHEAST FROM THE MAIN-
land of Alaska, the Southeast Region is a narrow strip of land with some
of the most spectacular scenery and mild temperatures found in the
state. In the north, between Icy Bay and Cross Sound, the coast is regular, with
a coastal plain largely covered by glaciers; settlements are sparse. South of Cross
Sound, the Alexander Archipelago consists of hundreds of mountainous islands interlaced with deep fjords. The mainland, with even higher mountains
ranging up to 10,000 feet in height, has major river systems originating in
Canada.

Southeast has a maritime climate, with small temperature variations, high
precipitation, and considerable cloudiness. Precipitation ranges from 80 to 200
inches in the region. The cool, moist climate produces a lush forest growth,
mostly spruce and hemlock, with some red and yellow cedar.

The wealth of fish and fur-bearing animals contributed to the relative prosperity of the Tlingit and other Northwest Coast Indians who settled in this
area. The highly sophisticated architecture developed by the Tlingit reflected
the ready availability of lumber. The region also attracted the Russians, who,
after stiff resistance from the Tlingit, finally established their capital at Sitka in
1808. The Russians found the rest of Southeast unprofitable, however, and
essentially ceded control of the trade here to the British and the Americans in
the 1820s.

After the acquisition of Alaska by the United States, Southeast received little
notice except for gold strikes in British Columbia, reached through Wrangell.
Discovery of gold in Juneau in 1880 produced the first Alaskan stampede, and
with the gold strike in the Klondike in 1896, Alaska was on the map. Thousands of would-be miners poured into Skagway, the closest port. Although there

156

Southeast Region

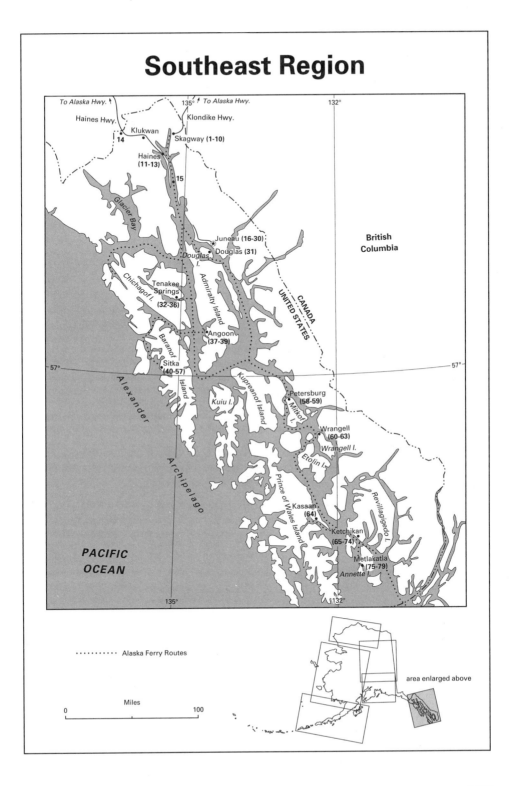

To Alaska Hwy.   135°   To Alaska Hwy.   132°

Haines Hwy.
Klukwan
14
Skagway (1-10)
Klondike Hwy.

Haines
(11-13)
15

Glacier Bay

Juneau (16-30)
Douglas (31)
Douglas I.

British
Columbia

Chichagof I.
Tenakee
Springs
(32-36)

Admiralty Island

Baranof Island

Angoon
(37-39)

CANADA
UNITED STATES

57°   57°
Sitka
(40-57)

Kuiu I.

Kupreanof Island

Mitkof I.

Petersburg
(58-59)

Alexander

Archipelago

Wrangell
(60-63)
Wrangell I.

Etolin I.

Prince of Wales Island

Kasaan
(64)

Revillagigedo I.

Ketchikan
(65-74)

PACIFIC
OCEAN

Metlakatla
(75-79)
Annette I.

135°   132°

.... Alaska Ferry Routes

Miles
0   100

area enlarged above

157

were subsequent strikes in the early twentieth century, the fishing industry became increasingly important to the economy, the first cannery having been built in Southeast in 1878. Although lumber did not become an export industry until after the Second World War, the lumber of Southeast did go into much of the construction within the region. More than 70 percent of the land of Southeast is administered by the U.S. Forest Service as the Tongass National Forest. Within the Tongass are twelve designated wilderness areas where logging is not permitted.

The lack of roads in Southeast underlies its dependence on boats for transportation and reinforces the maritime character of the region. Only two major towns, Skagway and Haines, are linked to the rest of Alaska by road, and both of those go through Canada; other roads join some towns, but by and large, each is fairly isolated.

Settlements hug the shoreline, where the land is flat. The grid plan is usually forsaken because of the irregularity of the coastline and the terrain. The buildings face the water, not only to see incoming traffic but also for the spectacular views.

Skagway

Skagway, the site of the Klondike Gold Rush National Historical Park, retains the finest collection of false-fronted commercial buildings in the state. A gold-rush boomtown, Skagway had several advantages that ensured its survival. Rather than being the site of a gold strike, Skagway was a major entry point to the Klondike and to the head of the Yukon River. Located at the origin of the arduous White Pass trail to the Klondike, the town competed directly with Dyea, 3 miles west at the foot of the steep Chilkoot Trail. Although the Chilkoot was the more popular route for stampeders, Dyea became a ghost town in 1899. With the completion of the White Pass and Yukon Route railroad to Lake Bennett, Skagway provided the easiest access to the Klondike. Growing from a homestead in 1896 to a population of 3,117 in 1900, Skagway saw thousands of people pass through the area in a very short time. Most of these travelers needed temporary accommodations and equipment for their journey, and that is what Skagway provided—hotels, bars, supplies, and prostitutes. The U.S. Army stationed several hundred troops here until 1904, when they removed to Fort Seward, near Haines. Although activity in the Klondike soon subsided, for about ten years Skagway flourished with all the excitement and adventure of the gold rush.

Capt. William Moore, the original homesteader who was determined to profit from his fortunate location, staked his claim and built a wharf. He encouraged investors to build a sawmill, which they did in 1897, ensuring that Skagway would be a wood-frame town. The constant traffic of steamboats from Seattle to Skagway provided a steady supply of other building materials. Thus the

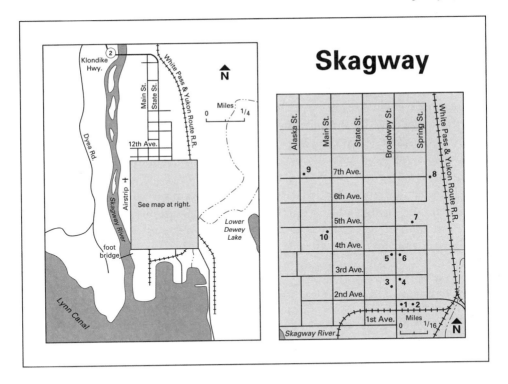

wood-framed buildings were ornamented with pressed metal, plate glass, and canvas awnings. Although rapid construction resulted in some shoddy buildings, the application of false fronts to commercial buildings was part of an effort to create the appearance of substantiality—in the short term in order to instill confidence on the part of the customer, and in the long term to ensure the survival of the town.

Skagway sits on the flat land at the mouth of the Skagway River, which drains White Pass. Disregarding Captain Moore's prior claim to the land, Skagway's streets were laid out in a grid pattern. Otherwise they were unexceptional, except that Broadway was 80 feet wide, as compared to 60 feet for the others. The White Pass and Yukon laid its tracks right down the middle of Broadway, and they were not rerouted until 1946. Boardwalks elevated the pedestrians off the muddy streets, and commercial buildings crowded the boardwalks. Residential buildings tended to be set back from the street with side yards.

In 1908, after the turmoil of initial growth had subsided, community leaders made an effort to clean up the town by demolishing deteriorating shacks and moving surviving commercial buildings to Broadway, giving it an appealing density of commercial blocks. By this time, Skagway was already attracting tourists, the mainstay of the economy today. Klondike Gold Rush National Historical Park includes several blocks of downtown Skagway, and the National

Park Service has restored, or is in the process of restoring, about a dozen buildings.

Many of Skagway's gold-rush-era buildings survive. Broadway is still the main commercial thoroughfare; false-fronted buildings still line the street. The early commercial buildings ranged in width from less than 10 feet to 25 feet or so, and examples of all sizes survive. None is particularly tall, although the verticality is emphasized by the narrowness of the false fronts and the application of turrets on corner locations. The boardwalk sidewalks add to the turn-of-the-century atmosphere; Skagway's streets were not paved until 1983 (these photographs were taken in 1982).

Residential buildings are located on all streets other than Broadway. Although the impression of spacious lots is new to Skagway—with a population much less than at its peak, vacant lots abound—the houses are true to their gold-rush-era origins. Most are one story, often built in an L-plan, with hipped or gable roofs. Decorative woodwork, projecting bays, and porches add a touch of Queen Anne to the overall appearance. Both commercial and residential buildings in Skagway employ wood expressively, from varied wall surfaces to applied ornament.

SE001 White Pass and Yukon Route Depot (Klondike Gold Rush National Historical Park Visitors' Center)

1898. Broadway and Second Ave.

The construction of a railroad over the White Pass to the Klondike in 1898–1899 ensured Skagway's survival as a town and doomed Dyea, the entry point for the Chilkoot Trail, to oblivion. The first railroad in Alaska, this line connected to the upper Yukon, by which interior Alaska could be reached. Although other, all-Alaska routes were soon developed, the White Pass and Yukon Route was an important early gold-rush era transportation route.

In Skagway, the railroad ran from Moore's Wharf, curved over to Broadway, and ran straight out Broadway. The White Pass and Yukon Route Depot was built in 1898 on the south corner of Broadway and Second Avenue; the west corner of the building was clipped to accommodate the tracks, forming a five-sided building. The two-story, wood-framed depot was constructed hurriedly, evidenced by packing crates and other second-hand lumber used in the construction. The exterior was finished with beveled siding, with paneling dividing the first and second stories. Elaborate brick chimneys pierce the hipped roof, which originally had wider eaves, cut back in 1907, probably to allow more light to the upper stories.

On the interior, the ticket office was located in the Broadway and Second Avenue corner, surrounded by the waiting room. The Canadian Customs Office occupied the west corner room, while the baggage room was in the rear corner. The second floor housed offices; the dispatcher's is marked by an oriel on the Broadway side of the building, affording a view of the trains. Throughout the building, there is a high wainscot of vertical boards, which was originally painted; the walls above were covered with cloth.

Upon construction of a new depot and office building in 1969, this depot was vacated and sold to the National Park Service. The building now serves as a visitors' center for Klondike Gold Rush National Historical Park.

SE002 White Pass and Yukon Route Railroad Building

1900, Henry Dozier. Second Ave., between Broadway and Spring St.

More sophisticated architecturally than the hastily erected depot, the general office building constructed in 1900 was designed by Seattle architect Henry Dozier. The forthright

SE001 White Pass and Yukon Route Depot (right); SE002 White Pass and Yukon Route Railroad Building (left)

Classical Revival design features a balustraded and pedimented parapet, modillioned cornice, swag-and-garland frieze, and shouldered architraves on the second-story windows. Fluted box columns on the first level frame the storefront windows. Lettering declaring this the "Railroad Building" built in "1900" is of galvanized iron, as are many of the moldings.

The rest of the two-story building is wood, covered with a variety of vertical and horizontal sidings. The office building was connected to the depot by a second-level passageway. In 1908, the first floors were connected in the rear, enlarging the baggage and freight rooms. A band of windows in the rear at the second level illuminated the drafting room. Interior finishes in this building were also more sophisticated than for the depot. Here, the vertical-board wainscot was stained and varnished, while the walls were lathed and plastered. A two-story fireproof vault held gold shipments and company papers. At its completion in May 1900, the newspaper declared it "by far the finest wooden structure in the city."

SE003 Arctic Brotherhood Hall

1899; 1900, facade. Broadway, between Second and Third avenues

An extraordinary example of Rustic architecture, the facade of the Arctic Brotherhood Hall is composed of driftwood sticks arranged in various patterns and constructions. The second-level balcony, pediments over the windows, parapeted cornice, and hood over the doorway are all constructed of these sticks.

The wall is faced with them as well; tiny sticks arranged in a basket-weave pattern give an interesting texture to the wall. Behind this false front is a gable-roofed, wood-framed building covered with novelty siding on the sides and rear.

On the interior, most of the structure was devoted to a two-story hall, 30 feet by 50 feet, with a balcony at the second level. Stick and driftwood furniture lined the walls; some of it can be seen today in the city museum.

The Arctic Brotherhood was a fraternal organization founded by a group of gold seekers on board a steamer bound for Skagway in 1899. Once on land they formalized the arrangement, making Skagway the first

SE003 Arctic Brotherhood Hall

camp, as the driftwood sign "Camp Skagway No. 1" on the front of the building notes. The building was constructed in 1899, but the driftwood facade, credited to Charles O. Walker, was not built until 1900. Rustic architecture is usually associated with urbanites "discovering" the wilderness, and its appearance in a sawmill-equipped town is no less ironic than a group of gold seekers forming an Arctic Brotherhood even before they had reached Alaska, much less the Arctic. A self-consciousness about the great adventure of the gold rush permeated Skagway.

SE004 **Mascot Saloon and Pacific Clipper Line**

1898, corner and adjacent buildings. 1937, two-story addition. Broadway and Third Ave.

Two of these three two-story buildings, now with a unified paint scheme, were built the same year in radically different styles. The 25-foot-wide building on the corner was constructed in March 1898 by the Northern Trading and Transportation Company. The gable-fronted building had an angled entrance at the corner which led into the Mascot Saloon. Steamship company offices occupied the remainder of the first floor. The next year, the Mascot's owners purchased the building and expanded the saloon so that it occupied the entire first floor.

In July–August 1898, the Pacific Clipper Line built the adjacent 15-foot-front building in a fancier style. A second-story oriel ornaments the facade, and a parapeted pent roof adds the texture of wood shingles to the clapboard- and bevel-sided walls. The first floor has a show window and two doors, one of which leads to the upstairs rooms. In 1904, Albert Rienert, then sole owner of the Mascot, bought the Pacific Clipper Line building and expanded the saloon. The corner entry was removed. In 1916, with the adoption of local prohibition, the Mascot was converted to a drugstore.

The 10-foot-by-20-foot two-story addition on the south was constructed in 1937 by Perry Hern, who had acquired the other two buildings in 1918. The clapboard-covered building with the same parapeted pent roof as the Pacific Clipper Line building next door has a show window and door at ground level and one window above. The similarities and differences in these buildings serve as interest-

ing documentation of their overlapping histories.

SE005 **Pantheon Saloon**

1897. Broadway and Fourth Ave.

The Pantheon Saloon was built as a plain board-and-batten hotel in 1897. After briefly being used as a hotel, the building served as a hardware store. It is most notable for its Rustic storefront, added in 1903 when it became the Pantheon Saloon and a substantial addition increased its size from 18 feet by 28 feet to 21 feet by 48 feet. Charles O. Walker, who had designed the Rustic front of the Arctic Brotherhood Hall, designed this one, which features driftwood logs as columns and cobblestone sections of wall, as well as the driftwood-stick decoration seen on the Arctic Brotherhood Hall.

The building has been altered frequently. The double doors of the Pantheon were replaced by a single door, and some of the cobblestones were removed to enlarge the show windows. A 23-foot-wide building was added to the south in 1943. Yet the unusual Rustic storefront, hailed as "artistic" when constructed, remains.

SE006 **The Trail Saloon and Lynch and Kennedy Store**

1904, 1900. Broadway and Fourth Ave.

The false front of this three-story building, the largest in Skagway, hides plain buildings and a fascinating history. In 1908, amid a movement to consolidate commercial buildings onto Broadway, Chris Shea and Fred Patten bought some barracks left by the U.S. Army in 1904, when it had transferred its troops to Haines. A two-and-a-half-story, 25-foot-by-100-foot barrack, which had been built in 1904 on Sixth near Broadway, was cut in half and moved to this corner site; the two halves were positioned with their gable ends facing Broadway, creating two separate buildings. Another barrack, with dimensions of 25 feet by 50 feet when it was built in 1900 and later increased 15 feet in length, was moved next to them. A false front was constructed over the first two buildings as part of its conversion to The Trail, a tourist resort and saloon. The first floor was devoted to a series of storefronts, while the upper stories were

SE004 Mascot Saloon and Pacific Clipper Line

SE006 Trail Saloon and Lynch and Kennedy Store

clad with clapboards and crowned with a bracketed cornice below an ornamented parapet. A two-story turret with a steep roof marked the upper two floors of the corner. The blank space with the false arch at the third level is between the two barracks; thus no window could be installed.

The third building, the 65-foot-long barrack, was leased to John J. Kennedy and Henry J. Lynch, who established a haberdashery. Removing the front of the building and constructing a 9-foot-wide connector to The Trail, Lynch and Kennedy built a false front to match the one next door. (The paired windows in the third floor are centered in the gable of the old barrack; those windows are off-center in the finished building because of the connector.) The first-floor sales room was the largest in Skagway, at 34 feet by 50 feet.

Neither business met with great success. The Trail venture went bankrupt in 1909. Soon after, Kennedy sold out to Lynch, who continued the clothing store until his death in 1915. The exotic building illustrates the vagaries of commercial enterprise, the mobility of Skagway buildings, and the nature of false fronts: a peek at the rear of this ensemble shows three, distinct, barracklike buildings.

SE007 Moore Cabin and House

1888, cabin. 1897 and later, house. Fifth Ave. between Broadway and Spring St.

The Moore cabin and house, at one time incorporated into the same structure, illustrate the typical if quixotic evolution of a frontier building, in this case, the earliest structure in Skagway. Capt. William Moore (1822–1909) established a homestead on the site of the future town of Skagway in 1887. An ardent backer of the White Pass route to the Yukon and foreseeing that a gold strike would eventually occur there, in 1888 Captain Moore built a one-story log cabin measuring 16 feet by 16 feet. The saddle-notched cabin had a gable roof covered with shakes.

The interior was lined with vertical planks covered with newspapers, but the building was left unfinished and was probably built primarily to hold the claim. In 1896, Captain Moore and his youngest son, J. Bernard "Ben" Moore (1865–1919), finally installed doors, a window, and flooring, and moved in.

By 1897, the Alaska and Northwest Territories Trading Company had built a sawmill in Skagway as part of its support for the White Pass route. In the summer of that same year, with sawn lumber now available, Ben Moore added a 14-foot-by-16-foot one-and-a-half-story wood-framed addition to the front of his cabin; he made still other additions in the fall and winter. In 1900, however, the Moores detached the log cabin and moved it to its present site 50 feet north of the house, placing it on a wood post foundation. Apparently, they already foresaw its tourist potential as the first cabin in Skagway.

The wood-framed house continued to grow and was inhabited by Ben Moore until he left Alaska in 1906. Except for the front porch, which dates from 1914, the house looks much as he left it, a one-and-a-half-story core surrounded by one-story, shed- and hip-roofed additions. Although not neat, the house illustrates the random growth typical of early buildings not only in Alaska but also throughout frontier America. The cabin has been restored and placed on a new foundation by the National Park Service, which plans to restore the house as well.

SE008 **City Hall** (Trail of 98 Museum)

1898–1900. Seventh Ave. and Spring St.

One of the few stone buildings in Alaska, Skagway's city hall began as a Methodist school but served for over fifty years as a federal courthouse. The two-story building is constructed of random-course granite in three colors. The basement of gray granite is topped by a 16-inch band of green granite, above which are the white granite walls. Halfway up the second story, the structure turns to wood frame and is finished with clapboards. The hipped roof has a cross gable on each side. A square tower, centered on the front, houses the stairwell and supports a louvered belfry. The Gothic-arch windows on the second story, fish-scale shingles in the gables, and an oriel window on the south contribute to the variety of forms and textures.

The Methodist school was the brainchild of Rev. J. J. Walter, superintendent of missions in Alaska for the Methodist church. When he arrived in Skagway in the summer of 1899, local Methodists were scraping together money to build a church. Walter felt that Skagway, with four hundred children and no public school, had more need for a school than for a church. In addition, a school would be easier to fund and could contain a chapel for community use. Walter soon raised $5,000, and ground was broken on 23 August 1899. The school, to be named after Bishop C. C. McCabe, would have four classrooms on the first floor, each measuring 28 feet by 19 feet. The second floor would hold a chapel and two recitation rooms, all of which could be opened into one auditorium.

Just at the time the school was ready to open in the fall of 1900, the U.S. Congress adopted legislation enabling license fees and taxes to support public schools in incorporated towns in Alaska. Suddenly, a Methodist school was no longer necessary. Walter sold the newly completed school building to the U.S. District Court for $9,000. After paying what was owed, the Methodists had $5,000 with which to build a church.

The U.S. District Court occupied the building, using the second floor as a courtroom, until the 1950s, when the City of Skagway acquired it. Municipal offices occupy the first floor, while the second floor houses a museum.

SE009 **Houses**

Seventh Ave. at Alaska St.

Next door neighbors on Seventh Avenue,

these two Queen Anne cottages have rectangular towers, set at an angle to the building. A similar scale and irregularity of plan also make them compatible partners. Typical in size of most of Skagway's early houses, these are more ornamental, giving a picturesque appearance, but their Queen Anne references represent a style already outmoded in the United States.

SE009.1 Guthrie House

1898–1902. Seventh Ave.

The house closer to the center of the block was built in 1898 for Lee Guthrie, a saloon owner. By 1902 it had gained its present configuration, a one-story cottage with a cross-gable roof, projecting bay windows, and rounded entry porch. The clapboard exterior contrasts with square shingles at the second level, ornamental shingles in the front gable, scrolled brackets on the bay windows, and spindlework and piercework ornament on the porch. The house has been extended considerably toward the rear, but it maintains its 1902 front.

SE009.2 Case House

1902. Seventh Ave., corner of Alaska St.

The house on the corner was built in about 1902 for Alice Case, who owned the property, and her husband W. H. Case, a photographer. A Swedish carpenter named Lindahl is credited with the construction. The irregular plan of the one-and-a-half-story cottage is emphasized by the cross-gable roof and two-story tower. The clapboard exterior is interrupted by a band of fish-scale shingles between the stories. Entrance is through a sun porch on the front. William J. Mulvihill, chief dispatcher for the White Pass and Yukon Route railroad, and his family lived here from 1909 until 1949. Mulvihill served as mayor of Skagway for an incredible sixteen terms.

SE010 Presbyterian (formerly Methodist) Church

1900. Main St. and Fifth Ave.

After the Methodist church sold its granite school building to the U.S. government for a tidy profit in 1900, the congregation built this church. The gable-roofed rectangular building has a corner tower and seems simple in form, but the interior is surprising. The nave is octagonal in plan, an arrangement popular with nonconformist denominations in the late nineteenth century. The altar was apparently recessed in the wall opposite the gable end; this wall has been closed off and the altar is now in the adjacent bay. The opera-house chairs, with cast-iron frames and wooden seats and backs, are original to the building.

On the outside, the church has features of the Shingle style. A Gothic arch is set in the gable end; the inset framed by the arch is clapboarded, while the gable is wood shingled. The two-story tower on the corner has fanciful raised corners at the base of its steeply pitched pyramidal roof. Entrance is through the base of the tower and on the side of the building; both have elaborate door hoods supported by bracketed box columns.

In 1917 the Methodist church ceased operation in Skagway and sold this building to a group of Presbyterians. That congregation occupies it today. A basement has been added, but the building has been largely unchanged.

Haines

Haines was founded as a Presbyterian mission in 1879 near the site of several Chilkat Tlingit villages. The land was deeded to the Presbyterians by the Chilkats and lies 10 miles southeast of Skagway on the opposite shore of the Lynn Canal. In 1881, Rev. Eugene Willard and his wife, Caroline, arrived, and the settlement was named after Frances Electra Haines, secretary of the Presbyterian National Committee of Home Missions. By 1885 eighty-five students attended Haines Mission, which developed into both a boarding school and day school under contract to the government.

Discovery of gold in the Porcupine District 35 miles northwest of Haines and the town's propitious location near the origins of the Chilkat, Chilkoot, and White Pass routes into the Klondike further increased its importance at the end of the nineteenth century. The construction of Fort William H. Seward here in 1902–1904 and the development of several salmon canneries in the area contributed to Haines's prosperity.

The town has a variety of early twentieth-century houses, ranging from modest one-story cottages to more elaborate bungalows. Main Street is lined with commercial buildings and extends down to the water. Architecturally, however, Haines is dominated by the adjacent military post, Fort Seward, a cohesive collection of imposing structures.

SE011 **Fort William H. Seward** (Chilkoot Barracks)

1902–1904

Fort Seward was the last of eleven military posts built in Alaska between 1897 and 1904 in response to the intense activity surrounding the gold rush. Located at Haines because of its proximity to the three major paths to the Klondike, the post was staffed with two companies previously located at Skagway. Never fortified, the post was renamed Chilkoot Barracks in 1922 and remained the only active military post in Alaska until 1940. After World War II, Chilkoot Barracks was declared surplus and sold to private owners. Arranged around a rectangular parade ground, the post's setting on the side of a small hill contributes to the impact of the neatly arranged buildings.

Aside from those mentioned below, other buildings at the fort included the hospital and administrative offices on one side of the parade ground and a guardhouse and quarters on the other. Toward the water were more functional buildings, such as the stable, cook house, and blacksmith shop. Off to one side was housing for noncommissioned officers and civilians. Most of these secondary buildings survive.

Although somewhat plain in design, the number of these buildings and their strict alignment make an undeniable impact. The granite ashlar used in foundations, clapboards covering wood-framed walls, and brick in the chimneys are materials common to military buildings of this period but unusual in Alaska. The post remains virtually intact, with only the loss of the barrack and the stables detracting from a fine collection of early twentieth-century buildings. Private owners have converted several buildings into a hotel and bed-and-breakfasts, and the Tlingit plank house and trapper's cabin (SE011.3) serve as tourist attractions. Most jarring about these reconstructions, however, is their placement in the parade ground, a planned open space. Detached from their proper surroundings, they detract considerably from the grandeur of the military post. Yet the regularity of the plan and the size of the quarters—far larger than most residential buildings in Southeast—are not lost and still stand as a firm declaration of a military presence.

SE011.1 **Officers' Quarters**

At the top of the parade ground, parallel to the waterfront, is a series of six officers' quarters. Five are designed for two families, one side a mirror of the other. They consist of two and a half stories with cross-gable pavilions and generous porches. The single house at one end was assigned to the chief surgeon and the larger house at the other end, just off the parade ground, was the bachelor officers' quarters. Next to the latter, on the downhill side, was the commanding officer's quarters (built in 1906), now converted to a hotel and linked to a neighboring building.

SE011.2 **Barrack**

Opposite the officers' quarters, on the downhill side of the parade ground, were two large U-shaped barracks, of which only one survives. The one-story porch across the front and Palladian windows in the gables added touches of grace to these large structures and helped to relate them to the officers' quarters.

SE011.3 **Tlingit Plank House**

1957–1964

As part of an effort to turn Fort Seward into a tourist attraction, a Tlingit plank house was constructed in the parade ground in 1957–1964. Based on a combination of original plans and the drawings of George T. Emmons, this 40-foot-square house is constructed of hammer-finished horizontal planks, notched into corner posts. There are a few accommodations to modern times: two doors have been added on the sides, the corner posts are set in concrete, and the planks are drift pinned. As the house is used for salmon bakes, tables and chairs occupy the space usually devoted to the fire pit and benches. The exterior has carvings on the corner posts as well as the front, with a totem pole incorporated into the rear facade.

The trapper's cabin to one side was built at the same time; it was intended to illustrate the architecture of the first whites in the area. The one-story cabin is constructed of logs sawn flat on three sides. On the other side of the plank house is a new building, used as a kitchen for the salmon bakes, that has the same dimensions as the plank house but is of simple modern construction.

SE012 **U.S. Government Indian School**

1905. 381 First Ave.

The U.S. government built this school for Indians as part of the segregated educational system in Alaska. The U.S. government provided education for Natives until the 1980s, whereas schools for non-Natives were funded by the locality or territory. The responsibility for Native education shifted from the U.S.

Bureau of Education to the U.S. Bureau of Indian Affairs in 1931.

Measuring 71 feet by 30 feet, this two-story building, which is larger than any private residential building in town, has large double and triple windows that further distinguish it as a school. Colonial Revival in design, the school has gable dormers and cornice returns on the gable ends. A small gable-roofed enclosed projection on the front (similar to one still extant on the end) contained the main doorway; this has been removed and the door converted to a window. Asphalt siding has been applied over the original beveled siding and the foundation covered with metal. The use of the Colonial Revival style—an unmistakably American style, although one rooted in the eastern United States—was a deliberate statement about the American education that was offered inside. The school was closed in 1947, and the city now uses the building for social service agencies.

SE013 **Chisel Building**

1916. Second and Main streets

An unusual poured concrete structure, the Chisel Building was constructed in 1916 by a merchant, Joseph H. Chisel. Chisel mixed and poured his own concrete, devising a system of temporary ramps. The three-story building is rough finished but ornamented by inset panels above the windows, a belt course between the first and second stories, and concrete dentils at the cornice. The upper stories housed a hotel and the first floor Chisel's store, with a mezzanine level. An idiosyncratic venture, the building is still a landmark in town.

Klukwan

Just northwest of Haines is Klukwan, a Chilkat Tlingit village that shuns publicity and does not welcome visitors. It is the only survivor of four Chilkat villages. The Chilkat were the most prosperous of the Tlingit because they controlled access to the Interior through the Chilkat, Chilkoot, and White Pass routes. Trade with the Athapaskans, particularly in eulachon oil, was dominated by the Chilkat, who grew rich from these endeavors. In the 1890s, the village of Klukwan consisted mostly of traditional plank houses facing the Chilkat River, including the famous Whale House described by George T. Emmons in 1916 as "the most widely known and elaborately ornamented house . . . in Alaska."

Because of the influx of whites into the region during the gold rush, the Chilkat lost control of the routes to the Interior but earned money instead by serving as guides. The villagers of Klukwan grew rich freighting supplies to the Porcupine mining district, 12 miles upriver. One Klukwan resident remembered earning $25,000 annually at this time. The architecture reflects this prosperity—large, two-story, wood-framed houses replaced the plank ones. These large buildings, which are recognized as clan houses, exhibit a sophistication of design unusual for Alaska at this time. Interspersed with more modest ones, they are visible in the village today, although most of the larger clan houses have been abandoned. Set in a line along the riverbank, most of the clan houses are two-and-a-half-story buildings, three bays wide with center doors and gable fronts that further increase their impact on the waterfront. Clad with beveled siding, they are ornamented with fish-scale shingles, bay windows, bracketed door hoods, and moldings. One house has a denticulated pediment, cornice returns on the gable, corner pilasters, and a carved eagle ornament below the gable window. Another, the Whale House (the direct descendant of the Whale House described by Emmons) is one and a half stories with the first story of poured concrete. The second story is covered with shingles, ornamented with a bracketed cornice.

New housing in the village has been built away from the river. Klukwan continues its prosperous ways: in 1990 the village corporation was named the most successful village corporation in the state, and in the top ten of all Alaskan corporations.

U.S.-Canada Border

SE014 Dalton Trail Post

Between 1891 and 1896. Mile 40 Haines Hwy.

The log building on the Canadian border was constructed by Jack Dalton, who negotiated with the Chilkat Tlingit and obtained access to the Chilkat pass to the Interior. Dalton kept tight control of this trail, establishing trading posts such as this one and setting up a toll road in 1899. With discovery of gold in the Klondike, the trail was used a good deal, but its use diminished with the construction of the White Pass and Yukon Route railroad to the Interior from Skagway. By 1914 a wagon road led from Haines to the border, following Dalton's trail; in 1943 the Haines Highway was constructed along this same route.

Operated as a roadhouse until the early 1970s, the Dalton Trail Post is a one-and-a-half-story building, 34 feet by 24 feet, constructed of horizontal round logs, saddle notched at the corners. A lower, one-story wing on one end is constructed of the same materials. The gables originally were finished with vertical planks; they now have wood shingles. In 1980, the building received a new roof and foundation.

Haines Vicinity

SE015 Eldred Rock Lighthouse

1906. Lynn Canal, 55 miles northwest of Juneau, 20 miles southeast of Haines

Combining keeper's quarters with the light itself, this two-story octagonal structure is the only one of the first twelve lighthouses in Alaska that has not been substantially altered.

Between 1902 and 1906 the Board of Lighthouses constructed a dozen lighthouses in Alaska, four of them in Lynn Canal, in response to the unprecedented traffic to the goldfields. Eldred Rock, the last of those twelve, was completed in 1906.

The first Alaska lighthouse to be constructed of concrete, the building has a concrete first floor and wood-framed second floor. An irregular octagon in plan, 52 feet in diameter, the structure has a cupola rising from the peak of its pyramidal roof, to a total height of 56 feet. The fourth-order light, displayed 91 feet above high water, was visible for about 15 miles. In 1973, Eldred Rock was unmanned and downgraded to a minor light.

Juneau

Occupying one of the most beautiful settings of any state capital, Juneau is nestled at the foot of a mountain on the shores of the Gastineau Channel. The buildings of the city seek the flat land at the base; only mining structures venture very far up the mountainsides. Although basically a grid plan, many of Juneau's streets curve and dodge to accommodate the terrain. At places, the hills are so steep that dedicated streets turn into wooden stairways. Despite a few large postwar office buildings, the architectural character tends toward wooden, two- and three-story commercial and residential buildings.

Juneau was founded by Richard Harris and Joe Juneau in 1880, after an Auke Indian from Admiralty Island gave them the tip that led to their gold

Juneau

strike. Harris and Juneau laid out a townsite, initially called Harrisburg, but then changed to Rockwell in honor of the naval commander who kept order in the town, and finally to Juneau, after Harris had left town. (Rockwell pulled out the next day.) The Auke Indians settled in a community of their own on what is now Village Street, west of downtown. Although miners and prospectors were initially attracted to the placer mining, it was the hard-rock mining that gave Juneau its staying power. Capital from San Francisco and other cities enabled large-scale operations to extract the ore, separate the gold with stamp mills, and process it on site. The first of these ventures, the Treadwell group, at its peak in 1915 crushed 5,000 tons of ore daily, averaging $2.50 of gold per ton. Treadwell was soon superseded by the Alaska Gastineau and the Alaska Juneau mining companies. The first two closed in the early 1920s, and Alaska Juneau in 1944, but during their operating years these three mines produced $158 million in gold.

In 1900 the capital of the district of Alaska was moved from Sitka to Juneau, responding to Juneau's burgeoning population of 1,864 and to its proximity to the Klondike goldfields. In 1912, Alaska became a territory; its territorial legislature first met here in 1913. The territorial buildings seem to have had little effect on the architecture of the town; brick-clad buildings such as the capitol are rare in Juneau, and the Colonial Revival style of the governor's mansion never achieved great popularity. Finally, in 1959 Alaska attained statehood, and Juneau became the capital of the new state.

While government has been a mainstay of the city's economy, tourism has achieved growing attention. When threatened in the mid-1970s with relocation of the capital to a site closer to the population center, Juneau citizens took an objective look at their city. What had been a seedy waterfront area was cleaned up, with utilities placed underground; a historic district was instituted, and the buildings obviously profit from design review. In addition to neighborhoods with high architectural quality, Juneau has one of the best preserved historic commercial areas in Alaska.

SE016 Alaska Governor's Mansion

1912, James Knox Taylor. 1936, altered. 716 Calhoun Ave.

On 1 January 1913, Territorial Governor Walter E. Clark and his family moved into this house, then Colonial Revival in appearance. Already under construction in 1912, when legislation was enacted providing that Alaska would be a territory and Juneau its capital, this house is the first building of the territorial government. The appearance of the house has been altered significantly since its original construction, as seen in the two accompanying photographs.

James Knox Taylor, the supervising architect of the Treasury, took a personal interest in the governor's house, meeting with Clark and his wife and entertaining suggestions from them. In 1910, Taylor had designed a 42-foot-by-42-foot house, much along the lines of that finally constructed; when the site was determined, however, Clark pointed out that the interior arrangement would have to be reversed and that the building could be enlarged. Accordingly, the house as constructed was approximately 58 feet by 60 feet. The entrance was on the east, from Calhoun Avenue, but the aesthetic front of the house faced south, with a view down a steep hill and across the city. On the south were the drawing room and library, the entrance hall and

Juneau, Douglas, and Vicinity

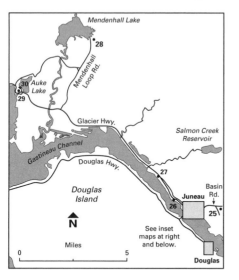

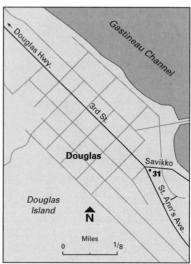

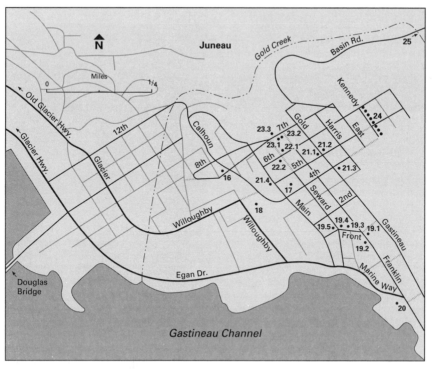

SE016a Alaska Governor's Mansion (historic view)

SE016b Alaska Governor's Mansion (current view)

dining room behind them, and the kitchen and an office on the rear. The second floor had four bedrooms, while the third floor was intended for servants and the territorial museum.

Built by Christ Kuppler from Seattle, the wood-framed building had clapboard siding and two small bay windows on the front. The steep gable roof had three irregular gable dormers; the modillioned cornice returned on the gable ends. Across the center third of the front was a two-story portico, with paired columns topped by a balustrade. Although the portico was somewhat ungainly, the overall effect was a twentieth-century version of a New England colonial house.

Construction supervisor William Neville Collier was charged with completing the project within the $40,000 allowed, and he made several changes. The house was originally in-

tended to be partially brick; Collier suggested that it be stuccoed wood. That too was eliminated, and the house was finished with clapboards. Pilasters on the exterior and parquet flooring on the interior were also eliminated. Despite Clark's interest in the building, he lived there only four months, being replaced as governor in April 1913.

In 1936 the appearance of the building was radically changed. The portico was replaced with a far grander one, six Corinthian columns (changed to Doric in 1963) stretching across the front of the house. The gable dormers were replaced with three segmental-arch dormers, evenly spaced. The entrance, on the gable end, was altered to accommodate a porte-cochère. The building was finally stuccoed, and pilasters were added. Now painted a gleaming white, the house has a commanding site, visible from much of the city.

SE017 **Alaska State Capitol** (Federal and Territorial Building)

1929–1931, James Wetmore. Fourth and Main streets

Little more than utilitarian in design, the state capitol is easily overlooked. Lacking a dramatic setting, the building is further compromised by its consistent floor-to-floor heights, which fail to denote any significant spaces within. The concrete frame is clad with a buff-brown brick; only the sumptuous marble columns at the entry hint that this building is anything special.

In 1910, Congress authorized $200,000 for a federal building. James Knox Taylor, supervising architect of the Treasury, preferred to wait for a larger appropriation rather than build an inadequate building. That larger appropriation was not made until 1928, when $775,000 was set aside (including the $177,500 remaining from the 1910 appropriation after purchase of the site). James Wetmore, acting supervising architect of the Treasury, is credited with the design (although as a lawyer he did no design work), and the contractor was N. P. Severin Company of Chicago.

Occupying an entire block, the building is six stories in front; because of the sloping site, it is five stories in the rear. Also deceptive is the capacity of this building, with dimensions of 169 feet by 118 feet, which is U-shaped in plan and therefore not as large as it appears. The first two stories are faced with Indiana limestone, with pilasters between the bays. A three-bay, two-story Tuscan portico has fat unfluted columns of Alaska marble supporting a plain architrave and balustrade. The third through fifth stories are faced with brick and arranged in a pier-and-spandrel pattern, with spandrels of Moderne design. Above the sixth story the modillioned cornice has been removed.

When it was dedicated in February 1931, the building housed the post office and federal offices on the first floor, the territorial legislature and museum on the second floor, and the governor's office on the third floor. U.S. courts occupied the fifth floor, and other federal offices were located in the rest of the building. The hallways were finished in native marble, with marble baseboards, stairways, and bathrooms.

Although there have been no major additions or alterations to this building, the modernization of the assembly rooms and offices is disappointing. Dropped ceilings, fluorescent lighting, and cheap paneling predominate. The site, too, continues to be a problem and was first recognized as such in 1930. The capitol fills the block and looks south, down the hill across the city. But the existence of the large courthouse building, designed by CCC/HOK in the 1970s, directly across the 30-foot-wide street effectively blocks the views to and from the capitol. Although built as the Federal and Territorial Building, the building was immediately recognized as the Capitol, and with statehood thirty years later, finally attained that status.

SE018 **Alaska State Office Building**

1974, John Graham Company in association with Linn A. Forrest Architects. Fourth and Calhoun streets

The eleven-story State Office Building nestles into the hillside and refuses to dominate the city. Linn A. Forrest also designed the Federal Building, an upright slab at Ninth Street and Glacier Avenue. That 1962 building, a concrete high-rise in a small-scaled city, provides a stark contrast to the State Office Building, which leans against the hillside, adjusting its plan to the uneven terrain. The first four floors, accessible only from Willoughby Street on the downhill side, house a parking garage. Most of the upper floors, which contain offices, are not located directly over the garage. Irregular in plan, they are arranged around an irregularly shaped atrium. Entrance is at the eighth level, on the Calhoun Avenue side, adjacent to the Capitol. Although the 1970s harsh concrete exterior does not conform to 1980s contextualism, the building's form is nicely sympathetic to its setting.

SE019 **Downtown**

In the 1880s, Front Street was the high-tide line of the Gastineau Channel. By filling this land, Juneau's developers created marketable lots on the water side of Front Street and South Franklin Street, thus providing space for half of this downtown district, as well as dock facilities. The Marine Park built in 1979 and cruise-ship facilities continue this seaward expansion.

Downtown Juneau, particularly South Franklin and Front streets, has a wealth of turn-of-the-century commercial buildings in remarkably unaltered condition. The curving streets, the canopies that extend over the sidewalks (giving much-needed shelter in an incessantly rainy climate), and the narrowness of the roadways contribute to the pedestrian quality of the area. The setting is perfect for these two- and three-story, wood-framed buildings, which feature storefronts at the ground level, some form of horizontal siding at the second and third levels, and a modillioned or bracketed cornice above. Dating mostly from 1890 to 1920, the buildings are painted in a variety of colors—probably not original—and the downtown has great appeal as a shopping area.

SE019.1 **Alaskan Hotel**

1912–1913. 167 South Franklin St.

The Alaskan Hotel has a residential quality

SE019.1 Alaskan Hotel

manifest in the two-story oriels on the front of the building. The three-story, wood-framed building has a stuccoed front and commercial storefronts at street level.

SE019.2 Alaska Steam Laundry Building

1901. 174 South Franklin St.

Across the street from the Alaskan Hotel is the Alaska Steam Laundry Building, constructed for E. R. Jaeger and his wife, who ran a lucrative business in a town full of single men. The corner turret is all the more unusual because the building is not on a corner lot; the turret projects 3 feet and is crowned by a conical patterned-shingled roof. The two-story, 39-foot-by-60-foot building has show windows on the first floor, paired windows on the second, and a modillioned cornice. The Jaeger family originally lived in the apartment on the second floor.

SE019.3 20th Century Gross Building

1939. 210 Front St.

The 20th Century Gross Building was constructed of reinforced concrete. The vertical grooves in the spandrels and the geometric designs above the windows of this five-story building allude to the Art Deco style.

SE019.4 Valentine Building

1905. 1913, addition. 202 Front St.

On the same block as the Gross Building, the Valentine Building occupies the oblique-angled corner of Front and Seward streets. Emery Valentine, a jeweler who served six terms as mayor, built the first part of the building on Seward Street in 1904; when it was extended to wrap around the corner to Front Street in 1913, it doubled in size. Two stories on a steeply sloping site, the building has a partial mezzanine level and plate-glass windows. On the second level, the windows are separated by fluted pilasters; above them, a modillioned cornice crowns a deep entablature with a denticulated architrave. On the interior, the original ornamented ceiling is exposed in the corner store, while the rest of the building still has drop ceilings.

SE019.5 McDonald's (First National Bank Building)

1899. 130 Front St.

This McDonald's deserves recognition for its sensitive adaptation of an existing commercial building; the tiny golden arches in the frieze are an in-joke more than an advertisement. Built to house the First National Bank, the two-story, wood-framed building was constructed in 1899. All of the siding, window surrounds, and cornice had been removed before the recent restoration.

SE020 Juneau Public Library

1988–1989, Minch Ritter Voelckers Architects. 292 Marine Way

An unlikely place for a library, the fourth floor of this parking garage also has a surprising sophistication of design. Added in 1988–1989 to a pre-existing parking garage, the library has vast expanses of glass to take advantage of the views in three directions. To break away from the boring regularity of a rectangular structure, a curving path from the corner elevators leads through the heart of the library, creating interesting spaces and glass-enclosed conference rooms as it goes. Designed by Minch Ritter Voelckers Architects of Juneau, the library is an unexpected haven in the bustling waterfront.

SE021 Churches

A number of interesting churches are located in a small neighborhood in Juneau.

SE021.1 Saint Nicholas Russian Orthodox Church

1893–1894. 326 Fifth St.

The only remaining octagonal-plan Russian Orthodox church in Alaska, Saint Nicholas Russian Orthodox Church was the first Russian Orthodox church in Juneau. Post-dating by several decades the Russian occupation of Alaska, the congregation was founded when Tlingit Chief Ishkhanalykh contacted the priest at Sitka to tell him that he wished to convert. In 1892, Bishop Nicholas visited Juneau and

SE021.1a Saint Nicholas Russian Orthodox Church (exterior)

SE021.1b Saint Nicholas Russian Orthodox Church (iconostas)

baptized the chief as Dimitrii. Dimitrii offered land, lumber, and labor to construct a church, while the bishop provided $2,000.

Although the precise origin of the design for this church is unknown, it is constructed in the form of several of the first churches or chapels, such as those at Sitka (1816), Unalaska (1808), and possibly Saint Michael (1840s). Unfortunately, none of the other octagonal churches survived even long enough to be photographed. Saint Nicholas's is painted white with royal blue trim, with small gable dormers and jigsawn trim giving it a picturesque air. The church is about 27 feet in diameter, wood frame with novelty siding. The sanctuary is contained within the main block of the building, while the vestibule extends on the west side. The polygonal roof rises to an octagonal cupola, which is topped with an onion dome, and over the vestibule there is a picturesque bell tower, added in 1905. On the interior, the seven-bay iconostas stretches across the eastern three sides of the building, with the end panels angled back slightly.

The church is oddly located on the site in order to follow the dictates of placing the altar toward the east. Closer to the corner is the priest's house, a one-and-a-half-story, wood-shingled dwelling.

SE021.2 Roman Catholic Cathedral of the Nativity of the Blessed Virgin Mary

1910. Fifth and Gold streets

The Canadian Catholic order of the Sisters of Saint Ann built the church here in 1910 and soon after added a hospital at Fifth and Harris streets. That hospital was converted to a school when a new hospital was constructed in 1912–1914.

SE021.3 Holy Trinity Episcopal Church

1896. 411 Gold St.

One block away from the Roman Catholic church is the Holy Trinity Episcopal Church. It is distinguished by its steeply pitched gable roof. Bishop Peter Trimble Rowe brought stock plans for the church, which never had a steeple. Wide wood shingles cover the walls, with smaller ones in the gables; the roof is covered with shingles as well. Gothic windows with colored glass pierce the walls, and entrance is through a vestibule on the side. The simple wooden interior features wooden scissors trusses. The church was extended and a parish hall added in 1956.

SE021.4 Christian Science Church

1906. 1924, moved. Fifth and Main streets

Built as a Presbyterian church, this church was moved to its current site in 1924 by the Christian Scientist church. The shingled building is L-shaped, with a tower and entrance porch filling the re-entrant angle to complete a nearly square plan.

SE022 Sixth Street

Between Gold and Seward streets

Montgomery and Frances Davis built several houses on Sixth Street, one for themselves and the rest to rent. J. Montgomery Davis was an English-born prospector and miner who came to Juneau in 1891 as bookkeeper and assistant manager of the Nowell Gold Mining Company. He soon married Frances Brooks, a wealthy English painter who had come to Juneau to observe the gold rush.

Between 1892 and 1912, the Davises built a number of houses for rental, including those located at 132, 136, 226, 232, and 238 Sixth Street. These are one and a half stories with a gable front and are sided in clapboards, beveled siding, or shingles. The three houses at 312, 312A, and 312B Sixth Street are set sideways to the street. Also one-and-a-half stories with gable fronts, these houses have front bay windows on the downhill sides. The

juxtaposition of owner-occupied and rental housing is made clear by the architectural distinction between the two; there is no doubt which is the owner's house.

SE022.1 J. Montgomery Davis House

1893. 1900, west wing. 202 Sixth St.

The first house the Davises built on Sixth Street is this one-and-a-half story wood-framed house with a steeply pitched gable roof, three round-arch windows, and patterned shingles in each gable. A one-story porch on the downhill side was enclosed with glass shortly after construction. The west wing, which gives the house an L-plan, was added in about 1900.

SE022.2 Frances House

1898. 137 Sixth St.

Also a part of the Davises' domain was the Frances house, a wood-framed, two-and-a-half-story house with patterned shingles and beveled siding. Almost square in plan, the house measures 30 feet by 34 feet and has a hipped roof intersecting with cross gables. Within each gable are paired windows set below a round arch. The house was built for Jerry Eicherly, postmaster, but leased to the superintendent of Perseverance Mine. In 1927, the house was threatened with demolition, as it was located on the proposed site of the Capital School. Frances Davis purchased the house and moved it to its present site 50 feet away, where it continued to be used as rental property but became known by her name.

SE023 Seventh Street

SE023.1 Wickersham House

1898. 213 Seventh St.

Built for Frank Hammond, owner of the Sheep Creek Mining Company, this house is best known for its association with James Wickersham, who lived here from 1928 until his death in 1939. Before Wickersham acquired the house, others connected with the mining industry had owned it, including John Malony, lawyer for Alaska Treadwell Gold Mining Company, and Bartlett Thane, manager and director of the Alaska Gastineau Mining

SE023.1 Wickersham House (dining room)

Company. In 1928, it was acquired by James Wickersham, a former judge who had been Alaska's third delegate to Congress and one of the most effective. In 1912, Wickersham obtained a territorial legislature for Alaska, in 1914 a government-funded railroad, in 1917 Mount McKinley National Park, and also in 1917 a state university. Wickersham's retirement to Juneau was interrupted by an additional, nonconsecutive term in Congress in 1931–1933.

After Wickersham's death in 1939, the house passed to his widow, the former Grace Bishop, and then to her niece, Ruth Allman, who opened it to the public. Today it is owned by the state of Alaska, and the nonprofit Wickersham Society conducts tours of the house, which is interpreted as a museum to James Wickersham.

Located at the top of one of Juneau's precipitous hills, where the streets become stairways, the two-and-a-half-story house has some elements of the Queen Anne style. The building is arranged in an irregular plan, with a bay window looking out over the city and a cross-gable roof. There are a variety of exterior materials including clapboards, beveled siding, and fish-scale shingles. On the interior, varnished woodwork enhances the double-parlor plan.

Significant changes were made during Wickersham's ownership when Seventh Street was opened up. Previously, entrance had been off the boardwalk on Seward Street, toward the front door on the downhill side. The main stairs led up from the front hall; the parlors would have been on the right, and a door behind the stairs led to the dining room. Wickersham turned this plan around, creating a sun porch around the original main

door. A porch on what had been the rear was enclosed, creating a new front door, with entry into the dining room. Wickersham also added hot-water heat and took out a partition on the second floor, creating a large bedroom on the downhill side. Although not elegant, the Wickersham House remains the best example of a home of the well-to-do in Juneau.

SE023.2 **Faulkner House**

1914. 227 Seventh St.

Next door to the Wickersham house is a house built on a similar scale, but in the Colonial Revival style. The two-story, wood-framed building is covered with clapboards and has a hipped roof with dormer. Columns and a decorated soffit add to its character. The house was built in 1914 for Herbert Faulkner, a deputy U.S. marshal and lawyer. L. O. Sloane, a doctor, also lived here.

SE023.3 **Thane-Holbrook House**

c. 1916. 206 Seventh St.

Across the street is a more modest house, built for Bartlett L. Thane. This classic bungalow has a gable roof with shed dormer, brackets in the gable ends, and exposed rafter ends. Willis S. Nowell, president and manager of steamship companies, lived there, and after 1922 Wellman Holbrook, a U.S. Forest Service official, and his wife, Mary.

SE024 **Kennedy Street**

1913-c. 1915. Between Fourth and Sixth streets

The neighborhood of Starr Hill was one of the first residential areas to develop after the original townsite. In the first few decades of Juneau's development, the hard-rock mining companies provided housing for their workers, until local businessmen recognized it as an opportunity. In 1913 city leaders requested the Alaska Juneau Mining Company not to build such housing, preferring to leave it to the free market. The mining company complied, and much of the newly developing Starr Hill neighborhood, near the mines behind Juneau, was constructed as speculative, rental housing.

SE024.1 Bungalows

1913. 500 block of Kennedy St.

One obvious example of the rental housing built for mine workers is the 500 block of Kennedy Street, where six once-identical bungalows sit in a line on the uphill side. Built in 1913 for Conrad W. Fries, a miner, and Ernest R. Jaeger, owner of the Alaska Steam Laundry, the houses are one-and-a-half-story bungalows, with gable fronts and Craftsman-style brackets. Most of the one-story front porches have been altered, but they were originally one-bay gable-roofed vestibules.

SE024.2 Mine Workers' Houses

c. 1915. 421, 431, 435, and 439 Kennedy St.

These houses were built about 1915 for the B. M. Behrends Company. B. M. Behrends was a merchant and banker, with some real estate investments, and these houses were probably also built for mine workers. Similar in scale to the 500 block, they are one-story front-gable houses with vestibules. They are set at a slight angle to the street, however, creating a more varied streetscape.

SE025 Last Chance Basin

1911. Basin Rd.

The Alaska Juneau Gold Mining Company opened an adit, or horizontal access, to its mines here in 1911 in an extraordinarily dramatic gorge. At the portal were several buildings housing machinery, such as compressors for drilling and repair facilities for the ore cars and locomotives. Dormitories, a mess hall, and a changing room served the workers, although some of them elected to live in town in new developments such as those on Kennedy Street within walking distance (SE024). Several buildings of the portal camp remain, together with marked sites of others along a walking trail, that still offers an evocative sense of mining life.

SE026 AWARE Shelter

1985–1986, Miller/Hull Partnership and Frank Maier Architect. 1547 Old Glacier Hwy.

This two-story, wood-framed building provides a temporary home for victims of domestic violence. AWARE, Aiding Women from Abuse and Rape Emergencies, sought a distinctive design, but one reminiscent of residential architecture in Southeast Alaska. The architects, the Miller/Hull Partnership of Seattle and Frank Maier Architects of Juneau, provided a rectangular building with a distinctive rounded, windowed, north end, where a meeting room is located. Decks on the south and west are accessible from adjacent first-floor rooms, and the building can house forty-eight women and children. Set on a wooded hillside, the building is clad in wood siding.

SE027 Gastineau Salmon Hatchery

1989, Jensen Douglas, Inc. 2697 Channel Dr.

A suitable successor to the picturesque earlier wooden industrial buildings on the waterfront, this new salmon hatchery is a clean, modern metal building. The hatchery incubates 162 million salmon eggs per year. Most of the salmon are released in other streams for eventual harvest by commercial and sport fishermen; the rest of the four species of salmon return to the hatchery to be used for brood stock. The hatchery includes a large visitor center with a window for viewing underwater.

SE028 Mendenhall Glacier Visitors' Center

1962, Linn A. Forrest. Mendenhall Loop Rd.

The first visitors' center built by the U.S. Forest Service, the dramatic, curving glass-walled facility at the Mendenhall Glacier was built according to designs by former U.S. Forest Service architect Linn A. Forrest, then in private practice. Sweeping views of the majestic glacier are enhanced by the semicircular stone-walled open area and the cantilevered, glass-walled enclosure above it. It is a classic example of the modern movement of the period responding to a dramatic setting.

Juneau Vicinity

SE029 Chapel by the Lake

1954–1958, Harold Foss and Linn A. Forrest. Auke Bay

A large and dramatic example of Rustic architecture brought into a suburban setting, the Chapel by the Lake features exposed log rafters, trusses, and walls. Most notable, though, is the large window behind the altar looking across Auke Lake to the Mendenhall Glacier, which must pose a special challenge to the minister. The Presbyterian church was built to a design by Juneau architects Harold Foss and Linn A. Forrest.

SE030 University of Alaska Southeast, Auke Lake Campus, William A. Egan Library

1990, Jensen Douglas, Inc., and Broome, Oringdulph, O'Toole, Rudolf, Boles and Associates. Auke Bay

Occupying a beautiful natural setting on Auke Lake, the campus buildings harmonize easily with their surroundings. The five earlier two-story wooden buildings are stepped into the hillside, linked in a meandering row by covered porches and walkways. The most recent building, dedicated in 1990, is the three-story William A. Egan Library. Built of wood, steel, and concrete, the new library, designed by Jensen Douglas, Inc., of Juneau, and Broome, Oringdulph, O'Toole, Rudolf, Boles and Associates of Portland, is a forceful yet compatible addition to the campus, which successfully adds steel and concrete to the prevailing wood palette of the campus. This building adds dramatic interior architectural spaces to the equally dramatic natural setting.

Douglas

SE031 Mayflower School

1933–1934, N. Lester Troast. Saint Ann's and Savikko streets

Across the Gastineau Channel on Douglas Island were the enormously profitable Treadwell Mines. The considerable operations included housing for the workers and even a swimming pool, as well as the stamp mills and mining operations. The mines started closing in 1917, and only ruins remain, but the small town of Douglas survived.

Besides the white Americans who dominated the mining industry, Treadwell had attracted a number of Tlingit Indians in the 1880s to work in the mines. While others moved on, the Indians stayed. In 1933–1934, the U.S. Bureau of Indian Affairs built this Colonial Revival-style Mayflower School, designed by N. Lester Troast, a BIA architect.

Set prominently at the end of Third Street on a sloping site, the school was designed as a community center as much as a school. On the ground floor were a kitchen, recreation room, laundry facilities, and showers, all intended for use by the community. The second floor housed the classroom, library, and facilities for home economics. The attic story had living quarters for the teacher.

Two-and-a-half stories in height on the downhill side, the rectangular clapboard-covered building is enlivened by Colonial Revival doorways, an architectural textbook application on an otherwise ordinary structure. The main entrance, on the long, uphill side of the building, has a scrolled pediment. On one gable end there is a pedimented doorway with fanlight, and on the long, downhill side a segmentally arched pediment. All of the doorways have paneled jambs, but the original doors have been replaced with ill-fitting, modern ones. The fourth side, which has no doorway, has a Palladian window in the gable. Removal of a small bell tower and the shutters has destroyed some of the character of this building. In addition, a set of three windows in the gable end has been removed, impairing the symmetry. But the ornamented doorways remain.

Tenakee Springs

Tenakee Springs is located on an inlet on Chichagof Island just west of Admiralty Island and, because of its natural hot springs, it has served as a modest resort since the nineteenth century. Miners wintered in Tenakee Springs beginning in the 1880s, but a measure of stability was not achieved until the establishment of Snyder Mercantile in 1899. Its owner, Ed Schneider, also built rental cabins continuing to attract a transient clientele. By 1902 enough permanent residents existed to establish a post office. In 1917 a cannery opened, the first of several salmon and crab canneries that operated until 1974. Today, the community is primarily a vacation and retirement center with a population just over one hundred.

The town consists of a single street occupying a thin strip of land along the shore of the narrow inlet, with hills rising steeply behind on the north. The town stretches for a mile or so along the road, from which automobile and truck traffic are prohibited. The street, varying from about 4 feet to 12 feet wide, is a slightly meandering path for pedestrians and small vehicles. Small, simple houses line both sides of the road, standing on high pilings on the water side, with a commercial center near the port facilities. There are no public utilities, and Snyder Mercantile, operating a noisy generator, sells electricity to the community.

There are two distinctive vernacular house types. One type is known locally as the cannery cottage because buildings of that type were moved from elsewhere on Chichagof Island where they were built to house cannery workers. They are wood-framed buildings ranging from 10 feet by 10 feet to 12 feet by 20 feet, with one or two rooms. Entry to the one-story buildings is through a distinctive inset corner. One has been adapted to serve as the post office. The other common house type is a log cabin, similar in size and shape to the cannery cottages. They are mostly built of hewn logs and have various types of notched corners. In the context of these simple buildings, the recent Tenakee Inn, though picturesque from a distance with its mansard roof, seems an inappropriate addition to the waterfront when seen up close. The dramatic setting and hot springs combine with the very simple buildings of Tenakee Springs to create an unusual and appealing town.

SE032 Port Facilities
1977

Two large docks, a small ship dock, a sea plane dock, and a helipad, built by the Alaska Department of Transportation, give Tenakee Springs thoroughly modern port facilities.

SE033 Bathhouse
1940

The mineral springs, at the center of the community, are free to the public and serve as a recreational and social focal point. The springs have been improved for bathing several times beginning about 1900. The present concrete building with concrete tub was built by the Civilian Conservation Corps. To it is attached a frame changing house.

SE034 Snyder Mercantile Company

c. 1899

Just next to the bathhouse is the Snyder Mercantile Company, still the commercial lifeline of the town. It is a large, two-story, wood-framed building on piling with false fronts on both the water and road sides.

SE035 Mineral Springs Cafe

early twentieth century

This early building, just east of the Snyder Mercantile Company, is similar to it in construction, again with two false fronts.

SE036 Tenakee Springs School

c. 1987–1988, Minch, Ritter, Voelkers, Architects

The state school program provides this tiny community with a large, modern school building serving a handful of students in grades kindergarten through high school. The award-winning, distinctively angular wooden building is located high up a long flight of steps from the street on a site leveled at great expense.

Angoon

Across the Chatham Strait, on the west shore of Admiralty Island, the Tlingit community of Angoon retains a mix of buildings that demonstrates its architectural growth. It was originally a community of traditional plank houses, facing the beach, but the settlement was shelled by the U.S. Navy after a misunderstanding in 1882. The clan houses that were built to replace those that were destroyed still line the beach today. Constructed in part by a nearby whaling company, the houses are gable fronted like the plank houses, but wood frame with horizontal siding, featuring windows and doors. Interrupting this purely American architecture, however, are hints of lingering traditional ways. Some of the houses were one open room, maintaining the plan of the plank houses, if not the structure. In addition, paintings on the fronts of the houses continue a long tradition, as do the gable fronts, the small platforms at the entrance, and the orientation toward the water.

In 1917, a community hall—a plain, warehouselike building on pilings—was constructed. With the founding of a local chapter of the Alaska Native Brotherhood in 1921, it became the ANB Hall. It is now the City Hall and has new siding on three sides. In 1918, a Presbyterian church was constructed. In 1928, after the nearby village of Killisnoo burned, many of the survivors moved to Angoon, bringing their Russian Orthodox religion with them. Recent houses have been constructed on the bluff, and the older houses along the shoreline have received new sidings and additions, but Angoon's architectural heritage is still apparent in the gable-fronted houses lining the shore.

SE037 Killer Whale House

1880s

The Killer Whale House, which features an exterior painting of two whales facing away from each other, was photographed in 1890 and remains remarkably unchanged. It is a one-and-a-half-story, wood-framed house with beveled siding and a gable front. Paired windows flank the central door. Modifications include a shed dormer, new window sash, and additions to the side. When constructed, the

SE039a Saint John the Baptist Russian Orthodox Church (exterior)

house was one large room, reflecting the traditional arrangement for dwellings, but partitions were added in the early twentieth century. The painting on the front was obscured in 1928, when the village was preparing to host a meeting of the Alaska Native Brotherhood, which at that time advocated the adoption of modern ways. The killer whales have been repainted in recent years.

SE038 Presbyterian Church

1918–1919. 1979, addition

The Presbyterian Church is a small, gable-roofed building. Wood framed with beveled siding, the building has a square bell tower at one corner of the front, through which is the entrance. Triple windows ornament the gable front and exposed rafter ends and brackets in the gable enliven the roofline. A large addition to one side, constructed in 1979, gives the building its current L-plan.

SE039 Saint John the Baptist Russian Orthodox Church

1929

Set on a bluff, slightly apart from the village, Saint John the Baptist was constructed in 1929. After the nearby village of Killisnoo burned, survivors from the village, who were

Russian Orthodox, moved to Angoon and established this church. The tall, gable-roofed church is rectangular, with the sanctuary incorporated into the main block of the nave and lit by windows in the east end. The rafter ends of the steeply pitched gable roof are exposed, and there are brackets in the gable end. The roof is crowned by a hexagonal belfry with round-arch openings, and an elongated onion dome rises from its peak. The nave and sanctuary rise to a tray ceiling of narrow beaded boards, which cover the wainscot as well.

SE039b Saint John the Baptist Russian Orthodox Church (iconostas)

Sitka

Sitka lies in a protected harbor on the western shore of Baranof Island. Once the capital of Russian America, its architecture represents elements of the three cultures—Native, Russian, and American—that are the legacy of Alaska. A group of Tlingit lived in the area and resisted the Russian-American Company's first attempt to establish a stronghold here in 1799. Those Natives were finally driven out by the company in 1804, however, and it was not until the 1820s that they were permitted back on the island. They then established a community on the northwest side of town, just outside a stockade built by the Russians. They replaced their traditional plank houses with American-style dwellings by the 1890s, and a few of these second-generation buildings remain—large gable-fronted buildings on Katlian Street.

The Russians occupied Sitka in 1804 and in 1808 moved the capital here from Kodiak. As the hub of government, trade, and religion in the Russian colony, Sitka was also the cultural center. Visitors commented on the Russians' lavish hospitality; at the governor's house, parties featured music, dancing, and imported liquors. Most importantly, Sitka was a port city, with shipbuilding facilities and a steady stream of visiting vessels.

The buildings were generally constructed of hewn logs of large Sitka spruce that had been logged locally and ranged from one-room houses to three-story barracks. In 1816, Sitka's first church was built, but it was replaced in the 1830s and again in 1844–1848. The latter was a cathedral. Located in the center of the main street, it was an impressive cruciform structure featuring an octagonal dome at the crossing and an 84-foot bell tower.

Russia's transfer of Alaska to the United States in 1867 was marked by a small ceremony in Sitka, at which the Russian flag was lowered and the Stars and Stripes raised. The site of this event, Castle Hill, has been designated a National Historic Landmark. The Russian governor's mansion dominated the city from atop this promontory; it was destroyed by fire in 1894. Sitka's main street was named Lincoln Street, and after an initial frenzy of entrepreneurial activity, Sitka settled into quiet times, although it served as the capital of Alaska until 1900. Sheldon Jackson, the indefatigable Presbyterian missionary, made Sitka the focus of his efforts beginning in 1882, running a vocational school for Natives, founding a museum of Native artifacts, and advocating the replacement of Native dwellings with modern American ones.

By the early twentieth century, salmon canneries and commercial fishing were the mainstays of the town's economy, as they continue to be today. The Naval Operating Base on Japonski Island across Sitka Harbor caused a flurry of activity in Sitka during the Second World War; after the war the base was turned over to the Bureau of Indian Affairs, which established a Native boarding school there. Previously connected by ferry, the island is now served by the O'Connell

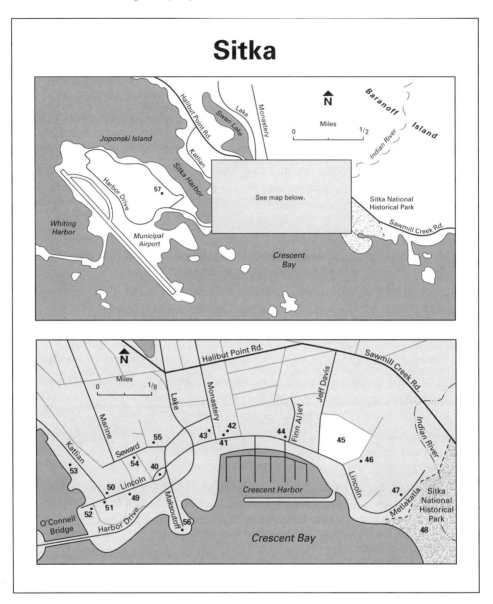

Bridge, the first cable-stayed, girder-span bridge in the U.S., completed in 1972. The construction of a pulp mill in 1960 further broadened Sitka's economic base.

Although the commercial heart of town continues to be Lincoln Street, which runs parallel to the shoreline, a devastating fire in 1966 destroyed the cathedral and neighboring commercial structures. Consequently, the street does not have the architectural cohesion found on most main streets. It still functions as the main street, however, stretching about a mile east to west, from a collection of totem poles on a battleground, past the former missionary school (now Sheldon Jackson College), past a residential area and a recreational harbor, past the rebuilt cathedral in the commercial center to the working harbor near the original Indian Village. To walk it is to walk through time and cultures, as reflected in the buildings.

SE040 Saint Michael the Archangel Russian Orthodox Church

1966, Sergei Padukov (after Bishop Innocent's design for the 1848 church). Lincoln and Maksoutoff streets

As the center of Russian Orthodoxy in Alaska, Saint Michael's Cathedral is appropriately large, prominently placed, and Russian in appearance. Faithfully reconstructed after the 1966 fire, the building was designed originally by Bishop Innocent and completed in 1848. Its cruciform plan, large octagonal dome, and division into elements of sanctuary, nave, and bell tower are hallmarks of Alaskan Russian Orthodox churches.

Before Bishop Innocent arrived in Sitka, he had spent ten years at Unalaska, where he had earned the admiration and respect of the Aleuts, made many converts, and designed and built a church. In 1834 he was assigned to Sitka, where a new church had just been constructed. In 1840, he was consecrated as Bishop Innocent, the first Bishop of Kamchatka, the Kurile and Aleutian Islands. The seat of this bishopric was Sitka, so a cathedral was required. Bishop Innocent designed it himself; the Russian-American Company financed construction. The cornerstone was laid in 1844, and on 20 November 1848, the cathedral was dedicated.

Although the administration of Russian Orthodoxy in Alaska has changed over the years, Sitka has remained the spiritual and administrative center of the church in Alaska, and Saint Michael's Cathedral is its physical embodiment. In 1960–1961, the Historic American Buildings Survey drew the building from measurements taken in the 1940s. It was the first building documented by HABS in the territory. In 1962, Saint Michael's was designated a National Historic Landmark. Just four years later, on 2 January 1966, the cathedral burned to the ground in a fire that destroyed much of downtown Sitka. Although most of the icons were saved, the

SE040a Saint Michael the Archangel Russian Orthodox Church (exterior)

SE040b Saint Michael the Archangel Russian Orthodox Church (iconostas)

building was a complete loss. The Russian Orthodox people rallied, however, and the building was reconstructed. The loss of the cathedral even provoked a resurgence of the faith, which had been in decline.

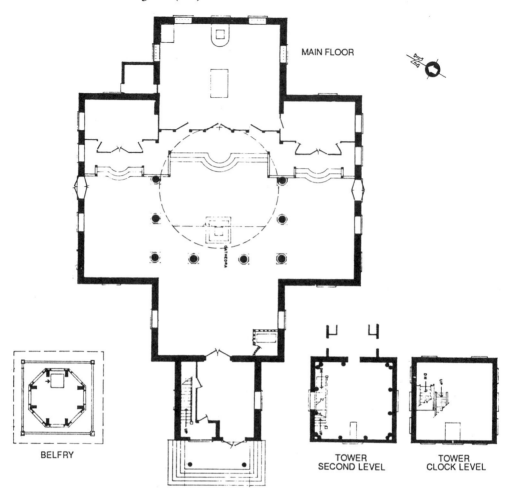

MAIN FLOOR

BELFRY

TOWER
SECOND LEVEL

TOWER
CLOCK LEVEL

SE040c Saint Michael the Archangel Russian Orthodox Church (floor plan)

The HABS drawings proved invaluable in the reconstruction of the church. Restoration architect Sergei Padukov of Toms River, New Jersey, adhered to the drawings as closely as possible, substituting fireproof materials for the original log construction. The building measures 67 feet by 97 feet and is in the plan of a Greek cross, with a squarish (15 foot by 18 foot) bell tower on the west end. Originally log, the building is now constructed of steel and concrete, but gray, beaded clapboarding covers the exterior, as it did originally. At the crossing of the gable-roofed nave and transepts, a large octagonal drum, 22 feet in diameter on the interior, supports a copper-clad dome, on top of which is a much smaller cupola and onion dome. The four-story bell tower, with different fenestration at each level,

supports an octagonal belfry, on top of which is an attenuated onion dome. The profile of these various domes, rising out of a low mass, is striking and distinctive.

On the interior, there are three altars. The main altar, located in the sanctuary projecting from the rear of the building, is screened by an elaborate seven-bay iconostas. Light is shed on this iconostas from windows in the dome above, which rises nearly 40 feet from the ground, in sharp contrast to the 11-foot height of the rest of the nave. Four Doric columns, as opposed to the original eight, support the ceiling at the base of the dome. The side chapels are located in the transepts, which are open to the nave. In each side chapel, the iconostas is slightly unusual; the paired royal doors are in the center, but the secondary doors are perpendicular to the royal doors, rather than being in the same plane. The south altar is dedicated to Saint Innocent the Apostle to America (Bishop Innocent was canonized in 1977), and the north chapel to Our Lady of Kazan.

The interior finish of the cathedral, which consists of linoleum on the floor and sailcloth tacked to the walls, only serves to heighten the beauty of the iconostas and icons. The iconostas is white with gold trim. The gilded royal doors are particularly stunning, and behind them, the altar is a shimmering gold. The main icons on the iconostas are covered with silver rizas. The cathedral's icon collection is particularly rich; two of them depicting Saint Michael the Archangel originally hung in Sitka's first church, constructed in 1816. In addition to those on the iconostas, the cathedral has five exhibit cases of icons. During the fire, all of the icons were rescued, except one depicting the Last Supper, which hung over the royal doors.

Saint Michael's has the air of a big-city cathedral, with tourists constantly strolling in and out and a low hum of activity. The setting is also reminiscent of a metropolitan cathedral, being in the heart of downtown Sitka, with the cathedral dividing Lincoln Street and traffic passing by. Neighboring buildings range from one-story stores to an eight-story apartment building, but Saint Michael's Cathedral has an unmistakable presence and manages to silence them all.

SE041 **Russian Bishop's House**

1842–1844. Lincoln and Monastery streets

One of only a handful of Russian-era buildings extant in Alaska, the Russian Bishop's House is a superbly restored two-story log building. Designated a National Historic Landmark, the building is operated as a museum by the National Park Service and open to the public.

The Russian-American Company constructed this building for the bishop to use as a residence and school. Adolph Etholen, the Finnish general manager of the company from 1840–1845, responding to a directive that the company provide adequate housing and maintenance for the clergy, undertook a building campaign during his tenure. Bishop Innocent, the first occupant, directed the design. The bishop's quarters and a chapel were on the second floor, while the first floor accommodated a seminary for Creoles—those of mixed Russian and native blood—as well as the offices of the church. The building remained an ecclesiastical and educational center in Alaska until the mid-twentieth century.

Because of the extensive research and restoration work undertaken by the National Park Service, more is known about this building than any of the other Russian buildings in Alaska. Of particular interest are its form, its structure, and its heating and ventilation systems, all of which were, if not widely used, at least familiar to builders. The main block of the two-story building has a hipped roof and a nine-bay front; it measures 64 feet by 43 feet. There are entrances on either end, shed-roofed galleries, heavy timber-framed two-story stairway and entrance halls. The front of the building, which with the galleries extended over 90 feet, faced south, toward the water, and was covered with horizontal boards and painted a yellow ocher color. The roof was clad with metal and painted red.

Like most of the Russian buildings, this one was constructed of hewn logs laid horizontally. Set on stone foundations, they were hewn to a depth of 8 1/2 inches and ranged from 10 inches to 19 inches in height. The logs were joined at the corners by a double lap joint; grooved on the bottom to fit snugly over the log below, they were chinked with moss and oakum. Vertical wooden dowels or driftpins were occasionally placed in the long expanses of logs to keep them from slipping. Supported by an intricate system of beams and joists, running in opposite directions on the first and second floors, the flooring consisted of planks running north-south on the first floor and east-west on the second, adding rigidity to the structure.

The methods of insulating, heating, and ventilating this building also shed light on standard Russian building practices of the time. Heat loss was prevented through the galleries, which functioned as air locks; there was no direct entry into the living quarters of the house. Between floors, there was a 3-inch layer of sand and wood shavings supported by a layer of planking. The building was heated by metal stoves on the first floor and masonry ones on the second. The metal stoves, none of which survived, were cylindrical, riveted sheet iron, lined with firebrick. The masonry stoves radiated heat through the brick

SE041a Russian Bishop's House
(exterior)

SE041b Russian Bishop's House
(parlor)

when the chimney was closed. Ventilation was aided by the use of partitions—7-foot-high plank walls—rather than full-height walls to divide rooms. Particularly high thresholds, from 1 inches to 6 inches, were used to reduce drafts between rooms. Fortochkas (brass tubes with caps) were used to penetrate the exterior walls and admit fresh air.

The only major change to the building over the years has been the replacement of the galleries, which occurred in 1887. At that time, they were decreased in height somewhat and brought under the slope of the extended hip roof. In its restoration the National Park Service reconstructed the original, two-story, shed-roofed galleries. The west gallery had windows, while the east gallery did not, although windows were painted in to preserve the symmetry.

Today, the first floor functions as exhibit space, while the second floor is a house museum, restored to the 1842–1853 period of Bishop Innocent's occupancy. On the first floor, one room has been peeled away to reveal the layers of construction. Flooring has

been removed to show the beams, insulation, and subfloor. Cloth, which would have then been painted or wallpapered, has been removed from the walls to show the logs, and cloth covering the ceiling has been removed to show planks and beams. Much of what is exposed is new wood; during restoration 75 percent of the front (south) wall had to be replaced up to the level of the second-floor window sills. Instead of logs, the Park Service used three 3-inch-wide planks (for a total width of 9 inches), half-lapped. Overall, about 70 percent of the building is the original wood. At the corners, logs were joined with simple lap joints, bolted.

On the second floor, the parlor is in the center of the north side (shown in the accompanying photograph), while the chapel is in the southwest corner. The Chapel of the Annunciation, the oldest Russian Orthodox chapel in Alaska, has exposed log walls and an uncarpeted floor, as it had originally. The iconostas is wallpapered, and most of the icons were in the chapel when it was acquired by the National Park Service. The chapel was reconsecrated after restoration, and is maintained by a warden from Saint Michael's Cathedral. Old inventories have been used to guide the furnishing of the rest of the second floor; some items have been replicated, while others are original. Wallpaper has been reproduced to replicate the original. Carpeting and upholstery are modern-day equivalents of materials likely to have been used. The ceiling is sailcloth.

The care that has been taken in this restoration reflects the significance of this Russian-era building and the relatively unaltered condition in which it remained. The quality of the meticulous restoration should stand as a model for other such projects in Alaska. Besides the obvious result of the restoration—the presence of this historically accurate building—our understanding of Russian-American architecture has been advanced immeasurably.

SE042 **Russian Orthodox School**

1897. Lincoln St.

This two-story, simple wood-framed house was constructed in 1897 adjacent to the Bishop's House and served as a Russian Orthodox school until 1922, when it became a public school. The gable end of the building is toward the street, but the entrance is in the long side, which is four bays long. The novelty-sided building measures 33 feet by 18 feet. Constructed by James Shields, the building cost $700. An enclosed stairway was added on the north, probably in about 1908, when the building received $300 worth of repairs.

When the school was rented to the city for use as a public school in 1922, the entrance on the west side, next to the Russian Bishop's House, was closed and a new one added to the east side. Partitions were added on the interior, perhaps when the building was rented for housing. The National Park Service has restored the exterior of the building, changing the entrance back to the east side.

SE043 **House 105**

1887. Monastery St.

Constructed by the Russian Orthodox church for rental income, the small house just northwest of the Russian Bishop's House was built by Peter Callsen, along with two other build-

ings for a total of $2,600. The 32-foot-by-24-foot building has a wood frame, covered with clapboards. The one-and-a-half-story, gable-roofed structure is three bays wide. The first floor has a center hall and two rooms on each side, while the attic is one room, lit only by windows in the gables.

Deriving its name from the building it replaced, which was designated no. 105 on the map drawn at the time Alaska was transferred to the United States, the house was originally located directly north of the Bishop's House. It was moved to its present site in the 1950s or 1960s. The exterior has been restored by the National Park Service, but the interior is not open to the public.

SE044 **Saint Peter's-by-the-Sea Episcopal Church**

1899, H. L. Duhring, Jr. 611 Lincoln St.

The newly named Episcopal bishop of Alaska, Peter Trimble Rowe, had this church built in 1899. Rowe took ideas for its designs back east, where Philadelphian George C. Thomas, treasurer of the Board of Missions of the Episcopal Church, hired architect H. L. Duhring, Jr., also of Philadelphia. John W. Dudley supervised construction, which was completed by Thanksgiving 1899.

One of the few stone buildings in Alaska, Saint Peter's Church has the heavy timbering, random rubble stone, and wood shingling characteristic of small ecclesiological churches

SE045 Sheldon Jackson College

of the late nineteenth century. Set on a stone foundation, the church is constructed of a heavy timber frame, filled with rubble stone nogging. (The accompanying photograph is historic, probably taken soon after construction; at some time, all of the stone was removed and relaid, and some diagonal bracing was removed.) Stone buttresses help support the walls. Windows of the nave have round arches, and there is a rose window in the front gable, set in a large pointed arch framed by the gable. This motif—characteristic of many small Richardsonian churches—is repeated in the small vestibule directly below. A square belfry, now equipped with louvers, but originally open, rises from the front of the gable roof and is topped with a tall pyramidal roof. The shingles on the roof are unpainted, whereas the shingles covering the gable end and the sides of the belfry are painted brown.

On the interior, the ceiling is supported by exposed wooden scissor trusses. The dark wood diagonal boards of the ceiling contrast with the white walls. Stained-glass windows and the original wooden pews create a subdued atmosphere. The reredos, added in 1932, was designed by Lester Troast, an architect who taught at the Sheldon Jackson School before setting up his architectural practice in Juneau.

SE044.1 See House

1905, H. L. Duhring, Jr.

Just behind the church is the See House, the home of Bishop Peter Trimble Rowe. Al-though designed by Philadelphia architect H. L. Duhring, Jr., at the same time he designed the church, construction was delayed on the house. Finally, in 1905, Rowe built his house, doing most of the construction work himself.

The house is a splendid example of the provincial Shingle style, complementing the church. Two and a half stories in height and irregular in plan, the wood-shingled building has a variety of projections, bays, and oriels. The wood-shingled hip roof and a stone chimney add to the rustic textures.

Rowe and his family did not stay here long. Faced with the decline of Sitka as the center of Alaska's trade and politics and desiring better medical care for his ailing wife, Rowe moved his office to Seattle in 1912, although he was buried in Sitka after his death in 1942. This house served as the rectory for the church—one of the grandest houses in the town.

SE045 Sheldon Jackson College

1910–1911, Ludlow and Peabody. Lincoln St.

The formally planned campus of Sheldon Jackson College is one of the few assemblages of buildings in Alaska axially arranged around an open space. The formality of the campus reflects the training of the architects, the New York firm of Ludlow and Peabody. Charles F. Peabody studied at the Ecole des Beaux-Arts while his partner, William Orr Ludlow, had worked in the office of Carrère and Hastings. Ludlow and Peabody formed a partnership in 1909 and the next year designed this campus. Five major buildings, symmetrically placed in a half-quadrangle plan, look south toward the water and present a fine appearance to the harbor. The central building, Allen Memorial, housed a gymnasium-auditorium on the first floor and four classrooms on the second. Adjacent buildings were dormitories. The two-story buildings share a similar massing, emphasized by hip roofs with jerkinhead gables; they have wood frames, covered with shingles on the first floor and board-and-batten siding on the second. Edwin Crittenden, the current campus architect, has described their architectural recipe as "Eclectic Tudor Gothic mixed a little with Eastern Stick and a pinch of Greene and Greene's Bungalow Craftsman stirred in with some Adirondack Lodge."

Founded as the Sitka Mission in 1878, the school is the oldest educational institution in the state. The boarding school, providing an eighth-grade education, was established by John G. Brady to train Native boys in American vocations and ways. Brady was a Presbyterian missionary who later became governor of Alaska. But it was the force and energy of the untiring Sheldon Jackson, another Presbyterian missionary, who saw to the school's survival. When its building burned in 1882, Jackson undertook a fund-raising campaign, cleared a new site, used lumber from an abandoned cannery 6 miles away, and constructed a 50-foot-by-100-foot, three-story building on this site. In 1884 the Presbyterian girls' school was transferred to Sitka from Wrangell, and construction continued through the 1880s and 1890s.

In 1910–1911, most of the then-existing buildings were demolished and the present campus constructed. At the same time, the school changed its name from the Sitka Industrial and Training School to the Sheldon Jackson School. In 1917, Sheldon Jackson High School was established, in 1944 the junior college opened and non-Natives were admitted, and in 1976 it offered its first four-year program.

Additional buildings have since been added in a way that respects the 1910–1911 Ludlow and Peabody design. One pre-existing building, the Sheldon Jackson Museum, stands off to the southeast; nearby a library designed by Waldron and Dietz, architects from Seattle, was constructed in 1974. Other new buildings are generally located behind the original five. The harmony of the original buildings and the compatibility of the later ones combine with an unusual respect for the landscape to make this an extremely attractive campus.

SE046 Sheldon Jackson Museum

1895, John J. Smith. Lincoln St.

The first concrete building in Alaska, this octagonal building was constructed in 1895 to house the collections of the Alaskan Natural History and Ethnology Society. Presbyterian missionary Sheldon Jackson was fascinated by Native artifacts, even as he was persuading Natives to abandon their traditional ways, and he was an avid collector. With a group of like-minded people in Sitka, he formed the society in 1887. Jackson had the first museum building constructed in 1888, a simple wood-framed building painted to resemble a Tlingit plank house.

John J. Smith, an architect from Boston, designed the replacement building. Concrete was chosen as the construction material for its fireproof qualities, important for a museum. Smith also recommended, however, that concrete—a material that was inexpensive because most of its ingredients were locally available—be used for Native houses as well. The octagonal plan, 67 feet in diameter, provided for a spacious interior with easy circulation. The original design called for a Georgian Revival doorway, but it was constructed with a Gothic motif, with concrete crenellations. This ornament has been removed, and the original entrance is now reserved for emergency exit use.

Artifacts, many collected by Sheldon Jackson between 1888 and 1898 and most predating 1930, represent all of the Native cultures of Alaska. They are arranged in original display cases, which include stacks of drawers as well as the usual glass-topped cases.

Sheldon Jackson College operated the museum until the state acquired it in 1983. In 1984–1985, restoration of the building included the installation of a new, steel-framed roof above the original wood-framed one. An addition to the rear of the building provides an entrance and space for offices. Painted a dark brown color to conform to the buildings on the adjacent Sheldon Jackson College campus, the museum retains a woodsy appearance, despite its material and unusual shape. Still exhibiting Jackson's Native artifacts, the museum is an intriguing illustration of the antiquarian impulse.

SE047 **Model Cottage**

late 1880s. 105 Metlakatla St.

In order to accommodate graduates of the Sitka Industrial and Training School, the Presbyterians set up a revolving-loan fund, enabling these Natives to build American-style houses for themselves. In theory, the young men, trained as builders, married the young women, schooled in the household arts. With these loans, they could build their own houses, eight of which were constructed on Metlakatla and Kelly streets in the 1880s and early 1890s.

The one-and-a-half-story houses were three bays wide, with a central door. Square in plan, 24 feet on a side, the houses had side-gable roofs that extended to cover a lower rear portion. The wood-framed buildings were covered with beveled siding, and there was scalloped ornament at the cornice. On the interior, the living room stretched across the front, with the kitchen, pantry, and wood closet behind; the stairway was in the center of the rear. The second floor had two bedrooms.

Only one of these houses survives, but it has been little altered. The one-bay porch at the front door has been enclosed, and the building has been extended in the rear about 4 feet. A large addition on one side is under construction, but the original scale and charm are still apparent in this model cottage, built to display Native abilities, while instilling an American way of life.

SE048 **Totem Poles and House Posts**

Sitka National Historical Park, 106 Metlakatla St.

The Sitka National Historical Park has an impressive collection of totem poles and house posts. Although detached from their houses and their history, the poles are an aesthetic achievement within themselves, and a remnant of an important aspect of Native architecture. Although many have been replicated, no original totem poles or house posts in Alaska remain on their original sites with their traditional dwellings. Although the park has some fragments of older poles in its collection, all of the poles displayed outdoors date from the 1930s or later.

Totem poles, which are usually about 30 feet tall (although the tallest here is 55 feet), are carved, freestanding cedar or spruce poles, representing a story or commemorating an individual or event. They were made by both the Haida and the southern Tlingit. Both Haida and Tlingit placed house posts—carved planks—on the outside corners of their houses or used them as interior structural members. Memorial or mortuary poles might have one image at the top relating to the clan of the person thus memorialized. Other poles and posts had a progression of carved or painted images, which do not convey a story as much as refer to one that is known by the intended viewers.

The poles at Sitka National Historical Park originated with a group amassed by Gov.

John G. Brady in 1901–1904. In 1903, Brady collected poles from Haida and southern Tlingit to exhibit at the Louisiana Purchase Exposition in Saint Louis. After the fair, some of these poles found their way back to Sitka, where they were exhibited in this park with others.

As the poles stand outdoors and are planted in the ground, they are subject to deterioration. In 1939–1940, the U.S. government supported a program to replicate poles, employing Native carvers with Works Progress Administration and Civilian Conservation Corps funds. Seven of these reproduction poles survive. Additional poles have been replicated by master carvers in the last decade or two. The National Park Service held a design competition for a bicentennial pole in 1976; it is the only contemporary piece.

The outdoor poles are set in a dense grove of mature spruce, lining a path along the shoreline that leads to the site of the Tlingit fort and 1804 battleground. The serenity of the location provides a romanticized setting in which to examine and contemplate these always intriguing and frequently haunting images.

SE049 Russian-American Company Building No. 29

1850s. 202–206 Lincoln St.

One of the few Russian-era buildings in Alaska is hidden behind clapboarding, altered fenestration, and additions. Designated Building No. 29 on the map that accompanied the transfer of Alaska to the United States, this structure was built by the Russian-American Company, probably in the 1850s.

The two-story log structure was originally three bays wide, with a gable roof. The logs were grooved on the bottoms to fit over the ones below; they were also marked with both Roman and Arabic numerals and dovetailed at the corners. Shortly after construction, a two-story, shed-roofed gallery was added to the west end, functioning as an entrance, stairway, and air lock, as at the Russian Bishop's House. In the 1880s another two-bay addition was constructed at the west end, incorporating the gallery under its gable roof. Four gable dormers were added to what had become a six-bay structure. In the 1960s, a storefront window and entrance at the northeast corner were introduced, eliminating one of the original window openings.

In 1867, the Russian-American Company sold this building to William Dodge, acting customs collector and first mayor of Sitka. Through the years, the building has passed through several hands and has been primarily used as commercial retail space on the ground floor and as a residence above. During a recent renovation, a layer of sand suspended in canvas nailed to the ceiling was removed. Large brick bake ovens are still in the basement.

Although the origins of this building are not readily apparent, Building No. 29 is a rare survivor of the Russian-American Company's governance of Alaska. It has been designated a National Historic Landmark.

SE050 Pioneers' Home

1934–1935, Heath, Gove and Bell. Katlian Ave. and Lincoln St.

Pioneers' Homes, state-supported old-age homes for men, were first legislated in 1913. After using abandoned military buildings in Sitka, the Pioneers' Home began construction on new buildings in 1934. Heath, Gove and Bell of Tacoma, Washington, designed the complex.

Of concrete construction, the main three-story building is in an open U-plan. The stucco walls, painted yellow, contrast with the red-tile hip roof. A corbeled cornice and various projections, including a sun porch across the front, give the building a slightly ungainly appearance, but as the largest building in Sitka, located on a spacious lot across from a park on the water, it is undeniably prominent. Auxiliary structures, such as the manager's house and nurses' quarters, were built in 1935 in a compatible style; a 1956 addition in the rear was constructed to accommodate women. The statue *The Prospector,* sculpted by Alonzo Victor Lewis in 1949, stands in front of the building.

SE051 U.S. Post Office and Court House

1937–1938, Gilbert Stanley Underwood. Lincoln St. and Katlian Ave.

Built to replace the previous federal building, which had been destroyed by fire, the Sitka Post Office and Courthouse is a Moderne, concrete structure. Designed by Gilbert Stanley Underwood, the building was constructed by J. B. Warrack Company for $155,888. The main block of the building is five bays long and rises two stories above a raised basement. The first- and second-floor windows are joined vertically by slightly recessed, ornamented spandrels. A shallow belt course across the tops of the second-story windows and flat circles framing the lettering across the top of the building constitute the only other ornament on the facade. The roof is flat and there is no cornice. At either end of the main block are one-story wings, one bay wide. On the interior, the post office lobby on the first floor has quarry tile flooring and wainscoting. At present, the post office has moved out and the building's future is uncertain.

Concrete construction was introduced to Alaska at the Sheldon Jackson Museum, located at the other end of Lincoln Street. It reached its culmination in this building, a sleek, modern structure that makes the most of its flat surfaces by presenting a pure form.

SE052 Cable Office

1904. 2 Lincoln St.

WAMCATS, the Washington-Alaska Military Cable and Telegraph System, succeeded in linking military bases in Alaska with those in the rest of the country (without going through Canada) through both underwater and overland cables. Sitka proved to be a pivotal location on the system, a link between Seattle and Valdez, all served by submarine cable. At Valdez, the system went overland as far as Saint Michael on Norton Sound. It was altogether an engineering triumph that was authorized by Congress in 1900; by August 1904, Seattle and Sitka were linked, and two months later Valdez and Sitka.

This building was constructed, probably in 1904, to house the telegraph terminal and switching equipment, although it has a distinctly residential character. The square house, 40 feet on a side, is two stories, with a pyramidal roof with wide bracketed eaves. Its wood-framed construction is now clad with aluminum siding, but the simple lines of the building have been maintained. By 1931, the cable had been replaced by a network of radio stations, but the building continues to operate as a communications center.

SE053 Alaska Native Brotherhood Hall, Sitka Camp No. 1

1914. Katlian St.

Founded in Sitka in 1912, the Alaska Native Brotherhood fought widespread discrimination against Natives. The Brotherhood, initially a Tlingit organization, operated through local camps, of which this one in Sitka was the first. Built in 1914 by Sitka Camp No. 1, this Craftsman-style structure is a two-story, wood-framed building extending out over the water; the building has a metal-covered gable roof. The first story and gable are clad with green-painted wooden shingles, while the second story has clapboards, painted white. Exposed rafter ends and brackets supporting the purlins add further decorative effect. On the interior is an auditorium with a stage at the far end and a shallow balcony around the other three sides. As a symbol of the political power of the Natives, this building has interest far beyond its architecture.

SE054 U.S. Coast and Geodetic Survey House

1916. 210 Seward St.

This building housed the U.S. Coast and Geodetic Survey staff, who monitored a magnetic observatory located on Observatory Street; when that observatory was linked to the house by a remote hookup, readings could be taken within the house. After a seismometer was installed in the basement in 1929, seismic readings were taken here as well. In 1940, this operation moved to new, larger quarters on Geodetic Way. The U.S. Forest Service has occupied the house since 1961.

This gambrel-roofed cottage measures 36 feet by 26 feet and is one and a half stories tall. A large, pedimented gable dormer centered in the front and a small shed-roofed vestibule below add to the size of this wood-framed, clapboarded dwelling.

SE055 May Mills House

1911–1913, Clyde A. Maclaren. 315 Seward St.

Occupying a prominent site overlooking downtown Sitka, the Colonial Revival-style May Mills house is a two-and-a-half-story, wood-framed structure with clapboard siding. The gable roof extends to cover a two-story, two-level porch across the front of the house, featuring four box columns at each level, delineating the three bays of the front facade. The first level of the porch has been enclosed with glass. Colonial Revival details include three Palladian windows, two in the gable ends and one in a gable-roofed dormer located in the center of the front. The house was designed by Seattle architect Clyde A. Maclaren for May Mills, sister of Sitka merchant and banker W. P. Mills.

SE056 W. P. Mills House

1916, Louis L. Mendal. 1 Maksoutoff St.

Set on a small island in the harbor, the W. P. Mills house is connected to Sitka by a 400-foot-long causeway, constructed in 1961. Previously, a succession of bridges performed that function. Designed in 1915 by architect Louis L. Mendal of Seattle for Sitka merchant and banker W. P. Mills (brother of May Mills), the house is best known for its views in all directions. The wood-shingled, wood-framed, one-and-a-half-story, gable-roofed house, constructed by local builder Tim Demedoff and completed in 1916, has large gable dormers and projecting bays. The thick stone foundations of this house survive from a Russian saltery, which had fallen into ruin long before the house was erected here.

SE057 Naval Operating Base

1939–1942. Japonski Island

Construction of the navy's first air station in Alaska began in Sitka in 1939. The facility received the designation of Naval Operating Base in 1942. With the Pacific theater moving farther away, the base was decommissioned in 1944. Since the war, Mount Edgecumbe School, a boarding school for Natives, has operated in these buildings. The surviving buildings and the setting still powerfully evoke the character of the air base of half a century ago.

The facilities were designed primarily for seaplanes, evidenced by two concrete ramps leading into the water. Because of the lack of level land, a short runway for wheeled planes, which survives, was equipped with arresting gear and catapults similar to those on an aircraft carrier. Other facilities associated with the Naval Operating Base include two metal-clad hangars (recently re-sided), a concrete two-story administration building, and a concrete auditorium. Most of the other buildings are residential in nature. One two-and-a-half-story barrack has shed-roofed dormers and clapboard-covered walls. It is connected to a two-story concrete barrack, which in turn is connected to the one-story concrete mess hall. The bachelor officers' quarters is a three-story concrete building, located near five du-plexes for officers and four single-family houses for higher-ranking officers. These smaller buildings, with gable roofs and clapboard sidings, have a domestic appearance enhanced by their location on the north side of the island, removed from the hangars and enlisted men's barracks.

Petersburg

One of the most picturesque villages in Southeast, Petersburg on Mitkof Island was founded in 1897 by Norwegian Peter Buschmann, who built a saw-mill and cannery here. Fellow Norwegians followed to create a flourishing fishing community. The population remained predominantly Norwegian until the mid-twentieth century, and the town's fishing industry is still a mainstay of the economy. The clearest remnant of the town in its early days is Sing Lee Alley, a narrow, curving street with a handful of false-fronted buildings, some of which are among the oldest in town. The waterfront is also lined with docks and canneries, and there are even some boathouses that have been converted to houses. Rising from the waterfront in a grid pattern, the rest of the town is characterized by neat bungalows with a pronounced frequency of shed-roofed dormers.

In an attempt to enhance Petersburg's reputation as Alaska's "Little Norway," a group of local women began doing rosemaling. This Norwegian folk painting tradition, usually reserved for furniture and wooden plates and bowls, met with a revival in the United States beginning in the 1930s. In the early 1970s, the Muskeg Maleriers began applying rosemaling to storefronts downtown and to shutters on residential buildings, giving Petersburg a distinctive appearance and thus creatively laying claim to a Norwegian heritage without drawing directly from it. At the same time, in a more general way this town of simple wooden buildings in a grandly picturesque setting rising behind a crowded harbor of small and large boats is similar to many coastal towns in Norway.

SE058 Sons of Norway Hall

SE058 Sons of Norway Hall

1912. Indian St.

Set on pilings over the water, this barnlike building was constructed in 1912. Lacking a public meeting place, Norwegians—who comprised the bulk of the population—constructed this hall for dances, basketball games, banquets, and conventions. It was renovated in 1985.

The two-and-a-half-story building, measuring 55 feet by 105 feet, has a gambrel roof with gable dormers. The wood-framed structure is covered with beveled siding. There is a hooded double door to the main hall and, along one side, a covered walkway and exterior stairway. On the other two sides, shutters decorated with rosemaling adorn the windows.

SE059 Machine Shop

1913. Harbor adjacent to downtown

Considering Petersburg's orientation toward the sea, one of the most expressive buildings in town is a purely functional one—a floating machine shop. This odd building was constructed on a barge, putting it level with the boats whose machines it is repairing regardless of the tides. The wood-framed building has beveled siding and a bowstring-truss roof. Still a functioning machine shop, it has always been tied up at this dock.

Wrangell

To the southeast on Wrangell Island, and connected by ferry to Petersburg and other points to the north and Ketchikan to the south, is the modern village of Wrangell. Although Wrangell has a fascinating history as the domain of four nations, its architectural character today is largely of the twentieth century. Fires in 1906 and 1952 have destroyed the cohesion of its commercial area. Today an architectural mixture of houses, ranging from early twentieth-century bungalows to modular prefabs, rises from the irregular shoreline. In a nod to Wrangell's heritage, a number of totem poles—all replicas—are sprinkled around town.

Once home of the Stikine Tlingit, Wrangell was occupied by the Russians in 1834. In an effort to prevent the British from gaining free access to the Stikine River, the Russians built Redoubt Saint Dionysius at the mouth of the river. In 1840 they leased it for ten years to the Hudson's Bay Company in return for provisions and furs; this lease was renewed periodically until 1865.

Under the British, the site was known as Fort Stikine, and with the discovery of gold up the Stikine River in Canada in 1861, it grew in importance as a supply point. After Alaska was acquired by the United States in 1867, the United States stationed troops here and named it Fort Wrangell, after the island on which it sat, which was named for the Russian Vice Admiral Baron von Wrangel. In the 1870s, gold strikes in the Cassiar region, also in Canada, were also reached through Wrangell, and for a few months each year Wrangell was the busiest town in Alaska, as recounted by historian Hubert Howe Bancroft. It was also exceedingly unimposing:

> The main street is choked with decaying logs and stumps and is passable only by a narrow plank sidewalk. Most of the habitations contain but one room, with sleeping rooms arranged round the walls and a stove in the center, and many of them have neither windows nor openings, except for

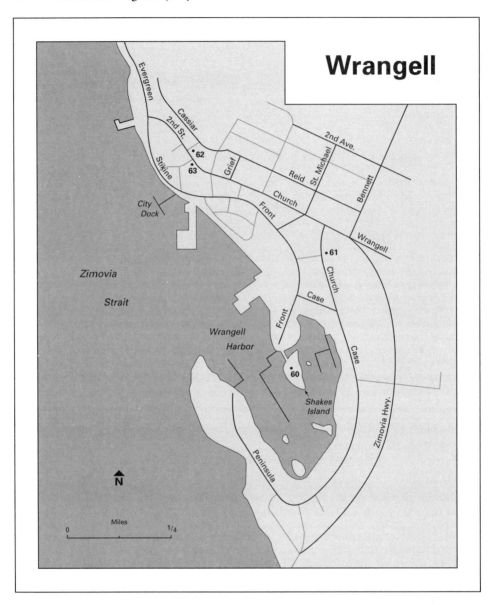

the chimney and a single door. (*History of Alaska, 1730–1885* [New York: Antiquarian Press, 1886], p. 678)

John Muir was even less impressed during his visit in 1879:

> The Wrangell village was a rough place. . . . It was a lawless draggle of wooden huts and houses, built in crooked lines, wrangling around the boggy shore of the island for a mile or so in the general form of the letter S, without the slightest subordination to the points of the compass or to building laws of any kind. (*Travels in Alaska* [1915; reprint, Boston: Houghton Mifflin, 1979], p. 25)

As one of Alaska's first boomtowns during the American period, Wrangell was a disorderly and uncivilized town. In 1877, the Presbyterian church attempted to counteract the deleterious effect of the wild Americans by establishing its first missionary effort in Alaska here in Wrangell, when Amanda R. MacFarland opened a school for Native girls. By 1880 it required five teachers, but in 1884 the boarding school was moved to Sitka.

Wrangell, no longer the roughest town in Alaska, continues to serve as a center for supplying and equipping outlying canneries and lumber mills.

SE060 Chief Shakes Community House

1939–1940, Linn A. Forrest. Shakes Island

As part of a program to preserve totem poles, the U.S. Forest Service, which since 1907 has administered most of the land in Southeast Alaska through the Tongass National Forest, constructed three traditional plank houses in southeast Alaska in 1939–1940. The work was directed by Linn A. Forrest, a young Forest Service architect, and executed by a Civilian Conservation Corps team of Native carvers trained by older Native carvers who recalled traditional carving techniques.

The traditional Tlingit dwelling was an intricate construction, with interior posts supporting the principal purlins of the gable roof. The plank walls were pierced by only one opening, in the center of the front. By the 1930s, Chief Shakes's House was the only traditional Tlingit dwelling remaining in all of Southeast Alaska, and it had a "modern" front, with windows and a door. The first clan house had been built on this site in 1834 and had been replaced twice before the present reconstruction.

This plank house is a complete reconstruction, using only the dimensions of the previous building, 40 feet by 43 feet. Vertical logs, hidden behind house posts, support the principal purlins; these then support the principal joists which, in turn, carried the minor purlins. The vertical plank walls, carefully adzed to resemble the original, are held with countersunk screws and pegged, unlike the original construction, which would have been pegged only. An intricate carving of a brown bear with many faces is applied to the front of the building, and entry is through its belly. This carving replicates one that adorned the clapboarded and windowed wall of the original house.

On the interior, the early nineteenth-century house posts that originally adorned this reconstruction were removed to the Wrangell Museum and replaced with replicas in 1985. The screen at the far end is a carving of a Chilkat blanket design. Three levels of flooring surround the central fire pit. Tools used in the construction of this house are on display in the back of the building.

There are also eight freestanding totem poles on the site, seven of them 1940 copies of historic poles; the eighth is a later one. A ninth pole, depicting three frogs, awaits replication.

SE061 Saint Philip's Episcopal Church

1903. 446 Church St.

Saint Philip's Episcopal Church has a design as unusual as its history. It is, in effect, a T-shaped cottage. The crossbar of the T is the front, accented by a side-gable roof and a double outside stairway (the latter dating from 1934). The entrance is through a pointed-arch doorway beneath a fish-scale-shingled cross gable. The nave of the church extends as the stem of the T. It is covered by a high hip roof, the front plane of which is a continuation of the roof over the entrance. Awkwardly placed at the peak of these roof planes is a small octagonal belfry. The building has beveled siding and tall windows with two-over-two lights that contain stained glass.

Built by Oscar Carlson and H. D. Campbell in 1903, the church was constructed as the Peoples' Church, a bold attempt to integrate the Presbyterian congregations. Rev. Harry P. Corser arrived in Wrangell in 1899 as minister for the First Presbyterian Church, a missionary church organized in 1879 for Tlingit, and for the Second Presbyterian Church, organized in 1898 for Americans. Leading a faction composed primarily of Tlingit dissatisfied with the discriminatory policies of the Presbyterian church, Corser founded a new congregation, which constructed this building in 1903 and named it the Peoples' Church.

Finally rejecting the Presbyterian church altogether, the Peoples' Church affiliated with the Episcopalians and in 1905 was renamed Saint Philip's. Corser was ordained an Episcopalian priest in 1907 and continued to serve this church until retirement in 1934.

SE062 **Wrangell Museum** (Wrangell Public School)

1906; 1912, enlarged. 126 Second St., corner of Bevier

The Wrangell Museum was built as a public school. It is one story, H-shaped in plan. Two wings face the front, connected by a recessed entryway reached by a double flight of stairs. Constructed in 1906, the building was enlarged in 1912, when both wings were extended toward the rear for an overall length of 83 feet. A bell tower in the center of the roof and ornamental shingles in the gables are the only decoration on an otherwise plain, bevel-sided building.

When the school building was converted to a museum in the 1960s, several partitions

SE062 Wrangell Museum (Wrangell Public School)

were removed. Windows in one half of the building have been painted over to protect the museum's collection.

SE063 **U.S. Post Office and Customs House**

1940, Hendrick P. Maas. Church St.

A handsome yet austere example of Moderne architecture, the Post Office and Customs House, designed by consulting architect Hendrick P. Mass, is constructed of reinforced concrete. The walls have been left rough finished, while the water table and spandrels are smooth. Eleven bays of windows are inset in panels, with recessed spandrels between the stories. The piers between them are ornamented with vertical lines. The roof is flat.

Despite the obvious addition of some mail boxes, the interior is virtually unaltered, with copper mail boxes, quarry tile floor and wainscot, and highly varnished wood-paneled walls. At one end there is a mural painting depicting Wrangell's history, signed by Marianne Appel and Austin Mecklen and dated 1943.

Kasaan

Old Kasaan, on Prince of Wales Island, was inhabited by the Kaigani Haida. In 1902–1904 the villagers moved to a new site a few miles away, attracted by the employment opportunities of a copper mine and a salmon cannery. The Kasaan Bay Mining Company built new cottages for the villagers. At the old site, traditional plank houses and totem poles were left, testifying to an abandoned way of life. Vandalism and outright thievery of the totem poles was so depleting this collection of artifacts that the U.S. Forest Service designated the site a national monument. By the time the wheels of the federal government had turned, however, it was too late: the village was destroyed by fire on 25 August 1915. The site was designated a monument over a year later; apparently officials in Washington had not been informed of the disaster. After years of uncertainty concerning the proper treatment of Old Kasaan, restoration was judged impossible or impractical, and the designation was revoked in 1955.

SE064 Chief Son-i-hat House

1880; 1938–1939, reconstruction, Linn A. Forrest. Totem Park

In 1880, Chief Son-i-hat left Old Kasaan, moved to a site close to what would become New Kasaan, and built a plank house. In 1938 the U.S. Forest Service found the house posts

and purlins still standing (as evidenced by the accompanying photograph) and decided to reconstruct the dwelling. Linn A. Forrest, architect for the Forest Service, based the plans for the reconstruction on the ruins of the house and instructed that as many parts as possible of the original dwelling be reused. Chief Son-i-hat's son, James Peele, was consulted about details, and the work was carried out by experienced Haida carvers, familiar with Native design and craftsmanship.

This Haida plank house is similar in design to the Tlingit, with four interior house posts carrying the framework of the roof. The building is about 44 feet square, with two levels around a fire pit. The vertical plank walls, split on the exterior and adzed smooth on the interior, are notched into sill and wall plates. Although Chief Son-i-hat's house is a 1938 construction, its careful adherence to a pre-existing building makes it an extremely faithful reproduction.

Ketchikan

Poised on the Tongass Narrows, at the site of a Tlingit fish camp, Ketchikan first attracted whites in 1887; the lure was both salmon and gold. With a population of 459 in 1900, Ketchikan was incorporated as a city, and by 1940 it was the second largest city in Alaska, with a population of 4,695. By then, interest in gold mining had been superseded by the fishing and lumber industries.

The city's architecture is dominated by the terrain. Because there is so little flat land, some buildings have been built on pilings over the water while others cling to the hillsides. Roads often dissolve into wooden stairways or boardwalks on trestles. The houses, which are either wood framed or concrete, are in the forms of cottages and bungalows. Basements are often exposed, although left unornamented. The houses abound with porches and picture windows—everyone gets a view of the water. Yards are most likely to be multilevel rock gardens.

There are a number of totem poles around town, including a fine collection at the Totem Heritage Center. Most notable is Chief Johnson's pole, in the

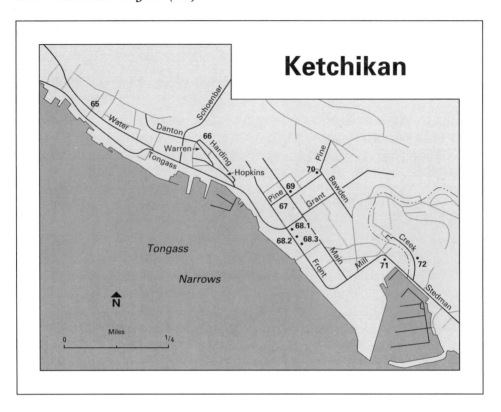

center of town at the corner of Steadman Street and Totem Way. Carved by Israel Shotridge and erected in 1989, it replicates the pole that stood on the site from 1901 to 1982 and was removed to the Totem Heritage Center for preservation.

Ketchikan's steep terrain and irregular street pattern create distinct, and sometimes tiny, neighborhoods, often with identifiable characteristics.

SE065 Captains' Hill

1904–1925. 1100–1400 blocks of Water St.

One interesting neighborhood because of its accommodation to terrain is Captains' Hill The houses are mostly bungalows in a variety of forms, each clinging to the cliff in its own way. The inhabitants were associated with the fishing industry, through the docks below, and many of them were Norwegian. Carl Foss, a Norwegian carpenter, is credited with building many of the houses. Although most of the buildings have been altered and none is a perfect example of a bungalow, their variety is appealing. The Norwegian community built the First Lutheran Church at the foot of Water Street in 1930.

SE066 Harding Street

Another peculiar neighborhood is that around Harding Street, where bungalows are tightly packed. Streets here are named Warren, G, and Harding, in honor of that president's visit to Ketchikan in 1923. Harding dissolves into Bayview Street, which is completely planked and built on a trestle. Several of the buildings have side-gable roofs with bracketed purlins in the gables.

SE067 Knob Hill

early twentieth century. 400 block of Front St.

Knob Hill has slightly larger houses than most

of those in Ketchikan. They were built early in the twentieth century for Ketchikan's merchant class. The buildings range from a shingled bungalow to a Tudor-style house with sweeping roofline. Front Street ends in a stairway down to the commercial area.

SE068 **Front Street**

1920s and later. 300 block Front St.

At the front edge of the commercial area facing the water, four buildings constructed in the 1920s and later, all faced with concrete or stucco, form a harmonious composition.

SE068.1 **Masonic Temple**

1947–1950. 352 Front St., corner of Grant St.

This handsome three-story building with a flat roof and rounded corners was built as a Masonic temple and still serves that purpose, with offices on the ground floor. Porthole windows at the end and sweeping aluminum marquees accent the Art Deco qualities of this unusual building.

SE068.2 **Citizens Light, Power and Water Company**

1925–1926, J. R. Nevins. 334 Front St.

This four-story building housing the public utilities and city hall was built as the Citizens Light, Power and Water Company Building in 1925–1926. Designed by Seattle architect J. R. Nevins, the flat-roofed building is divided by continuous piers into eight bays on the upper stories. The fourth story was a later addition, and the first story has been altered with a glass block storefront.

SE068.3 **Gilmore Hotel**

1926–1927, C. Frank Mahon. 326 Front St.

The Gilmore Hotel is a three-story building with Classical Revival ornament in the form of a modillioned cornice crowned by a red tile roof below the parapet. The 71-foot-long facade is divided into three bays, with four windows per bay.

SE069 **Burkhart House**

1904. 500 Main St., corner of Pine

Built in 1904 for H. Z. Burkhart, builder of Ketchikan's first large sawmill, this towered, Queen Anne style dwelling was probably intended as an advertisement for the merits of lumber. Set on a hillside so steep the street is not cut through, the two-and-a-half-story house has a prominent basement on the downhill side. Hip-roofed, with one cross gable, the building's mass is accented by a two-story round tower projecting from the front corner of the building. The wood-shingled conical roof contrasts with the narrow hori-

SE068 Front Street

zontal siding of the walls, set off by wider belt courses and diamond-shaped shingles in the east gable; the basement is shingled.

The house is compromised somewhat by later additions. The Burkharts enclosed a porch on the west, creating a sun porch. Capt. Walter C. Dibrell was the second owner, acquiring the house in 1916; Dibrell was the first superintendent of the U.S. Bureau of Lighthouses for Alaska. He added the large one-story portion on the east, also with a prominent basement. More recent alterations include removal of the original sash from the windows, creating larger voids than were originally intended. Despite these changes, the original building is easily recognizable as a prominent, exuberant expression of early twentieth-century entrepreneurship, even if its Queen Anne style was somewhat out of date by 1904.

SE070 **Norman R. Walker House**

1920. 541 Pine St., corner Bawden

An excellent example of the Craftsman bungalow, the house was built in 1920 for Norman R. "Doc" Walker, a druggist with a distinguished career in the territorial legislature. Carl Foss, a local master carpenter, constructed the one-story, wood-framed house, which measures 25 feet by 46 feet and is clad in wood shingles. The low, irregular massing, deep overhangs, and variety of materials characterize the Craftsman bungalow, which is found throughout this neighborhood. The details of this building make it an outstanding example of the style, one that holds its own in comparison with bungalows in California or elsewhere in the Lower 48.

The cross-gable roof has exposed rafter ends and purlins, the latter embellished with brackets. Each side of the house has a different porch or projection. On the front, it is a porch across the facade, with battered brick piers, low-arch openings, and wood-shingled walls. On the south side, a one-bay entrance vestibule projects from a slightly projected, gable-roofed element, nestled into the main block of the building, next to an exterior brick chimney. On the north side, a steeply pitched shed roof shelters a slightly projecting bay window. All of the eaves extend 2 feet or 3 feet beyond the walls. The windows vary in shape, but many have small lights above the transoms.

SE071 **Federal Building**

1937–1938, Garfield, Stanley-Brown, Harris, and Robinson. Mill St., corner Steadman St.

Built on landfill, Ketchikan's Federal Building is an unusually vertical version of 1930s government architecture in Alaska. The Cleveland, Ohio, architectural firm of Garfield, Stanley-Brown, Harris, and Robinson designed a terracotta-embellished, semi-hexagonal building in 1933. When construction bids exceeded the allotted amount, the firm redesigned, ending up with this five-story, reinforced concrete building. Construction of the 50-foot-by-117-foot building, with a one-story 49-foot-by-51-foot section on one side, was begun in 1937 and completed one year later for $326,000. The concrete on the exterior is smooth finished and unornamented, except for horizontal lines at the levels of sills and lintels and vertical lines between windows, characteristic of the austere style of the federal buildings in frontier Alaska. The building housed the post office, courthouse, customhouse, and jail. Today the visitors' center of the U.S. Forest Service occupies the first floor, with offices and courtrooms above.

SE072 **Dolly's House**

by 1906. 24 Creek St.

Creek Street was the red-light district of Ketchikan from 1902 until 1954. Due to an ordinance prohibiting more than two ladies in a brothel, the houses were small. Built largely on pilings, the houses were reached by a boardwalk.

SE072 Dolly's House

The one-and-a-half-story building at number 24 is wood framed, covered with beveled siding. The gable front has a bay window at the first story, and two doors, the one on the left added later. On the interior, there is a double parlor on the right side and stair hall and kitchen on the left. The upstairs has two bedrooms.

The building is open to the public, interpreted as a museum concerned with the life of Dolly Arthur, a prostitute. She lived here from 1919 until 1973, and the furnishings—most of them her own—include pieces from all of the decades she lived here, the typical accumulation of a lifetime.

Ketchikan Vicinity

SE073 **Totem Bight Community House**

1940, Linn A. Forrest. Mile 9.9 North Tongass Hwy.

Constructed by the Civilian Conservation Corps for the U.S. Forest Service in 1940, this traditional Tlingit plank house was designed by U.S. Forest Service architect Linn A. Forrest to be part of an entire reconstructed village. The village was never completed. Built by a crew of Native craftsmen under the supervision of Charles Brown of Saxman, this traditional plank dwelling of the Tlingit measures 40 feet by 44 feet. Four interior house posts, independent of the exterior walls, support principal purlins, which support the rafters. Exterior walls are vertical planks, anchored by large posts at the two front corners, and smaller ones at the rear corners and midpoints.

The front of the dwelling has a wealth of ornamentation, all executed by Charles Brown: the entire house front is carved and painted, the corner posts are carved and painted above the roof, and there is a tall totem pole at the center of the front, through the base of which is the main entrance to the dwelling. The front of the house is overdecorated; this center post is a hallmark of the Haida, not the Tlingit, and probably would not have been combined with a painted house front. Human figures, which adorn the corner posts, are rare in totemic art, animals being preferred.

On the interior, a fire pit in the center is surrounded by three levels of planked flooring. All four house posts are highly ornamented, but there is no screen and no other ornament. The building is crowned by a movable smoke-hole covering. A doorway near the west corner is an obvious accommodation to the public.

Also on site are thirteen totem poles, all of them replicas from the 1930s and later. Poles depicting the Master Carpenter and Man Captured by Otters were executed by John Wallace of Hydaburg and erected in 1941 and 1947. Wallace, who was eighty-three years old in 1940, had learned carving from his father and then repudiated it when he joined the church, even to the extent of cutting down and burning totem poles in Klinkwan. Late in life he returned to carving. Other poles are copies of originals taken from nearby Tlingit and Haida villages and carved by CCC Native workers.

SE073 Totem Bight Community House

Saxman

SE074 **Tribal House**

1990. 2 miles southeast of Ketchikan

This traditional plank house, measuring 47 feet by 76 feet, was completed in 1990. Built by Saxman residents, the house is far larger than other reconstructions. Planks on the front and rear are vertical, while on the sides the planks are vertical on the lower 3 feet of the walls and horizontal above. The planks are pegged and have been given an adze finish. The carving on the front of the building and the house posts and screen inside were crafted by local carvers.

The collection of twenty-four totem poles was assembled in the 1930s from neighboring Tlingit villages of Old Tongass, Cat Island, Village Island, Pennock Island, and Cape Fox. Many inhabitants of these deserted villages moved to Saxman. The U.S. Forest Service employed Civilian Conservation Corps workers—Native carvers—to restore or duplicate old poles.

Linn A. Forrest, Forest Service architect, located the totem poles in a formal setting. A roadway lined with poles leads up from the water, then divides into two stairways, one framed by Raven totems, the other with Bear. The other totem poles are arranged in a circle, at the top of which is the new tribal house. The legends of the poles and their origins are known and are recounted in Viola Garfield and Linn A. Forrest, *The Wolf and the Raven* (Seattle: University of Washington Press, 1961).

Metlakatla

Father William Duncan, a Church of England lay missionary, arrived in Port Simpson, British Columbia, in 1857, where he began an extraordinary career among the Tsimshian Indians. Requiring absolute devotion from his followers, he established a new community, Metlakatla, where he insisted on industry, education, western habits, and "neat houses." Although the community was largely self-sufficient, it was also isolationist; contacts with outsiders were carefully regulated, and alcohol was particularly suspect. Duncan learned the Tsimshian language, educated the people, and developed a society that was as much entrepreneurial as it was religious.

In 1887, after a falling-out with the Anglican church and the Canadian government, Duncan moved the entire community to Annette Island in Alaska, south of Ketchikan. Here, at New Metlakatla, he built a new community, beginning with a sawmill. By 1891 the villagers had constructed ninety-one houses, one- and two-story buildings with a variety of ornament. The picket-fenced yards were full of flowers, and the houses were painted a rich variety of colors. Duncan laid out a grid plan, dividing each block into four 80-foot by 90-foot lots, so that each house was on a corner lot. Although a fire in 1893 destroyed about twenty houses, the Metlakatlans rebuilt.

The public buildings were distinctive in appearance. A twelve-sided, twelve-gable building served initially as a church, and then as the town hall. In 1893–1896 a Gothic church was constructed: 70 feet by 100 feet, 43 feet high, with two 80-foot-tall towers. It burned in 1949. An octagonal guest house, completed in 1897, a four-gabled school, and a combination jail, engine house, and library building—the first story painted red for the engine house, the second story white for the library, and the cupola blue—built in 1905 completed the odd array of public buildings. Some of them can be seen in the undated photograph on page 208.

Today none of the oddly shaped public buildings survives. Most of the original two-story houses have disappeared as well, having been replaced with bungalows and cottages in a variety of forms. There are two churches in the community, reflecting a split in the village after Duncan's death.

Although not as outlandish architecturally as it once was, with four-, eight-, and twelve-gable buildings, Metlakatla still stands apart from most Native villages, especially in its grid plan and bungalows and cottages. Duncan's experiment has resulted in a thriving village with new schools, a nearby lumber mill, and a new runway. And it still has "neat houses."

SE075 William Duncan Memorial Church

1957

The William Duncan Memorial Church was built on the site of the church that burned. The large, twin-towered building with Gothic windows and buttresses is covered with clapboards. The church joined the Assembly of God denomination in the 1980s.

SE076 Presbyterian Church

1922

The other church in Metlakatla is the Presbyterian church, with one tower in the center of the front. The congregation was established in 1920, comprised of graduates of the Sheldon Jackson School, and construction of the church began in 1922. A large addition, giving the church an L-plan, was constructed in the 1980s.

SE077 Town Hall

early twentieth century

The Town Hall, a T-shaped building with a large hipped roof and a gabled projection in front, and ornamented with fluted columns, was built by members of the Metlakatla Athletic Club, a basketball team that needed a gymnasium. The gym occupies the portion under the hip roof, while the front of the building was devoted to town offices.

SE078 Cannery

1891; 1918, rebuilt

The primary source of income for Metlakatla is its cannery. Built in 1891, it was destroyed by fire and rebuilt in 1918. Located next to the town dock, the cannery is composed of long, gable-roofed buildings extending over the water. As a federal reservation, Metlakatla operates fish traps, the only legal ones in the state.

SE079 Father Duncan's Cottage

1891

The most notable house in town is Father Duncan's Cottage, now a museum honoring the founder of Metlakatla. Built for Father William Duncan by his Tsimshian followers, the house is a one-story, gable-fronted cottage measuring approximately 36 feet by 30 feet. Across the front, four pilasters support an architrave that defines the low pediment, in which is a curious fleur-de-lis ornament. A small entrance vestibule, looking like an afterthought, protrudes from the center of the

Metlakatla

front. The wood-framed building is covered with novelty siding.

The interior is divided into eight rooms, without halls. Two large rooms are in the middle, front and back, with pilastered fireplaces sharing a chimney. The walls are vertical beaded boards, and the ceiling follows the slope of the gable roof, creating a spacious interior. On each side of these public spaces are three small rooms, entered through doors with large transom windows.

The kitchen, located in an ell, was entirely rebuilt when the building was restored in 1972–1975. It now serves as offices for the museum. The house is open to the public, and full of Father Duncan's possessions, including books and clothing. This unusual building once housed an unusual man.

Interior (IN)

INTERIOR ALASKA INCLUDES THE EASTERN PART OF THE STATE drained by the Yukon and Kuskokwim rivers. Located between the Alaska Range on the south and the Brooks Range on the north, the lowlands and rolling hills of the Interior are divided by streams and rivers. Because of the discontinuous permafrost that appears throughout the region, there are thin forests of spindly spruce known as taiga. Tundra, wet ground with low vegetation, is found in the northern and western parts of the Interior.

The Interior has a semiarid climate with annual precipitation of only 12 inches, but because of the permafrost much of this precipitation stays near the ground's surface, creating a boggy land and excellent breeding ground for mosquitoes. The Interior has the greatest temperature extremes in the state, ranging from −50 and −60 degrees in winter to 80 or even 90 degrees in the summer.

Most of the Interior was inhabited by Athapaskan Indians, who led a nomadic life centered on hunting. Isolated trading posts established by the British Hudson's Bay Company and the Russian-American Company created a market for furs and introduced material goods into Native culture. The gold rush, however, changed the lives of the Natives radically; they were introduced to a market economy and to the ready availability of manufactured goods, processed foods, and liquor.

White Americans prospected for gold in the Interior before the Klondike strike. Most successful was the strike at Birch Creek, which resulted in a stampede to Circle City on the Yukon River in 1896. But the thirty thousand gold seekers who poured into Canada's Klondike region after 1897 dramatically increased the population of Interior Alaska. Many of the gold seekers, disappointed in the Klondike, floated down the Yukon to try their luck in Alaska. At the same time, the Klondike attracted increased traffic going up the Yukon on river

209

steamboats from Saint Michael, where passengers transferred from ocean-going vessels. Subsequent gold strikes sent this hopeful population rushing back and forth across the Interior: to the Koyukuk in 1898, to Nome in 1900, to Fairbanks in 1902, to Ruby in 1911, to Chisana in 1913. Log cabin towns were born and died overnight.

Permanent institutions of government and religion rushed to keep up with this new and peripatetic population. The Third Judicial Court was established in Eagle in 1900 but moved to Fairbanks in 1903. The U.S. Army set up a post at Fort Egbert, near Eagle, in 1899, but it was practically deserted by 1910. The Episcopal church, which was active in the Interior before the strike in the Klondike, invested $1,800 in a church in 1896 in Circle, which was a ghost town two years later. The Episcopalians established several missions along the Yukon, with ministering to the Natives as their priority over the needs of the miners. They were joined by the Roman Catholics, who established a mission at Holy Cross and a church in Fairbanks, among other places.

Although few buildings are known to exist from before the Klondike strike, a fair number remain from the turn of the twentieth century. On the creeks, log cabins were built with the sole purpose of immediate shelter, for one winter or as long as the gold held out. Usually constructed with sill logs laid directly on the ground, and with a disregard for permafrost, these buildings were only semi-permanent. As towns were built, construction reflected conflicting aims: the appearance of stability versus practicality in what would probably be temporary boomtowns. Inexpensive log cabins sat beside wood-framed houses, and mill-sawn false fronts were attached to log buildings.

Overland transportation improved in response to the needs of the population of the Interior. The Valdez-Eagle and Valdez-Fairbanks trails were established, then upgraded. Along those and other frequented routes, roadhouses were constructed every 20 miles or so, providing shelter and food to travelers. Larger than their residential neighbors, roadhouses and stores are usually the only two-story log buildings to be found. The Alaska Railroad, completed in 1923, provided a linkage to Anchorage and the South-Central Region.

Although easily obtained placer gold was not mined in small-scale operations with much success after about 1910, well-capitalized outfits brought a second generation of mining—dredging and extensive hydraulic operations—to the goldfields in the 1920s and 1930s. Military buildup during World War II and after also helped the local economy, as well as sparking construction of the Alaska Highway: at last, Alaska was joined to the rest of the continent by road. Construction of the oil pipeline in the 1970s resulted in another boom, comparable to the gold rush in the population it attracted and the modernization it provoked.

Interior Region

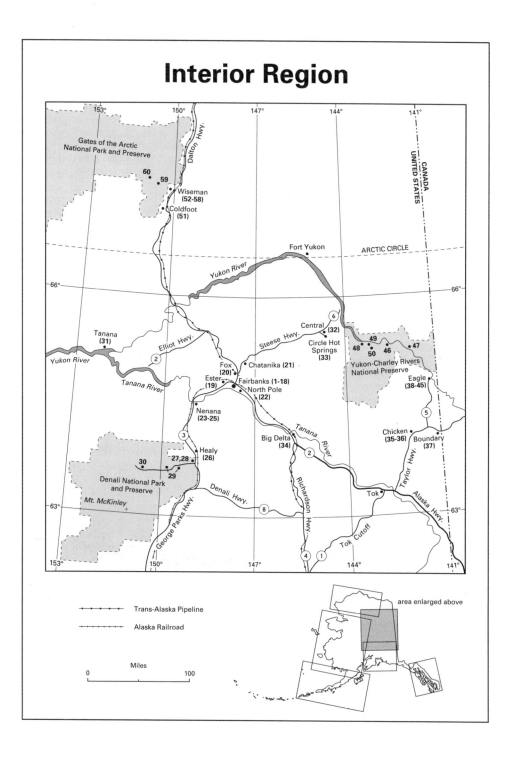

Trans-Alaska Pipeline

Alaska Railroad

Miles

0   100

area enlarged above

Fairbanks and North Star Borough

Fairbanks

Fairbanks might have been just another gold-rush boomtown had it not been for several actions by the federal government. James Wickersham's decision to locate the Third District Court here in 1903 was pivotal; it also caused Wickersham to make Fairbanks his home, and he was a particularly effective advocate for the city through the years. The U.S. government's purchase of the Tanana Valley Mines Railroad, to add to the Alaska Railroad, further advanced Fairbanks's viability. The location of the future University of Alaska at a nearby site brought students and faculty, and the establishment of Ladd Field brought a population of U.S. military personnel. But it was the gold that started it all.

Elbridge Truman Barnette established a trading post on this site in 1901, when his steamboat could travel no farther up the Chena River. The site proved to be fortuitous, for that winter gold was found on creeks north of the Chena, and the closest navigable point was Fairbanks (named by Barnette at Wickersham's urging in honor of a Republican politician who never visited Alaska). In its early years, Fairbanks vied for prominence with the town of Chena, located 7 miles downstream at a spot on the Chena River where navigable river levels were more reliable. But when Falcon Joslin built the 45-mile Tanana Valley Mines Railway in 1904 and connected the goldfields with both Chena and Fairbanks, the future of Fairbanks was ensured.

The population of the Fairbanks Mining District soared to about ten thousand; between 1902 and 1909, $50 million in gold was produced. By the 1910s gold production lagged, and population dropped as prospectors moved on to other gold strikes, or back to the U.S. during the First World War. Revitalization came in the 1920s with the Fairbanks Exploration Company, a well-capitalized outfit that brought five dredges into the area by 1930 and began mining on a large scale.

Located on the south side of the Chena River, Fairbanks was platted in an elastic grid plan, bending where the river bent. Barnette's trading post, which he sold to the Northern Commercial Company in 1904, dominated the waterfront. On the north side of the river were the railroad depot and roads to the goldfields. Although the initial buildings of the town were of log construction, a sawmill was in operation by 1904, and from then on most of the buildings were wood-framed, one-story bungalows or cottages, with a few two-story foursquares. A May 1906 fire devastated much of the commercial center of the city, but Wickersham, who had built a wood-framed house in 1904, felt that its effects were beneficial overall. When he returned to Fairbanks in July 1906, he noted in his journal:

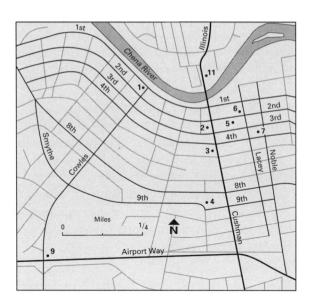

Fairbanks

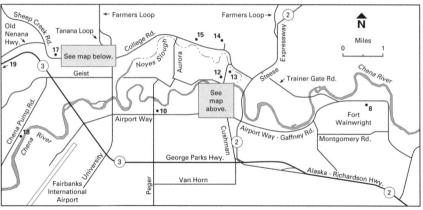

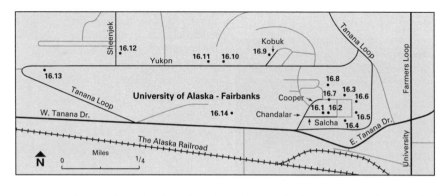

University of Alaska - Fairbanks

The town looks fine—as usual a big fire hurts individuals, but helped the town very much. The old log cabins—unsightly spots—the different sorts and styles of buildings have gone—and whole blocks of well-built buildings occupy the places. The streets have been widened—in the fire-swept division—the banks, stores and business houses all rebuilt and the town looks better than ever.

Fairbanks today has a mix of architecture. The downtown area lacks cohesion, with parking lots and unsympathetically altered buildings interrupting the streetscape. Concrete buildings from the 1930s are the finest survivors in the commercial area downtown, while cottages and bungalows from Fairbanks's first decade are found in neighborhoods east and west of the commercial center. Postwar expansion is seen in two early high rises downtown, as well as in suburban growth. In the last few decades, good new architecture has been built at isolated spots around town, as well as at the university, which provides a catalog of architecture from the last three decades.

IN001 First Avenue and Cowles Street

The houses and commercial buildings in this area, close to downtown Fairbanks, date from the first two decades of Fairbanks's history. Both First Avenue and Cowles Street have cohesive streetscapes, but even isolated buildings on neighboring streets serve to illustrate the early years of Fairbanks. The houses are one or two stories in height, of log or wood-frame construction, with gable or hip roofs. Porches and vestibules animate the fronts of the buildings, and the yards are wooded. The commercial buildings along First Avenue maintain a domestic scale.

IN001.1 George C. Thomas Memorial Library

1909. 901 First Ave.

The George C. Thomas Memorial Library is the outgrowth of a church library. Episcopalian missionary Hudson Stuck started a library in a portion of Saint Matthew's Church in 1906. George C. Thomas, a Philadelphia banker, heard of this library and donated $4,000 toward a building for it. The designer is not known, but the log building is in a distinctly bungalow form.

Constructed in 1909, the one-story building is 40 feet square and constructed of 6-inch logs, sawn flat on three sides and nailed at the corners. Punctuated by eyebrow dormers, the hip roof extends on two sides to cover a porch. The large windows had leaded glass. Spiral-fluted galvanized-metal columns supporting the porch roof have recently been replaced.

The Episcopal church sold the library to the city in 1942; the city turned it over to the Fairbanks-North Star Borough in 1968. The library moved to a new building in 1977, and this one now houses a credit union.

IN001.2 Saint Matthew's Episcopal Church

1948, Bell and Upjohn. 1022 First Ave.

Saint Matthew's Episcopal Church is the same basic design as that of the previous church on the site. Archdeacon Hudson Stuck had built a log building with a gable front and a gable-roofed vestibule in 1905; it was destroyed by fire in 1947. The new church,

IN001.2 Saint Matthews Episcopal Church

designed by Bell and Upjohn of New York City, is built with logs sawn flat on three sides. The belfry is on top of the vestibule, nestled under the peak of the gable, rather than on the nave roof. There is a large, recent addition in the rear, but the rustic character of this church prevails.

IN001.3 **Mary Lee Davis House**

1916. 410 Cowles St.

Built by miner Arthur Williams, the Mary Lee Davis House is a one-and-a-half-story, novelty-sided bungalow, with a low hip roof and overhanging eaves. The porch across the front is also covered by the main roof; the porch's half-walls and box columns add solidity. Two hip-roofed dormers as well as the main roof are ornamented with carved brackets. Leaded-glass sidelights and a transom window contribute to the bungalow charm.

Author Mary Lee Davis, who bought the house in 1923, described it in hyperbolic fashion:

A man who had been a wanderer, an adventurer, made quite a little fortune in Dawson in the early days, married a young wife who loved the bright lights of the city and its ways, and then came to our town to live. The wife longed for 'Frisco, but the husband—for reasons which I suspect, but which he alone knew best—did not care to leave the North. He proposed a compromise, so I have been told. If she would remain contented in Alaska for ten years, he promised to build her the finest house that the Territory had known! She considered this. Having had, perhaps, some former experience with the futility of masculine promise, she went to her attorney and had him draw up the plans

and specifications of a house such as her fondest dream had imaged. It was to have a real lawn, first and foremost—that unknown, luxurious thing in a land of moss; and it must have a real fireplace, a thing until then unknown in the Interior. It must have hot-water heat, even though a man had to come from Seattle to install it, and an oak floor (another import!), oak trim and doors, a large porch all screened and roomy, a double garage, and the best plumbing obtainable, with all-porcelain fixtures. This house was to be really warm—not a log cabin to be chinked anew each year, to sag in the corners when the frost moves, and "with cracks you can stick the stovepipe through." Oh, no! This was to be one frame house set inside another frame house, complete, with six full inches of sawdust in the space between the outer walls and also in the ceilings, making it absolutely frost proof in winter and heat proof in summer. (*Uncle Sam's Attic: The Intimate Story of Alaska* [Boston: W. A. Wilde, 1930]), 308–9)

According to Davis, Williams died before the house was completed, and she and her husband bought it.

IN001.4 **Falcon Joslin House**

1904. 413 Cowles St.

Built when Fairbanks was just a fledgling town, the Falcon Joslin house is a two-story four-square building. A one-story enclosed porch across the front and a one-story addition to one side have somewhat obscured the upright quality of the house. The wood-framed house with novelty siding and corner boards has a shallow-pitched hip roof with a hip-roofed dormer.

Falcon Joslin played a crucial role in the battle for survival between Chena and Fairbanks. Joslin, who had built a 12-mile railroad near Dawson, came to the Fairbanks area to build a railroad to the goldfields. In 1904 he plotted a spur line from Chena to Fairbanks, thereby giving Fairbanks, which was plagued with low water, easy access to the deeper waters of Chena, while at the same time making Chena nothing more than a transfer point. Joslin's construction of his house in Fairbanks in 1904 illustrates this commitment to the community. By 1907 his Tanana Valley Mines Railroad, a narrow-gauge line, ran 45 miles from Chena to Chatanika, with a spur to Fairbanks. Once the gold rush was over, however, the railroad had financial difficulties. Joslin sold the line to the U.S. government in 1917; he had left Fairbanks the year before.

IN001.5 Odd Fellows Hall

1907. 825 First Ave.

Built as a bathhouse, the Odd Fellows Hall is a tall, narrow, wood-framed building fronting on a wider, one-story building. The two-story front portion has novelty siding and cornice returns on its gable front. Cora Madole lived on the second floor, and her associate "Doc" Overgaard had his office and living quarters on the first floor. In the one story portion was the bathhouse, with a long hallway with bath stalls off of it.

In the winter of 1909–1910 the water and steam pipes froze, putting Cora Madole and Doc Overgaard out of business. They sold the building to the Odd Fellows, who still use it as a meeting hall.

IN001.6 Masonic Temple

1906. 809 First Ave.

The Renaissance Revival-style facade of the Masonic Temple is an unusually ambitious if awkward composition. Executed in pressed metal, it was originally painted a light reddish tan. Round-arch openings on the first floor (two of which have been altered), a one-story tetrastyle Ionic portico (which had an elaborate cornice with balustrade above), swags and garlands in the frieze, a modillioned cornice, and a nameplate in the pediment all present a grand appearance to the street. Behind this facade is a simple two-story, wood-framed building.

The Fairbanks Masons began as a club in 1904, receiving their charter in 1908. That year, they bought this building, which had been· constructed in 1906 for the Tanana Commercial Company. The Masons ex-

tended the building to the rear, giving it its present dimensions of 32 feet by 60 feet. They also raised it in 1913 in order to create a basement and added this facade in 1916.

IN002 U.S. Post Office and Court House

1932–1933, George Ray. Cushman St. between Second and Third avenues

Occupying one whole block in downtown Fairbanks, the three-story U.S. Post Office and Court House is an Art Deco monument symbolic of the federal government's role in establishing Fairbanks. In 1903, Judge James Wickersham decided to move the seat of the Third Judicial Court to Fairbanks, thus ensuring the survival of that fledgling town. He immediately ordered that a wood-framed courthouse be built, which was succeeded by another in 1906. As a delegate to Congress from 1909 to 1917, Wickersham attempted to obtain funding for a replacement. In 1914 the Fairbanks postmaster noted that Fairbanks was "the commercial center for a radius of more than 300 miles," and with the coming of the government railroad, a new building "will be a positive necessity." The postmaster recommended concrete construction, even at that early date.

Funding for the building was not obtained until 1931 (when James Wickersham was once again Alaska's delegate to Congress), but several years earlier, the office of the Supervising Architect of the Treasury inquired into the feasibility of concrete as a construction material in Fairbanks's harsh climate. Joseph M.

Story, an architectural engineer, described successful concrete buildings in Fairbanks, and Roy B. Earling, assistant manager of the Fairbanks Exploration Company, described that company's concrete-block building (IN012.1) as showing "no evidence whatever of settling or heaving after four years' use."

With that advice, George Ray, a Washington, D.C., architect, was hired to design a reinforced-concrete building. The recessed center block of the building is four stories high. On either side, three-story blocks are brought forward. Each of the three blocks is three bays wide, with similar fenestration, which includes aluminum spandrels between floors and strong piers between the bays. The piers rise above the aluminum-capped cornice. All of the aluminum trim has Art Deco detailing. Entrance is through a one-story portion in the center of the facade, below green marble panels. The lobby has fluted pilasters executed in a dark-stained wood, ornamental plaster ceiling, and marble baseboards and borders on the terrazzo floor. The courtroom on the third floor (now fourth) has a coffered ceiling.

In March 1932 the supervising architect let a contract for the construction of the building to the William MacDonald Construction Company of Saint Louis, Missouri, for $393,000. Most of the building was completed and occupied fourteen months later, with only the aluminum trim causing a delay. The post office, courts, and other federal offices occupied the building until 1977, when they moved to new quarters. The building has been renovated for private office space.

IN003 City Hall

1933. 410 Cushman St.

This two-story concrete building is in a modernized Classical Revival design. Contrasting paint colors—a most un-Classical convention—highlight the modernized Classical ornament, consisting of horizontal gouges representing quoining and a stylized cornice below a paneled parapet. The appearance of the building is further harmed by the installation of offices in the space originally occupied by the fire department, garage doors having been replaced with windows.

IN004 Main School

1933–1934, Joseph D. Boyer and Tourtellotte and Hummel. Eighth Ave. and Cushman St.

After fire destroyed the previous school building in December 1932, reinforced concrete was the material of choice for the new school building. With one eye on the U.S. Post Office and Court House, then under construction, city leaders used the same material, derived cost estimates from the federal building experience, and even drew on the design.

Main School has a two-story central block flanked by two-story hyphens and wings. Each window bay, divided by concrete piers that rise above the roofline in a contrasting dark color, has large windows separated by concrete spandrels with bas-relief panels. Vertical gouges above the windows are repeated on the piers. The blank front walls of the wings have slightly recessed and raised panels; the sides have the same fenestration and ornament as the front of the building. On the interior, classrooms are arranged in a U-plan on the perimeter, with the auditorium in the center of the building expressed by a rounded element on the rear. In 1939, a large addition to the rear of the south wing was constructed with Public Works Administration funds. In 1948 a similar addition was made to the north wing.

Joseph D. Boyer, the engineer supervising construction of the U.S. Post Office and Court House, devised schematic plans for this building that were then fully drawn by a Portland, Oregon, architectural firm. It is not known who contributed what to the design, but its resemblance to that of the federal building indicates that Boyer's influence was strong. The William MacDonald Construction Company, which also had the federal building, contract, was hired to construct the building for $117,000 in May 1933. The building was occupied in January 1934 and was used as a school until 1976. It now houses school district offices.

IN005 Empress Theatre

1927. 535 Second Ave.

Although bizarrely reinterpreted by a landscape mural depicting the Alaskan wilderness on its second-story front facade, the Empress Theatre remains important because of its concrete construction and its association with Austin "Cap" Lathrop. In 1927, Lathrop had this movie theater built as part of his chain of theaters throughout Alaska. As fire is a constant concern with theaters, he had it built of steel and concrete.

The first floor of the facade has been altered by a new storefront, but the second floor retains two round-arch windows and a denticulated cornice. The theater, which seated 670 people, was one of the largest buildings in town and repeatedly used for large gatherings. It served as a movie theater until 1961, when it was converted to a drugstore.

IN006 Lacey Street Theatre

1939, B. Marcus Priteca; interior, Frank Zallinger and Frank Hollineck. Second Ave. and Lacey St.

The Lacey Street Theatre is the finest Art Deco building in Fairbanks. The two-story concrete building rises to a four-story tower at the corner, which supports a vertical metal and neon sign, reading "Lacey St." Incised vertical lines between the windows are complemented by horizontal lines stretching the length of the facade; the tower has this same ornament, as well as some zigzag decoration. The theater entrance was on Second Avenue, not on the corner; a standard marquee surmounts the theater entrance. The corner housed a bank.

One of Austin E. "Cap" Lathrop's string of movie theaters, the Lacey Street Theatre was constructed in 1939. B. Marcus Priteca, the Seattle architect who also designed the Fourth Avenue Theatre in Anchorage for Lathrop, designed this one. The interior, which was destroyed in a 1966 fire, was designed by Frank Zallinger and Frank Hollineck.

Rebuilt after the 1966 fire with minimal changes to the exterior, the building was renovated in 1970 with further interior alterations. The theater closed in 1981, but the building remains, an excellent example of the Art Deco style.

IN007 Northward Building

1951–1952. Block bound by Lacey, Third, Fourth, and Noble

The Northward Building is famous as the Ice Palace popularized by Edna Ferber's 1958 novel. The eight-story building is steel framed with reinforced concrete floors, clad with metal siding. Undeniably plain, it exhibits the same austerity of design found in concrete buildings of Alaska. The building, in a rough H-plan, contained 210 apartments above stores on the first floor and a garage in the basement.

Although Ferber's Ice Palace was a glass-block marvel, her description of its reputation points to this building:

Alaska's first apartment house. People fought to live in it. Townsmen, dwelling in their frame houses and wrestling with the regional problems of heating, lighting, plumbing, water, were madly envious of Ice Palace tenants. There never was a vacancy unless a tenant accommodatingly died, rashly built a new house, or left permanently for Outside.

Later, a character explains:

It's an apartment house—kind of an apartment hotel, really. We're quite petted on it, and brag a lot. Maid service, restaurant, elevators, laundromats in the basement with twenty machines. Drugstore. Supermarket. The works. It's a town under one roof. (*Ice Palace* [Garden City, N.Y.: Doubleday, 1958], 18, 57–58)

Nearby is another early high-rise, the eleven-story Polaris Building, at the corner of First and Lacey. Now a hotel, the reinforced concrete building had 144 apartments above the first floor. Together, these two buildings changed the skyline of Fairbanks and the way of life—a self-contained Le Corbusier utopia for the Alaska frontier.

IN008 Fort Wainwright (Ladd Field)

1938 and later

Construction began on the first U.S. Army airfield in Alaska in 1938. During World War

II, Ladd Field served as a cold-weather experimental station, as an air depot for the repair and testing of aircraft, and as the principal base for the Air Transport Command, which transferred almost eight thousand military aircraft to the Russian front for use by Russian crews. The initial construction effort was concentrated on a 5,000-foot runway, with auxiliary buildings to the north. Because of the harsh weather, all of the buildings at the original post were permanent construction, not standardized temporary buildings. The original, permanent garrison was located on the north side of the runway in buildings arranged in a horseshoe-shaped plan, and most of them were occupied in 1941. The Quartermaster Corps completed 80 percent of the buildings before its duties were shifted to the Corps of Engineers in January 1941. Because additional functions were assigned to Ladd Field in 1943, there was additional construction. The runway was extended to a length of more than 9,000 feet, and a second, parallel runway was built to a length of 7,200 feet.

Additional hangars were constructed on the south side of the runway, and the coast artillery garrison was housed in buildings haphazardly arranged on the southwest side of the runway. By 1945, there were seventy-five buildings on the base.

In 1961 the Air Force transferred Ladd Air Force Base to the army, which was then named in honor of Lt. Gen. Jonathan M. Wainwright, the hero of Corregidor. The base has continued to expand in postwar years, most recently with the assignment of the Sixth Infantry Division (Light) to Fort Wainwright. The new construction is concentrated west of the original portion and is generally standardized and undistinguished. One exception is the housing area northwest of the runways, where slightly Postmodern housing is arranged on cul-de-sacs.

IN008.1 **Quarters No. 1**

by 1941

At the core of today's base, which has been much expanded, is a horseshoe-shaped plan. At the head of the horseshoe is Quarters No. 1, the commanding officer's quarters. This is a two-story, hip-roofed house, now covered with vinyl siding. Arrayed around the horseshoe are officers' quarters, twelve-unit, two-story buildings with hip roofs and gable-roofed vestibules. These also have been covered with vinyl siding.

IN008.2 **Murphy Hall** (Building 1045)

by 1941

The bachelor officers' quarters is a hip-roofed building with a gable front. Fluted and curved doorjambs, visible in this view of the side and rear, and octagonal windows on the front hint at its 1940s origins.

IN008.3 **Headquarters Building** (Building 1555)

1943

Just south of Murphy Hall is the Headquarters Building, which recently underwent a $7 million renovation for use as the 6th Infantry Division (Light) Headquarters. The U-shaped building was constructed in 1943 as the post exchange, hospital, theater, barracks, mess

IN008.2 Murphy Hall (Building 1045)

hall, and administrative space. Gabled entrance pavilions break up the long, hip-roofed faces of this building.

IN008.4 Hangar No. 1 (Building 1557)

by 1941

At the open end of the horseshoe, across the parade ground from Quarters No. 1, is the largest building on the old base, Hangar No. 1. With a low gable roof and corner towers, the building now has a dropped ceiling and a removable interior partition. Offices have been added to the outside walls.

IN009 Noel Wien Memorial Library

1977, CCC/HOK. 1215 Cowles St.

Virtually unornamented on the exterior in the modern aesthetic, the library benefits from simple lines and geometric forms. Completed in 1977, the library was designed by the Anchorage firm of CCC/HOK. The one-story building is steel framed with vertical cedar wood siding. Windows are few in proportion to wall space, responding to a climate whose bitter cold in winter and excessive sunshine in summer discourage the extensive use of glass, but despite a low ceiling the interior is light, open, and appealing. The irregular plan accommodates public library space, stacks, auditorium, and administrative offices, centered on a skylit court. There is also indirect lighting from second-story windows above the lobby.

IN010 Alaskaland

Alaskaland, the site of the Alaska 67 Centennial Exposition, combines amusement park with re-created historic areas, using buildings moved in from other sites. A Goldrush Town, Native Village, and Mining Valley are arranged around picnic areas and a civic center.

At the main entrance is the 237-foot steamboat *Nenana,* built in 1933–1935, now set in a dry pond. On railroad tracks that go nowhere is the Harding Railroad Car, in which President Harding rode while visiting Alaska at the completion of the Alaska Railroad.

The Native Village is an assortment of reconstructions of various Native dwellings from throughout Alaska. The Tlingit plank house is miniature in scale, while the others appear to be full sized. The proximity of the different forms of Native architecture and the lack of relative proportion between them make this an especially confusing exhibit. The Mining Valley contains some relocated miners' cabins and some new construction to accommodate the salmon bake offered there. A collection of mining equipment, with different levels of interpretation, is scattered about the site.

The Goldrush Town, an array of more than thirty buildings linked by boardwalks and asphalt streets, contains both new and old structures. The historic buildings, including both log and wood-framed examples, are all open to the public, although most of them contain shops. Most of the log buildings are one story, with saddle notched corners and gable fronts. Only four of the buildings are not primarily shops today (IN010.1–IN010.4).

IN010.1 Wickersham House

1904

Appointed district judge for the Third Judicial District, James Wickersham moved to Eagle in 1900. In 1903 he moved the court to Fairbanks, both foreseeing and ensuring the permanence of that boomtown, and built this house for his family in 1904. Located at First and Noble streets, the house was originally just two rooms. The 14-foot-by-16-foot living room was the one-story, gable-roofed section that serves today as the dining room. A shed-roofed kitchen was attached to what is now the right end of the house; it was removed when the house was moved to Alaskaland, and the present kitchen was reconstructed.

In 1905, Wickersham added electricity to the house and set up his phonograph. The outhouse off of the kitchen was connected to the house. In 1906, he added two sections to the house. On one side of the living room,

IN010.1a Wickersham House (exterior)

IN010.1b Wickersham House (interior)

he added two rooms covered by a cross-gable roof, forming a T-plan with the original section. The addition was about 16 feet by 28 feet and became the new living room with a bedroom behind. Behind the old living room he added another room, reconstructed after the move. With the addition of a "heating plant," Wickersham pronounced that "Our new home is done. We now have six good rooms—plenty." Later, however, yet another shed-roofed addition was constructed in front of the bathroom.

The house as it stands today looks far tidier and more rational than its construction history would indicate, as though it were designed to be a three-room, T-shaped, gable-roofed cottage with kitchen wing. The gable roof extends to cover the entryway and is supported by turned columns; at one point this porch was enclosed, but it is now open. The wood-framed house is covered with novelty siding and has a wood-shingled roof.

The furnishings are as they would have been in Wickersham's time, with some original pieces. The hardwood floors are not orig-

inal, and would have been softwood, but in general the house gives the visitor a good picture of the judge's life-style.

The house is set in a grassy yard with a picket fence. The picket fence was original to the house; Wickersham built it even before the house and was quite proud of it. The theme-park setting is unfortunate for such a carefully interpreted historic house museum.

IN010.2 Presbyterian Church

1904

The Presbyterian Church has a steep gable roof and round-arch windows. As built in 1904 at the corner of Seventh Avenue and Cushman Street, it had a stronger medieval revival character. A large stained-glass, pointed-arch window was located where the gable-roofed vestibule is now; entrance was through the corner tower, now gone, which had a belfry and tall steeple. The simple interior of this church is particularly striking in contrast to the fairgrounds outside.

IN010.3 Kitty Hensley House

1914

The Kitty Hensley House took its present form in 1914 when Captain Smythe remodeled a one-story log cabin by adding a tall gambrel-roofed second floor. The house is small, with a bay-windowed living room on the first floor, a kitchen in a one-story, board-and-batten room in the rear, and one room on the second floor.

IN010.4 Georgia Lee House

1916

Alaskaland's offices are in the Georgia Lee House, a hip-roofed bungalow with hip-roofed dormer, built in Nenana for the Alaska Railroad. In 1928 it was moved by rail to Fairbanks to occupy the site at 829 Fourth Avenue until it was moved to Alaskaland in 1967.

IN010.5 Pioneer Hall

1967

The Pioneer Hall is a new construction; the wood-framed building is designed to read as six separate buildings, but inside it is one, giving new meaning to the term "false front." About half of the building contains historic artifacts that would be more meaningfully displayed in the historic buildings.

IN011 Immaculate Conception Roman Catholic Church

1904. 115 North Cushman St.

Father Francis Monroe, S.J., arrived in Fairbanks in 1904 and had this 30-foot-by-65-foot wood-framed church built on the edge of the original townsite. In 1906, a Catholic hospital was built on Garden Island, just across the Chena River. Five years later, the buildings of the Catholic church were consolidated at that site; the church was moved across the frozen river. In 1914, the church was altered considerably by the raising of the roof 5 feet, the addition of the bell tower and vestibule,

and the construction of a two-story priests' rectory on one side of the church.

The novelty-sided church has a steeply pitched gable roof and narrow round-arch windows on its gable front. A bell tower rises from the center of the facade; its open belfry is topped by a pyramidal roof. The one-story vestibule across the front has a flat roof and flat-arch windows; it lacks the light and soaring quality of the rest of the church.

On the interior, the walls and ceiling are covered with highly ornamental pressed tin. The ceiling pattern is coffered, while that on the walls resembles large panels between the windows. There is a handsome wood wainscot and stained glass in the windows. In sharp contrast to the rest of the church, the altar wall is plain, unornamented wood. There is a meeting hall in the lower level of the church.

IN012 Fairbanks Exploration Company Complex

1926. 700 block Illinois St.

The Fairbanks Exploration Company, a subsidiary of the United States Smelting, Refining and Mining Company (USSR&M), bought up most small gold-mining operations in the Fairbanks area by 1925 and began an extensive prospecting and drilling program. With considerable capital, the company was able to bring in dredges and to construct the 90-mile-long Davidson Ditch to provide water for the dredging operations. Between 1926 and 1940, the Fairbanks Exploration Company employed close to one thousand men each year, bolstering the Fairbanks economy. The company built an extensive industrial complex on the north side of the Chena River, and many of those buildings remain today.

IN012.1 Office Building

1926

The two-story building, 80 feet by 40 feet, has a reinforced-concrete frame with an exterior wall of rock-faced concrete blocks. The water table, doorway, and molded cornice and parapet were of smooth concrete. Behind the office building is the assay office, a one-story building constructed of the same rock-faced concrete blocks and trimmed with the same smooth concrete, giving a nod toward architectural refinement in spite of the coarse appearance of the utilitarian materials.

IN012.2 Machine Shop—Electrical Shop—Foundry

c. 1926

Behind the Assay Office, on the other side of the railroad tracks, is the large Machine Shop—Electrical Shop—Foundry, a one- and two-story, steel-framed structure, clad with corrugated iron, another utilitarian material, on wood sheathing. Other buildings, most of them warehouses, were wood framed, some with corrugated iron siding. The power plant, located north of the assay office, no longer stands, but the complex is otherwise remarkably intact. Some of the buildings are being used by USSR&M's successor, the Alaska Gold Company; others are vacant.

IN013 Fairbanks Exploration Company Housing

c. 1927. 505, 507, 521, and 523 Illinois St.

In about 1927, the Fairbanks Exploration Company built four one-story houses for its management-level employees, across the street from its Fairbanks complex. Hip-roofed with front porches, the wood-framed houses have bungalow characteristics. Numbers 507 and 521 face Illinois Street, with mirror-image plans. Behind 507 is 505, which faces south. Number 523, behind 521, is set at an angle, meant to face a semicircular drive that was never built. Each house has a greenhouse; one four-bay garage serves all of the houses. These four houses of a type, in a planned setting, clearly have a different origin than most houses in Fairbanks. Their role as company housing is clearly expressed in their similar designs.

IN014 Joy Elementary School

1960, Lee S. Linck of Alaska Architectural and Engineering Company; 1989, addition and renovation, ECI/Hyer and Patricia Piersol. 24 Margaret St.

Recognized at a joint meeting of the American Association of School Administrators and the American Institute of Architects in 1962, this unusual circular school was designed in 1960 by the Fairbanks firm of Alaska Architectural and Engineering Company, headed by architect Lee S. Linck. A central multipurpose room is covered with a low saucer dome; the fourteen classrooms on the perimeter have gable roofs. A corridor encircles the multi-purpose room; above this central room was the kitchen and cafeteria. The exterior walls, originally constructed largely of glass, had pointed panels of formed metal, in a variety of colors, beneath the gable roofs. That appearance has since been altered.

In 1986 the school was closed for construction of an addition and the removal of asbestos. The original building was clad with a reinforced fabric covering and several inches of insulation, and window area was reduced, making the building easier to heat. The upper level of the multipurpose room was converted into a viewing area, and the dome of the roof is visible. The addition, half again the size of the original building, picks up the angular motif of the gable roofs and is faceted in plan. The addition is sympathetic, and the building remains an odd but attractive piece of architecture.

IN015 Creamer's Dairy

early twentieth century. Creamer's Lane, between Farmer's Loop and College Rd.

Owned and operated by one family from 1904 to 1965, Creamer's Dairy is a collection of farm buildings dating from all decades of the first half of the twentieth century. The farm was founded by Charles Hinckley, who had brought three cows to the boomtown of Fairbanks, which he recognized as a likely spot for a dairy. In 1920, Charles Creamer, who had grown up in Fairbanks, married Rosanna Goldman, Hinckley's sister-in-law, in Tacoma, Washington. For seven years they operated a chicken farm there, then returned to Fairbanks with a load of chickens. Hinckley sold the farm to Creamer, who continued to operate it until his wife died in 1965.

In addition to the main house and barns, just to the west of the farm complex, is the manager's house, a gable-roofed, one-story house with a gable-roofed vestibule, constructed in 1956, and the two-story, bevel-sided bunkhouse, constructed in 1957. Attached to the east end of the bunkhouse is a one-story garage.

IN015.1 House

1904; 1922, second story

The main house is one of the oldest structures, but like the complex it grew over time.

IN014 Joy Elementary School

The first section was built in 1904, the second story added in 1922, and a rear addition in 1930. As completed, it is a one-and-a-half-story, wood-framed house, covered with novelty siding, with a gable roof and two gable wall dormers.

IN015.2 **Barns**

early twentieth century

The barns are the most prominent buildings on the site. The tallest section, measuring 36 feet by 110 feet, with an ogee-arch roof, was constructed in 1937, while the similarly shaped, 36-foot-by-102-foot section was added later. The roofs are framed with built-up wood trusses, diagonally braced. Perpendicular to them is the older, unpainted barn, a gable-roofed building with dimensions of 40 feet by 104 feet. In front of the barns is the processing building, built in several sections in the 1920s and 1930s, with the most recent constructed of concrete blocks.

IN016 **University of Alaska**

The decision to locate the Alaska College of Agriculture and School of Mines near Fairbanks in 1915 was a factor in Fairbanks's survival as a permanent town. The legislation was introduced in Congress by James Wickersham, a steadfast supporter of Fairbanks, who specified a site near the Agricultural Experiment Station, which had been established in 1906. An appropriation from the territorial legislature was not forthcoming until 1917, when the first building was constructed, although there were not enough funds to furnish it.

With the appointment of Charles E. Bunnell as president in 1921, the college received the boost it needed. Bunnell was a dynamic leader, and the college grew steadily. Classes began in 1922, and the college graduated its first student, a transfer, in 1923. By 1925, there were eleven buildings constituting the campus. In 1935, the college was named the University of Alaska.

Set on a commanding ridge, the architecture of the university does not always take advantage of the site. The plan often seems haphazard; buildings are not connected, despite the severe weather, and recent buildings have been constructed in an extended campus a mile away, and joined by a shuttle-bus service. The permafrost that underlies much of the campus renders certain sites unsuitable for building. In addition, the U.S. Geological Survey owns 40 acres near the middle of campus, preventing expansion to adjacent sites.

No major buildings remain from the initial building program, which concentrated on expedient, wood-framed structures. The second generation, from the 1930s, included several reinforced-concrete structures with modified Art Deco detailing. Postwar expansion has had the greatest effect on the campus, and oil-boom buildings of the 1970s and 1980s are some of the best.

IN016.1 **Eielson Building**

1934, first floor, N. Lester Troast; 1940, completed, Foss and Malcolm

The Eielson Building, officially named the Col. Carl Ben Eielson Aeronautical Engineering Building, represents the building style of the 1930s and also the difficulties the fledgling university encountered. Ben Eielson, a Fairbanks schoolteacher turned pioneering pilot, had been a local hero ever since he took the first air mail contract in 1924, delivering mail from Fairbanks to McGrath. In 1928 he gained further fame when he flew across the top of the world. In 1930 he was killed while trying to rescue the *Nanuk*, a ship caught in Siberian ice.

This building was planned as a memorial to him, but by 1934 only $12,000 of the estimated $100,000 needed for construction had been raised. Nonetheless, construction went forward on a two-story-plus-basement reinforced-concrete building. As designed by N. Lester Troast of Juneau, the 54-foot-by-84-foot building had two-stage buttresses delineating each bay, a corner tower, and Jacobean hood molds on the third-floor windows. That first year, only the first floor was completed, and a temporary gable roof was constructed.

When the building was completed in 1940, Foss and Malcolm were credited with the design, which had taken on a distinctly Art Deco appearance. Troast's buttresses became piers with vertical gouging at the tops. There were also vertical gouging between the first and second floors and zigzag ornament along the cornice. The octagonal corner towers on the west side were left unfinished.

IN016.2 Signer's Hall

1935; 1985, alteration, Roger Cotting

Adjacent to the Eielson Building is Signer's Hall. This concrete building was constructed as the gymnasium, serving later as the museum. A recent renovation has given it a Victorian appearance, incredibly enough.

IN016.3 Elmer E. Rasmuson Library

1970, Manley and Mayer

At the north side of the quadrangle at the heart of the campus is the Elmer E. Rasmuson Library. Along with the similar and adjacent Fine Arts Complex, it was constructed to a design by Manley and Mayer. The library has a concrete and pebble-dash exterior. The flat roof with wide eaves seems to float above the building on a row of windows at the cornice.

IN016.4 Bunnell Building

1959, Manley and Mayer

Across the quadrangle from the library is the Bunnell Building. The Bunnell Building re-placed Old Main, the original main building of the campus, which was located just in front of this building. The Bunnell Building's curtain wall of enameled panels and glass terminates in concrete bays at either end.

IN016.5 Duckering Building

1964, Alaska Architectural and Engineering Company; 1985, addition, Ellerbe Alaska

Designed by the firm of Fairbanks architect Lee S. Linck, the Duckering Building, next door to the Bunnell Building, is similar to it in appearance. An addition to the rear, which in contrast to the many-windowed front of the building uses bold lines and a flat facade, was designed by Ellerbe Alaska, now Design Alaska.

IN016.6 Brooks Building

1952, Foss, Malcolm and Olsen

Next to Duckering is Brooks Building, a concrete monolith caught between Art Moderne and Brutalism.

IN016.7 Gruening Building

1973, Graham, Knorr, Elliot

Across from Brooks is the large, cube-shaped Gruening Building, combining concrete anonymity with jarring fenestration.

IN016.8 Constitution Hall

1956, Foss, Malcolm and Olsen

North of Gruening is Constitution Hall, a two-story concrete building, with a dramatic one-story portion.

IN016.9 President's House

1958, Edwin B. Crittenden

There are several buildings of interest along Yukon Drive. One of them, the President's House, is a long, low building, one story in the front and two in the rear, due to its sloping site.

IN016.10 Moore, Bartlett, and Skarland Halls

1964, Alaska Architecture and Engineering Company

(Skarlana); 1966, 1970, Crittenden, Cassetta, Wirum, and Cannon (Moore and Bartlett, respectively)

Each building in this group of high-rise dormitories has a similar pebble-dash exterior and narrow windows.

IN016.11 Rainey's Cabin

1936

Just west of that complex is Rainey's Cabin, a sentimental favorite. Built in 1936, Rainey's Cabin is of most interest as an example of the Rustic style, a consciously nostalgic attempt to recapture frontier Alaskan dwellings. Like such houses, this one is one story and built of log, but the similarities end there. The asymmetrical gable roof and the sheer number of windows, including an odd one with a pointed arch, are unusual, and the stone, open fireplace in the center of the living room is completely anomalous. Open fireplaces are not effective heating mechanisms, and stone was laborious to transport. Located in the midst of the concrete and high-rise buildings of the university, the cabin was built by T. S. Batchelder for the first professor of anthropology on the campus, Froelich Rainey, and his wife. It still houses an occasional visiting anthropology professor.

IN016.12 University of Alaska Museum

1981, CCC/HOK

There are two buildings in the collection at the west end of campus that are of particular interest, the Butrovich Building and the University of Alaska Museum. The museum is a stark white assemblage of geometric shapes. Well composed, it sits comfortably on its hillside, overlooking the valley below.

IN016.13 Butrovich Building

1989-present, Design Alaska

Also on the west end of campus is the newest building at the University of Alaska. Like the museum, it is very white. A low, horizontal building, it hugs the hillside, its horizontality further emphasized by long concrete retaining walls at either end. It remains only partially occupied.

IN016.14 Patty Gymnasium

1963, Linn A. Forrest; 1979, addition, Ellerbe Alaska

At the bottom of the hill, providing a weak entrance to the campus, is the Patty Gym. Designed by Linn A. Forrest and constructed in 1963, it has a large addition designed by Ellerbe Alaska (now Design Alaska) and completed in 1979.

IN017 Agricultural Experiment Station

1911–present. West Tanana Dr.

Few buildings remain from the early days of this Agricultural Experiment Station, established in 1906. By 1911, 93 acres had been cleared, 70 of which were under cultivation. A log barn, 30 feet by 32 feet when built, was extended 30 feet. Two log cabins had been converted to provide housing, and in 1911 a new cottage was built, perhaps the one that stands there now. In 1914, a 25-foot-by-40-foot hog house was built. Using earth as insulation between studs, it was covered with corrugated, galvanized iron.

The station was one of the more successful of the U.S. Department of Agriculture's Alaska stations, and buildings appear to have been replaced as needed. The present dairy barn has a concrete block first floor (probably in response to dairy laws) and a gambrel roof. All of the other barns have plywood siding with a saw kerf textured siding called T1-11 and gable roofs. When the government closed all the agricultural experiment stations in Alaska in 1932, this one was acquired by the University of Alaska, which continues to administer it today.

Fairbanks Vicinity

IN018 Chena Pump House

1933. Chena Pump Rd.

Water was a critical element in advanced gold-mining operations. High-pressure water stripped the muck overburden, steam thawed the frozen gravel, and water dredged and sluiced it. The Chena Pump House took this badly needed water from the Chena River and pumped it over the Chena Ridge to the Cripple Creek operations near Ester, 6 miles east of Fairbanks.

Constructed by the Fairbanks Exploration Company in 1933, the pump house is a simple wood-framed building, measuring 20 feet by 108 feet, with a corrugated-metal covering and a gable roof. Inside, the machinery included ten 14-inch double-suction centrifugal pumps, which delivered water through three 26-inch pipelines. Once over the ridge, the water flowed through a 3-mile ditch to the mining operations, where it was used for stripping and dredge ponds.

In about 1958 the pump house went out of service. Twenty years later, the building was rehabilitated for use as a restaurant. All of the machinery has been removed.

Ester

IN019 Cripple Creek

1930s

In 1905–1906, Ester was the site of a mining camp that had three hotels, five saloons, and two general stores. After the richer areas had been mined, however, the population quickly dropped off and little is left of this early camp. Most of the buildings still standing date from the 1930s, when the Fairbanks Exploration Company set up a large camp on the site. The company used corrugated metal, a quick, inexpensive, and fireproof way to cover a building, and other similarly expedient materials, resulting in a utilitarian appearance. Working with a dredge and aided by water pumped over the Chena Ridge from the pump house on the Chena River, the company began mining operations in 1935–1936. In 1940 they brought in a second dredge, and that winter three hundred men were working the site. After closing temporarily during World War II, the camp continued operating until 1958. It is now run as the Cripple Creek Resort.

IN019.1 Mess Hall-Bunkhouse

1934, Arnold Nordale; 1936–1937, moved to current site

The mess hall-bunkhouse, now the restaurant and hotel, was constructed in 1934 at the

IN019.1 Mess Hall-Bunkhouse

Fairbanks Exploration Company's camp at Fox and moved to Ester in 1936–1937. Built according to plans by Arnold Nordale, a company employee, the two-story, hip-roofed building measures 37 feet by 72 feet. The wood-framed structure was sided with boards, tar paper, and corrugated metal; Celotex was placed on the interior. About one third of the first floor was devoted to kitchen facilities; the rest was the dining room and rooms for the cooks and foreman. The second floor had twelve rooms housing four men apiece. During a twenty-six-day strike in 1941, the men demanded indoor toilets (among other things), so a one-story, shed-roofed bathroom was added to one side. Today the building serves as a hotel and restaurant. The dining room has been enlarged by one bay by removing the cooks' and foreman's rooms. The bedrooms on the second floor each have two beds and a bath.

IN019.2 Assay Office / Superintendent's Office and Blacksmith Shop

1906

The assay office/superintendent's office (now the gift shop) and the blacksmith shop (now the mining museum) both date from about 1906, the time of Ester's first wave of settlement. Both are one-story, gable-roofed structures, the assay office sided with horizontal planks and the blacksmith's shop with corrugated metal. The false fronts were added in about 1958 to make their appearance more picturesque. Between them is the Malemute Saloon, a reconstruction; the original burned to the ground in 1969.

IN019.3 **Bunkhouses**

late 1930s

Clustered north of the mess hall are additional bunkhouses. The shed-roofed one was built to house twelve men in three rooms, each 12 feet by 16 feet. The three exterior doors are similar in arrangement to the ATCO trailers popular during pipeline construction days in the 1970s. The other three bunkhouses were built to house sixteen men. They have center doors, with four rooms opening off the center hall. Both the twelve- and sixteen-man bunkhouses are covered with corrugated metal, a prefabricated building material.

IN019.4 **Wanigans**

1930s

Just west of the bunkhouses are two wanigans, portable housing built by the Fairbanks Exploration Company for men patrolling segments of the Davidson Ditch. These wood-framed buildings have shallow-pitched gable roofs and tar paper covering the exterior walls. They were built on skids, designed to be moved.

Fox

IN020 **Goldstream Dredge No. 8**

1928

The Fairbanks Exploration Company's Dredge No. 8 went into operation at Goldstream Creek

11 miles north of Fairbanks in 1928. In the next thirty years, it moved only 4 1/2 miles, yet it shifted tons of earth and recovered 7.5 million ounces of gold. The dredge itself, five stories high, remains virtually unaltered from when the operation shut down in 1959. The site is open to the public.

The dredge is essentially a metal clad, floating building of utilitarian design. The Bethlehem Steel Company manufactured the dredge in Bethlehem, Pennsylvania. It was then shipped across the country by train and floated to Fairbanks and assembled. The structure of the dredge is steel framed, with metal siding on wood studs. Sixty-eight buckets, each with a capacity of 6 cubic feet, scooped schist and brought it on board. The schist was placed in a trommel, a perforated cylinder, which rotated. Smaller pieces fell out into sluice boxes, where water caused excess particles to float and gold to sink, catching on riffles. The gold was finally picked up with a mercury amalgam.

Processed schist was expelled out the back of the dredge into tailings piles. Powered by electricity generated in Fairbanks by the United States Smelting, Refining and Mining Company, which owned the Fairbanks Exploration Company, the dredge floated in its own pond and moved by means of winches in a zigzag pattern. Eight people were required to run the dredge, which operated for about eight months of the year, three shifts a day. Six more people worked on the ground, preparing the area to be dredged by removing overburden with hoses and melting permafrost with cold-water thawing. Core samples were taken to aim the dredge.

IN020.1 **Bunkhouse**

1928

Near the dredge is a two-story, hip-roofed bunkhouse, constructed by the Fairbanks Exploration Company. Measuring 37 feet by 73 feet, the wood-framed structure was covered with corrugated metal, as were most of the FE Company's camp buildings. The first floor contained the kitchen and dining room, while the second floor had twelve bedrooms. The bunkhouse was moved to its present site in 1983 from its original location on the other side of Steese Highway. The adjacent smaller bunkhouse was also an FE Company structure, moved to this site more recently.

Chatanika

IN021 **Chatanika Gold Camp**
1925

Chatanika served as the base camp for the Fairbanks Exploration Company's operations on the Chatanika and Cleary creeks, 28 miles north of Fairbanks. In 1928, mining was assisted by the completion of the 90-mile Davidson Ditch and by the two dredges built on Goldstream Creek, evidenced by the tailings piles on the north side of Steese Highway. In preparation for this effort, the FE Company constructed the Chatanika camp in 1925.

The remaining buildings from that time are all wood framed and clad with corrugated metal. The largest are the two bunkhouses at the top of the hill. The thirty-six-man bunkhouse-mess hall, a gable-roofed building, now serves as a restaurant and hotel. There is a screened meat cache off the back end of this building. The fifty-two-man bunkhouse has a hip roof and a one-story bathroom addition. The blacksmith shop, boiler house, and garage also survive from this period. Wood-sided buildings at the site date from a later period.

North Pole

IN022 **North Pole High School**
1985, Design Alaska. Eighth Ave. and Old Richardson Hwy.

North Pole is 15 miles southeast of Fairbanks, developed after the Second World War due to an oil refinery, nearby military bases, and a recognizable postmark. The newness of the surrounding community is reflected in the high school, a bold and colorful building in an often bleak landscape.

The North Pole High School was designed by the Fairbanks firm of Design Alaska. The austere concrete walls are enlivened by a variety of geometric shapes painted different colors and separated by red and blue lines. The tall, windowless block in the center of the front is the fly for the stage; the auditorium behind it seats 450. Classrooms are arranged on hallways on two sides of the building. Near the entrance is the cafeteria, open to the corridors, and the gymnasium is in the block to the right. Displaying a lively use of concrete, the design has won awards from the Alaska chapter of the AIA and American Society of School Administrators in conjunction with the AIA.

South and West

Nenana

At the turn of the twentieth century, Nenana was an Athapaskan Indian village. James Duke set up a trading post here in 1906, and Nenana's history would have been unexceptional if it had not been for the Alaska Railroad. With a strategic location at the confluence of the Tanana and Nenana rivers, Nenana was originally intended as a construction camp where materials to build the railroad to the south could be unloaded from steamboats. The Alaska Engineering Commission built some substantial buildings: an office building, bachelors' quarters, mess hall, and hospital, all two-story, foursquare, hip-roofed buildings; none of them survives. On B Street, however, are a number of one-story, hip-roofed cottages that appear to date from the railroad's construction. Although some have been altered, each had a front porch covered by the main hip roof and a hip-roofed dormer.

The AEC platted a townsite here in 1916, and lots sold unexpectedly well. Originally, the railroad was to cross the Tanana at the west side of town, where the Parks Highway Bridge (built in 1967) now crosses. When the crossing east of town was decided, engineers made a distinct effort to route the tracks through town, ensuring Nenana's financial viability. Just east of town, the tracks make a large loop to the south before turning north across the bridge. By 1921, Nenana's function as a construction camp had ended, and the Alaska Engineering Commission withdrew most of its personnel. The construction of the bridge over the Tanana, completed in 1923, brought another spurt of activity. President Warren G. Harding came to Nenana to drive the golden spike marking completion of the railroad on 15 July 1923.

A fire in 1935 destroyed most of the buildings in the heart of the city, so few of the earlier commercial establishments survive. The depot at the foot of A Street and the railroad that still runs through the heart of town stand as vivid reminders of Nenana's past.

IN023 Alaska Railroad Depot

1922. Front and A streets

Designed by the Alaska Engineering Commission, the depot at Nenana was constructed in 1922 by contractor Hartley Howard at a cost of $24,000. Based on the same design as the station in Seward, Nenana's was 4 feet longer at either end and a bit wider to accommodate more insulation. The overall dimensions are 98 feet by 24 feet, with a 30 foot wide section in the middle. The wood frame was covered with wide clapboards below the window sills and wood shingles above. The low hipped roof, hip-roofed dormers, wide overhangs supported by brackets, and exposed rafter ends are identified with the Craftsman style and stem ultimately from the stations that H. H. Richardson designed for small towns in New England four decades earlier.

The interior is finished with a pressed-tin ceiling and vertical board wainscoting. A slight change in plan from the Seward station provided for a hallway from the waiting room to baggage room, between the ticket agent's office on the track side and the bathrooms on the road side.

In 1937 a second story was added to the west end of the building to provide quarters for the station agent. The addition, clad with narrow clapboarding, is topped with a hipped roof. The station today is occupied by a museum and gift shop.

IN024 Saint Mark's Episcopal Church

1907; 1955, moved to present location and rebuilt. Front and Market streets

Saint Mark's, a log church measuring 22 feet by 28 feet, was built in 1907 at the site of a mission 1 mile upriver. About 1955 it was moved to its present site, where it sits at a slight angle to the intersection, and was probably largely rebuilt at the same time. Nonetheless, the log construction, gable front, and bell tower so favored by the Episcopalians are preserved. Although log construction was not necessary—sawn lumber being readily available—the logs gave the church a picturesque appearance, at the same time being exotic enough to appeal to potential donors in the Lower 48. The gable-roofed church is constructed of logs sawn flat on top and bottom, saddle notched at the corners, ends projecting. The Gothic windows have stained glass. At the front of the shake-covered roof is a pyramidal-roofed open belfry.

The Episcopal mission was founded a distance from the Native village, on the opposite side of the river, in order to segregate the pupils from the negative influences of the village. The Episcopal church built a boarding school that attracted some forty Natives from the region. With the "usual inducement" of doors and windows, Natives moved near to the mission and created a "proper village," in Rev. Hudson Stuck's words. When the Alaska Engineering Commission platted a townsite a mile away, Stuck expressed concern that the influences of a railroad town were even more nefarious than those of a

Native village. Stuck requested the Alaska Engineering Commission to move the mission and surrounding village to a new site, but they declined. Ironically, after the closing of the boarding school in 1955, the church was moved into the railroad town that Stuck so deplored.

IN025 **Mears Memorial Bridge**

1922–1923, Modjeski and Angier, engineers

When built, this bridge over the Tanana River was among the longest single-span truss bridges in the United States. The 704-foot-long, pin-connected, through-truss railroad bridge was designed by Modjeski and Angier of Chicago, consulting engineers. Designed to avoid the necessity for piers in the river, which were subject to damage from ice floes in the spring, the bridge was also elevated to allow river traffic to pass. As a result, the southern approach was extensive, including a 2,880-foot-long timber trestle and a steel viaduct that featured a 120-foot-long Warren deck truss. A steep bluff at the north end of the bridge required only one short approach span. The American Bridge Company fabricated the bridge at its Ambridge works outside of Pittsburgh and transported the bridge parts by rail to Seattle and by boat to Alaska. Construction of the bridge was closely supervised by Col. Frederick Mears, chairman of the Alaska Engineering Commission. He was

replaced as chairman in March 1923, three months before the bridge opened, completing the 470-mile length of the Alaska Railroad.

Healy

IN026 **Historical Healy Hotel**

1946; 1986, moved to present location. Mile 248.8 Parks Hwy.

Built in 1946, the Healy Hotel takes the form of a 1940s Moderne building, but in place of the usual concrete, the materials here are those of a traditional railroad structure. The wood-framed building is two stories, rectangular in plan, with a flat roof and no cornice. The walls are covered with horizontal and vertical beveled siding, alternating in bands, in an almost Stick-style application. The center section of the building, containing the lobby and main stairway, projects, and there is a one-story restaurant projecting from the rear. A corridor runs longitudinally, with rooms on the front and back.

The hotel was originally located next to the railroad tracks in Healy and housed railroad employees based there as well as train crews passing through. In June 1986, the hotel was moved about a mile to its present site. The only alterations to the exterior were vestibules at the end of each building, but on the interior, thirty-two bathrooms were added.

Denali National Park and Preserve

Established as a national park in 1917, just one year after the National Park Service was founded, Mount McKinley National Park was centered on the towering, 20,320-foot Mount McKinley. The 2,200 square miles of the park included the crest and northern slope of the Alaska Range, and at the time was the United States' second largest park, second only to Yellowstone. Advocates also hoped that the park would protect the local populations of caribou and Dall sheep, threatened by the imminent completion of the Alaska Railroad, and would encourage tourism to the central part of Alaska.

The park was expanded to 3,030 square miles in 1932. In 1938 the National Park Service built a two-story, flat-roofed hotel; it burned in 1971. The park's name was changed to Denali in 1980, in recognition of the Native name for the mountain, and the park was expanded to 6 million acres. The first national park in Alaska, Denali has always been one of the more accessible, located directly on the Alaska Railroad. Encompassing such vast expanses of wilderness, Denali has been seen as the essence of Alaskan national parks.

While the architecture is truly secondary to the natural splendors for which the park was founded, Denali's buildings illustrate an evolving Rustic style. Buildings in the park harmonize with the landscape through siting, indigenous materials, unobtrusive sizes, and an openness to the outdoors.

IN027　Visitor Access Center

1990, ECI/Hyer. Riley Creek

The Visitor Access Center at Riley Creek borrows from Rustic architecture and railroad buildings. The two-story building is large, with a high gable roof with gable dormers, covered with standing-seam metal. The walls covered with beveled siding, alternating with bands of vertical planks, recall railroad architecture. A hip-roofed porch with a log-handrail balustrade on three sides of the building and cross-gable entrances with exposed log bracing in the gables are elements of the Rustic style.

Most of the interior is opened to the full two-story space, lit by a large window in the gable end. At the other end is a 250-seat theater, and along one side there are offices on two levels. The function of the building is to process visitors, sending them in appropriate directions, while at the same time giving them an introduction to the park. This handsome building is an appealing beginning to a visit.

IN028　Headquarters Buildings

1925–1937

The naturalistic setting, unobtrusive size of the buildings, and use of native materials in the construction of the headquarters buildings are all hallmarks of the Rustic style. Foremost is the setting, which is on a hillside, set in a spruce forest, with winding roads and trails. While the complex is composed of two dozen buildings, the small size of the buildings and their compatibility to their setting serve as a camouflage. None of the buildings is more than two stories tall; most are constructed of round logs; all are painted dark brown.

Construction of the headquarters at the present site started in 1925, but no money was allocated for building construction until 1928. In these early years, park rangers themselves built the buildings of logs, locally

cut, and of found materials such as pieces of surplus railroad buildings.

During the years 1928–1937 there was dramatic expansion of the park facilities and the further implementation of the Rustic style. By 1937, there were eighteen buildings at headquarters. The new buildings were designed by Park Service landscape architects and featured round logs as structural frame or as whole walls, rough-sawn board-and-batten siding, and exposed rafters and purlins in the gable ends.

Between 1938 and 1941, the Park Service used Civilian Conservation Corps personnel and funding to continue the building program, as well as to improve roads and sewers throughout the park. Park Service architects designed buildings with a variety of finish materials, departing somewhat from their previous commitment to traditional materials. The five surviving buildings from this period (see IN028.3, IN028.4, and IN028.5 for examples) are clad with clapboards, stone, and reinforced concrete, as well as the traditional logs.

Recent construction in the compound has been generally compatible architecturally, and the rustic feeling of the place is preserved.

IN028.1　Office Building (Building No. 22)

1926

One building remaining from the first period, when the rangers built their own buildings, is Office Building No. 22, which served as the superintendent's office, a one-story, gable-fronted building of round logs square notched at the corners. The building, which is about 20 feet on a side, has been moved twice and the porch reconstructed, but its appearance is essentially the same as when it was built.

IN028.2 **Building No. 21**

1934–1935

An example of the Rustic buildings designed by Park Service architects, Building No. 21 features a large shed dormer and a stone chimney. The first-floor walls are built of round logs, laid horizontally, while the second floor is clad with vertical rounded planks; the building has a concrete foundation. Built as a dormitory for rangers, it now serves as the administrative office, and the interior has been substantially altered.

IN028.3 **Building No. 102**

1939

Built of concrete—not usually a Rustic material—this garage has clapboards in the gable. There is a large addition to one side.

IN028.4 **Building No. 23**

1940–1941

This employees' residence has a steep gable roof with shed dormer. The foundation is concrete, the first floor is of horizontal round logs, and the upper story wood-framed with vertical log planks.

IN028.5 **Building No. 111**

1939

The superintendent's garage, this building is unusual for its stone-veneered concrete walls. The superintendent's house, which stood nearby, burned, and the garage has been converted to a residence, which involved a large addition and the filling in of the garage doors.

IN028.5 Building No. 111

IN029 **Patrol Cabins**

1924–1925. Denali National Park and Preserve

Fourteen cabins constructed within Denali National Park from 1924 to 1935 survive. Built as winter quarters for rangers who patrol the park to prevent poaching and illegal trapping, the cabins are simple log structures. Patrolling in the winter is still done by dog sled. The cabins are spaced 10 to 15 miles apart, equivalent to one day's journey.

Six of the cabins were built along the McKinley National Park Road, the 86-mile road that goes through the heart of the park, from the Alaska Railroad station to Kantishna (see IN029.1 and IN029.2). The Alaska Road Commission and the National Park Service cooperated to construct the road, and the cabins along it are also a product of their partnership.

Along the park's north boundary, six boundary cabins constructed by carpenters contracted to the park service in 1930–1932 survive. The 12-foot-by-14-foot cabins are constructed of round logs saddle notched at the corners; log ends are battered. Two later boundary cabins were built in 1932 and 1935 (IN029.3).

IN029.1 **Savage River Cabin**

1925

The first cabin completed along the road was the Savage River Cabin, and from there the cabins were spaced every 10–15 miles. Like most of the cabins, this one is 12 feet by 14 feet, of logs hewn flat on three sides, square notched at the corners. As with all of the

IN029.2a Pearson Cabin (exterior)

IN029.2b Pearson Cabin (sections and floor plan)

IN029.2c Pearson Cabin (cache)

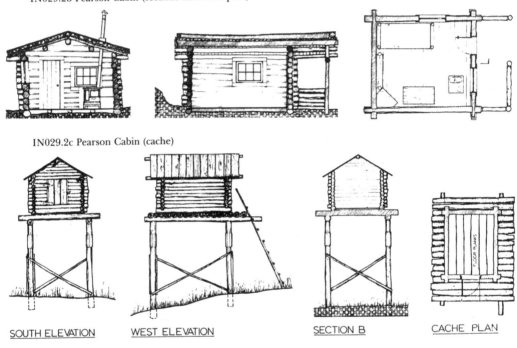

SOUTH ELEVATION   WEST ELEVATION   SECTION B   CACHE PLAN

IN029.2d Pearson Cabin (doghouse)

EAST ELEVATION   SOUTH ELEVATION   SECTION C   DOG KENNEL PLAN

patrol cabins, the gable roof extends in the front to cover a porch.

IN029.2 Pearson Cabin

1927

An exception to the typical design is the first cabin at the Toklat River, known as the Pearson Cabin, built by park service personnel. Grant Pearson, one of the rangers who constructed the building, went on to become park superintendent. The 12-foot-square building is constructed of round logs, saddle notched at the corners. Wood for the floor, doors, and window frames was whipsawn by the rangers. The outbuildings include a log cache, raised nearly 10 feet off the ground. Small-diameter round logs form the walls, roof, and floor. Four two-room doghouses, constructed of round logs with shed roofs, would have housed eight dogs, enough for a team.

IN029.3 (Lower) Windy Creek Ranger Station and Moose Creek Ranger Cabin

1932, 1935

Two later boundary cabins, the (Lower) Windy Creek Ranger Station from 1932 and the Moose Creek Ranger Cabin from 1935, were designed by Park Service landscape architects. Like the others, they are built of round logs saddle notched at the corners, but they exhibit a higher degree of finish and each has two rooms. Sill logs are laid on concrete foundations, and the interiors have tongue-and-groove flooring and built-in cabinets.

IN030 Wonder Lake Ranger Station

1939. Denali National Park and Preserve

Built by Civilian Conservation Corps workers, the Wonder Lake Ranger Station is a one-story, L-shaped building. Set on a raised, concrete foundation, the wood-framed building is clad with clapboards up to the window sills and board-and-batten siding above. A porch across the front wraps around one side of the ell; posts are ornamented with rudimentary fan brackets. This example of the Park Service's Rustic architecture has one of the finest views of Mount McKinley from its front porch.

Tanana

IN031 (Episcopal) Church of Our Saviour

1897–1906

Overlooking the Yukon River in splendid isolation, the Church of Our Saviour is an outstanding example of the Shingle style in the wilderness. With a dramatic cross-gable roof, the T-shaped building is further enhanced by round arches set in three of the four gables. Within each round arch is a triplet of round-arch windows, the center one taller than its neighbors. The walls are a combination of log and wood-frame construction, a particularly strong illustration of the combination of frontier and high style that characterizes so much Alaskan architecture. The logs, hewn flat on three sides, are lap jointed at the corners; above them, wood shingles cover a wood frame. The shingled walls are painted red, while the shake roof is painted green. A bell tower at the crossing has a modillioned cornice and a pyramidal roof, also covered with shakes. Several details point to a sophisticated builder: the wood-shingled walls slope out slightly, to cover the lintels of the windows, adding a plastic quality to the walls. Each round arch has two rows of shingles, slightly inset, serving as voussoirs.

When it was intact, the interior was equally dramatic, with walls and ceilings covered with a beaded, tongue-and-groove redwood siding. The siding was laid vertically as a wainscot, over 5 feet high, and diagonally on the walls above. The altar was on a raised platform on the east side, and on the north was a library and mortuary. There was a choir balcony in the north transept.

The Episcopal mission was founded by Bishop Peter Trimble Rowe and Reverend Jules L. Prevost in 1896, who located the mission near the confluence of the Yukon and Tanana rivers, across from a Native village. A church supporter named Mary Rhinelander King, from New York, donated the money for the church. Although the origin of the design is not known, it shares the Shingle style of Saint Peter's in Sitka (SE044, p. 000); Rowe himself helped construct both of them. Judging by these two churches, Bishop Rowe believed in architecturally sophisticated churches that would make an impact on their communities. Within a few years, however, the Episcopalians resorted to more functional log churches, little different from log cabins. Perhaps the difficulties encountered in the construction of this church accounted for the shift in policy. Construction of this church, sometimes halted because of lack of materials, took about nine years, and at least two professional carpenters worked on it. The building was finally consecrated in October 1906.

By 1910, the mission included a church, hospital, sawmill (established in 1898), cemetery, rectory, school reserve, and thirteen Native houses. Three miles downriver was the trading post and primarily non-Native town of Tanana, and beyond that, Fort Gibbon. The mission was abandoned in the 1940s, when most of the inhabitants moved to the downriver town.

The Church of Our Saviour is currently being restored by the village, which recognizes it as a landmark. In 1981, the foundation was replaced, the building raised several feet, and some new logs installed on the lower part of the walls. The roof was also repaired at that time. The restoration work has not been completed, however; doors and windows are covered temporarily with plywood and plastic, and on the interior the floor remains plywood and the wainscoting has been removed, exposing the logs and studs.

IN031.1 Saint James Episcopal Church

1940s

Saint James Episcopal Church was established in Tanana in the early twentieth century for the non-Native population. The church, dating from the 1940s, is a gable-roofed log building, with a central, front bell tower. It has an active congregation.

East

Central

IN032 Central House

1926. Mile 128 Steese Hwy.

Built on the road from Fairbanks to Circle, the two-story log roadhouse is in a deteriorated condition but still conveys its former grandeur. Riley Erickson and Henry Stade built the 20-foot-by-52-foot building in 1926 to replace the original roadhouse, dating from 1894. The building is constructed of round logs, saddle notched at the corners, and well-chinked with moss. The gable roof is supported by four purlins but no ridgepole; it is covered with sod on planks. There is a large one-story addition on the south side.

When the Steese Highway was under construction in 1927, Erickson and Stade made sure that the highway would go right by their door. But travelers in automobiles had less need for roadhouses than those traveling by dogsled, and after Erickson's death in 1948, the roadhouse closed. It now has garage doors in its gable end, signifying a new use as an outbuilding.

Circle Hot Springs

IN033 Arctic Circle Hot Springs

1930

A few miles south of the road to Circle is an area of natural hot springs, which had long been used by miners, and before them, Natives. The area was not developed into a formal resort until 1930, when Frank and Emma Leach built the two-and-a-half-story hotel. The gable-roofed building, with a three-and-a-half-story cross gable at one end, has gable dormers. The pool is adjacent, as are a number of log cabins, some dating from before construction of the hotel. Recent additions include ATCO trailers—prefabricated four-room trailers used during pipeline construction—covered with logs and serving as motel rooms.

Big Delta

IN034 **Big Delta State Historical Park**

1907–1926

Big Delta State Historical Park, located on the Valdez-Fairbanks Trail on the south bank of the Tanana River, includes several buildings that reflect the transportation and communications functions that developed around this pivotal location.

The transportation hub flourished until the Second World War, when the Alaska Highway was built, connecting with the Richardson Highway (the old Valdez-Fairbanks Trail) south of this site. During the subsequent upgrading of the Richardson Highway, it was rerouted west of the roadhouse, and a bridge replaced the ferry across the Tanana River.

The site is now a state park, interpreting several phases of Alaska's transportation and communications history.

IN034.1 **Signal Corps Building**

1907

Near a roadhouse that had been constructed in 1904 ran the Washington-Alaska Military Cable and Telegraph System (WAMCATS), the overland communications system linking military bases to each other and to the contiguous United States. In 1907, the U.S. Signal Corps built several cabins here for their staff. One Signal Corps building survives: a simple log structure, square notched at the corners, with the log ends painted a trademark red and white.

IN034.2 **Rika's Roadhouse**

1909–1910

In 1909–1910, the Alaska Road Commission upgraded the Valdez-Fairbanks Trail from a sled trail to a wagon road. At that time, John Hajdukovich replaced the original one-story roadhouse with the two-story, gable-fronted structure known today as Rika's Roadhouse. The eave line continues across the gable front, giving the three-bay building a pedimented look. The construction is round logs, saddle notched at the corners.

In 1917, Hajdukovich hired Rika Wallen, a recent Swedish immigrant, to run the roadhouse; he sold it to her in 1923. In 1926 she added the side-gable portion. She had a flourishing farm here, witnessed by the several outbuildings, as well as a post office and the roadhouse. Bypassed by the upgraded Richardson Highway, Wallen closed her roadhouse in 1947 but lived here until her death in 1969. The roadhouse has been restored. The interior has been remodeled as a gift shop, although a piece of packing-crate flooring remains.

IN034.3 **Ferryman's Cabin**

1929

The Alaska Road Commission ran a ferry across the Tanana River here, constructing a log cabin for the ferryman in 1929. The ferryman's cabin still stands at the water's edge, with a gable roof extended in front. Another log building on the site was constructed as a storage shed for the ARC in 1914.

Chicken

IN035 **Chicken Creek Hotel**

1906

In the Fortymile Mining District, on the Valdez-Eagle trail, was the mining town of Chicken, distinguished by the two-story Chicken Creek Hotel, constructed by Harvey Van Hook in 1906. When the territory acquired the building in 1925 to use it as a school, the second story was removed. In 1946, the building was used again as a roadhouse. Seven years later, the Fairbanks Exploration Company acquired it and still owns it but does not use it. Active mining occurs near the townsite, which is now private property.

The log building is constructed of squared logs, butted at the corners and nailed into corner boards. There are two rooms across the front, each with a door and two windows in the front of the building, and one room across the rear. The building has a low gable roof, covered with corrugated metal.

Chicken Vicinity

IN036 **Jack Wade Dredge**

1907. Mile 86 Taylor Hwy.

The rusting heap of Jack Wade Dredge, sitting next to the highway in a rearranged dredge pond, is a visible reminder of the intense gold mining that took place in this region beginning at the end of the nineteenth century. The Fortymile district, of which this is a part, experienced a gold rush in 1887 and continued to flourish, receiving spillover miners from the Klondike after 1897.

One of the first dredges in the area, the Jack Wade Dredge was brought into the Fortymile in 1907, first working Walker Fork and Uhler Creek. A tin-covered building on pontoons, the dredge is considerably larger than most buildings of its time in Alaska, with about half the capacity of the Goldstream Dredge in Fox. In 1934, when it was brought to Jack Wade Creek, the hull and bucket line were replaced. The dredge worked until 1941; it has since been abandoned.

Boundary

IN037 **Boundary Cafe and Lodge**

1930s, cafe; 1926, lodge

Located almost at the Canadian border on the road to Dawson, the town of Boundary consists of two historic log cabins. The larger of the two still serves as a cafe; it is constructed of round logs, saddle notched at the corners. The gable roof, constructed of sod on poles, covered with metal, extends in the front about 3 feet. The lodge, near the road, is also a log building with saddle notching and a gable roof extended in front. Constructed of both indigenous and found materials, products of their wilderness setting, the buildings continue to function as a way station for travelers.

Eagle

Set on the Yukon River 8 miles from the Canadian border, Eagle was founded as a mining town but owes its survival to its role as a transportation and communications hub. The U.S. Army established a post here in order to have a presence on the border, and the U.S. government established a customs office here as well. Finally linked to the road system in 1954, Eagle is a community with about one hundred buildings, nearly half dating from the first decade of the town's life. It is one of the more accessible places in Alaska to see and understand the frontier life through the architectural record.

Of the thousands of hopefuls who poured into Canada's Klondike Region in 1897–1898, many moved down the Yukon or up the Fortymile River when they found the grounds already staked. Eagle was founded in 1898 as a gold-rush boomtown, near claims on American and Mission creeks. Initially, it had a population of 1,700, but within a year it had dropped to 400, and Eagle's role shifted to serving as an American trading post on the Yukon River for the Fortymile region to the south. Winding 1,300 miles through the heart of Alaska and on into the Yukon Territory of Canada, the Yukon River gave access to the Klondike gold-rush town of Dawson. Over a hundred steamboats a year plied the upper Yukon River in summer, most of them stopping at the transfer point of Eagle. Laid out in a grid plan, the town soon had large commercial buildings on the river and small, one-story log cabins on lots behind. When it incorporated in 1900, Eagle's population had declined to 300.

In 1899 the U.S. Army located a company of men at the post known as Fort Egbert. Besides keeping the peace among the gold stampeders and establishing a U.S. presence on the border, the army also extended the Washington-Alaska Military Cable and Telegraph System (WAMCATS) to Eagle and built the Valdez-

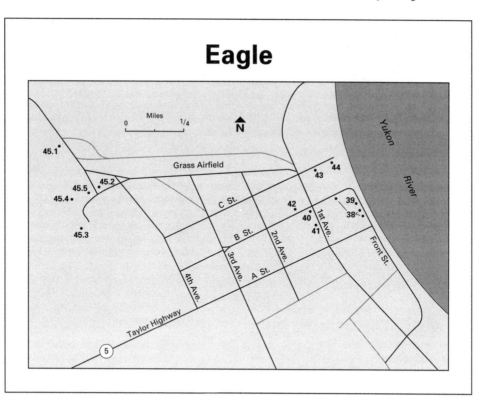

Eagle trail, known as the Trans-Alaska Military Road. In 1900 Eagle was named the seat of the Third Judicial District Court, and Judge James Wickersham arrived to build a courthouse and home. In 1903 a customs station opened in Eagle.

Eagle's importance faded quickly, however. The army built the Valdez-Fairbanks trail in 1902–1906. In 1903, Wickersham moved his court to Fairbanks. By 1911 Fort Egbert had been mostly abandoned by the army, and by the 1920s steamboat traffic had fallen to only a few regular runs. In 1939, only 26 people voted in a local election in Eagle, and today fewer than 200 people live there.

Eagle began as a log cabin town, but the presence of a sawmill by 1900 changed its appearance. Many of the older buildings—mostly log, many covered with novelty siding salvaged from the fort—survive.

A few miles upriver from Eagle is Eagle Village, the home of the Han Athapaskans native to the area. Little about their architecture is distinctly Athapaskan; it consists mostly of log buildings similar to those in Eagle. The linear layout of the houses, however, their orientation to the river, and the existence of outbuildings such as smokehouses, which are illustrative of subsistence lifestyles, are characteristic of Native villages.

Eagle

IN038 Northern Commercial Company Buildings

1898–1899

Three buildings in Eagle are identified with the Northern Commercial Company, the biggest trader in the Interior, created by the merger of the Alaska Exploration Company and the Alaska Commercial Company in 1901. A corrugated-metal-covered warehouse on Front Street and a store next door were built in 1898–1899 for the AE Company, while around the corner on Berry Street the AC Company built another store. The Front Street store has an elaborate false front, featuring multipaned storefront windows, recessed entrance, and a stepped, parapeted roofline with a denticulated cornice. It is attached to a building constructed of logs sawn flat on three sides, square notched at the corners. The building stands vacant, but its former grandeur measured by this remote setting is readily apparent.

The store on Berry Street, known as the Taylor Building, has the same storefront, with a recessed entry and multipaned windows, surmounted by a gable instead of a false front. The building is wood-framed, covered with novelty siding.

IN039 U.S. Customs House

1900. Front St.

Built as housing for noncommissioned officers at Fort Egbert, the customs house was moved down to Front Street in 1915 when it was acquired by the customs service. In 1989, it was moved back from Front Street about 15 feet, and up out of the reach of the river.

The front gambrel roof that extends to cover a small entrance porch at an inset corner is a distinguishing characteristic of this one-and-a-half-story, wood-framed building.

A two-story, wood-framed building, the U.S. Courthouse was constructed in 1901 due to the efforts of Judge James Wickersham, who collected business license fees and court fines to finance its construction. The windows and doorway have pedimented surrounds, and there is a balustraded porch across the front. The large blank space between the two windows at the second floor of the gable front denotes the judge's bench on the interior. The entire second floor of the building was occupied by the courtroom, while the first floor was used for a variety of federal offices. Whereas the federal government regularly asserted an architectural presence with customs houses and courthouses, often combining them in one structure along with the post office to allow greater monumentality, in Eagle a domestic appearance was adequate. Still, this is by far the largest building in town. This building, like the customs house, is now a museum, open to the public.

A similar building still stands on the grounds of Fort Egbert (IN045.1). Slight differences include the column at the corner (turned wood at the fort, paneled box column here) and the patterning of the shingles in the gable. Here the shingles are in a diamond pattern; the rest of the building is covered with novelty siding. At the time of the first move, a one-story, hip-roofed wing on the side was moved to the rear; a ghost remains on the dormer. The building functions as a museum, with different themes of Eagle's history conveyed in different rooms.

IN040 U.S. Courthouse

1901. First Ave.

IN041 Well House

1909; 1910, wind generator; 1913, belfry. First Ave.

Next to the courthouse is a public building of another kind. The well house, a two-story, wood-framed structure with a pyramidal roof and a bell tower, covers a 60-foot deep well, still used by village residents. The second floor houses a holding tank. This building was constructed in 1909, and an old well house on the north became the firehouse. The wind generator was added in 1910, and the belfry, housing a fire bell, in 1913. The building serves as a meeting place and town landmark.

IN042 Wickersham House

c. 1900. Berry St.

Built as a 16-foot-by-24-foot log building, the Wickersham house has been covered with novelty siding, probably salvaged from Fort Egbert, as have many of the log buildings in town. Located across from and behind the courthouse where he worked, Judge James Wickersham's house cost $75 for the logs and $100 for the lot. The gable roof was constructed of split logs covered with more than 1 foot of moss and sod, which has since been covered with corrugated metal. The kitchen was housed in an 8-foot-wide shed-roofed

IN040 U.S. Courthouse (right); IN041 Well House (left)

IN042a Wickersham House (historic view)

IN042b Wickersham House (current)

portion in the rear. The gable-roofed vestibule is curiously tucked under an extension of the roof, an original feature.

IN043 **City Hall**

1901. C St.

The one-story log building that has served as Eagle's city hall since 1901 is typical of the log cabins built in the town and surrounding area. The structure consists of round logs, saddle notched at the corners and chinked with moss and mud. Earth is piled around the foundations for additional warmth. The gable roof is constructed of rafters supporting planks, on which corrugated iron has been placed; sod roofs were probably more typical. A recent addition to the rear is approximately the same dimensions, but taller. Constructed of logs sawn flat on three sides, it is an exceptionally compatible addition.

IN044 **Episcopal Church**

1940s. Front St.

The Episcopalians rebuilt their church here in the 1940s, purchasing logs for $100 from Fort Egbert's hospital building. The original church, similar in design, had been built by the Presbyterians in 1900 and acquired by the Episcopalians in 1905; it now operates as a nondenominational church. Crowned by an open belfry, the current church is constructed of logs sawn flat on three sides, square notched at the corners. There is a gable-roofed vestibule with a splayed lintel on the doorway and molded panels on the door. A smaller, one-story hyphen connects the church to the two-story rectory, also constructed of logs. The rectory, larger than the church, shows some architectural sophistication, with a low shed dormer in its gable roof, slightly pedimented molded lintels, and exposed rafter ends reminiscent of the bungalow style.

IN045 **Fort Egbert**

By establishing Fort Egbert in 1899, the U.S. Army accomplished several objectives. Serving as a law-enforcement authority in a district that was legally unable to govern itself, the army was charged with keeping the peace in the frenzy of the gold rush, and Fort Egbert was located in the midst of the Canadian and American stampedes. Fort Egbert's location 8 miles from the Canadian border also established an American presence at a critical site. In addition, the army provided the important functions of communications and of transportation. It built a telegraph and a cable line that linked all of its posts with the contiguous United States without going through Canadian territory and constructed the Trans-Alaska Military Road from Valdez to Eagle. Although Fort Egbert flourished for only about ten years, its presence helped Eagle survive as a permanent town.

Although the initial buildings at Fort Egbert were of log, a sawmill was soon constructed and the post began to take on a more finished look. The post eventually had forty-five buildings, arranged in a grid plan around a parade ground and connected by boardwalks. Today only five survive, and the original plan of the fort is obscured by building relocations and the construction of an airstrip at an angle through the site. The five buildings that remain, however, were carefully restored by the Bureau of Land Management in 1974–1979.

IN045.1 **Noncommissioned Officers' Quarters**

1900; 1902, addition

The noncommissioned officers' quarters was originally a one-story building constructed of wood frame with beveled siding. In 1902 the second story was added, making the building

IN045.1 Noncommissioned Officers' Quarters

a one-and-a-half-story, gambrel-roofed house. A small entrance porch is recessed at the corner. In 1907 a one-story, hip-roofed addition was made on one side. There are shingles in the gable, patterned near the peak. The first-story windows, with four-over-four-light sash, are unusually tall. The building is virtually identical to the house that was moved from the fort to become the customs house (IN039).

IN045.2 **Quartermaster's Warehouse**

1899

The 25-foot-by-81-foot quartermaster's warehouse was constructed of logs. Six years later it was sheathed in novelty siding. With a gable roof covered with corrugated metal, the building has a three-bay front and six-over-six-light windows.

IN045.3 **Mule Barn** (Quartermaster's Stables)

1900

The mule barn is a large two-and-a-half-story structure covered with beveled siding. Small, square windows denote each stall. There is a three-bay front, with hay doors at the second and third levels.

IN045.4 **Granary** (Quartermaster's Storehouse)

1903

The one-story building with board-and-batten siding held 200 tons of feed.

IN045.3 Mule Barn (Quartermaster's Stables)

IN045.5 **Water Wagon Shed**

1907

The water wagon shed also served as the firehouse. The wood-framed building has a paper-composite exterior, held with battens. The building was originally located closer to the barracks (no longer extant), near the surviving noncommissioned officer's quarters. A shed-roofed addition was built in 1909.

Yukon-Charley Rivers National Preserve

IN046 **Ed Biederman Fish Camp**

1916 and later. Left bank of Yukon River, opposite and .5 mile downstream from Kandik River

Max Adolphus "Ed" Biederman had the mail contract between Eagle and Circle for about twenty years beginning in 1912 and made the 160-mile trip by dog sled in six days, with a layover at each end, thirteen times a winter. This camp, located halfway between Eagle and Circle, served as his stopover on the third night out, where he switched dog teams. On other nights he stayed at roadhouses or shelter cabins, places where he had stashed goods ahead of time. The winter trail that he maintained was used by other travelers as well and served to link the linear community of the scattered residents on the Yukon and its tributaries between Eagle and Circle.

Biederman kept about twenty-four dogs and in the summer maintained an active fish camp here to feed them all. Virtually useless in the summer, dogs belonging to miners and trappers in the region would also board at Biederman's, so he might have as many as sixty dogs at a time. Biederman had two fish wheels with 12-foot-wide baskets reaching 8 feet into the water and once caught nine hundred salmon in 12 hours. The fish would be cleaned, then smoked over a fire. Biederman would sell the fish, baled in 65-pound bundles for dog food, in Circle and Eagle.

The cabin and outbuildings at this fish camp are evidence of Biederman's way of life. The main cabin, built in 1916, is one story, of round logs saddle notched at the corners. The cabin is divided into two rooms by a log cross wall, but the exterior logs run the full length of 31 feet. The entry, originally an open porch, has since been enclosed with a variety of found materials. The roof is sod on split poles and covered with corrugated metal.

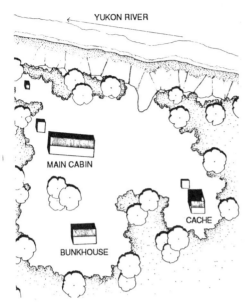

IN046a Ed Biederman Fish Camp (site plan)

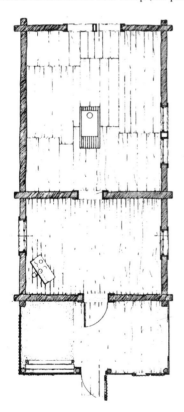

IN046b Ed Biederman Fish Camp, main cabin (floor plan)

Other buildings at the site include a bunkhouse, built in 1918, a one-story, one-room log structure. There is a cache, raised 6 feet on posts, with wood-framed diagonal-plank walls; a greenhouse, 8 feet by 10 feet, with partial walls and the frame of a gabie roof; a meat cellar; and various A-framed dog houses. Accompanied by his wife and five children, Biederman used this camp until his death in 1945. The complex is within the Yukon-Charley Rivers National Preserve, but privately owned.

IN047 James Taylor Cabins

c. 1924. Right bank of Yukon River opposite mouth of Fourth of July Creek

James Taylor was a miner turned trapper who built himself an intricate set of buildings on the north side of the Yukon River, probably in about 1924. In 1908, he was prospecting on Fourth of July Creek, on the south side of the Yukon. In 1919 he sold his claims to a larger outfit, one that was able to develop the necessary hydraulic operation. Five years later he moved across the river and turned to trapping.

Taylor first constructed a 12-foot-by-13-foot one-story log cabin. The round logs are hewn on the interior and fastened into corner posts. The roof of sod on poles was replaced in 1984. After about five years, Taylor built another cabin to live in, and the old one became the shop. That main cabin, which was destroyed by fire in 1968, was remembered for its ingenious conveniences, such as a dumbwaiter that serviced the root cellar and was operated by a crank in the kitchen; a wood box that was filled by using a chute and a trapdoor; and papier-mâché-like chinking.

Other buildings at the site are similarly ingenious. The dog barn, a low cabin with saddle-notched log walls, has six stalls with vertical-pole walls. Each stall has its own door, operable by an outside lever. Taylor also built individual doghouses out of logs and extensive vertical-pole corrals that led down to a stream.

Taylor left Alaska in 1933 and died shortly thereafter. He left his place to Ed Biederman.

IN048 George McGregor Cabin

1938. Left bank of Yukon River, approximately 2 miles downriver from Coal Creek

IN048 George McGregor Cabin (section)

A one-room log cabin in a remote setting, the George McGregor cabin is a good example of a solitary trapper's cabin. Measuring 12 feet by 13 feet, the one-story cabin could have been built by one person. The walls are constructed of round logs, unpeeled but hewn slightly on the interior, saddle notched at the corners. The floor had rough-sawn planks on poles; there was a small root cellar in the center. The gable roof was constructed of round poles running perpendicularly to the ridgepole. On top of these was a layer of sod, which supported a plank roof and tar paper. The ridgepole extended in front to support corrugated metal that covered a porch. Although no stove remains, there is a stovepipe. Outbuildings included two caches and the ruins of another cabin or tent frame.

In the 1920s, George McGregor was a prospector, staking claims on Woodchopper Creek and a tributary, Mineral Creek. In the mid-1930s, he sold out to Gold Placers, Inc., and turned to trapping. He built this cabin in 1938, probably using it as his home base during the winters, and also constructed other cabins on his trap line. Dogs were his means of transport in the winter, and in summer he caught fish to feed them, using this cabin as his fish camp. In 1954, McGregor moved to Eagle, where he held several elective offices before leaving Alaska in 1963.

This basic log cabin is probably little different from the cabins of the 1898 gold stampeders. Its one-room plan and indigenous materials, characteristic of the frontier, are enduring.

IN049 Slaven Roadhouse

1930. Left bank of Yukon River at mouth of Coal Creek

Constructed in 1930, the Slaven Roadhouse was built by a man who spent about thirty years prospecting claims in the same creek. Typical of small-scale miners, Frank Slaven never struck it rich but he made enough to get by. Born in Ohio, he started staking claims on Coal Creek and its tributaries in 1905. Thirty years later he sold out to Gold Placers, Inc., who brought in a dredge and other equipment and mined the creek on a large scale.

Slaven built this roadhouse in about 1930, when he was sixty years old. The two-story building consists of a 21-foot-by-21-foot log section with unusually fine craftsmanship. The round logs are hewn flat on the interior and grooved on the bottoms to fit snugly over the ones below. This technique, seen in Russian Alaskan architecture but not associated with the American gold-rush period, is attributed to Sandy Johnson, a Finnish immigrant who

IN049a Slaven Roadhouse (exterior)

IN049b Slaven Roadhouse (section)

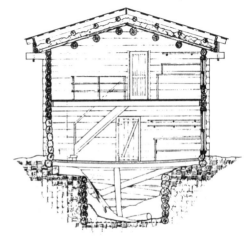

assisted in the construction. The corners are neatly square notched.

A wood-framed section, 21 feet by 16 feet, was added soon after. The drop siding on the exterior and the beaded-board siding on the interior probably came from Fort Egbert, upriver, where buildings were being dismantled. The 14-inch-diameter purlins of the roof extend the full length of the structure and support split logs carrying 6 inches of sod. Atop this is a second roof structure, added in 1935, which consists of 6-inch-diameter purlins, rafters, planks, and corrugated metal. The additional purlins and planks provided a base on which to nail the metal; additional purlins, nestled in the sod, are common supports for metal coverings added to sod roofs.

An arctic entry on the south was added some time between 1935 and 1938 and has since been removed. On the interior, the first floor served as the kitchen on the south, and living room on the north. On the second floor, there was a dormitory over the living room and private rooms for Slaven and the cook, Mary Bissell, on the south.

The roadhouse venture was not entirely successful for Slaven. Located only 6 miles from Woodchopper Roadhouse, it was too close to be useful to travelers who hoped to make 20 or 25 miles in a day. When Gold Placers, Inc., started developing the Coal Creek claims in 1934, however, the roadhouse gained new life, as traffic up the creek increased. Materials would be unloaded from barges at the roadhouse at the mouth of Coal Creek and then transported overland up the creek. With the construction of an airstrip at the camp and with the growth of air travel in general, roadhouses like Slaven's were needed less and less. Slaven moved to Seattle in 1938. The roadhouse now serves as a ranger station and shelter cabin in the Yukon-Charley Rivers National Preserve.

IN050 Coal Creek Dredge and Camp

1936. Coal Creek

Although much more complex than the basic placer mining operations that preceded it on Coal Creek, the Coal Creek dredge and camp are representative of a simple dredging operation. Unlike the Fairbanks Exploration Company, which invested $10 million before

IN050 Coal Creek Dredge and Camp

dredging began and which brought eight dredges into the Fairbanks area, Gold Placers, Inc., was initially a one-dredge operation, and complex pumping and ditch building were not employed.

Ernest Patty, who had founded the School of Mines at the University of Alaska, and Gen. A. D. McRae of Vancouver formed Gold Placers, Inc., in 1934. They brought a dredge, diesel tractor, and hydraulic mining equipment into Coal Creek, barging them to the mouth of the creek and taking them overland in winter. By 1936 they had also set up a dredge on Woodchopper Creek, a neighboring drainage, and had built an airstrip on Coal Creek. They employed forty men at Coal Creek and thirty on Woodchopper.

The camp at Coal Creek, originally located about 6 miles from the mouth of the creek, consisted mostly of wanigans, or one-story, wood-framed buildings on skids for easy moving. About a dozen buildings remain: bunkhouses and mess hall, office and assay shop. The machine shop burned in 1951 and was replaced with a quonset hut.

The dredge was designed by mining engineer Charles Janin of San Francisco; it was constructed by the Walter W. Johnson Company of Oakland. The dredge was then disassembled and shipped via Skagway, down the Yukon River, and nearly 7 miles up Coal Creek where it was reassembled in 1935. The 4-cubic-foot buckets, powered by a diesel motor, moved the dredge downstream, chewing up the gravel streambed as it went. The camp followed. The camp is now located about 3 1/2 miles from the mouth, and the dredge, which was last operated in 1975, is about a mile from the mouth.

North

Coldfoot

Located above the Arctic Circle, on the southern slopes of the Brooks Range, Coldfoot was a classic gold-rush boomtown, flourishing in 1902 and all but deserted in 1906. That year, many of the residents moved north to Wiseman, taking some of the Coldfoot buildings with them. Coldfoot today has been mostly reclaimed by the land, with only two buildings remaining.

Coldfoot had an extraordinary second life, as well, as a construction camp for the Trans-Alaska Pipeline in the 1970s. Remaining from its second life is a truck stop, on the opposite side of the Haul Road, where surplus ATCO trailers have been turned into a hotel.

IN051 James Minano Cabin

c. 1915. North side of the road heading toward the river

The Minano cabin is still standing, but half of its roof has caved in. Built after the first boom, the Minano cabin dates from about 1915. It is constructed of round logs, saddle notched at the corners, with dimensions of approximately 16 feet by 22 feet. The roof is constructed of sod on planks; on top of this more planks and flattened fuel cans were laid. There is an arctic entry, 7 feet by 7 feet, on the front and a root cellar under the building. There is also an unusual amount of whipsawn lumber, seen in the flooring, walls of the cellar, and ceiling; this may have been removed from other buildings in the ghost town of Coldfoot.

James Minano was a Japanese trader who married Sucklarlalook, an Eskimo from Barrow. They came down to Coldfoot about 1903, raising a family and cultivating extensive gardens in the more than twenty hours of sunlight on a summer day.

Across the road is a small shed constructed of squared logs nailed into corner boards. It, too, has a gable roof covered with flattened fuel cans. Without a chimney or sod roof, it was probably constructed as an outbuilding.

Wiseman

By following the river systems, prospectors reached beyond the Interior of Alaska to the Brooks Range. Like the rest of the Interior, the temperature range is extreme, but the nearly constant sunlight in the summer creates a verdant landscape that belies its arctic location. The foothills of the Brooks Range are forested, although the spruce are small. Located on the middle fork of the Koyukuk River at Wiseman Creek, the town of Wiseman was founded about 1906, providing access to diggings on both Nolan and Hammond creeks. The Koyukuk District, centered at Wiseman, produced nearly $5 million worth of gold between 1900 and 1930. Wiseman flourished until 1916 but, instead of disappearing after the initial rush, continued to survive. In the winter of 1930–1931, Robert Marshall, an explorer and forester, lived in Wiseman and undertook a study of the town, focusing on the cultures and compatibility of the Eskimos and white Americans. Written in the vein of the then-new sociological study *Middletown,* Marshall's *Arctic Village* is an affectionate portrayal of a remote village.

Bypassed by the road to Prudhoe Bay constructed in the 1970s, Wiseman still retains many of its early log structures. Arranged in a seemingly random plan on the west bank of the Middle Fork of the Koyukuk River, the town is bisected by Wiseman Creek. The log cabins are small—one or two rooms, usually—and low, with berms around their foundations. Sod roofs, covered with metal, and arctic entries are favored in this northern climate.

Materials are frequently reused in remote areas such as this, and the metal roofs are a good example. Five-gallon fuel cans (the trade name Blazo being the most popular) are flattened and form large shingles, which are then layered on a roof. Sometimes the cans are applied only to the ridges of roofs or are used to wrap the legs of caches so that porcupines cannot climb them. Other cans, such as butter tins, served for smaller jobs. Wherever they are used or whatever kind of can, they rust to a uniform brown color, adding an interesting texture to an otherwise organic structure.

IN052 **Northern Commercial Company Store**
c. 1910

The largest building in Wiseman is the two-story Northern Commercial Company Store. Located on the river bank for easy unloading, the log structure had corrugated-metal additions, which have since been removed. The round logs are square notched at the corners, and the building is neatly made. The Northern Commercial Company constructed this building about 1910, when it moved here from Coldfoot; it was one of three stores in town.

IN053 **Gus Larson Cabin**
c. 1940

The craftsmanship exhibited in this small building makes it a good example of the type. The gable-roofed building has a smaller, gable-roofed entry that serves as an unheated storage area. All of the living takes place in the main room. The round logs, saddle notched at the corners, the sod roof with a covering of flattened fuel cans, and the compactness of the building are typical features of one-man log cabins. When these photographs were taken in 1984, the cabin was occupied by one man, whose neatly arranged possessions illustrate a compact way of life in a small space.

IN054 Heppenstall-Green Cabin

c. 1915

Larger than most cabins in Wiseman, this cabin has three rooms. Its distinguishing feature is its hip-roofed front porch on the river side, featuring a spindlework frieze and a balustrade.

IN055 Schoolhouse

1919; 1928, moved to present location

The schoolhouse was constructed in Cold-foot, but moved to Wiseman in 1928. At that time, new joists, ridge pole, and roof poles were installed in the one-story, log building. The unusually large windows are the only features that differentiate this building from the residential cabins of the town. Recently, the school has received some large plywood additions. The cabin just behind it was the residence of the schoolteacher.

IN056 Pioneers of Alaska, Igloo No. 8

1910

The Pioneers of Alaska, a social and benevolent organization, founded Igloo No. 8 in Wiseman in 1914. *Igloo* was a colorful name for the individual lodges, emphasizing the northern location of the organization. Here the Pioneers bought a log saloon that had been built in about 1910 and used it for a community center, library, chapel, and dance hall. The round logs are square notched at the corners, and tin has been placed over the chinking. The building has a corrugated metal roof and a hip-roofed front porch.

Wiseman Vicinity

IN057 Sod House Frames

early twentieth century. Mile 195.3 and Mile 196.6 Dalton Hwy.

Close to the highway are remains of two sod houses associated with Natives in the area. At Mile 195.3, on the west side of the road, is the pole frame constructed by "Arctic John" Etalook. The simple post-and-beam frame, 12 feet by 12 feet, had vertical poles with a 1-inch to 3-inch diameter nailed to it. Canvas was stretched on the outside, and sod piled against it. The roof was a shallow gable, covered with poles and sod, except for a portion around the stovepipe, which was covered with flattened fuel cans. The interior was covered with canvas or cardboard. One wall and part of the roof have collapsed, and most of the sod has washed away, but the construction is still evident.

At Mile 196.6, on the east side of the highway, is a shelter built by Florence Jonas. The log structure is unusual, being a modified A-frame. The 5-foot-by-12-foot structure was covered with canvas, with sod laid on top. Inside, a stove made from an oil drum and a bunk remain. Although the shelter has not been inhabited for some time, it remains remarkably intact.

IN058 Cabin

c. 1920s. Mile 197 Dalton Hwy.

A log cabin on the banks of Gold Creek, on the west side of the highway, may have been built by the Alaska Road Commission as a shelter cabin. The cabin, measuring approximately 11 feet by 14 feet, is constructed of round logs, saddle notched at the corners. The gable roof, of sod on poles, has purlins but no ridgepole. A gap in the roof that is the length of the structure indicates where the ridgepole would have been; the eave poles, which usually held the ends of the roof poles, have also been removed. The cabin has sunk about 1 1/2 feet into the ground due to permafrost, resulting in a short doorway.

Gates of the Arctic National Park and Preserve

IN059 Charlie Yale Cabin

c. 1900. Approximately 8 miles west of Nolan, Glacier River

The cabin built by Charlie Yale has three rooms in an L-shaped plan. The main room, about 14 feet square, served as the living room, while the outer room, about 15 feet by 9 feet, was a drying room and work room. A shed-roofed addition to one side, about 7 feet by 9 feet, was probably used for storage. The walls are round logs, saddle-notched at the corners and chinked with moss. The gable roof is constructed of sod laid on round poles, then covered with flattened fuel cans.

There is a second, smaller cabin nearby displaying the same construction techniques. Other artifacts and features at the site are related to mining, Charlie Yale's occupation, and include a pipe rack, for the storage of steam pipes, a shaft opening, and a tailings pile. Yale sank a 168-foot-deep shaft to bedrock and drifted from there, but the mining was apparently not profitable. Yale was described by Robert Marshall as "an old hermit prospector" who lived on Glacier River for about ten years, then moved on. Since Yale's departure, the cabin has been used for shelter by travelers on the winter trail to Wiseman, which passed just behind this cabin.

IN060 Vincent Knorr Cabin

by mid-1930s. Mascot Creek, 3 miles above its juncture with Glacier River

Set on a high bank next to Mascot Creek, Vincent Knorr's cabin is a carefully constructed small log structure. Measuring about 13 feet by 14 feet (and now shifted to a

IN060a Vincent Knorr Cabin (gable)

IN060b Vincent Knorr Cabin (southwest elevation)

parallelogram rather than a rectangle), the round logs are saddle notched at the corners and chinked with moss. The roof is constructed of poles resting on the purlins and supporting a layer of moss; the purlins are pegged at the ends to keep the poles in place. The one-room cabin had a window in each wall, a stove in one corner, and a root cellar underneath. Nearby was a cache and an outhouse. Vincent Knorr, who signed his name in chalk over the doorway, built this cabin by the mid-1930s, when he had staked at least five claims on Mascot Creek.

The complex is within the Gates of the Arctic National Park and Preserve, but privately owned.

Northern Region (NO)

T HE NORTH SLOPE OF THE BROOKS RANGE, AS IT DESCENDS TO the Arctic Ocean, constitutes the Northern Region. The land is underlain with continuous permafrost, producing for the most part a moist tundra. Covered much of the year with snow and ice, in the summer the treeless tundra is revealed, melting 12 inches to 16 inches below surface. Thousands of temporary thaw lakes, which change from year to year, dot the tundra.

The Northern Region's nearly three months of total darkness in the winter is complemented by nearly three months of full sunlight in the summer. The climate is cold and dry. Although the temperatures can reach 70 degrees in the summer, it can snow on any day. Strong, constant winds make the winters even harder, as temperatures average below zero. Precipitation is only about 10 inches annually, but the land remains covered by snow and ice more than six months of the year.

The region was traditionally inhabited by both maritime and inland North Alaskan Eskimos. The former established villages on the coast, living off whales, seals, and walrus. Occasionally they would take hunting trips up the rivers, but they were for the most part a sea-oriented people. The inland Eskimos relied on caribou for subsistence; as hunters, they traveled widely. The first whites in the area came by sea: whalers and explorers approached the northern coast in the mid-nineteenth century, and they established a trading relationship with the Eskimos. Missionaries followed, but the remoteness of the area discouraged significant white settlement, until the development of the Prudhoe Bay oil fields. Today, airplanes are the most common means of traveling to or among villages.

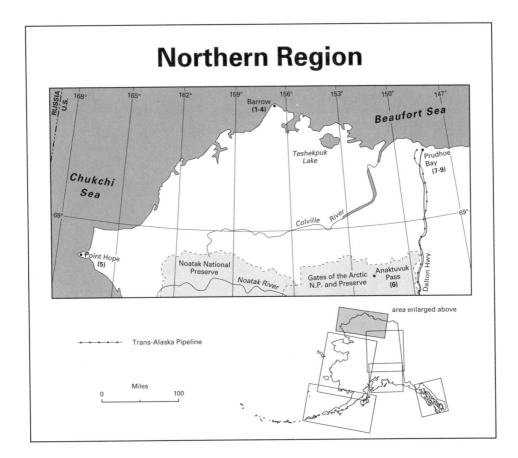

Northern Region

Trans-Alaska Pipeline

Miles
0   100

area enlarged above

Barrow

The northernmost town in Alaska, Barrow was traditionally the trading point for the Alaskan Arctic coast. Today it is the seat of the 88,000-square-mile North Slope Borough and maintains its primacy among the coastal villages.

Long an Eskimo village, Barrow became a major trading post after 1826 when whites first visited the village. British and American explorers and whalers frequented the coast east of Barrow, and whaling remained a profitable outside trade until the end of the nineteenth century. A Presbyterian mission was established in 1890 under the auspices of Sheldon Jackson.

Barrow received unprecedented attention in 1935 when Will Rogers and Wiley Post crashed and died about 15 miles south of it on their flight from Fairbanks to Siberia; a monument near the airport stands as a memorial. In the 1940s, oil exploration on the North Slope caused Barrow's population to triple. The 1970s oil boom brought a similarly prosperous boost to Barrow.

Today Barrow encompasses two sections—the old town of Barrow is on the southwest, while the trading post of Browerville is northeast—joined by a sand spit. Because the North Slope is treeless and Barrow is exceedingly remote, building materials are valuable. Remnants of traditional sod dwellings, both historic and prehistoric, are near the southwest end of Stevenson Street; they appear as grass-covered mounds. Both Barrow and Browerville have a mix of architecture, with houses of found materials such as packing crates and driftwood side by side with manufactured housing. A few large public buildings constructed in the last two decades represent Barrow's recent prosperity.

NO001 Point Barrow Refuge Station
(Cape Smythe Whaling and Trading Station)

1889. Building 3220, Browerville

The oldest wood-framed building standing along Alaska's Arctic coast, the Point Barrow Refuge Station was a manned refuge station for shipwrecked whalers. After 1854, American whalers began hunting east of Point Barrow, with frequent losses of ships and men. On 2 August 1888, thirty whale ships anchored off Point Barrow were waiting for the ice pack to open so they could enter the Beaufort Sea. A gale blew up, sending ships crashing into one another and breaking up in the heavy seas. Great loss of life was avoided only because the U.S. revenue cutter *Bear* and the *U.S.S. Thetis* were nearby and rescued sailors; the value of the lost ships exceeded $100,000. That tragedy resulted in the construction of this station.

Whalers from San Francisco and New Bedford, Massachusetts, petitioned Congress for a series of refuge stations along the coast but received only this one. Built near the site of an old U.S. Signal Corps station, 11 miles south of Point Barrow (and now within the boundaries of Barrow), the building originally was 30 feet by 48 feet with a large

central room with bunks for fifty men. It had a shallow-pitched gable roof and a shed-roofed vestibule on the southwest end. A 20-ton coal bunker was attached to the northeast side.

During the seven years that it functioned as a refuge station, there were no major shipwrecks to require its services. The shady business dealings of the station's first superintendent probably also contributed to the closing of the station in 1896. The next year, more than one hundred men sought shelter for eleven months at Point Barrow when four ships were crushed by ice and four others were icebound for the winter. The Pacific Steam Whaling Company, which had bought the station, had rented it to a naturalist, Edward Avery McIlhenny, for the winter; he helped shelter the shipwrecked sailors.

In 1898, the building was sold to the Cape Smythe Whaling and Trading Company, whose manager was Charles Brower. Around 1920, he raised the roof, steepening the pitch, and added a cross gable in the front. Later, a lower addition was made to the southwest front, and other additions to the rear. The three windows across the northwest side, which faces the ocean, have been enlarged and plate glass installed. A restaurant in the building is still operated by family members.

NO002 Brower House

1905. Building 3129, Browerville

Charles Brower built a one-and-a-half-story wood-framed house for his Eskimo wife, Asianggataq, and their growing family in 1905, next door to his trading post. According to his daughter Sadie Brower Neakok, who was born in 1916 and grew up in the house, the first floor was one big room, with a cookstove in the center. On the second floor, where everyone slept, the older children's quarters were partitioned from the parents and babies. Since then, the roof has been raised to accommodate a second story, the pitch has been changed, and the building has received several additions.

NO003 Utkeagvik Presbyterian Church Manse

1929–1930. Building 1268, Momegana St., Barrow

Extraordinary in its setting, a wood-shingled Dutch Colonial house was constructed as the parsonage of the Utkeagvik Presbyterian Church. The church had been established by a Presbyterian missionary, L. M. Stevenson, in 1899. The present church building, a long low structure with a bell tower, was constructed about 1954, with the Christian education building behind dating from 1968. The manse is of more interest architecturally.

The previous manse burned down in 1925, and the pastor, Dr. Henry W. Greist, went on a fund-raising expedition Outside; on his return he stopped in Seattle to order lumber cut to the architect's specifications. The materials were shipped to Barrow and the house was erected in 1929–1930. Anne Morrow Lindbergh, who visited in 1930 while accompanying her husband to the Orient, described Greist's involvement in constructing the gambrel-roofed house:

He had built the manse in which we were staying. His son, "outside," had helped him to plan it. The doctor himself, directing the Eskimos, had measured and fitted every board and nail. . . . Aside from his work as architect and carpenter, he preached every Sunday, had a Bible class Wednesday nights, was doctor, surgeon, and dentist, and was preparing his boy for college.

Greist took special precautions with the permafrost: "He had placed special insulation in the floor, for it was impossible to have a furnace in the cellar. If you started to thaw out the ground underneath, the house might sink. And a furnace would require too much fuel in a fuel-less country."

The windows were triple paned, and a tube similar to the Russian *fortochkas* provided ventilation: "The windows, triple storm ones, were all nailed down. They were for light and not for ventilation. Windows that open and shut are always draughty. The rooms were ventilated by pipes which let in air indirectly but kept out rain and snow."

The rest of the house, as well as the water, was heated by downstairs stoves: "Heat from the kitchen went up through ventilators in the ceiling to the bedrooms above. There were big stoves in all the rooms. The doctor installed the water tank, connected it with pipes for running water downstairs, and heated it from the stove."

The values expressed by this American suburban home built in the Arctic were also captured by Lindbergh, here describing her entry:

I stamped my numb feet on the wooden steps of her home as she (Molly Greist) pushed open the door. The warmth of a kitchen fire, the brightness of gas lamps, and a delicious smell of sweet potatoes and freshly-baked muffins poured out around me and drew me in. A long table spread for our "Thanksgiving dinner" filled the living room. White cloth, rims of plates, curves of spoons, caught the light from swinging lamps above. I looked around quickly and felt the flavor of the American home—chintz curtains drawn aside, pictures of "woodland scenes" on the walls, bright pillows on the sofa, and there, in the window, a box of climbing nasturtiums. (*North to the Orient* [New York: Harcourt Brace, 1935], pp. 100–103.)

NO004 Agvik Street

Barrow

Several large office, commercial, and public buildings have been constructed in the last fifteen years on Agvik Street, making it the heart of the city and giving it the appearance of a downtown. In general, the buildings are large, high-tech, and brightly colored and take little from their bleak surroundings.

NO004.1 Stuaqpak

1976, Kelley Pittelko Fritz and Forssen

Operated by the Alaska Commercial Company, the Stuaqpak, or supermarket and general store, was constructed for the Arctic Slope Regional Corporation. Because of Barrow's

NO004.1 Stuaqpak (right); NO004.2 Arctic Slope Regional Corporation Office Building (left)

strong winds, the large building has little or-nament, but diagonal cedar siding contrasts with an orange cylindrical element across the front, sheltering the entrances—a high-tech arctic entry. Inside, second-level windows light the front of the first level, where it is open to the second. The building was designed in 1976 by Kelley Pittelko Fritz and Forssen of Los Angeles.

NO004.2 Arctic Slope Regional Corporation Office Building

1970s. Corner of Kiogak St.

A planned addition intended to be connected to the Stuaqpak but constructed as a separate building is the Arctic Slope Regional Cor-poration office building. The similarity of the design to Stuaqpak suggests that it had the same designers. Large, windowed walls, meet-ing at the corner, are framed on top and one side by the same diagonal cedar siding. A cylindrical entrance, near the back of the building on Kiogak Street, is also similar to Stuaqpak. The opposite sides of the building have the same design as the front.

NO004.3 Alaska Court System Building

1985. Corner of Kiogak St.

Across Kiogak Street from the Arctic Slope Regional Corporation office building is an-other large office building, which houses the Alaska Court System. Constructed in 1985, this three-story building also has an open corner with a cylindrical glass element shel-tering the entrances—a variant of the high-tech arctic entry. The gray-stained wood sid-ing is broken by banded windows.

NO004.4 North Slope Borough Office Building

1975, Pacific Architects and Engineers. Near Mome-gana St.

Painted a turquoise blue, the North Slope Borough office building is two stories, rising to three in the center, where there is a dra-matic open interior.

Point Hope

Claiming to be the oldest continually occupied site in North America, Point Hope, westernmost point of Lisburne Peninsula, in the Chukchi Sea, has a rich archaeological heritage. Four distinct sites within the radius of a couple of miles have been identified by archaeologists or are represented by standing build-ings. The site called Ipiutak, recognized as a National Historic Landmark, was occupied at least two thousand years ago. By 400 C.E., there was a settlement of eight hundred dwellings there, on the south shore of Marryat Inlet near the present cemetery. Excavated in 1939–1941, the Ipiutak houses were semisub-terranean, with a driftwood or whalebone superstructure supported by four posts inside the walls, and tunnel entrances.

A later settlement, called Old Tigara, was located west of Ipiutak, on the ocean's edge. Some artifacts found in the settlement that has since washed away dated to 500 C.E. to 700 C.E.; in ridges still remaining, evidence indicates a settlement from 1400 C.E. to 1750 C.E., a settlement that survived until after contact with whites. It has been estimated that as many as 800 people lived here in 1850. That number is probably high, but it was a substantial settlement.

Around the turn of the century, because of the beach erosion, the village moved less than a mile to the east, to the village of Tigara. Tigara had suffered a population decline during the measles epidemic of 1902 and probably experienced continuing decline from other diseases contracted through contact with whites. By 1908 it had a population of 179 in twenty-three households. A whaling station established in 1887 at a site called Jabbertown, 6 miles east, operated until 1910. A government school was set up at Jabbertown in 1904, moving to the village in 1924. An Episcopal mission was established 1 mile northeast of Tigara in 1890 and moved into the village in 1955. The cemetery northeast of Tigara, established due to the missionaries' influence, is fenced with whalebones and is thus extraordinarily evocative of its place. The houses at Tigara evolved from semisubterranean, sod-covered dwellings with tunnel entrances to American-style wood-framed houses. Because of the draftiness of wood-framed houses, however, sod was piled around them. By 1955, the village of Tigara had fifty houses, mostly frame.

In 1976, the village of Tigara was abandoned, again due to shore erosion. The entire community moved, for the last time, 2 miles to the east, establishing a new village called Point Hope. The informal linearity of the old village was abandoned in favor of a grid plan. In contrast to the grass-covered mounds of Tigara, the new houses at Point Hope are elevated, on an unvegetated gravel pad. While some of the wood-framed buildings were moved from Tigara, most of the buildings are new, manufactured houses.

At the site of Tigara, most of the original sod houses survive as mounds. Whalebone-framed entries lead to sod craters, as the lumber lining the dwellings was removed for reuse. Others have had their tunnel entrances removed and the skylight converted to a trap door; these are being used as cold-storage facilities by the villagers. A handful of wood-framed houses remains, some of them with sod piled around the exterior walls.

NO005 **Nanny Ooyahtona House**

turn of the twentieth century. Second row from south, Tigara Village

The most complete sod-covered house at Point Hope, one of the most extraordinary vernacular structures in America, was occupied until 1975. The house has extensive whalebone framing, as well as one lumber-walled room. The entire building is covered with sod, forming grassy mounds in the summer.

The house is approached on the level, via a path to the front door outlined with vertical whalebones. Through the doorway, which is framed with sawn driftwood, is a hallway 3 feet long and 2 1/2 feet wide. It opens into a large room, approximately 8 feet by 17 feet. The walls are densely lined with vertical whalebones. Whalebone posts against the interior of the walls support the wall plates, which are both whalebone and lumber. Lying crosswise on the wall plates are the whalebones that constitute the ceiling. The height of the dirt-floored room is about 5 1/2 feet. There is a square skylight.

At the back of this room is a hallway, also lined with whalebones. The hall, which is 3 1/2 feet wide, 4 1/2 feet high, and 10 feet long, leads to the back room, which is finished entirely with shiplap vertical planks. The room

NO005a Point Hope Cemetery

NO005b Nanny Ooyahtona House
(interior)

NO005c Nanny Ooyahtona House
(entrance)

measures 11 feet by 14 feet. There were two parallel 6-inch-diameter ridgepoles, one of which has collapsed, leaving the room open to the elements. The height of the room from the plank-lined floor to the bottom of the standing ridgepole is 5 feet 8 inches. The ceiling was also shiplapped lumber.

A rare survivor, the Nanny Ooyahtona

House displays a combination of traditional and transitional building forms. The whalebone framing, sod covering, and lack of windows are the most striking traditional elements. But unlike traditional dwellings, this house is on grade—not semisubterranean—and it is reached through a hallway on the same level, not a tunnel with a trapdoor into the living space. The use of lumber is not unusual, although here it is machine sawn, reflecting technology from Outside. This wood-walled room may have been a later addition; a one-room living space would have been traditional. Although there are many grassy mounds at Tigara and other places, indicating abandoned dwellings, this one can be entered, enclosing the visitor with whalebones and sod.

Anaktuvuk Pass

Anaktuvuk Pass, on the north slope of the Brooks Range, is today the only settlement of Nunamiut Inupiat, the Inupiat Eskimo who were land oriented. The Nunamiut inhabited inland northern Alaska until whalers introduced guns, with devastating consequences to the caribou herds that formed the mainstay of the Nunamiut diet. In addition, alcohol and disease introduced by whites forced population shifts and a reordering of the Nunamiut existence. Their precontact population inland was estimated at fifteen hundred; by 1900, it was two hundred to three hundred. By about 1920, there were no Nunamiut inhabiting the inland; they had all dispersed to coastal settlements.

But also by 1920, the caribou population was on the rise, which eventually brought the Nunamiut back inland. In the late 1930s, a handful of families returned to live inland permanently, re-establishing the seminomadic existence they had had before. In the late 1940s, they settled at Anaktuvuk Pass, where there was an airstrip and a temporary school. Regular mail service, construction of a church in 1951, and the appearance of a permanent schoolteacher in 1960 were further inducements to abandon their seminomadic existence and settle at Anaktuvuk Pass year-round, permanently. Today, Anaktuvuk Pass has a population of more than two hundred.

The architecture reflects this shift to a permanent settlement. The traditional winter dwelling of the Nunamiut was a willow-frame structure covered with moss; none of these is known to survive. The summer dwelling was a willow frame covered with caribou skins, which by the late 1950s was discarded in favor of the canvas-walled tent. In the late 1940s or early 1950s, the traditional winter dwelling gave way to the sod-covered house, which had an inner frame of larger logs, as opposed to branches, and was covered with squares of sod. Some of these buildings were standard horizontal log cabins, covered with sod. In the mid-1960s, the sod-covered houses were gradually replaced with plywood-covered frame houses, and more recently with manufactured houses.

NO006 House

1960

Although Anaktuvuk Pass has half a dozen sod-covered houses, only one is still occupied. Situated in the middle of town, it is a log cabin constructed of logs hewn flat on three sides and lapped at the corners. Measuring about 15 feet square and covered with sod, it was built in 1960 at a site about 25 miles south of Anaktuvuk, and moved to this site shortly after. At that time, a second room, about 14 feet by 15 feet, was added to the first. The house is semisubterranean, set about 1 1/2 feet to 3 feet into the ground. The gable roof has a ridgepole and two purlins, on which are closely laid rafters, hewn flat on one side, supporting canvas on which sod was piled. The floor was composed of end panels from gas crates. The door was small, about 2 1/2 feet by 4 1/2 feet.

After having sat vacant for a few years, the house was renovated by the present resident. He replaced a few rafters, then laid corrugated aluminum roofing on top, and sod on top of that. He also built a plywood arctic entry and replaced the flooring with plywood. He insulated the roof on the inside and put a vapor barrier and a new covering on the interior walls. The house is one of the last inhabited sod-covered dwellings in Alaska.

Prudhoe Bay

A 400-square-mile oil field, Prudhoe Bay has become synonymous with the wealth that Alaska experienced in the 1970s. After discovery of oil in 1968 by ARCO, the eleven companies owning leases selected ARCO and BP to operate the field jointly on their behalf. BP controls the western half, and ARCO the eastern. There are four additional oil fields currently in production, all connected to Prudhoe Bay and all feeding oil into the pipeline.

All of the facilities and roads are constructed on gravel pads, which provide a solid base while insulating the permafrost. Wells are clustered on these pads, and drilled outward. Untreated oil is sent to the gathering center (in BP's terminology) or flow station (ARCO's) where the oil, gas, and water are separated. The oil goes to the pipeline, where it travels the 800 miles to Valdez. Liquid gas is also sent in the pipeline, while other gas is reinjected into the oil reservoir. Water, too, is reinjected, to maintain pressure in the reservoir and to enhance recovery.

At Prudhoe, the work force numbers between five thousand and six thousand, most working for contractors to the two oil companies. At BP and ARCO, most people work a twelve-hour day, seven-day week, rotating off for seven days. No one lives permanently at Prudhoe; instead, the companies provide transportation to Barrow, Fairbanks, or Anchorage for the weeks off. Single bedrooms are shared by counterparts on the other shift. BP and ARCO have approached the construction of their residential facilities slightly differently, and both have adjusted their approaches over time.

The main operations centers were prefabricated Outside and barged to Prudhoe Bay. The port is ice free only three weeks a year, necessitating a carefully planned sea lift to unload all the pieces, and in the right order. They were then "crawled," using bulldozer-type tracks, to the site.

The stresses that the modular units received during barging and crawling were greater than those at the site. Once installed, wind was of more concern than cold, as heat is generated at the oil fields and is essentially a free commodity. Although snow accumulation is not a problem because of the wind, drifting can be. Most drifting snow travels close to the ground, so the buildings are elevated to permit snow to blow under them. The cold climate and long hours of darkness have resulted in an interior focus. The operations centers contain control facilities for oil production, offices, and maintenance facilities, as well as residential, dining, and recreation areas, so that many people live and work in the same building. The self-sufficiency of the operations centers lends them a futuristic or unearthly quality.

NO007 **BP Base Operations Center**

1973–1974, Wallace, Floyd, Ellenzweig

Barged in during the summer of 1973 and erected by March 1974, the original section of BP's Base Operations Center has a slightly better than functional design, focused on a glass atrium. Wallace, Floyd, Ellenzweig, a Cambridge, Massachusetts, architectural firm with arctic experience, designed the five units, which when assembled originally housed 140 workers. Because of the severe winds on the North Slope, there is no exterior ornament, not even overhanging eaves. The top of the building has a low gable roof. To minimize snow drifting, the building is raised 7 feet above ground, and the bottom edge is chamfered. Raising the building also removes it from the permafrost. Pilings 22 inches or 28 inches in diameter are set some 30 feet into the ground and backfilled with a sand slurry, which freezes around the piling. Concrete pile caps prevent the transfer of heat through the piling to the permafrost.

Total prefabrication was the key to the composite building concept. Four prefabricated modules, each weighing approximately 750 tons, three stories high, and measuring 126 feet by 150 feet, are U-shaped in section. The central portion is a one-story cast concrete box, flanked by three-story wood-frame sections. The structure rests on a 5-foot-thick steel-frame skid. Above the concrete section is the atrium, devoted to recreational uses (including a swimming pool that doubles as a fire reservoir), that has a steel roof truss and glass roof and walls. On either side are the bedrooms in double-loaded corridors. Seventy 16-foot-by-20-foot suites contain two separate bedrooms and a bathroom. The structure here is a conventional platform frame, with gypsum wallboard on the interior, a vapor barrier, polyurethane insulation, plywood, and on the exterior prefinished corrugated steel sheeting. The triple-glazed windows are a standard wood casement with sash that open.

The skids for the modules were manufactured in Texas and shipped through the Panama Canal to Seattle where the modules were constructed on them. They were then taken by crawlers to the barge, shipped to Prudhoe

NO007a BP Operations Center (exterior)

NO007b BP Operations Center (interior)

Bay, and crawled onto shore 18 miles and assembled. The units were placed 1 1/2 feet apart and joined with plywood and metal panels, leaving room for expansion to accommodate the temperature range.

Other sections, which house the garages and service areas, were constructed on site from knock-down, prefabricated components. Total prefabrication is cost-effective only for modules in which there is a great deal of equipment or interior finish work. As labor costs on the North Slope are high, it is cheaper to do this finish work elsewhere and ship the module completed. The site-built structures, which did not require much finish work, were also built on grade.

In 1976 an addition was made to the south, adding 140 beds. In 1980–1981, a second addition provided 236 more beds and a movie theater. The dining room was moved from the original building to this addition. The end walls of these additions, in this farthest outpost of civilization, have a nearly symmetrical arrangement of windows, doors, and stairways. Wallace, Floyd, Ellenzweig were again the designers.

NO008 ARCO Operations Center

1975, CCC/HOK

In 1975 ARCO constructed its Prudhoe Bay Operations Center as an addition to the original operations center, which consisted of wood-framed structures assembled on site. The new PBOC provided four residential

wings off of a recreational central building, all two stories tall, housing 224 people. At the same time, the original operations center converted all of its double rooms to single occupancy.

The new PBOC was prefabricated in modules in Tacoma, Washington, and barged to the site. Elevation from the ground prevented heat transference to the permafrost, provided access for the crawlers, and lessened wind action on the structures. The bottom edge of the modules was chamfered to funnel the wind. Steel trusses support a concrete deck, and the entire structure is enveloped by steel-clad urethane panels.

The central module is 70 feet by 190 feet by 40 feet high, providing an activities center with gymnasium, lounge areas, and auditorium. It also serves as a spine; the four residential modules run perpendicular to it. They are each 40 feet by 144 feet by 36 feet high, with two-room suites on a double-loaded corridor.

ARCO's philosophy, which produced a relatively spread-out complex, has changed recently. The cost of constructing gravel pads has induced it to build more compact facilities. The operations center will be moved and consolidated with the one at the Kuparuk oil field; the transportability of the structure is now proving to be one of its great advantages.

NO009 BP Base Operations Center

1987, Ralph M. Parsons Company. Endicott

Located 10 miles northeast of Prudhoe Bay, the Endicott oil field went into production in 1987. BP's Base Operations Center, a self-contained community providing room for 150 workers, was designed by the Ralph M. Parsons Company, an engineering firm, and constructed in prefabricated modules by ATCO, a Calgary company. In a departure from precedent established at its Prudhoe Bay operations center, the modules were hauled in by truck, rather than by barge. As at Prudhoe, residential rooms are arranged around a public core—here, two stories of dining room, lounge areas, theater, and gymnasium. All of the bedrooms are on the exterior.

Western Region (WE)

T HE WESTERN REGION, THE WEST COAST FROM KOTZEBUE
Sound down to Bristol Bay, including the lower Yukon and Kuskokwim
rivers, is underlain with discontinuous permafrost, producing a moist
tundra. The tree line remains several hundred miles in from the coast except
near Norton Sound and Bristol Bay. Between them are the deltas of the Yukon
and Kuskokwim rivers.

The climate is generally maritime, with temperatures considerably warmer
toward the south. Total precipitation is about 20 inches annually. The flat lands
and seashore setting are subject to an unremitting wind.

The region north of Norton Sound was traditionally home to the Inupiat
Eskimo, and to the south, Yupik Eskimo. With diets based largely on fish or
sea mammals, the Eskimo lived near the shore or on rivers. Occasional hunting
forays inland would provide meat. The Russians established redoubts and trading posts on the Nushagak, Kuskokwim, and Yukon rivers. Their influence is
apparent in the number of active Russian Orthodox churches in the villages
along these rivers. Usually set slightly apart from the houses, higher if possible,
the three-part plans of the churches are visible in their silhouettes, which are
often crowned with onion domes and three-bar crosses.

Change occurred rapidly near the end of the nineteenth century, when the
wealth of salmon in Bristol Bay was discovered by white Americans. Canneries
were soon built at every river mouth, threatening the Natives' subsistence patterns and bringing in new people.

Gold had an even greater effect on the Seward Peninsula. The first strike
was at Council City in 1898. When gold was found in creeks 80 miles to the
west, near present-day Nome, stampeders came rushing to the scene. And in
1900, after gold was found to be lying on, or just under, the beaches, thou-

Western Region

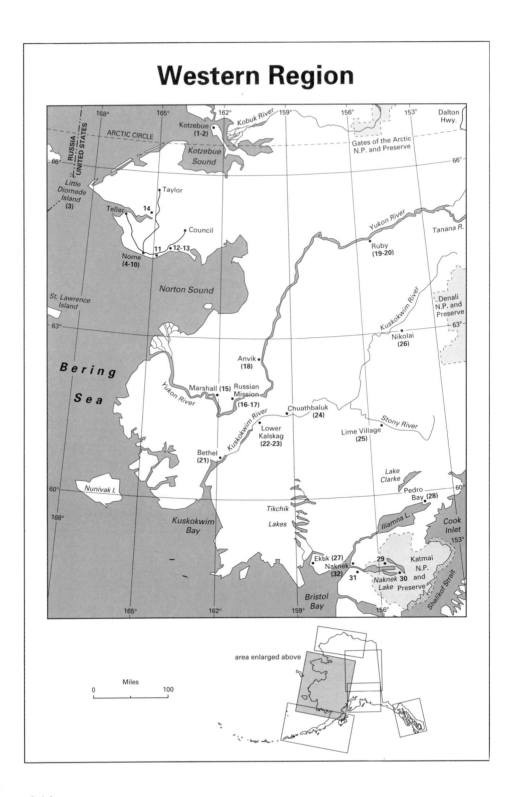

RUSSIA / UNITED STATES

ARCTIC CIRCLE

168° 165° 162° Kobuk River 159° 156° 153° Dalton Hwy.

Kotzebue (1-2)

Gates of the Arctic N.P. and Preserve

Kotzebue Sound

66° 66°

Little Diomede Island (3)

Taylor

Teller 14

Council

Yukon River Tanana R.

Nome (4-10) 11 12-13

Ruby (19-20)

Norton Sound

St. Lawrence Island

Kuskokwim River

Denali N.P. and Preserve

63° 63°

Nikolai (26)

Anvik (18)

B e r i n g

S e a

Yukon River

Marshall (15) Russian Mission (16-17)

Chuathbaluk (24)

Stony River

Kuskokwim River

Lower Kalskag (22-23)

Lime Village (25)

Bethel (21)

Lake Clarke

60° Nunivak I. Pedro Bay (28) 60°

168°

Tikchik Lakes

Iliamna L.

Cook Inlet

Kuskokwim Bay

153°

Ekuk (27) 29 Katmai N.P.

Naknek (32) 31 Naknek 30 Lake and Preserve

Shelikof Strait

Bristol Bay

165° 162° 159° 156°

area enlarged above

Miles
0   100

sands of gold seekers poured into Nome. Although relatively few stayed after the first season, when the easy gold was removed, subsequent strikes made gold mining profitable for about a decade. In the 1920s gold dredges and cold-water thawing made larger operations successful, and gold mining continues today.

There are few roads in the entire region, but the advent of the airplane has made most villages comparatively accessible. Settlements continue to be located along the shore or on rivers. Building materials—except for native sod and driftwood, which are rarely used today—must be imported into these treeless places, and prefabricated dwellings have found a special applicability here. Yet at least one traditional Native dwelling and many Native churches survive. Buildings constructed by white Americans at the turn of the twentieth century were not particularly responsive to the climate, tending to resemble buildings that would have been built elsewhere. They stand as evidence of gold-rush towns, of well-intended missions, of roadhouses along winter trails, and of remote settlements, reflecting the many reasons for building.

North of Norton Sound

Kotzebue

Kotzebue, on Kotzebue Sound of the Chukchi Sea, was a natural meeting place for Eskimo traders, and a village grew up here in the nineteenth century. In 1897 the Friends established a mission here, dominating the educational and cultural scenes for several decades. A minor gold rush to the Kobuk River area in 1898 and an influx of traders added to the white influences on the town. The older part of town, near Second Avenue and Mission Street, has a variety of one-story, wood-framed buildings with a handful of log structures.

In 1951, the U.S. Bureau of Land Management auctioned the publicly held land, which was most of downtown Kotzebue, to private owners, and the population doubled in that decade. Rapid growth continues and is reflected in the number of prefabricated, modular homes. Today, Kotzebue serves as a regional center and as headquarters of the NANA (the Northwest Alaska Native Association) Regional Corporation.

WE001 Rammed Earth House

1968. Building 836

The remnant of a well-intentioned government program to use indigenous materials in constructing low-cost housing, Building 836 was intended to be built of rammed earth. Earth, when compressed, becomes hard as brick, and rammed earth has served as a construction material in various parts of the world for centuries. Danish architect Vetle Jorgensen conceived this project in 1968. The Alaska State Housing Authority provided $8,000 for basic materials, such as the roof and windows, and VISTA volunteers provided the labor.

In Kotzebue, however, the earth was too sandy to be used effectively as rammed earth. The 4-foot-thick walls were finished to a height of only 4 feet. The current owner bought the unfinished house for $500 in 1969 and completed it with standard wood framing.

WE002 NANA Regional Corporation Building

1977, Alley-Haeg. Third Ave.

The NANA (Northwest Alaska Native Association) Regional Corporation Building is a two-story structure, with offices on the second floor and the NANA Museum of the Arctic on the first floor, displaying ethnological and natural history collections. The building is unusual in shape, coming to a sharp point at one end, with a serrated edge. Originally a dark brown natural color, the building has been painted baby blue.

WE002.1 Sod House

1977

Just beyond the point of the NANA Regional Corporation Building is a museum exhibit of a sod-covered house, the traditional dwelling of the Eskimos. An entrance passage leads to one large room, lit by an off-center skylight. The walls are formed by vertical half-logs; on the exterior is a thick layer of sod. The same materials are applied to the roof, which is supported on two ridgepoles.

Little Diomede Island, in the Bering Strait

WE003 John Iyapana Kugeri

early twentieth century. Ignaluk

The only traditional kugeri remaining on Little Diomede Island, John Iyapana's house was probably constructed in the early twentieth century. The kugeri—a community house, larger than individual dwellings—is a semi-subterranean dwelling with a tunnel entrance coming up through the floor. The interior is approximately 14 feet square. The walls are constructed of vertical planks, held by corner posts and horizontal logs; on the outside is a 10-inch-thick layer of sod, covered by a layer of stone. A bench runs around the four walls of the interior; other original furnishings include two stands for seal oil lamps and two drying racks. The walls have recently been painted white to conceal layers of soot. The skylight in the roof was traditionally covered with seal intestine; it is now covered with plastic and protected by a balustrade. The 28-foot-long tunnel entrance is framed with timber, plywood, and whale bones; near the entrance is a storeroom, approximately 5 1/2 feet square and about 4 feet 9 inches high.

When refurbished in 1945, wooden planks from Seattle were used to replace old wallboards and ceiling. The ceiling was raised about 2 1/2 feet. In 1977, a fuel oil stove and electric lights replaced the seal oil lamps.

WE003 John Iyapana Kugeri

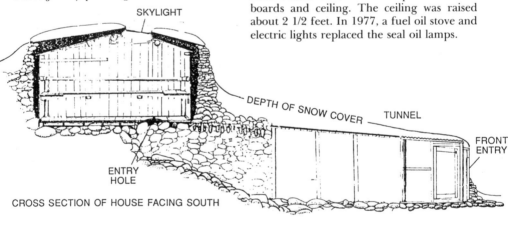

SKYLIGHT

DEPTH OF SNOW COVER   TUNNEL

FRONT ENTRY

ENTRY HOLE

CROSS SECTION OF HOUSE FACING SOUTH

Nome

Nome experienced one of the most dramatic gold rushes on the continent. Gold was discovered on nearby creeks in 1898, and 3,000 stampeders appeared in the new mining camp of Nome by July 1899. The discovery of gold on the

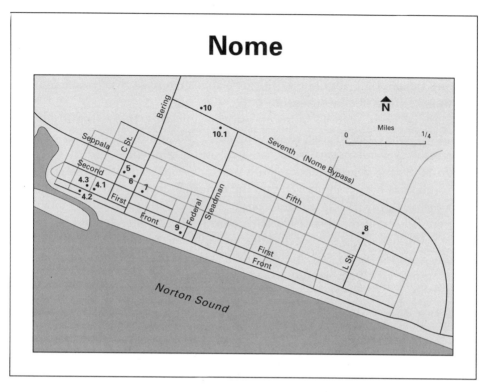

beaches that summer, however, sent thousands more hopefuls sailing to Nome. Located on Seward Peninsula, on the north side of Norton Sound, not only was Nome relatively easy to reach but the gold itself was also easy to reach, just 1 foot to 4 feet or more below the surface of the beach, where claims could not be staked. Shoulder to shoulder, gold-mining novices crowded together, needing only a shovel and a rocker to separate the gold from the sand.

The town itself was chaotic. Described as two blocks wide and 5 miles long, Nome originally consisted of tents and a few driftwood log cabins lining the seashore. In 1899 and 1900, the new wave of gold seekers shipped their own buildings to the treeless tundra, including 8 million board feet of lumber and a few galvanized-iron structures. Streets were narrow, and often occupied by buildings; sanitation was rudimentary; and 25,000 people swelling the small city produced near anarchy.

In the next decade, several strikes on ancient beaches east of town produced prosperity and some degree of permanence for the town, whose population settled at about 5,000. The buildings constructed at this time run the gamut of wood-framed structures in cottage, bungalow, and farmhouse forms. Like most towns in Alaska, Nome did not have a "richest man in town" house, an obviously wealthy man's house built to make a statement. Instead, the classes mixed freely—as wealth and status were dependent on the luck of the pay dirt—and the architecture had a certain uniformity of scale and lack of pretention. The houses are small and narrow, with gable roofs and clapboarding. Bay windows, arctic entries, and wood shingles ornament them. Because construction materials are so valuable, buildings tend to be adapted to new uses and the resulting changes on the exterior are not always flattering to the architecture. The numerous repairs and alterations with available materials give the buildings a patchwork, often shabby, appearance.

Nome has been battered by several storms and fires. In 1934, a fire devastated the commercial district, destroying all the buildings on twelve city blocks. As a result, several streets were widened and straightened; the street plans collide at Bering Street, marking the new and old sections. Although some older buildings have been moved into the eastern area, the town lacks the cohesion of steady growth. The seawall constructed in 1949–1951 and a timber and concrete jetty built in 1919–1923 have also drastically altered the appearance of the town, obscuring the beaches that made Nome famous. Several buildings remain, however, to give the architectural flavor of this westernmost gold-rush town. Mining continues west of Nome to this day.

WE004 First Avenue, West

First Avenue between Bering and F streets retains a collection of buildings that date from Nome's first decade of settlement. The wood-framed houses are mostly one or one and a half story, with gable roofs and bay windows. The houses are set on the street, without yards, and the road remains unpaved.

WE004.1 Discovery Saloon

1901. 197 First Ave. West

The only false-fronted building remaining in Nome, the Discovery Saloon is a two-story, wood-framed structure, now unhappily covered with aluminum siding. The building measures 18 feet by 36 feet and originally had plate-glass windows flanking a recessed doorway on the first floor. This entrance has been changed to an enclosed porch. At the second floor are two oriels, which originally were linked by a balustraded porch. At the third-floor level, a Palladian window, now converted to a simple square window, was set in the rounded pediment of the false front.

When opened by Max Gordon in 1901, the Discovery Saloon was one of forty-four saloons in town. Advertising billiards and card tables, Gordon operated the saloon until 1912. By 1940 it had been converted to a residence.

WE004.2 Orton House

1904. 220 First Ave. West

The one-and-a-half-story Orton house was built for Ira Orton, a lawyer from San Francisco, and his wife, Viola, in May and June of 1904. It has an L-plan, with a hip-roofed main block and a lower gable roof on the projecting ell. These rooflines, as well as that of the hip-roofed dormer, are topped with an unusual wooden cresting, creating an interesting profile. The wood-framed house is covered with clapboards.

WE004.3 William Moore House

by 1903. 201 First Ave. West

WE004.2 Orton House

William Moore worked at jobs such as clerk at the hotel, notary public, real estate broker, and stenographer as well as miner. By 1906 Moore had sold the house to Chauncey G. Cowden, who organized the Miners and Merchants Bank of Alaska. The one-and-a-half-story, wood-framed house has a gable front with a bay window in the center. Beveled siding contrasts with clapboards in the gable. The entrance is through an arctic entry, partly projecting to the side.

WE005 Celia Gilbert House

1907. 264 C St.

Built for dressmaker Celia Gilbert, the two-story, wood-framed house has two two-story bay windows, including one on the gable front. Sunburst ornament on the side of the entry enlivens the clapboard-covered exterior. There is a two-story, shed-roofed addition on one side, probably added after 1916, when the United Methodist Church bought the building to serve as a hospital. In 1922, when the church built a larger hospital, this building was converted to a nurses' residence. It served in that capacity until the late 1940s, when a larger hospital was constructed several blocks away. It is now a private home.

WE006 W. H. Bard House

c. 1906. 259 Bering St.

This foursquare house has a hipped roof with an eyebrow dormer. The wood-framed building, now sided with wide clapboards in contrast to the original narrow ones, was built for William H. Bard, who owned one third of the Bessie Bench mining claim, found in February 1906. A lawyer, Bard also served

Nome as mayor, councilman, municipal judge, and city attorney. By 1909, he had moved to Seattle.

WE007 Jacob Berger House

1904. 41 Second Ave. East

Probably the first two-story house on the Bering Sea coast, the house was built for Jacob Berger, a Jewish miner who made three rich strikes in the area. He sent away for architectural plans, building materials, and furnishings, and completed the house in 1904. The hip-roofed, one-and-a-half-story building has a two-story square tower in the center of the front, topped by a pyramidal roof. The wood-framed building is covered with clapboards on the first story and wood shingles on the second. From 1945 to 1958, it was the home of Sally Carrighar, a naturalist and ethnographer who wrote several books about Alaska.

WE008 Nome Elementary School

1987, CCC Architects Alaska. Fifth Ave. East and L St.

Bearing all the features of well-thought arctic design, the Nome Elementary School is raised on insulated piling above the permafrost. Beige metal panels cover the exterior, accented by orange trim and a red roof, bright contrasts against the bleak landscape. The entrances are enclosed and hooded, providing protection from the wind.

WE009 Old Federal Building

1937–1938, Gilbert Stanley Underwood. Front St. and Federal Way

Completely unrecognizable under its new exterior, the Old Federal Building was constructed in 1937–1938 at a cost of $374,000. Underwood, the consulting architect from Los Angeles, designed an H-shaped building with a three-story main block and two-story projecting wings. The wood-framed building was finished with asbestos board laid horizontally to resemble shiplap siding. The exterior was otherwise unrelieved by ornament, with steel-sash windows and a flat roof.

Today, the building is covered with wood siding, with wings raised to three stories; oriels are supported on scrolled brackets. The building houses a variety of offices, while the federal offices and post office have moved

across the street to a two-story, concrete
building constructed in 1956.

WE010 Hammon Consolidated Gold Fields Buildings

1920s. Seventh Ave. East and Bering St.

Between 1905 and 1917, about twenty dredges
were introduced into the goldfields at Nome,
none of them particularly successful. In 1922,
W. P. Hammon acquired the property of the
Pioneer Mining Company in Nome and
brought in two dredges. The next year Hammon sold his interest to the United States
Smelting, Refining and Mining Company (also
the owners of the Fairbanks Exploration
Company), and Alaska Gold Company continues the operations today.

To power the dredges, Hammon Consolidated Gold Fields (the name was retained
until 1938) built a diesel power plant just
north of the city limits, about 3 1/2 miles
from the dredge areas. The power plant complex includes a number of gable-roofed
buildings, sided and roofed with corrugated
metal.

WE010.1 Saint Joseph's Roman Catholic Church

1901

The most notable building in the Hammon
Consolidated power plant complex is Saint
Joseph's Roman Catholic Church. Although
serving the ignominious role of a gold-

WE010.1a Saint Joseph's Roman Catholic Church

company warehouse and stripped of its steeple, Saint Joseph's remains the only church
building from Nome's early history. Constructed in 1901, the 40-foot-by-60-foot church
had an 88-foot steeple that supported a large,
electrically lit cross serving as a beacon over
the tundra and sea. This cross was deemed
so important that the city paid the cost of
illuminating it. Originally located at Steadman and King's Place, the building was moved
to its present site in 1946 and oriented with
its back to the street. The building's rear
facade had a lower, gable-roofed sanctuary;
this sanctuary was removed and warehouse-
type doors were installed. On its original front,
two round arches surmount the double-leaf
doorway, and there is a rose window in the
gable. The tower has been chopped off above
the first story. The wood-framed building has
novelty siding; corner pilasters and buttresses
have been removed. When the Catholics built

WE010.1b Saint Joseph's Roman Catholic Church (floor plan)

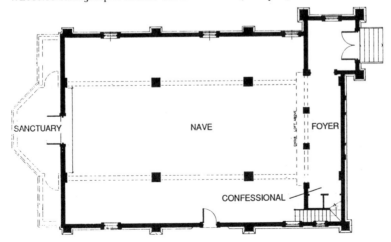

a new, smaller, more easily maintained church in 1946, the USSR&M Company acquired this one, a surprising choice for a warehouse.

Nome Vicinity

WE011 Cape Nome Roadhouse

c. 1900; 1913, moved. Mile 14 Nome-Council Rd.

Located one day's travel outside of Nome, the present Cape Nome Roadhouse replaced a log structure built in 1900. In 1913, after the latter was washed away in a flood, an abandoned building from Safety was moved to this site. The two-story, wood-framed building with a front-gable roof has a shed-roofed addition to the side, increasing the size of the house considerably. There is also a one-story portion in the rear. The cement asbestos shingles covering the building and the bay window across the front are not original. The building is now used as a residence.

WE012 Solomon Roadhouse

c. 1900; 1918, moved. Mile 33.5 Nome-Council Rd.

Although not at its original location, the Solomon Roadhouse still serves as the landmark identified with the old town of Solomon. After discovery of gold on the Solomon River in 1899, a dredge was brought in and extensive hydraulic mining was undertaken by 1904. The Council City and Solomon River Railway was constructed in 1904 to connect Solomon on the coast with the thriving gold-rush town of Council City. The railway's terminus was Dickson, on the east side of the river; Solomon, on the west side, was connected by a ferry and footbridge. In Dickson the company built offices, warehouses, and a hotel. The railroad was abandoned in 1907, and after Solomon was devastated by a storm in 1913, survivors moved the town across the river to Dickson.

In 1918, W. J. "Billy" Rowe moved one of the railroad buildings about a mile east of Solomon/Dickson on the Nome-Council road. Rowe used it as a horse barn. Pete Curran acquired it in 1939, at the same time that the new site of Solomon was being abandoned, again due to flooding. This building continued to serve as a roadhouse and store until Curran's death in 1958. Currently not in use, it is a two-story, wood-framed building with

novelty siding. One-story, shed-roofed additions at front and rear serve as arctic entries. The front-gable building has molded lintels on some windows.

WE013 Bureau of Indian Affairs School

1930s. Mile 33.5 Nome-Council Rd.

Across the street from the roadhouse is a Bureau of Indian Affairs school, probably built in the 1930s. The one-story building with carved bargeboards has the standard U-shaped form, with three doors, and incorporated teacher's quarters in the building.

WE014 Pilgrim Hot Springs

c. 1908, c. 1919. Mile 7 of road at Mile 53 of Nome-Taylor Rd.

An unlikely collection of buildings in a remote location, Pilgrim Hot Springs also has an unlikely history. Hot springs here create a favorable location for agriculture, and the land was homesteaded at the turn of the century. The springs also attracted miners and their ladies in search of recreation, and a roadhouse was built to accommodate them.

By 1918, the property was owned by the Catholic church, which established an orphanage for Native children at the height of the influenza epidemic. Father Bellarmine Lafortune directed the construction, as well as the orphanage. Local timber was supplemented with sawn lumber, floated in on the Pilgrim River. The hot springs heated some buildings, including the greenhouse, as agricultural production continued. For twenty years, Pilgrim Hot Springs served as an orphanage, with about one hundred children and twenty staff members, until closing in 1941. During World War II, the site was used by U.S. military forces as a rest and recreation center. The Catholic church still owns the complex but has leased it long-term to private interests. The farm continues to flourish today.

WE014.1 Roadhouse

c. 1908

The old roadhouse stands near the entrance. Constructed after the original one burned in 1908, it is a simple gable-roofed building with a large addition on one side. The wood-framed building has a variety of claddings, including novelty siding, horizontal planks, and board-and-batten. During the time that the site was an orphanage, the roadhouse served as the laundry.

WE014.2 Our Lady of Lourdes Church

c. 1919

Next to the roadhouse is Our Lady of Lourdes Church, a two-and-a-half-story, cross-shaped building with a bell tower. The wood frame is covered with galvanized iron clapboarding, with wood shingles in the gables and wooden pilasters at the corners. The first floor served as the main kitchen and priests' quarters, while the second story is the church. Box columns separate the lower side aisles from the nave. The painting behind the altar of Our Lady of Lourdes was executed by one of the orphans. A skylight, which is now closed off, illuminated the altar. There is stenciling on the walls and linoleum on the floors. Confessional booths line one of the side walls. The building is no longer used.

WE014.3 Dormitory

c. 1919

The other large building on the site is the dormitory, a long, one-and-a-half-story structure. The wood-framed building has vertical planks on the sides and novelty siding on the ends. There is a variety of windows and doors, indicating that the building has been used for a variety of functions over the years. It is now serving as a tool shed and machine shop. Its gable-roofed dormers are its most distinguishing feature.

WE014.4 Nuns' Quarters

c. 1919

Near the dormitory is the Nuns' Quarters, a gable-roofed building measuring 20 feet by 24 feet. The one-and-a-half-story building has exposed rafter ends at the eaves and is covered with a variety of horizontal sidings. The windows have been replaced with fixed sash.

Yukon and Kuskokwim

Marshall

WE015 Saint Michael the Archangel Russian Orthodox Church

1960

The plywood-covered Saint Michael the Archangel Church is a humble shelter for the spectacular icons inside. The icons were obtained from the Russian Orthodox church at Saint Michael on Norton Sound and appear to be among the oldest in Alaska.

Because the Yukon River is so braided at its mouth, Saint Michael served as an important access point to the river. Ocean-going vessels were anchored at Saint Michael, a sheltered harbor. Travelers then portaged over to the Yukon or, later in the nineteenth cen-

WE015 Saint Michael the Archangel Russian Orthodox Church (iconostas)

tury, transferred to river-going steamboats for the journey to the river mouth, and up the river. The Russians established a post at Saint Michael in the 1830s and in 1886 built a majestic log church. By the 1950s, that church was abandoned and deteriorating, and the icons were removed to the village of Ohogamiut, just a few miles upriver from Marshall, in 1957.

Named after Woodrow Wilson's first vice president, Marshall was a gold-rush town that experienced its big rush in 1913. The village is now inhabited almost entirely by Eskimos, who have moved in from surrounding villages. Marshall had no Russian Orthodox church before this one was built in 1960; the icons were moved from Ohogamiut at that time.

Russian Mission

Russian Mission, known to the Eskimos as Ikogmiut and to the Russians as Kvikhpak, was established by the Russians as a mission in 1845. Most of the other missions were located at trading posts, thus earning the protection of the Russian-American Company, but this mission was separate, located on the Yukon near a portage to the Kuskokwim. As such, it became the base of operations for the one missionary assigned to the vast region of the lower Yukon and Kuskokwim region, Iakov Netsvetov. The first church was built here in 1851.

In 1895, a new large church, approximating a cathedral in size, was constructed by Zachary Bel'kov. The log structure, with a hip-roofed square nave supporting a large octagonal drum, a three-stage bell tower, and a semioctagonal hip-roofed sanctuary, must have presented quite an appearance on the Yukon. It was demolished in 1938–1939 after construction on an adjacent hill of a smaller log church, modest in appearance but nonetheless well designed.

WE016 (Old) Elevation of the Holy Cross Russian Orthodox Church

c. 1937

Although smaller than its predecessor, this new church was also in the three-part form, with sanctuary, nave, and bell tower clearly expressed. The square nave, about 20 feet on a side, is topped with a hipped roof. The semihexagonal sanctuary also has a hipped roof, while the narthex and vestibule have gable roofs. From the roof of the narthex rises a bell tower. The hewn logs of the walls are dovetailed at the corners. The icons, which have been removed, were arrayed on the slopes of the ceiling as well as on the iconostas. Now abandoned, the church, though small, has a classic form.

WE017 (New) Elevation of the Holy Cross Russian Orthodox Church

1973–1975, Father Gabriel Gabrieloff

Dedicated in 1980, the new Church of the Elevation of the Holy Cross was designed by Father Gabriel Gabrieloff, a native of the village. It is located on the adjacent hill, on the site of the 1895 "cathedral." In its elements—a tall, cubical nave topped by a hipped roof, a large octagonal cupola over the nave, separate vestibule and sanctuary—it recalls the 1895 church, but the proportions of the plywood-covered church are not as graceful. Most notable in the new church are the icons, which probably first decorated the 1895 church. The nine-bay iconostas was purchased by Anisim Bel'kov, Father Zachary's brother, while the oil-on-canvas icons have a pre-Raphaelite appearance. Additional icons hang on the sides of the octagonal drum, as they had in the previous church. Still in use, this fourth church to be built in Russian Mission follows the traditions of its predecessors, architecturally as well as ecclesiastically.

Anvik

WE018 Christ Church Episcopal Mission

1888

Rev. Octavius Parker and Rev. John Chapman established an Episcopal mission near here in 1887. Recognizing that they had established the mission on an eroding site, they moved it the next year to a site about 2 miles down the Yukon to the mouth of the Anvik River. By 1889, when Parker left, they had a sawmill and had begun constructing buildings.

Included with the mission's role was that of school and hospital. The Episcopalians operated a boarding school at Anvik, attracting children from the region until the 1950s. One of the first female doctors in Alaska, Dr. Mary Glanton, was stationed here, arriving in 1894. The Natives gradually moved their village closer to the mission, constructing log cabins and abandoning their traditional semisubterranean houses.

WE018.1 Christ Episcopal Church

1892; 1927, moved

Christ Episcopal Church was built of round logs, dovetailed at the corners. A small gable vestibule on the front and the gables of the building were covered with board-and-batten siding. A square, open belfry was perched on top of the nave. The gable roof was covered with wood shingles. The windows had four-over-four lights and double-hung sash.

In 1927, the church was moved about 75 feet to the south due to erosion. At that time, the building was placed on a stone and concrete foundation, and the logs were covered with wood shingles; today, just the lower two or three courses are exposed. A hip-roofed

vestibule was added to the front of the building, with an offset square bell tower. The belfry was moved from the church onto the bell tower. In addition, a two-level semioctagonal addition was made to the altar end.

The interior of the church features a tray ceiling of narrow beaded boards, stained and varnished. The wooden altar is set in a proscenium arch. The pews are a variety of wooden benches, and there is a barrel stove in one corner. The apse is lit by second-story windows; stained glass was installed in these and the sidelights surrounding the front door during a 1985 restoration. The building is well cared for and is a pleasant and pristine example of a mission church.

WE018.2 Dormitory and School

1932

The two-story dormitory and school measures 72 feet by 36 feet. The first floor is of horizontal round logs, dovetailed at the corners, while the second floor is wood framed and covered with wood shingles. Three triangular dormers decorate the front of the building, as does a Rustic porch across the center portion of the front. There are brackets in the eaves of the gables.

The first floor contained a chapel, dining room/school room, and kitchen, while the second floor had bedrooms. Since the mission closed, it has functioned as a pool hall and movie theater; it is currently vacant. In the mid-1960s one third of the building was converted into a gymnasium, and the second floor was removed.

WE018.3 Rectory

1958

The rectory stands just east of the dormitory. It is a one-story log building, constructed of logs sawn flat on three sides. The building has a hip roof and a hip-roofed projection in the center. The rectory carries the log-construction tradition into the present, as many of the buildings in town are log cabins. One curious convention, perhaps adapted from the dormitory, is that several houses around town have a log first floor and a wood-framed second story, or upper portion of the first.

Ruby

Ruby, a gold-rush town that boomed from 1907 to 1918, is attractively set on a sloping hillside on the Yukon River, between two bluffs. Most of the buildings, which include both log and wood-framed construction, face the river. There are a number of log buildings, many quite recently built, constructed of logs sawn flat on three sides, perhaps products of the city-owned sawmill in the center of town. Only one false-fronted building remains.

In 1929 a fire destroyed twenty-three buildings on Front Street, effectively removing the gold-rush-era commercial area.

WE019 **Store**

1929

Immediately after the fire, Tom DeVane built the most dramatic building along the waterfront, a one-story log store. The long building, built of round logs squared and lap jointed at the corners, has a cross gable in both front and rear near the center of the building. Corrugated-metal additions on one end indicate that it was a successful store, requiring expansion, but it is now abandoned.

WE020 **Roadhouse**

1911, 1913, 1918 and later

The roadhouse, comprised of sections of different buildings, seems to reflect the history of the entire town. The oldest section is that built by Doc Frost, probably about 1911. It is a gable-roofed log building, measuring about 16 feet by 18 feet. In 1913, Oscar Tackstrom—bookkeeper for the sawmill—constructed a one-room building of wood frame, described as "the biggest, nicest home in town" by a long-time resident. About 1918, the two buildings were moved downhill by Judge William Growden to the present site and joined into a new building, with the gable roofs at right angles to each other. Growden located the U.S. commissioner's office, the U.S. Signal Corps station, and district courtrooms in the building. It is not known when the porch on two sides, covered by a hip roof, was added. In 1935, Sig and Mame Wiig, local miners, bought the building and converted it to a roadhouse, adding a section measuring 30 feet by 60 feet on the downhill side. A shed-roofed kitchen off of the Doc Frost building adds to the sprawl. Now covered with imitation brick asphalt siding, the building continues to be used as a roadhouse.

Bethel

WE021 **Yukon-Kuskokwim Delta Regional Hospital**

1980, Caudill Rowlett Scott

Modern and high tech, the Yukon-Kuskokwim Delta Regional Hospital is both responsive and alien to its surroundings. It is located in a remote town on the lower Kuskokwim River that was founded by Moravian missionaries and has evolved into a regional hub. Completed in 1980, the large one-story, steel-framed building is clad with bright yellow prefabricated panels accented with blue. Architects Caudill Rowlett Scott accommodated the permafrost by elevating the building on legs that are on H-shaped thermopiles, incorporating copper tubes of freon that passively extract heat from the tundra through convection. The elevation of the building also enables snow to blow under the building, rather than drifting around it. Rounded corners increase the aerodynamics or at least seem to visually. A dramatic, enclosed handicapped ramp at the primary entrance and hooded stairways on all sides of the building provide access to the bright interior. The fifty-bed hospital is oriented around a central concourse, which includes an open waiting room and courtyards to provide natural light.

Lower Kalskag

WE022 (Old) Saint Seraphim Russian Orthodox Chapel

1936

Also on the Kuskokwim River, 65 miles northeast of Bethel, the old church at Lower Kalskag, located precariously close to the eroding river bank, is a small log chapel. In the classic form, it is divided into three distinct parts—sanctuary, nave, and vestibule—all covered with gable roofs. The nave is square, measuring 19 1/2 feet on the exterior. The logs are hewn, dovetailed at the corners. The bells and the iconostas have been removed to the new church.

Lower Kalskag was first populated as a summer fish camp a few miles downriver from Kalskag. When the Russian Orthodox founders of Kalskag were joined by Roman Catholic Eskimos, conflicts developed. In the 1930s the Russian Orthodox villagers moved downriver, turning their seasonal fish camp into a year-round village.

WE023 (New) Saint Seraphim Russian Orthodox Church

1972–1975, Iftukim Evan

Located safely away from the river, on the other side of town, the new church in Lower Kalskag was constructed in 1972–1975. Iftukim Evan, a member of the church, was primarily responsible for the design, which he developed by looking at photographs of other churches. The square nave, measuring about 27 feet on a side on the interior, is covered with a hip roof, while the sanctuary and vestibule at either end have gable roofs. The wood-framed building is sided with a modern textured plywood paneling called T1–11, and the roofs are covered with corrugated metal.

The design and construction of this relatively recent church are probably typical of many of the older churches in this region. Iftukim Evan, with a third-grade education, was not trained as a carpenter, but as operator of the sawmill the construction of the church fell to him. He made no drawings but designed it in his head. The hipped roof gave him particular problems, as he had not had experience with any. The semicircular projection in the center of the amvon (the dais in front of the iconostas) was likewise tricky to design, and although he asked around, no one could tell him how it should be constructed. As a result, the three-step projection is unusual, with the bottom step more oblong than semicircular. Evan used a compass to design the cut-outs of the balustrades of the sides of the amvon. The crystal chandelier required electrification, which Evan was also able to effect. The construction team was composed of the villagers themselves, who donated their time as opportunity and inclination dictated.

Chuathbaluk (Little Russian Mission)

WE024 Saint Sergius Russian Orthodox Chapel

1955

Although this wood-framed, asphalt-sided building was constructed in 1955, it is in the same plan and form as the previous log church, which probably dated from 1891, when the village was founded as a Russian Orthodox mission. The village was abandoned in the 1920s but reoccupied in 1954. The church is in three distinct parts, reflecting interior functions. Most prominent is the nave, 24 feet by 27 feet, with a hipped roof rising to a cupola and onion dome. On the east end is a smaller, rectangular sanctuary with a gable roof and on the west end, a gable-roofed vestibule. Large double doors, reused from the previous church, are sheltered by a gable-roofed porch; there is also a secondary door on the south side of the vestibule. The iconostas, which was also apparently reused from the previous church, has several large oil paintings, and the three-step amvon (platform before the iconostas) adds to its presence.

A new church is currently under construction, intended to replace this one, which has foundation problems. The new church will be of log, the material of the earliest church, but will be rectangular in plan, without the sanctuary denoted on the exterior. Both churches sit on a hill above the village of Chuathbaluk, which recently adopted this Eskimo name, discarding its traditional but diminutive name of Little Russian Mission.

plan, measuring 17 feet along each exterior wall, constructed of round logs, square notched at the corners. On the interior, the sanctuary is not divided from the nave; instead, a sheet is stretched in front of the altar when the services call for this privacy. There is no iconostas as such; icons, apparently saved from the previous village, are attached to the rear wall. This church does not have any sort of vestibule, as entry is directly into the nave.

This unusual one-cell church may represent the earliest type of church built. As villages grew, a sanctuary would be added at one end, the altar moved into it, and a vestibule added to the other end. By its very simplicity, the Chapel of Saints Constantine and Helen may be most informative of long-past customs.

Lime Village

WE025 Saints Constantine and Helen Russian Orthodox Chapel

c. 1920s

Although the date of construction of this church is not known, Saints Constantine and Helen Chapel is unique among surviving Alaskan Russian Orthodox churches. Athapaskan Indians founded Lime Village in 1917 on the Stony River, a tributary of the Kuskokwim, after a forest fire destroyed the villagers' previous home about 20 miles upriver. This chapel was either built at that time, with a new roof added in the 1940s, or was perhaps entirely reconstructed in the 1940s.

The pyramidal-roofed church is square in

Nikolai

WE026 Presentation of Our Lord Russian Orthodox Chapel

c. 1929

Nikolai is a small Athapaskan village on the south fork of the Kuskokwim River. The three parts of this Russian Orthodox church—sanctuary, nave, and vestibule—are clearly expressed on the exterior of this structure. The nave, measuring about 18 feet by 24 feet on the interior, has a hipped roof. The sanctuary on the east end, less than 2 feet narrower and about 12 feet deep, has a gable roof, as does the vestibule on the west end, which is a little narrower than the sanctuary and about the same depth.

The wood-framed nave was constructed in about 1929, replacing a log structure built in 1915 when the village moved from its previous site a few miles away. The vestibule and sanctuary are constructed of thick planks and were added within a few years of the nave's construction. The building is crowned with three onion domes of varying shapes. On the interior, the iconostas across the east end of the nave is the focus of attention.

The church sits in a fenced churchyard with aspens and spruces. The wooden fences around each grave were painted colorfully in the spring of 1990. A shrine about 20 yards northeast of the church marks the site of the previous church.

Bristol Bay and Lake Iliamna

Ekuk

WE027 Saint Nicholas Russian Orthodox Chapel

1917

The fishing village of Ekuk is located on Nushagak Bay, off of Bristol Bay. A small simple chapel, Saint Nicholas was constructed in 1917. The materials of the building, which is wood-framed with clapboard siding, were probably donated by or obtained from the nearby cannery. The plan is rectangular, 16 feet by 34 feet, but the sanctuary on the east end is denoted by a hipped roof, while the west end is gabled. There is a small vestibule supporting a bell tower on the gable end.

John Huyano, who helped construct the building, may have been responsible for many of the ornamental touches. Decorative bargeboards, wooden sconces on the walls, and a chandelier constructed of wood, rope, and beads display the same craftsmanship as a picture frame found in the church, signed by Huyano. The small church is now used only during fishing season, when the nearly abandoned village of Ekuk fills with cannery workers and fishermen.

Pedro Bay, Lake Iliamna

WE028 Saint Nicholas Russian Orthodox Chapel

1940s

Deteriorating and abandoned, Saint Nicholas Chapel is a small but virtually unaltered example of the three-part form. The nave, which measures 14 feet by 17 feet on the interior, has a steep gable roof. On the east end, the sanctuary is in a semioctagonal form, with a high polygonal roof. The vestibule on the west end has a shed roof. The building is constructed of hewn logs, square notched at the corners. The church was said to have been moved from Old Iliamna in the 1940s, or built at that time. All of the icons have been removed for safekeeping.

WE028 Saint Nicholas Russian Orthodox Chapel

Katmai National Park and Preserve

WE029 Roy Fure Cabin

c. 1926. Bay of Islands, north side Naknek Lake

Roy Fure built this log cabin on Naknek Lake about 1926. Unlike the cabins of American trappers and prospectors of this period, the cabin has hewn logs, dovetailed corners, and exquisite craftsmanship. Measuring about 20 feet by 15 feet, the one-room cabin was constructed entirely of hand-hewn timbers, including the roof structure and the floor. The logs were grooved lengthwise on the bottoms to provide a tight fit over the logs below. The gable roof, originally sod on planks, was covered with corrugated metal in the 1930s. There is a window in each wall, and the door is in the long wall, rather than the gable end.

Born in Lithuania in 1885, Fure arrived in Alaska in 1912. He worked at canneries and at commercial fishing in the summers and came inland to trap in the winters. By his first wife, Anna Johnson, a Native, Fure had four children, two of whom did not survive childhood. After Anna's death in 1929, Fure married Fanny Olson, an Aleut, by whom he had a daughter. Fure had another cabin up American Creek and lived here sporadically until his death in 1962.

In 1986–1988, the National Park Service restored Fure's cabin. Sill logs were replaced and gravel laid around them to increase

WE029 Roy Fure Cabin

drainage. Other logs were replaced as needed, and the 4-inch-thick planks of the roof and the 3-inch-thick planks of the floor were replaced entirely. New corrugated metal was placed on the roof, and shutters were added to the windows as bear-proofing. Artifacts inside the cabin, which apparently date from Fure's occupancy, include a wooden lamp shade, now holding pieces of a 1927 *Saturday Evening Post,* a coffee can pierced to function as a shower head, an iron bedstead, and old cans and bottles.

The most prominent feature of the site, which slopes down to the lake's edge, is a 27-foot-high wind generator, scheduled for restoration. Other buildings on the site are an outhouse with walls and roof covered with flattened fuel cans and a storage shed covered with the same material. The craftsmanship and ingenuity evident in the buildings and artifacts contribute to an aura of self-sufficiency, typical of those who lived in the bush.

WE030 Eskimo Pit House

1968. Brooks River

Reconstructed according to the evidence provided by an archeological excavation, this Eskimo Pit House was built on the site of its 1300 C.E. prototype. University of Oregon archaeologists led by Don E. Dumond undertook the work for the National Park Service, using evidence found at the site as well as local Eskimos' knowledge of construction techniques.

This area along the salmon-rich Brooks River has been occupied by humans for centuries; in fact, the pit house sits on the site of a dwelling even earlier than the prototype. After testing a number of pit house sites, partially excavating two, and completely excavating three, this site was selected for reconstruction. It represents a semisubterranean dwelling built by Thule period Eskimos; flaked stone artifacts found at the site helped date the dwelling.

The building is only partially built, showing a dwelling theoretically under construction so visitors can see the structure. The dwelling portion, whose floor originally sat about 2 feet 6 inches below ground (ground levels change over time; here the ground level is about 1 foot higher than when the dwelling was originally constructed), is about 15 feet by 16 feet. The spruce-log structure has four center posts supporting a cribbed roof. Laid between the vertical half-logs that line the earthen walls and the horizontal logs supported by the center posts, split cottonwood logs, flat side up, form the roof, which would have been covered with sod and moss. The dirt floor has a central fireplace, vented through a central smoke hole. Along the back wall is a dirt bench, elevated about 8 inches; a log along the front of this bench was added to help the visitor see this change in levels. The dwelling is entered through a tunnel, which is about 2 feet lower than the dwelling, effectively trapping cold air. A skin across the doorway would have allowed air to travel under it, feeding the fire.

The pit house is enclosed in a prefabricated

log structure called Panabode. Although the enclosure destroys the original context, it effectively preserves a sod dwelling. The use of an actual site as well as the thorough research that went into this reconstruction make it a fine representation of an Eskimo semisubterranean dwelling.

Savonoski

WE031 **Russian Orthodox Church**

after 1912. South side of Naknek River

The gable-roofed rectangular church at Savonoski, measuring 16 by 40 feet, has several unusual features. Wood-framed with clapboard siding, the church has double doors with round-arch panels—a stock Victorian door, perhaps, but highly unusual in remote Alaska. Over the windows, sawtooth ornament is applied in the form of an exaggerated pediment, reminiscent of Russian ornament. A square cupola allows light into the nave.

Contained within the main rectangular block are three elements: sanctuary, nave, and narthex. The back quarter of the block, marked by a wide arch, serves as narthex, while through a single door in the rear is the vestibule, measuring 9 feet by 11 feet. There is a three-step amvon, or platform before the iconostas, which is currently decorated with faded paper flowers, having been stripped of its icons.

The church was built when the old village of Savonoski, which was once located closer to Katmai, evacuated to this site after the 1912 volcanic eruption. The village is now abandoned. Elaborate pickets form a fence around the church and its cemetery, which are reached by a long boardwalk snaking across the tundra from the site of the village on the Naknek River.

Naknek

WE032 **Saint John the Baptist Russian Orthodox Church**

1912

The village of Naknek is located at the mouth of the Naknek River, on the north side. Built in 1912, Saint John the Baptist is a rectangular block, 16 feet by 38 feet, incorporating both nave and sanctuary. Of wood-frame construction, the church's walls are covered with clapboard siding. The gable roof is decorated with three onion domes and crosses. The decoration of the interior is modest, although the royal doors of the iconostas feature circular oil-on-canvas paintings. Set in a fenced churchyard, on the edge of the river next to the original village of Naknek, the church is soon to be replaced by a new one, on another site.

Southwestern Region (SW)

T
HE ALEUTIANS ARE SAID TO HAVE THE WORST WEATHER IN
the world. Measurable precipitation falls more than two hundred days
per year. Although the range of temperatures is narrow and fairly temperate, storm winds occur in all months. The days are generally cloudy, wet,
and windy.

Southwestern Alaska includes the Alaska Peninsula, the Aleutian Chain, the
Pribilof Islands, the Shumagin Islands, and the Kodiak Archipelago. The Aleutian Chain extends in an arc 1,100 miles long, with over one hundred islands
in an active seismic zone. The Alaska Peninsula runs northeast from the Aleutians about 500 miles to Naknek Lake. Three hundred miles west of the peninsula is the small grouping of the Pribilof Islands, while on the east and south
sides are the Kodiak Archipelago and Shumagin Islands. Most of the region is
treeless; only the northern parts of the Kodiak islands and the Alaska Peninsula are forested.

Southwestern Alaska was the first area settled by the Russians, who were well
established here by the end of the eighteenth century. The Aleutian Chain had
been long inhabited by the Aleuts, and the Alaska Peninsula and Kodiak Island
by Pacific Eskimos, who strongly identify with the Aleuts. Russian domination
of these peoples was cruel but effective, and the Russians used Aleut labor to
establish a colony and to deplete the waters of the valuable sea otter.

After the United States bought Alaska in 1867, the Alaska Commercial Company followed in the footsteps of the Russian-American Company, operating
the fur trade in a virtual monopoly. By the turn of the twentieth century this
domination had ended, as had the prominence of the fur trade, when commercial fisheries took over. Southwestern Alaska received renewed attention
from the United States during World War II, when the westernmost islands

281

were the only part of U.S. territory occupied by the enemy. A military presence still exists due to the strategic location of the region.

Although no traditional Native dwellings are known to survive, one Russian-era building exists, the Russian-American Company *Magazin* in Kodiak. The synthesis of Russian and Aleut cultures is best seen in the number of Russian Orthodox churches that populate the landscape today. Generally the most conspicuous and architecturally elaborate building in any village, the churches exhibit the traditional three-part form, with sanctuary, nave, and bell tower (or often just a vestibule) delineated on the exterior. None dates from the period of Russian occupancy; the Natives adopted Russian Orthodoxy and continued its traditional architecture when building new churches. Domestic architecture is generally undistinguished, consisting of small houses of found materials that are steadily being replaced by manufactured housing. There are few roads in this part of the state, and building materials and household goods must be shipped or flown in. Settlements are scattered and oriented to the sea.

Kodiak Archipelago

Kodiak

Founded by the Russians in 1793, the town of Kodiak remained the seat of Russian interests in America until 1808. The Russians built a J-shaped fort and a number of other log buildings, although they deteriorated rapidly in Kodiak's wet climate. The Russians organized hunting parties from Kodiak, used it as a trading post, and undertook considerable farming in the area. The first Russian Orthodox church in America was established here in 1794, and the church maintains a seminary in Kodiak today. Facing depletion of the sea otter, the Russians were forced to look to the east and moved the capital to Sitka. Kodiak (called Pavlovsk, or Saint Paul's Harbor by the Russians) diminished in importance but remained Russia's second largest settlement in America.

After the sale of Alaska to the United States, the Alaska Commercial Company obtained most of the Russian-American Company's property and became the primary trader in the area. With the beginning of commercial salmon fishing in the 1880s, Kodiak Island gained new importance because one of the richest rivers in Alaska was located on the island. The fishing industry remains Kodiak's primary business; Kodiak is the second largest commercial fishing port in the United States.

During World War II, the U.S. Army and Navy both maintained posts on the south side of town. Construction of the Kodiak Naval Operating Base began in 1939, and at the time of the attack on Pearl Harbor it was the principal advance naval base in the North Pacific. Fort Greely was constructed at the same time and also maintained the subpost of Fort Abercrombie on the north

Southwestern Region

Katmai N.P. and Preserve

Afognak I.
Afognak (6)
Ouzinkie (3-5)
Kodiak (1-2)
Kodiak I.
Shelikof Strait

Bristol Bay

St. Paul I.
St. Paul (18)
Pribilof Islands
St. George (19-20)
St. George I.

Bering Sea

Pilot Point (10)

Karluk (9)

Old Harbor (7)

57°

Akhiok (8)

Trinity Islands

Alaska Peninsula

Sand Point (11)

King Cove (12)

Shumagin Is.

Islands

Unimak I.

Akutan (13)

Dutch Harbor (16)

Unalaska (14-15)

54°

Aleutian

Unalaska I.

Nikolski (17)
168°

165°

162°

159°

156°

153°

Pacific Ocean

Miles
0   100

area enlarged above

side of town. Today, the U.S. Coast Guard operates a facility that encompasses both the Naval Operating Base and Fort Greely; Fort Abercrombie is a state park.

The 1964 earthquake in Prince William Sound had considerable impact in Kodiak. Because the town is built on a rock foundation, the earthquake itself caused only minor damage, although the whole of Kodiak Island subsided 6 1/2 feet. The subsequent tidal wave, however, destroyed 80 percent of the downtown and all of the harbor. During reconstruction, low-lying land downtown was filled in and seawalls constructed. A recommendation that only concrete or masonry buildings be constructed in the downtown was rejected. The town has been rebuilt into a thriving community. Although few historic buildings remain, one of the few Russian-era buildings in Alaska is in Kodiak.

SW001 **Russian-American Company Magazin** (Baranof Museum, Erskine House)

between 1804 and 1808. 110 Marine Way

The oldest Russian building in Alaska, this is a fine example of the heavy log blocklike construction of the Russians. The hewn-log structure was built as a warehouse, or *magazin,* for the Russian-American Company, probably before 1808. As originally constructed, the one-and-a-half-story structure measured 67 feet by 33 feet and had a steep hipped roof. Dovetailed at the corners, the 12-inch wide logs are rough hewn, grooved on the bottom to fit over the log below, and chinked with moss. A log cross wall divided the building into two unequal portions. With its broad face positioned toward the water, the *magazin* was a substantial and solid structure.

Some time in the nineteenth century, several major alterations were made to the structure. The roof form was changed from hip to gable and a large pediment was added in the center of the front facade. The building was sided—perhaps first with vertical redwood siding and later with clapboards—and a one-story porch, incorporated under the roof, was constructed across the front.

The Russian-American Company, which had a monopoly on trade in Alaska, constructed this building as a warehouse. After the sale of Alaska, the Alaska Commercial Company bought most of the Russian-American Company's buildings, including this one. The Alaska Commercial Company dominated the fur trade in western Alaska, just as the Russian-American Company had done before it.

A bay window on one end, added around the turn of the twentieth century, indicates that the building was then being used as a residence. In 1911, the Alaska Commercial Company sold the building to its long-time employee, W. J. Erskine, who lived here with his family until 1948. During his ownership, the first floor was divided into about eight rooms. Erskine enclosed part of the front porch with glass in 1942. Since 1967, the house has been operated as a museum by the Kodiak Historical Society.

SW002 **Holy Resurrection Russian Orthodox Church**

1946–1947. Mission Rd. and Kashevaroff St.

Constructed to replace a church that had been destroyed by fire, this church maintains

SW001b Russian-America Company Magazin (Baranof Museum, Erskine House) (floor plan)

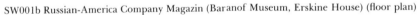

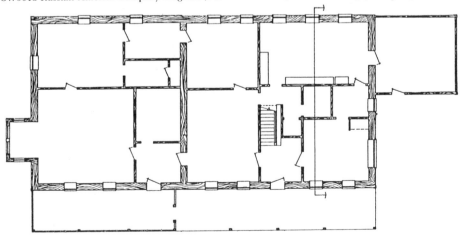

some of the same elements but in such proportions that it presents an entirely different appearance.

The previous church was constructed in 1873–1874 of hewn logs in the plan of a Greek cross. The cross-gable roof was topped by a large octagonal drum at the crossing; its pyramidal roof supported a cupola with an onion dome. The square bell tower supported an octagonal belfry, topped by a small onion dome. The windows were rectangular.

The present church is in the plan of a Latin cross, also with an octagonal drum at the crossing and a square bell tower. On this church, the transept is much shallower, the drum much smaller, and the two onion domes much larger. Windows have Gothic arches, a difficult form in log buildings, and thus reflecting the wood-frame construction. The sanctuary has a small, polygonal projection at the rear.

The interior is light and spacious. Most of the icons are new, the old ones having been lost in the fire. The iconostas is divided into five bays by stylized golden pilasters.

Spruce Island

SW003 Saints Sergius and Herman of Valaam Russian Orthodox Chapel

1895–1896. Monk's Lagoon

As the connections between communities on Kodiak Island are limited to sea or air transport, Spruce Island, just 10 miles north of the town of Kodiak, is closer and more easily reached from the town than are many other communities on Kodiak Island. Set back from the water about half a mile in sylvan surroundings, the small chapel is an exquisite piece of architecture. The nave is nearly square in plan, measuring about 19 feet by 21 feet; its double-pitched hip roof emphasizes its squareness. The sanctuary also has a hip roof, peaking near the nave, thus leading the eye inward and upward. The gable roof of the small vestibule echoes the pitch of the nave's roof. The interior is plain, finished in beaded boards, painted light blue. The iconostas is constructed of fixed doors, as part of the wall between the operable doors. There is no electricity, heat, or water. The building is located miles from the nearest community.

Although today the chapel is strongly identified with Father Herman, who in 1970 became the first American saint of the Russian Orthodox church, the chapel was originally built in commemoration of the one hundredth anniversary of the introduction of Russian Orthodoxy to America and named after the founders of the monastery at Valaam, where the missionaries originated. When they arrived in Alaska in 1794, missionaries met with hostility from Alexander Baranov, company manager at Kodiak. Despite these constraints, Father Herman founded an orphanage for Natives on Spruce Island and moved here permanently sometime after 1808. He died in 1837 and was buried here with a disciple, Hieromonk Ioasaph. Forty years later, the chapel was erected between their two graves.

Father Herman's memory began to be revived with the appearance of Father Gerasim on Spruce Island in the 1930s. Father Gerasim, who devoted his life to the memory of Father Herman, repaired the chapel and probably was responsible for having the two graves moved under the chapel. When Father Herman was canonized, his remains were moved to Kodiak. The chapel is used for special services a few times a year.

SW004 Father Gerasim's Cell and Chapel

1930s. Monk's Lagoon

Along the path to the Saints Sergius and Herman of Valaam Russian Orthodox Chapel stands a small complex of buildings, memorials to an apostolic life. In a commitment of

SW004 Father Gerasim's Cell

Ouzinkie villagers, has two rooms, a bedroom and a living room, still furnished and lined with icons and books. The small kitchen is in a lean-to addition. A frame chapel, measuring 12 feet by 14 feet, stands on the site of Father Herman's cell; it has a moss-covered gable roof and a plywood interior lined with icons. Nearby, a new well house protects a spring from which holy water is obtained.

Although long vacant, the cell and chapel of this priest, who spent his life in a way that few of us can understand, have an immediacy about them that makes visitors feel as though they have intruded on a very private life, and a very private mission.

faith that is rare in modern times, Father Gerasim devoted his life to the memory of Father Herman, who had been dead nearly one hundred years by the time Father Gerasim arrived on Spruce Island.

Born in Russia in 1888, Father Gerasim came to Alaska in 1915, serving at Sitka, Kodiak, and Afognak. In 1935 he was assigned to the other side of Spruce Island, where he spent winters at Ouzinkie. He spent summers in isolation at Monk's Lagoon, however, increasingly withdrawing from society and devoting his time and energies to the memory of a long-dead priest. After nearly losing his life in the 1964 tidal wave, Father Gerasim's health declined, and he died in 1966.

The small complex of buildings is an evocative memorial to his life of devotion. The small frame cabin he built, with the help of

SW005 Nativity of Our Lord Russian Orthodox Church

1906; 1939–1940, enlarged. Ouzinkie

Occupying a hilly site on a picturesque harbor, Nativity of Our Lord Church has the distinctive elements of an Alaskan Russian Orthodox church. The long nave, topped with an octagonal cupola, has a lower sanctuary at the east end and an even lower vestibule at the west end.

Constructed in 1906, the church looked slightly different before alterations in 1939–1940: the nave was shorter, almost square, measuring about 18 feet by 21 feet on the interior. The nave was two bays long; a change in the wooden siding marks the spot where the additional bay was added. A three-stage bell tower was at the west end; removed from the church and altered, the top two levels

SW005 Nativity of Our Lord Russian Orthodox Church

now serve as a detached gatehouse, while the first level is now the vestibule. On the interior, the octagonal cupola sheds light on the iconostas, which is divided into seven bays and painted white with gold trim.

Ouzinkie was founded by the survivors of a settlement on the other side of Spruce Island, established by Father Herman in the late eighteenth or early nineteenth century. Father Herman died in 1837, and twelve years later the settlement was devastated by disease; the survivors relocated to this site. Their first church, built just to the north of this one, was a low gable-roofed log structure. Members of the village built this new one in 1906. In the 1930s, the village was described as having two hundred people, mostly Aleuts; Russian was still spoken in the majority of the homes. The village had two canneries, one of which hired Native labor, probably accounting for the prosperity that encouraged them to enlarge their church in 1939.

Afognak, Afognak Island

SW006 **Nativity of the Holy Theotokos Russian Orthodox Church**

1905

The massive hewn logs of this structure are revealed at the east end, where the sanctuary has been removed, and on the north side, where some of the siding has been removed. The logs, dovetailed at the corners, range from 9 inches to 16 inches in height and are 12 inches wide.

Named after the Madonna (*Theotokos*, Greek for "God bearer," being a title given to the Virgin Mary since the time of the early church), this church had a sanctuary, nave, bell tower, and vestibule in the standard east-west alignment of Russian Orthodox churches. The community of Afognak was hard hit during the 1964 tidal wave and afterward elected to move to a new site. The congregation took with it only the iconostas and royal doors from this building to their new church at Port Lions. The belfry, with round-arch openings for the bells, had disappeared by 1975 and the vestibule soon after. Recently, as the ocean undermined the church, which now sits partially on the beach, the sanctuary has been dismantled and stored in the nave.

An interior dome, whose framing is visible

SW006 Nativity of the Holy Theotokos Russian Orthodox Church (detail of structure of dome)

in the attic (and shown in this photograph), supports an octagonal drum, which protrudes through the gable roof and is lit by several windows, which originally shed light on the iconostas below. Layers of wallpaper and oilcloth in the nave hint at past splendors, and the partially dismembered church remains an evocative sight in a desolate setting.

Old Harbor, Kodiak Island

SW007 **Three Saints Russian Orthodox Church**

1953

The 1953 Three Saints Russian Orthodox Church illustrates the persistence of the form of Russian Orthodox churches in Alaska. Although its proportions are somewhat wider and lower than earlier churches, it maintains the separate nave, sanctuary, and narthex/bell tower. Three onion domes supporting Orthodox crosses and the bright blue roof and trim further distinguish the building.

The gable roofs of the sanctuary, nave, and narthex are at different levels but share the same pitch. Out of the one-story narthex rises a square bell tower, which is only slightly higher than the ridge of the roof of the nave. The nave has a hexagonal cupola, and the sanctuary a square one; neither has windows. On the interior, the nave has a false dome

SW007 Three Saints Russian Orthodox Church

SW008b Church of the Protection of the Holy Theotokos (iconostas)

under the cupola; octagonal in shape, it rises about 3 feet to a flat ceiling. Despite the linoleum floors and plyboard walls of the nave, there are some features worth noting. Windows are topped with curlicued pediments, reminiscent of Chinoiserie—an unlikely find in an Aleut village. Two new large icons decorate the iconostas, which is divided into seven bays.

Located at the southwestern end of the village, the church is nestled among steeply rising hills. Shrines throughout the village are dedicated to each of the three saints—Basil the Great, Gregory the Theologian, and John Chrysostom.

Akhiok, Kodiak Island

SW008 Church of the Protection of the Holy Theotokos
1926

Set apart from the village, perched on a windswept hill, the green-trimmed Russian Orthodox Church of the Protection of the Holy Theotokos is an exceedingly well-proportioned wood-framed building. The gable-roofed nave measures approximately 20 feet by 30 feet, being three bays long. The sanctuary, with a lower gable roof of the same pitch, is about 14 feet by 15 feet. The two-story bell tower, with a pyramidal-roofed belfry with round-arch openings, measures about 10 feet by 12 feet.

The square belfry is matched by a square cupola over the nave. The entrance to the building, rather than being on the west end, is on the south side of the bell tower, respecting the strong winds. On the interior, the cupola above is matched by a false dome; the octagonal space, which has a flat ceiling space that is recessed into the main ceiling, is an obvious reference to the cupola above. The iconostas is a simple board wall with unpainted wooden moldings marking the seven bays.

Constructed by the Alitak Packing Company, owners of a nearby cannery, the Rus-

SW008a Church of the Protection of the Holy Theotokos (exterior)

sian Orthodox church provides shelter to two spruce trees, the only ones on the southern part of Kodiak Island. The bleak landscape is enlivened by this neatly maintained building, which, despite the absence of an onion dome, is unmistakably an Alaskan Russian Orthodox church.

Nearby is a reconstructed barabara, the traditional Aleut dwelling. Sod-covered and plank-lined, the building was constructed by the Kodiak Area Native Association in 1989.

Karluk, Kodiak Island

SW009 Ascension of Our Lord Russian Orthodox Chapel

1888

The highly styled Ascension of Our Lord Chapel features a three-stage bell tower with an open belfry and an octagonal cupola over the nave. Painted white with lime-green roofs and light blue trim, the church is on a bluff, high above the river and the cannery activity that took place on the spit of land below.

The wood-framed chapel, covered with clapboards, has three distinct elements—sanctuary, nave, and bell tower. The gable-roofed nave and the slightly lower gable-roofed sanctuary have pedimented windows, with crosses in the pediments. A large tent-roofed octagonal cupola, with two windows, rises from the ridge of the nave.

The bell tower has a pedimented and pilastered entrance reminiscent of the Greek Revival style in the Lower 48. At the second level there are bull's-eye windows. Rising from the pyramidal roof is a third level, an open belfry, with round-arch openings, covered by an ogee-shaped dome. The interior is spacious and well lit, thanks to windows in the west wall of the nave and the octagonal cupola, which measures 17 feet in diameter. The paneled wainscot is painted bright green, the beaded-board walls white, and the ceiling light blue. The nine-bay iconostas has stylized pilasters and is divided vertically into three parts, including a row of icons above the iconostas proper. Icons on the iconostas and others on the side walls of the nave are oil painted on canvas.

This church, on the far side of Kodiak Island, is the oldest extant Russian Orthodox church in Alaska, as well as being one of the most professionally designed. Its size and style are probably attributable to the prosperity afforded by the rich salmon runs in the Karluk River, which brought canneries to this site in the 1880s. The first cannery was built by Messrs. Smith and Hirsch in 1882 and organized in 1884 into the Karluk Packing Company. Five other canneries were constructed near the mouth of the Karluk River within the next ten years; this area had one of the greatest salmon runs in the state.

When the Karluk Packing Company began constructing new houses for the Natives, a Native named Melety requested that the company build him a church instead. A stenciled plaque in the church reads "Melety's Memorial Church, Built in 11 June 1888, by Charlie Smith Hursh, Karluk, Alaska." The canneries closed in the 1930s, and a severe storm in 1978 realigned the river and forced the removal of the village to a site about three-quarters of a mile upriver. The church was spared, however, and stands on a point of land as one of the most remarkable in Alaska.

Alaska Peninsula and Shumagin Islands

Pilot Point

SW010 Saint Nicholas Russian Orthodox Church

c. 1912

Overlooking a cannery on the flats below, Saint Nicholas Church was constructed about 1912. One of several very simple Russian Orthodox churches in Alaska, the wood-framed building is covered with clapboard siding. The main block of the building, which measures 15 feet by 36 feet, has a gable roof that is hipped over the sanctuary end. The iconostas features pairs of colonnettes marking each bay. The Royal Doors are pierced tin, while the deacons' doors are cotton, stretched on a wooden frame. Other decorative items include a carved wooden lampada, or hanging candle, and two carved candlestands. There is a recess in the ceiling, reminiscent of a dome, which abuts the iconostas.

Sand Point, Popof Island, Shumagin Islands

SW011 Saint Nicholas Russian Orthodox Chapel

1936; 1986, reconstructed

Although quite small, this is an exceedingly handsome church. The nave and sanctuary are combined under one gable roof in the three-bay-long main block. A square bell tower rises above the main block to its pyramidal roof, which supports a smaller, octagonal belfry. The building was constructed in 1936 but was rarely used and deteriorated rapidly. In the 1950s the icons were removed for safekeeping. In 1986 the building was reconstructed, following the original design carefully, but extending the length about 6 feet. Only the foundation, part of the tower, and part of the iconostas are original.

The interior reflects its relatively recent date. Finished in a light oak, the iconostas has spiral-topped columns separating the bays. The icons are from the original church. Light oak is also used for the wainscot and window trim.

King Cove

SW012 Saint Herman Russian Orthodox Chapel

1987

Although the church building is undistinguished—a gable-roofed rectangle covered with T1–11 textured plywood siding and a three-stage bell tower—Saint Herman's now contains the iconostas and icons from Belkofski.

Belkofski, founded in 1823 by sea otter-hunting Russians, is located 12 miles southeast of King Cove. When the church was built in 1887, the community was obviously prospering, as the church was particularly ornate, featuring three cupolas, pedimented window surrounds, and a Classical entrance portico. The village has been abandoned, as has the church.

The iconostas features horseshoe-arch openings, like the iconostas at Unalaska. The frame of the iconostas has moldings, incising, and carved grapes and leaves above the royal doors; the bottom 6 inches of the iconostas were cut off to fit it into the King Cove church. The iconostas holds large oil-on-canvas paintings, imported from Russia. The church also has four bells from Belkofski, marked "W. T. Garratt, S.F. Cal." and dated 1870 and 1881.

Although this splendid, nineteenth-century iconostas is somewhat incongruously placed in a 1984 church, the moving of iconostases follows a long tradition.

SW012 Saint Herman Russian Orthodox Chapel

Aleutian Islands

Akutan, Akutan Island

SW013 Saint Alexander of Nevsky Russian Orthodox Chapel

1918

The fishing village of Akutan sits in the shadow of volcanic Mount Akutan on one of the northern islands of the Aleutian chain. This small chapel is modest in size and exterior decoration. The sanctuary is incorporated into the gable-roofed main block, rather than being in a separate element; the main block measures 18 feet by 31 feet and is three bays long. A gable-roofed vestibule on the front is nearly as tall as the nave; it was widened by about 6 feet in the 1980s.

The interior is more elaborate than the exterior would suggest. The amvon, or dais before the iconostas, extends along both walls in a U shape, culminating in balustraded projecting ends. The iconostas, although a simple structure, has icons in three tiers; some of the icons appear to be quite old, perhaps by an Aleut artist. In the center of the nave ceiling is a square, flat recess, evocative of a dome.

Unalaska

Unalaska Island is one of the largest islands in the Aleutian chain. Long the home of Aleuts, it became the site of a Russian trading post in the eighteenth century. This settlement was located on the spit of land between Iliuliuk Bay and Iliuliuk River, which is also the original townsite of Unalaska. Today, the city encompasses a much larger area, including the better-known Dutch Harbor.

As far as is known, no Russian-era buildings survive, but one of the largest and most elegant of the Russian Orthodox churches is located here, representing the persistence of Russian influence. In the late nineteenth century, the Northern Commercial Company established a dock and warehouses on the Dutch Harbor side of the bay, and at the Unalaska townsite, the Alaska Commercial Company occupied the northwest end of the spit, now the site of a cannery. At the other end of Unalaska was the town's cemetery. In between, there was a mixture of small buildings constructed by public and private owners.

During the Second World War, both navy and army posts were located on the island. The army moved Fort Mears to Unalaska Valley and built a number of houses. These 16-foot-by-20-foot houses, known as cabanas, were sold to Natives in 1944–1945 for nominal amounts and moved down to the townsite on skids. Some have been attached and combined into bigger buildings.

SW014 Church of the Holy Ascension

1894

Set on a picturesque harbor, the Church of the Holy Ascension is one of Alaska's most impressive Russian Orthodox churches. Constructed in 1894, it is one of the oldest surviving, and with three altars it is one of the largest. The massing of the building, which defines the interior uses on the exterior, is striking and unusual.

In plan, the church takes the form of a Latin cross. With its hip roofs, however, the design focuses attention upward, not sideways. The two-story nave is crowned by a pyramidal roof, which is topped by a cupola with onion dome. The two side chapels and sanctuary are separate elements, with hip roofs

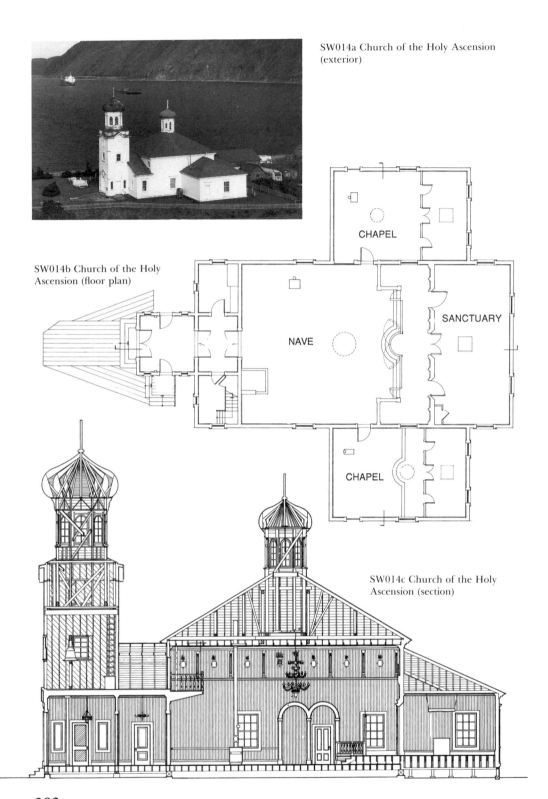

SW014a Church of the Holy Ascension (exterior)

SW014b Church of the Holy Ascension (floor plan)

CHAPEL

NAVE

SANCTUARY

CHAPEL

SW014c Church of the Holy Ascension (section)

292

echoing the pitch of the nave roof and with peaks near the nave. The narthex separates the mass of the building from the three-story bell tower, which also has a cupola and onion dome capped with an Orthodox cross. The wood-framed building with novelty siding is simply ornamented, with entablatures over the openings. The front doors and windows in the west front of the church are arched; all the others are rectangular. Some ornament has been removed from the bell tower, which had a belt course and false balconies at the second level.

The interior of the nave is cavernous in feeling, as much due to its size (36 feet by 41 feet by 22 feet high) as to the lighting. The side chapels, which measure 20 feet by 21 feet and are one story, seem almost miniature in comparison. On the interior, light is manipulated to focus attention on the iconostas and altar. The only windows to the outside are on the side walls, toward the rear, and on the west wall, high up; the latter were added shortly after construction. At the east end of the nave, windows borrow light from the side chapels to illuminate the iconostas. The sanctuary, by contrast, has four windows, so that when the doors in the iconostas are opened, light streams toward the altar and spills out into the nave in a dazzling display.

Unalaska received this cathedral-like church just after the Russian Orthodox church had divided Alaska into two districts, with Unalaska being the administrative center for the western half and Sitka for the eastern. Unalaska had previously served as a base for Russian Orthodox missionaries, particularly for Father Ioann Veniaminov, who was assigned here in 1824. Father Veniaminov traveled widely throughout the territory, translated the Bible into the Aleut language, gained the trust and respect of the Natives, and built the first Church of the Holy Ascension. In 1834, Veniaminov was transferred to Sitka; he was named a bishop and eventually became metropolitan of the church in Russia.

Because of Unalaska's traditional importance to the Russian church in Alaska, the church contains a wealth of icons, including two in the Byzantine style dating to 1821; an icon of scenes from the life of the Virgin said to have miraculous powers; and an icon of Saint Panteleimon covered by a silver riza. Icons along the top of the iconostas in the north chapel, dedicated to Saint Innocent of Irkutsk, are believed to have been painted by

Vasilii Kriukov, an Aleut artist, and to have been on the iconostas of the first church in Unalaska. Carved ornament on the iconostas, such as the swags above the icons and the lyres below, may date to the church built by Father Innocent in 1825.

Little is known about the origin of the spectacular design of this church. Bishop Nicholas arranged with Rudolph Newman, general agent of the Alaska Commercial Company, for its construction; the company charged $9,350. The bishop provided the company with plans, and the company hired an architect to turn them into detailed drawings, but the designer remains unknown.

SW015 Bishop's House

1882, Mooser and Pissis

Located about 150 feet northwest of the Holy Ascension Church, the Bishop's House is a small dwelling, unusual in Unalaska for its Victorian trim and variety of form. The house, commissioned by Bishop Nestor, was constructed by the Alaska Commercial Company. Part of Bishop Nestor's campaign to provide housing for his clergy, this residence was also built to be used by the San Francisco-based bishop in his visits to the western part of the district. With Italianate detailing popular in San Francisco at that time, the building was designed by the San Francisco architectural firm of Mooser and Pissis.

The wood-framed house has a two-story, hip-roofed main block, containing two rooms on each floor, with a central stairway. On each side is a one-story, hip-roofed section with two rooms, for a total of eight. The house differs somewhat from the architectural drawings. Although the drawings show a squared-off plan, the two-story section has semihexagonal ends, increasing the variety of the surfaces. Also in a departure from the drawings, the entrance is in the center, directly into a room designated as the parlor on the plan, rather than into a room in the wing. The bracketed cornice has wreaths in the fascia board, and the doorway has a bracketed hood. The novelty siding is painted gray with white trim.

Although it now stands virtually alone, accompanied only by a small outbuilding, the Bishop's House was one of several buildings near the church. Between the Bishop's House and the church was a customs house. West of the Bishop's House, a 30-foot-square school building was built at the same time as the house; it was extended, in about 1893, and finally joined to the Bishop's House. Farther west was the Alaska Commercial Company store.

In 1960 the school building was destroyed in a fire that also damaged the Bishop's House. Restoration of the house began in 1976, but work on the interior is not yet completed.

Dutch Harbor, Amaknak Island

SW016 Naval Operating Base and Fort Mears

1932, 1939–1944

Bombed by the Japanese in 1942, the military bases at Dutch Harbor, near Unalaska, served both the army and the navy and were the largest of the early bases in the Aleutians, pivotal to the defense of the Aleutian Chain. The United States military involvement in the Aleutians began in 1911 when the navy established a radio communication station. Although a naval aerology station was constructed in July 1939, serious buildup did not begin until the summer of 1940. Completed in 1944, the Naval Operating Base included seven docks and housing for 281 officers and 5,444 enlisted men. Albert Kahn and Associates of Detroit developed the original plan for the base, proposing a composite building with housing and work functions in connected structures. Although Kahn's plans stipulated reinforced concrete, suitable aggregate could not be found at Dutch Harbor. New plans proposed steel, but because of war shortages, wood-framed structures were finally decided upon.

The army facilities included housing for 9,976 officers and enlisted men. Here the Kahn composite buildings were shelved in favor of the standard army quartermaster plans, 700 series. These two-story, wood-framed buildings, each housing 63 men, were altered during construction to include drying rooms and arctic entries, interior wallboards, and blackout windows. Originally constructed on Amaknak Island next to the Naval Operating Base, Fort Mears expanded to Unalaska Island across the bay; eventually the army consolidated its facilities there and left Amaknak to the navy.

The hills around Dutch Harbor contain many concrete structures, half buried into the earth. Built between 1941 and 1944, these include battery command posts, two-level observation posts with rounded, concrete roofs, and the smaller pillboxes.

On 3 and 4 June 1942, the Japanese bombed Dutch Harbor, as a diversionary tactic to conceal their occupation of the islands of Attu and Kiska and as a defensive measure, to prevent attacks by the Americans against the Japanese mainland. Although 43 Americans died, the base was not appreciably damaged.

Since the navy's departure in 1947 and the army's in 1952, the extensive installation has fallen into ruin. Recent demolitions through the army's Defense Environmental Restoration Program have left only a few military buildings, some of which are mentioned below. The site was declared a National Historic Landmark in 1985.

SW016.1 Naval Radio Station Apartment Building

1932

Constructed as part of the Naval Radio Station, this apartment building has a brick exterior, the only one in the Aleutian Islands. The wood frame was veneered with bricks, which were painted olive drab after the bombing. The six-apartment building has steeply pitched gable roofs reminiscent of the Tudor Revival style.

SW016.2 Aerology Operations Building

1942

This L-shaped building has a two-story core in an octagonal—or square with chamfered corners—plan. The wings are of Loxtave construction—prefabricated, precut tongue-and-groove planks joined with a patented end connection. As in plank or log construction, the walls needed no studding or bracing. The building was erected as the meteorological station for the naval air facility.

SW016.3 Composite Buildings

1940–1944, Albert Kahn

The two-and-a-half-story, shed-roofed composite buildings were interconnected, enabling inhabitants to live and work in the same building. Such a concentration of activ-

SW017a Saint Nicholas Russian Orthodox Church (exterior)

ity made the arrangement vulnerable to bombing attacks, and the military soon adopted a more scattered approach.

Nikolski, Umnak Island

SW017 **Saint Nicholas Russian Orthodox Church**

1930

This church is particularly grand for such a small village. The form of the church is apparently based on that of the cathedral at Unalaska, about 100 miles to the northeast. Lacking wings, the church at Nikolski has a tall, hip-roofed nave framed by gable-roofed sanctuary and narthex. Entrance is through the base of a two-story bell tower. One odd detail is the same as at Unalaska: round-arch windows in the second level of the west end of the nave. Unlike Unalaska, however, this church has three windows on each side of the nave.

The interior of this wood-framed building is large, with the nave measuring 27 feet by 33 feet and the ceiling rising to a height of 17 feet. There is a three-step amvon, or dais in front of the iconostas, with projections along the sides. The iconostas is divided into seven bays and two tiers, ornamented with carving, piercework, and light bulbs. The building has an extraordinary amount of carving, attributed to Sergei Soroff, a member of the church. Ornament includes the fat balusters at the choir loft and amvon and narrower balusters around the warden's desk; candlestands; frames for icons on the iconostas, above it, and on the amvon balustrade; and a medallion in the nave ceiling, reminiscent in design of that at Unalaska, but here carved instead of painted.

The size and splendor of this church, funded and built by the parishioners, is unusual in a small fishing village. Nikolski, however, had a burst of prosperity in the 1920s, stemming from fox trapping on outlying islands. On Nikolski a sheep ranch established in 1926 survives today.

SW017b Saint Nicholas Russian Orthodox Church (iconostas)

Pribilof Islands (Saint Paul and Saint George Islands)

Located 250 miles north of the Aleutian Chain in the southern Bering Sea, the Pribilofs are four small islands, treeless and windswept, that have received unique treatment from the U.S. government. On one edge of each of the two occupied islands of the Pribilofs, buildings cluster together to form a town. The large wooden buildings (with some prebuilt additions) of the sealing industry are closest to the waterfront, and the houses are farthest away, up a hillside. Between them, churches, stores, community halls, and garages denote the center of town. The government-built houses are small, identical in appearance, neatly lining the streets, which are covered with a volcanic material called scoria. Their bungalow-like size and appearance indicate their 1920s construction date. In Saint Paul, the larger of the towns, the houses are concrete, often covered with new wooden siding; they face the same direction, looking downhill with their backs to the wind and water. In Saint George, the houses face each other across the streets. In both towns, the Russian Orthodox churches are the most visible structures; set in picket-fenced churchyards in the middle of town, they are built on a larger scale, with a distinctive shape and identifying cross.

Both the Russians and the Americans exploited the wealth of the fur trade in the Pribilof Islands, so the islands were a highly prized and specially administered resource. When the Russians recognized that the Pribilofs were a significant breeding ground of the northern fur seal (attracting 85 percent of the fur seal population), they settled the two larger islands with a group of Aleuts, taken from Atka and Unalaska in the Aleutians. Supervised by a handful of Russians, these Aleuts engaged in the harvest of the fur seal beginning in 1786. The Russian American Company, which obtained a trade monopoly for all of Alaska in 1799, took nearly one million furs from the Pribilofs in three years, devastating the seal population.

After Russian America was acquired by the United States, the United States granted a monopoly on the fur seals on the Pribilofs to the Alaska Commercial Company from 1870 to 1890 and to the North American Commercial Company from 1890 to 1910. In addition to paying a flat rate, the companies also paid the government a percentage of the take. The Pribilof Islands were extremely profitable for the government and its lessee; the company harvested $2.5 million of seals annually, and the government received $9.6 million during the first twenty years. The Alaska Commercial Company was also required to provide for the Aleut inhabitants; to this end, it replaced the barabaras with small, wood-framed houses in neat rows. By 1890 there were ninety-three of these houses on Saint Paul, and twenty-one on Saint George.

The population of fur seals was not inexhaustible, however; several attempts at conservation had been undertaken by the Russians, and during the United States' tenure the government put an annual ceiling on the number of furs. By the turn of the century, pelagic sealing had also taken its toll, and in 1910 the entire fur seal population was estimated at 130,000. Sealing was completely halted, and the U.S. government took over administration of the islands.

When sealing commenced again in the 1920s, the United States reconstructed all of the houses on both islands. Finding the two-room houses far too small, the government built three-, four- and five-room houses. At this time, all of the government-occupied buildings were also rebuilt; those occupied by government officials are generally larger than the Native dwellings. Buildings to shelter fur processing are large, wood, gable-roofed buildings, and the exteriors give little clue of the industry that went on inside.

Today, fur sealing has been halted; there is no market, worldwide, for the furs. Each year the Aleuts undertake a small subsistence harvest. The government no longer administers the islands but has turned them over to the Aleuts, who are attempting to diversify the economy. The inhabited portions of both islands have been designated a National Historic Landmark as the primary site of the world's fur seal industry.

Saint Paul Island

SW018 Saints Peter and Paul Russian Orthodox Church

1905–1906, Nathaniel Blaisdell

The oldest building on the island of Saint Paul, the church is a significant expression of the Russian-influenced Aleut culture. Although under U.S. domination for nearly fifty years when the church was built, the Aleuts held onto their faith, commissioning this church with their earnings from the seal harvest.

Constructed to replace an earlier building, the church was designed by Nathaniel Blaisdell, an architect from San Francisco. It is unlikely that Blaisdell ever visited Saint Paul; the priest there arranged with the agent of the North American Commercial Company, who was based in San Francisco, for its construction. Bishop Tikhon of the Russian Orthodox Church approved the drawings be-

SW018b Saints Peter and Paul Russian Orthodox Church (iconostas)

fore construction began in 1905. Four carpenters were sent from San Francisco to construct the church; they were aided by the church members themselves.

Originally, the church was far more ornate than at present. In the 1980s, cement asbestos

SW018a Saints Peter and Paul Russian Orthodox Church (exterior)

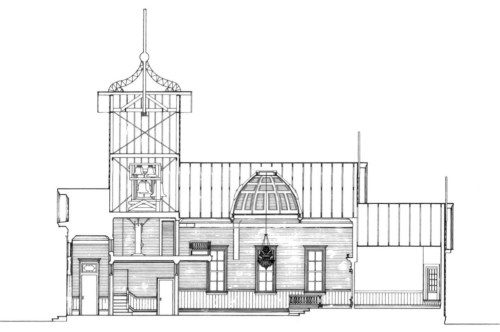

SW018c Saints Peter and Paul Russian Orthodox Church (section)

shingles were applied to the exterior, and much of the ornament was removed. Still, the basic form is unmistakable: sanctuary, nave, narthex and bell tower, and vestibule, each a distinct element on the exterior. Although each of these elements (except the bell tower) has a gable roof at a different level, the slopes of the roofs are identical, giving the exterior a harmonious appearance. Instead of the traditional onion dome, there is an open ironwork structure reminiscent of a dome, far more practical in the heavy winds of the Pribilofs.

The original Classical Revival detailing of the church—such as corner pilasters, cornice returns on the gable ends, and entablatures over every opening—has been lost on the exterior but is maintained on the interior, which features a spectacular iconostas. Divided into seven bays, the mahogany iconostas (which was retained from the previous church) features fluted, engaged Corinthian columns set on paneled bases. The central doors in the iconostas, the royal doors have latticework and a sunburst motif in the transom light. The doors are unpainted mahogany, while the iconostas itself has been painted white with gold trim to set off the icons. Above the iconostas, five large paintings emphasize the height of the nave.

A striking contrast to the remote, windswept island that can only be described as bleak, the sumptuousness of the interior of this church is startling. A building of such color, light, and beauty is tangible evidence of the persistence of faith and culture.

Saint George Island

SW019 Church of the Holy Martyr Saint George the Victorious

1935–1936

Unusual among Alaskan Russian Orthodox churches, the Church of Saint George features pointed-arch windows and an ogee-arch doorway. The origins of these Gothic elements are not known, and there is no known architect. Yet the form of the wood-framed, clapboard-covered building is traditional: sanctuary, nave, narthex, bell tower, and porch are all clearly expressed on the exterior. The bell tower is crowned by a large onion dome whose shape is reflected in the ogee arch of the doorway.

The interior contains another unusual and striking feature: a triple barrel arch extending the length of the nave. In the wall above

SW019a Church of the Holy Martyr Saint George the Victorious (exterior)

SW019b Church of the Holy Martyr Saint George the Victorious (iconostas)

the iconostas, a mural of the Madonna has been painted; the clouds and blonde angels, which look strangely like Hollywood starlets, add a surreal touch. The iconostas is traditional, divided into seven bays by engaged box columns, painted white. Colored light bulbs in porcelain sconces decorate both the vertical and horizontal elements of the iconostas.

The church was built by a local construc-

tion crew supervised by a carpenter named Pearson from Seattle and by Paul Swetzof, Sr., from Saint George. Like the earlier churches in the Pribilofs, construction was financed by the local Aleuts, from their earnings from sealing. Converted to Russian Orthodoxy by the Russians in the late eighteenth or early nineteenth century, the Aleuts have steadfastly held onto this religion, and this eccentric but striking church stands as witness.

SW020 Sealing Plant

1951

The sealing plant on Saint George retains most of its original equipment, although no furs have been taken from the island since 1985. Inside the large wood-framed U-shaped building, the processing equipment has changed little since the nineteenth century; only a portion was ever mechanized. The plant was used to process the furs for shipment to the Fouke Company plant in Saint Louis, Missouri, where they were further processed before sale. The seals, all immature males, were killed on the beaches and the furs brought to this building. The furs were first washed of blood and flesh in redwood tanks, then placed in kench tanks to preserve them before processing. Here they were layered with salt; several skins remain.

In the blubbering room, each skin was placed on a metal mold and stripped of its blubber with a curved knife. The blubber ran in a gutter to barrels outside, where it was retained for use in preserving the texture of the skins. The skins, moved around the plant via a cart and overhead track, were taken to the brining tank, where they were soaked in brine and agitated. After drying, the skins were rolled in borax and packed in barrels.

Without this industry, the Pribilof Islands would still be uninhabited. The sealing plant is the most poignant reminder of the reasons behind the human presence on the island.

Notes

1. In Alaska, the aboriginal peoples—Eskimos, Aleuts, Athapaskans, and Northwest Coast Indians—are generally referred to as Natives. The Northwest Coast Indians inhabiting Alaska are the Tlingit, Haida, and Tsimshian. The Haida and Tsimshian populations are small. *Native,* capitalized, refers to these people; lower-case *native* means indigenous.
2. Christy G. Turner II, "Ancient Peoples of the North Pacific Rim," in *Crossroads of Continents: Cultures of Siberia and Alaska* ed. William W. Fitzhugh and Aron Crowell (Washington, D.C.: Smithsonian Institution Press, 1988), 115.
3. William W. Fitzhugh, "Eskimos: Hunters of the Frozen Coasts," in *Crossroads,* ed. Fitzhugh and Crowell, 43.
4. Wendell H. Oswalt, *Alaskan Eskimos* (San Francisco: Chandler Publishing, 1967), 85–115.
5. Oswalt, *Alaskan Eskimos,* 99–100.
6. Aron Crowell, "Dwellings, Settlements, and Domestic Life," in *Crossroads of the Continents,* ed. Fitzhugh and Crowell, 195.
7. Frederick Whymper, *Travel and Adventure in the Territory of Alaska* (New York: Harper and Brothers, 1869), 175.
8. Ernest S. Burch, Jr., "Kotzebue Sound Eskimos" in *Handbook of North American Indians,* Vol. 5, *Arctic,* ed. David Damas (Washington, D.C.: Smithsonian Institution Press, 1984), 307; Oswalt, *Alaskan Eskimos,* 94–95.
9. Oswalt, *Alaskan Eskimos,* 110–11; Crowell, "Dwellings, Settlements, and Domestic Life," 198; James W. VanStone, "Mainland Southwest Alaska Eskimo," in *Handbook,* ed. Damas, 5:231.
10. Burch, "Kotzebue Sound Eskimos," in *Handbook,* ed. Damas, 5:307–8.
11. Oswalt, *Alaskan Eskimos,* 94–95.
12. Robert F. Spencer, *The North Alaskan Eskimo: A Study in Ecology and Society* (1959; reprint, Washington. D.C.: Smithsonian Institution Press, 1969), 47.
13. Whymper, *Travel and Adventure,* 165.
14. Robert F. Spencer, "North Alaska Coast Eskimo," in *Handbook,* ed. Damas, 5:328.
15. E. W. Nelson, *Eskimo about Bering Sea,* 244; Henry N. Michael, ed. *Lieutenant Zagoskin's Travels in Russian America, 1842–1844,* (Toronto: University of Toronto Press for Arctic Institute of North America, 1967), 115.
16. Riley D. Moore, "Social Life of the Eskimo of St. Lawrence Island," *American Anthropologist* 25 (1923): 346.
17. Moore, "Society Life of the Eskimo," 346–48; E. W. Nelson, *Eskimo about Bering Sea,* 259–60;

Charles C. Hughes, "Saint Lawrence Island Eskimos," in *Handbook,* ed. Damas, 5:271.
18. Timothy M. Sczawinski, "The Little Diomede Kugeri," *The Northern Engineer* 13 (Winter 1981): 22–23; Edward S. Curtis, *The North American Indian,* vol. 20 (1930; reprint New York: Johnson Reprint, 1970), 111–12; E. W. Nelson, *Eskimo about Bering Sea,* 256.
19. Curtis, *North American Indian,* 20: 99–100; E. W. Nelson, *Eskimo about Bering Sea,* 255; Peter Nabokov and Robert Easton, *Native American Architecture* (New York: Oxford University Press, 1989), 207.
20. Lydia T. Black and R. G. Liapunova, "Aleut: Islanders of the North Pacific," 54; Crowell, "Dwellings, Settlements, and Domestic Life," 199, both in *Crossroads,* ed. Fitzhugh and Crowell.
21. Fitzhugh, "Eskimos: Hunters of the Frozen Coasts," ibid., 50.
22. Donald W. Clark, "Pacific Eskimo: Historical Ethnography," in *Handbook,* ed. Damas, 5:191.
23. Black and Liapunova, "Aleut," in *Crossroads,* ed. Fitzhugh and Crowell, 54.
24. Cornelius Osgood, *The Han Indians: A Compilation of Ethnographic and Historical Data on the Alaska-Yukon Boundary Area* (New Haven: Yale University Department of Anthropology, 1971), 85.
25. Frederica de Laguna and Catharine McClellan, "Ahtna," in *Handbook of North American Indians,* vol. 6, *Subarctic,* ed. June Helm (Washington, D.C.: Smithsonian Institution Press, 1981), 645.
26. Osgood, *Han Indians,* 86–87, describes the structure as portable.
27. Robert A. McKennan, "Tanana," in *Handbook,* ed. Helm, 6:571; VanStone, "Mainland Southwest Alaska Eskimo," in *Handbook,* ed. Damas, 5:66, identifies the structure as semipermanent.
28. A. McFadyen Clark, "Koyukon," in *Handbook,* 6:596.
29. Osgood, *Han Indians,* 89.
30. McKennan, "Tanana," in *Handbook,* ed. Helm, 6:571.
31. Frederica de Laguna, "Tlingit: People of the Wolf and Raven," *Crossroads,* ed. Fitzhugh and Crowell, 59.
32. Crowell, "Dwellings, Settlements, and Domestic Life," ibid., 205–6.
33. Descriptions based on: Louis Shotridge and Florence Shotridge, "Chilkat Dwelling House," *University of Pennsylvania Museum Journal* 4 (1913): 86–89; George T. Emmons, "The Whale House of the Chilkat," *Anthropological Papers of*

the *American Museum of Natural History* 19 (1916): 18–24; Aurel Krause, *The Tlingit Indians* (Seattle: University of Washington Press, 1989), 86–87. The Shotridges and Emmons each describe a single house, which structurally appear to be identical; yet a few differences indicate that they are different dwellings. The dimensions vary (Emmons's is 49 feet 10 inches by 53 feet, while the Shotridges' dwelling appears to be more elongated), and the number of levels is different. Krause's description is more general.

34. Some front facades had vertical planks, others horizontal, others a combination; variations occurred within a single village. Joan Vastokas, "Architecture of the Northwest Coast Indians of America," (Ph.D. diss., Columbia University, 1966).

35. Bill Holm, "Art," in *Handbook*, 7: 606–7; Emmons, "Whale House," 18, 23–30.

36. Albert P. Niblack, *The Coast Indians of Southern Alaska and Northern British Columbia* (1888; reprint, New York: Johnson Reprint, 1970), 306.

37. Frederica de Laguna, *Under Mount Saint Elias: The History and Culture of the Yakutat Tlingit* (Washington, D.C.: Smithsonian Institution Press, 1972), 295–300; Niblack, *Coast Indians*, 305–7; Crowell, "Dwellings, Settlements, and Domestic Life," in *Crossroads*, ed. Fitzhugh and Crowell, 206–7.

38. Shotridge, "Chilkat Dwelling House," 94–98; de Laguna, *Under Mount Saint Elias*, 302–3.

39. de Laguna, *Under Mount Saint Elias*, 304.

40. Vastokas, "Architecture of the Northwest Coast Indians of America," 33.

41. Surviving traditional dwellings—albeit exhibiting transitional features—include the John Iyapana Kugeri, Little Diomede Island (see WE003, p.266), and the Nanny Ooyatahna Sod House, Point Hope (see NO005, p.257). Reconstructions include Chief Shakes House in Wrangell (see SE060, p.199), the Totem Bight Community House in Ketchikan (see SE073, p.205), and the community house in Kasaan (see SE064, p.201), all built by the Civilian Conservation Corps in the late 1930s. There have been a number of additional reconstructions since 1960.

42. Dorothy Jean Ray, *The Eskimos of Bering Strait, 1650–1898* (Seattle: University of Washington Press, 1975), 174.

43. Edwin S. Hall, "Interior North Alaskan Eskimo," in *Handbook*, ed. Damas, 5:344.

44. Richard K. Nelson, *Hunters of the Northern Forest: Designs for Survival among the Alaskan Kutchin* (Chicago: University of Chicago Press, 1973), 273–79.

45. Osgood, *The Han Indians*, 157.

46. Hudson Stuck, *Ten Thousand Miles with a Dog Sled* (1914; reprint, Lincoln: University of Nebraska Press, 1988), 70.

47. Nancy Yaw Davis, "Contemporary Pacific Eskimo," in *Handbook*, ed. Damas, 5:203.

48. Wallace M. Olson, "Minto, Alaska," in *Handbook*, ed. Helm, 6:708.

49. Margaret Lantis, "Aleut," in *Handbook*, ed. Damas, 5:167.

50. P. A. Tikhmenev, *A History of the Russian-American Company* (Seattle: University of Washington Press, 1978; orig. pub. 1861), 1:471.

51. Black and Liapunova, "Aleut," in *Crossroads*, ed. Fitzhugh and Crowell, 54.

52. Russell Sackett, *The Chilkat Tlingit: A General Overview* (Fairbanks: University of Alaska, Anthropology and Historic Preservation, Cooperative Park Studies Unit, 1979), 34–40.

53. Frederica de Laguna, *The Story of a Tlingit Community: A Problem in the Relationship Between Archeological, Ethnological, and Historical Methods* (Smithsonian Institution, Bureau of American Ethnology, Bulletin 172, 1960; Brighton, Mich.: Native American Book Publishers, 1980s), 189.

54. Dale C. Slaughter, "The Point Barrow Type House: An Analysis of Archeological Examples from Siraagruk and Other Sites in Northern Alaska," *Anthropological Papers of the University of Alaska* 20 (1982): 157.

55. James W. VanStone, *Point Hope, An Eskimo Community in Northwest Alaska* (Fort Wainwright, Alaska: Arctic Aeromedical Laboratory, 1961), 60.

56. James W. VanStone, *Eskimos of the Nushagak River: An Ethnographic History* (Seattle: University of Washington Press, 1967), 130, 145.

57. Vilhjalmur Stefansson, *My Life with the Eskimos* (1913; reprint, New York: Macmillan, 1951), 299.

58. Norman A. Chance, "Alaska Eskimo Modernization," in *Handbook*, ed. Damas, 5:646.

59. "Remote Housing Aided Many," *Building Alaska* (published by the Alaska State Housing Authority) 3 (July 1967): 4; Paul L. Gagnon, "The Beaver Report" (Alaska Rural Development Board, 1959), 6, 29.

60. "Kotzebue and Mountain Village Selected for Experimental Houses," *Building Alaska* (August 1968): 6.

61. Examples include the sod-covered dwelling in Kotzebue erected by the NANA museum (see WE002, p.266), the plank house at Saxman (see SE074, p.206), and the barabara in Akhiok.

62. Svetlana G. Fedorova, *Ethnic Processes in Russian America* (Anchorage: Anchorage Historical and Fine Arts Museum, 1975), 8.

63. James R. Gibson, "Russian Expansion in Siberia and America: Critical Contrasts," in *Russia's American Colony*, ed. S. Frederick Starr (Durham: Duke University Press, 1987), 34. The pre-contact population of Aleuts was estimated at between 12,000 and 15,000. Margaret Lantis, "Aleut," in *Handbook*, ed. Damas, 5:163. In 1842, Sir George Simpson, governor of the Hudson's Bay Company, estimated the Aleut population at barely one tenth of its pre-contact size. S. B. Okun, *The Russian-American Company* (1939; re-

print, Cambridge: Harvard University Press, 1951), 193.

64. Svetlana Fedorova, *The Russian Population in Alaska and California, Late 18th Century—1867*, trans. and ed. Richard A. Pierce and Alton S. Donnelly (Kingston, Ontario: Limestone Press, 1973), 217–18.

65. Arthur Voyce, "National Elements in Russian Architecture," *Journal of the Society of Architectural Historians* 16 (May 1957): 7.

66. Martin Sauer, *An Account of a Geographical and Astronomical Expedition to the Northern Parts of Russia Performed by Commodore Joseph Billings in the Years 1785, etc. to 1794* (London, 1802), 40, cited in Anatole Senkevitch, Jr., "The Early Architecture and Settlements of Russian America," *Russia's American Colony*, ed. Starr, 161.

67. Fedorova, *Ethnic Processes*, 10.

68. P. A. Tikhmenev, *A History of the Russian American Company*, vol. 2, *Documents*, trans. Dmitri Krenov, ed. Richard A. Pierce and Alton S. Donnelly (Kingston: Limestone Press, 1979), 11. Baidaras, called umiaks by the Eskimos, are small, skin-covered boats holding twenty to twenty-five people. Baidarkas, or kayaks, are similar but smaller, holding one, two, or three people.

69. Tikhmenev, *Russian-American Company*, 2:11.

70. Fedorova, *Russian Population*, 218.

71. Barbara Sweetland Smith, National Historic Landmark nomination: Russian-American Company *Magazin* (Washington, D.C.: National Park Service, 1986).

72. Manuscript reproduced in Colin Bearne, trans., Richard A. Pierce, ed., *The Russian Orthodox Religious Mission in America, 1794–1837*, (Kingston, Ontario: Limestone Press, 1978), 117. Confirmed by Rezanov two years later in his report to the Company Board of Directors, 15 February 1806, Tikhmenev, *Russian-American Company*, 2:188.

73. Archimandrite Ioasaph to G. I. Shelikhov, Kodiak Island, 18 May 1795, *Documents Relative to the History of Alaska* (hereafter *DRHA*) 3:151.

74. P. A. Tikhmenev, *A History of the Russian-American Company*, trans. and ed. Richard A. Pierce and Alton S. Donnelly (Seattle: University of Washington Press, 1978; orig. pub. 1861–63), 1:87.

75. Tikhmenev, *Russian-American Company*, 1:87.

76. Tikhmenev, *Russian-American Company*, 2:188.

77. Ibid., 2:77.

78. Baranov referred to it as the "new church" in 1796, see Tikhmenev, *Russian-American Company*, 1:47.

79. Bishop Gregory, "The Orthodox Church in Alaska," *Orthodox Alaska* 5 (1975): 15.

80. Innokentii Veniaminov, "The Condition of the Orthodox Church in Russian America" (originally published 1840); trans. and ed. Robert Nichols and Robert Croskey, *Pacific Northwest Quarterly* 63 (April 1972): 43–44.

81. Order, Lieutenant-General Ivan Peel to G. I.

Shelikhov, Irkutsk, 12 May 1794, *DRHA* 3:161.

82. Shelikhov to Baranov, Okhotsk, 9 August 1794, Tikhmenev, *Russian-American Company*, 2:54–7.

83. Cited in Fedorova, *Russian Population*, 216.

84. Okun, *Russian-American Company*, 33.

85. Tikhmenev, *Russian-American Company*, 1:33; Hubert Howe Bancroft, *History of Alaska, 1730–1885* (1886; reprint, New York: Antiquarian Press Ltd., 1960), 329–31; Timothy L. Dilliplane, "Industries in Russian America," *Russian America: The Forgotten Frontier*, ed. Barbara Sweetland Smith and Redmond J. Barnett (Tacoma: Washington State Historical Society, 1990), 131.

86. Rezanov to Emperor, Unalaska, 18 July 1805, Tikhmenev, *Russian-American Company*, 2:149; 1:88. Another motive for the temporary halting of the fur seal harvest is given by historian S. B. Okun (*Russian-American Company*, p. 61), who notes that the furs had flooded the market, driving the price down and that the company destroyed 700,000 skins to inflate the price.

87. Rezanov to Baranov, 20 July 1805, *DRHA*, 3:184.

88. Cited in Bancroft, *Alaska, 1730–1885*, 467.

89. Tikhmenev, *Russian-American Company*, 1:160.

90. Inventory of the Russian American Company, no date but probably 1815, *DRHA* 3: 253.

91. Sokolov to Board of Directors, Sitka, 1 June 1817, *DRHA*, 4:129.

92. Fedorova, *Russian Population*, 222.

93. William H. Dall, *Alaska and Its Resources* (Boston: Lee and Shepard, 1870), 8–9.

94. Tikhmenev, *Russian-American Company*, 1:174–75.

95. Okun, *Russian-American Company*, 85–86.

96. Creoles were of mixed blood, Russian and Native.

97. Whymper, *Travel and Adventure*, 153.

98. Michael, *Zagoskin's Travels*, 185.

99. Bishop Innokenty to Novo-Arkhangelsk Ecclesiastical Consistory, Novo-Arkhangelsk, 22 February 1849, *DRHA*, 1:374–75. Because Kvikhpak was no longer the site of a Russian-American Company post, the church had to finance construction itself.

100. Alaskan Russian Church Archives, Manuscript Division, Library of Congress, microfilm reel 151.

101. Innokenti Veniaminov, "The Russian Orthodox Church in Alaska" (originally published 1858), trans. Robert Croskey, *Pacific Northwest Quarterly* 66 (January 1975): 17.

102. Cited in Michael Oleska, ed., *Alaskan Missionary Spirituality* (New York: Paulist Press, 1987), 246–248.

103. James R. Gibson, *Imperial Russia in Frontier America: The Changing Geography of Supply of Russian America, 1784–1867* (New York: Oxford University Press, 1976): 37–38.

104. Tikhmenev, *Russian-American Company*, 1:374.

105. Ibid. Pavel N. Golovin, *The End of Russian*

America, (originally published 1982) trans. Basil Dmytryshyn and E. A. P. Crownhart-Vaughan (Portland: Oregon Historical Society, 1979), 49, also describes this sawmill.

106. Whymper, *Travel and Adventure,* 97.

107. Dall, *Alaska and Its Resources,* 255. Actually, the town was sixty years old.

108. Chistiakov to Stepan Iakovlevich [Nikiforov], 23 February 1827, Records of the Russian-American Company, Correspondence to the Governors General, Communications Sent, 5:44.

109. Tikhmenev, *Russian-American Company,* 1:200.

110. Ibid., 1:386, 411; *DRHA,* 2:4.

111. Golovin, *Civil and Savage Encounters,* 137–38.

112. Board of Directors to Administrator-General, Captain of the second rank Nicholas Yakovlevich Rosenberg, 31 August 1851, *DRHA,* 4:381–2.

113. Bishop Gregory, "The Church in Alaska after 200 Years," *Orthodox Alaska* 6 (July 1977): 10. The church moved its diocesan seat to San Francisco in 1870, after Alaska was sold to the United States. In 1905, responding to Eastern European immigration in the East, the administrative base of the church moved to New York. The Russian church continued to support its Alaska parishes, on a reduced level, until the Russian Revolution, when all support from Russia ceased. After some upheaval within the church, the American church's members formed two new churches; the Alaskan parishes are a part of the Orthodox Church in America. Barbara Sweetland Smith, *Orthodoxy and Native Americans: The Alaskan Mission* (Syosset, N.Y.: Orthodox Church in America, 1980), 17–19; Basil M. Bensin, *The Russian Orthodox Church in Alaska, 1794–1967* (Russian Orthodox Greek Catholic Church of North America, 1967), 3–4.

114. Fedorova, *Ethnic Processes,* 23. Russian "peasants' customs" and folklore are also mentioned in Helen A. Shenitz, "The Vestiges of Old Russia in Alaska," *Russian Review* 14 (January 1955): 55–59.

115. Wendell H. Oswalt, *Napaskiak: An Alaskan Eskimo Community* (Tucson: University of Arizona Press, 1963), 124.

116. In a study of five Aleut (Pacific Eskimo) villages after the 1964 earthquake, Nancy Yaw Davis found the concern for the church buildings and identification with the Russian Orthodox church to be a uniting and powerful force. Nancy Yaw Davis, "The Role of the Russian Orthodox Church in Five Pacific Eskimo Villages as Revealed by the Earthquake," *The Great Alaska Earthquake of 1964: Human Ecology* (Washington: National Academy of Sciences, 1970), 125–46.

117. Voyce, "National Elements in Russian Architecture," 11.

118. The origin of this form may relate to the Russian *trapeznaya,* or meeting room, which had been a separate structure, and was incorporated into the churches as a larger vestibule, or meeting place. The octagon shape did not adapt well to additions; occasionally the *trapeznaya* was wrapped around three sides of the nave. To accommodate additions, a square or rectangle was employed at ground level, rising to form an octagon. Alexander Opolovnikov and Yelena Opolovnikova, *The Wooden Architecture of Russia: Houses, Fortifications, Churches* (New York: Harry N. Abrams, Inc., 1989), 18.

119. Modern construction materials also include concrete, as in the reconstructed Saint Michael's Cathedral (1977).

120. Betty John, *Libby: The Alaskan Diaries and Letters of Libby Beaman* (Boston: Houghton Mifflin, 1989), 48.

121. While precise comparisons to Orthodox churches in Russia cannot be made, it is worth noting that Alaskan churches were probably far simpler. Elements identified with Russian wooden churches include multiple onion domes, clustered like an upside-down bunch of grapes; ornately shingled onion domes; highly decorated eaves and bargeboards; extended, carved brackets; and prominent exterior stairways. None of these is found in Alaskan churches.

122. U.S. Treasury Department, Bureau of Statistics, "Commercial Alaska in 1901," in *Summary of Commerce and Finance for May 1902* (Washington, D.C.: Government Printing Office, 1902), 3949; *Progress of Alaska Since Purchase: How Its Industries Began* (Juneau: Alaska Bureau of Publicity, 1917), 6. The machinery at Sitka was moved to Cook Inlet after the 1879 season, and the cannery buildings were used in the construction of the first building at the Sitka Industrial Training School in 1882.

123. "Commercial Alaska in 1901," 3945.

124. Ted C. Hinckley, *The Americanization of Alaska, 1867–1897* (Palo Alto: Pacific Books, 1972), 189.

125. "Commercial Alaska in 1901," 3944.

126. Alfred Hulse Brooks, *Blazing Alaska's Trails* (1953; Fairbanks: University of Alaska Press, 1973), 299.

127. Ibid., 304–5. David Stone and Brenda Stone, *Hard Rock Gold: The Story of the Great Mines that were the Heartbeat of Juneau* (Juneau: City and Borough of Juneau, Juneau Centennial Committee), 11, 24.

128. James Wickersham, *Old Yukon: Tales—Trails—and Trials* (Washington, D.C.: Washington Law Book Company, 1938), 122.

129. William R. Hunt, *North of 53: The Wild Days of the Alaska-Yukon Mining Frontier, 1870–1914* (New York: MacMillan, 1974), 18.

130. Pierre Berton, *The Klondike Fever: The Life and Death of the Last Great Gold Rush* (New York: Alfred A. Knopf, 1958), 33.

131. Wickersham, *Old Yukon,* 122.

132. Ibid., 46.
133. Neal A. Armstrong, "Sheldon Jackson Scenes: A Documentary History of Sheldon Jackson Junior College, Sitka, Alaska, 1878–1967" (M.A. thesis, George Peabody College for Teachers, 1967), 94.
134. Sheldon Jackson to Mrs. Sara T. Kinney, 5 August 1888, cited in Theodore Charles Hinckley, Jr., "The Alaskan Labors of Sheldon Jackson, 1877–1890" (Ph.D. diss., Indiana University, 1961), 175.
135. Ibid.; Alice Palmer Henderson, *The Rainbow's End: Alaska* (Chicago: Herbert S. Stone and Co., 1898), 219.
136. Armstrong, "Jackson Scenes," 95, notes that the subdivision, called "Westminster Addition," was designed by Presbyterian missionary Eugene Willard.
137. *Report of the Governor of Alaska For the Fiscal Year 1886* (Washington, D.C.: Government Printing Office, 1886), 941.
138. *Report of the Governor of Alaska for the Fiscal Year 1888* (Washington, D.C.: Government Printing Office, 1888), 32.
139. *Report of the Governor of Alaska for the Fiscal Year 1902* (Washington, D.C.: Government Printing Office, 1902), 23.
140. Peter Murray, *The Devil and Mr. Duncan: A History of the Two Metlakatlas* (Victoria, B.C.: Sono Nis Press, 1985); Phyllis Bowman, *Metlakahtla—The Holy City!* (privately printed, 1983).
141. Robert Laird Stewart, *Sheldon Jackson* (New York: Fleming H. Revell, 1908), 363.
142. Brooks, *Blazing Alaska's Trails*, 493. Jackson somewhat neglected the education of whites; in 1890, there were only two schools for white children, at Sitka and at Juneau. Ten years later, legislation was enacted that enabled communities to set up their own public schools. Jackson's downfall concerned a rather odd project that he undertook as commissioner of education, to import domestic reindeer as an industry to feed Eskimos.
143. "Commercial Alaska in 1901," 3985.
144. Berton, *Klondike Fever*, 417.
145. Hunt, *North of 53*, 99.
146. Robert L. S. Spude and Sandra McDermott Faulkner, comps., *Kennecott, Alaska* (Anchorage: National Park Service, Alaska Region, 1987), 3.
147. As far as is known, Native population stayed relatively constant, but statistics on Native population are not always reliable.
148. The sources for this data are Claus-M. Naske and Herman E. Slotnick, *Alaska: A History of the 49th State* (1979; reprint, Norman: University of Oklahoma Press, 1987), 301 and the U.S. Bureau of the Census.
149. *Aids to Navigation in Alaska History* (Alaska Division of Parks, 1974).
150. Claus-M. Naske, *Paving Alaska's Trails: The Work of the Alaska Road Commission* (Lanham, Md.: University Press of America, 1986), 15.
151. Naske and Slotnick, *History of the 49th State,* 90.
152. G. Marion Burton, "Automobiling on the Valdez Trail," *Collier's Outdoor America* (16 July 1910): 21.
153. By early 1919, the AEC had built about four hundred buildings along the line, ninety-six of them in Anchorage. AEC Summary of Detailed Estimates, compiled by L. L. McPherson, Engineer, 31 March 1919, National Archives and Records Service, RG 126, Office of the Territories Classified Files 1907–1951, file 9–1–3.
154. James Wickersham, journal, 22 May 1904.
155. Wickersham journal, 24 May 1904.
156. Robert L. S. Spude, *Skagway, District of Alaska, 1884–1912: Building the Gateway to the Klondike* (Fairbanks: University of Alaska Cooperative Park Studies Unit, 1983), 47–65.
157. Stuck, *Ten Thousand Miles with a Dog Sled: A Narrative of Winter Travel in Interior Alaska,* 368–69.
158. C. A. (Bert) Bryant, "Another Man's Life," (Alaska Historical Library, typescript, 1937), 163.
159. William D. Moore, "From Peru to Alaska" (University of Washington Manuscript Collection, typescript, [1923]), unpaginated, but describing events in 1889.
160. William Douglas Johns, "The Early Yukon, Alaska, and the Klondike Discovery As They Were Before the Great Klondike Stampede Swept Away the Old Conditions Forever by One Who Was There" (University of Washington Manuscript Collection, typescript, [1939]), 125.
161. James Wickersham to his mother, from Circle City, 25 August 1900, James Wickersham correspondence, University of Alaska-Fairbanks, Archives.
162. A. W. Greeley, *Handbook of Alaska: Its Resources, Products, and Attractions* (New York: Charles Scribner's Sons, 1909), 13. The first homestead act allowed entries only on surveyed lands—of which there were none in Alaska, and not even meridian lines or monuments from which to survey. Hinckley, *Alaskan*, 183.
163. Brooks, *Blazing Alaska's Trails*, 514–16.
164. Ernest Gruening, *The State of Alaska* (New York: Random House, 1954), 273, 277.
165. Orlando W. Miller, *The Frontier in Alaska and the Matanuska Colony* (New Haven: Yale University Press, 1975), 200.
166. Gruening, *Alaska*, 298.
167. James R. Shortridge, "The Alaskan Agricultural Empire: An American Agrarian Vision, 1898–1929," *Pacific Northwest Quarterly* 69 (October 1978): 145–58.
168. *Knik, Matanuska, Susitna: A Visual History of the Valleys* (Matanuska-Susitna Borough, 1985, 1986), 170.

169. Gruening, *Alaska*, 291.
170. Clarence C. Hully, *Alaska: Past and Present* (Portland, Oreg.: Binsford and Mort), 316.
171. Cited in Michael Carberry and Donna Lane, *Patterns of the Past: An Inventory of Anchorage's Historic Resources* (Municipality of Anchorage, 1986), 95.
172. Naske and Slotnick, *History of the 49th State*, 122.
173. Hulley, *Alaska: Past and Present*, 335.
174. The "T" or Kodiak hangars could also be constructed with Howe trusses, and steel trusses could also be in a bowstring form. James D. Bush, Jr., "Narrative Report of Alaska Construction, 1941–1944" (U.S. Army Corps of Engineers, 1944), 313–15.
175. Ibid., 278–79.
176. Hulley, *Alaska: Past and Present*, 361.
177. Gruening, *Alaska*, 316.
178. Miller, *Matanuska Colony*, 200.
179. *The Alaska Almanac: Facts About Alaska—1990 Edition* (Anchorage: Alaska Northwest Books, 1989), 145.
180. *The Alaska Almanac*, 148.
181. "The Trans-Alaska Oil Pipeline: The Whole Story," *Alaska Construction and Oil*, Special Pipeline Report (September 1975), 20.
182. Stan Cohen, *The Great Alaska Pipeline* (Missoula, Mont.: Pictorial Histories Publishing, 1988), 133.
183. *The Alaska Almanac*, 150.
184. Martha Frey, "Nuts About Huts," *Anchorage Historic Properties News* 2 (Summer 1989):3.
185. *What's Doing in Anchorage* (Anchorage, 1955), 32; Stephen M. Dunn, "Prebuilts and Conventional Construction: A Comparative Analysis of Single-Family Residential Development in Alaskan Metropolitan Areas" (typescript, 1972), 33.
186. Lloyd E. Hixon, "How to Design Against Earthquakes," *AIA Journal* (October 1965): 81–82.
187. "Two San Francisco firms win competition to design a new capital city for Alaska," *Architectural Record* 163 (February 1978): 40–41; "SF firms design Alaska capital building," *Progressive Architecture* 59 (March 1978): 40; "Alaskans to vote on plan for building capital city," *AIA Journal* 67 (June 1978): 72; David Littlejohn, "Dream Town in the Wilderness," *Atlantic Monthly* (October 1978): 83–94.
188. Axel Carlson, "Why Build A Log House?" *Alaska* 42 (August 1976): 16–18.

Sources Consulted

This list of sources begins with the general references. They are listed according to the three cultural eras in Alaska—Native Alaskan, Russian Alaskan, and American Alaskan—followed by interviews. The sources used for the entries for individual properties follow, listed by region and then alphabetically by locale within region.

For researching the individual sites, the best histories were those compiled by state and federal agencies. Local surveys and over two hundred nominations to the National Register of Historic Places, representing an impressive and exceedingly useful body of work, were undertaken or supervised by the state historic preservation office, Division of Parks and Outdoor Recreation, Department of Natural Resources.

The Alaska Regional Office of the National Park Service has undertaken nominations to the National Historic Landmark program, Historic Resource Studies of areas in and near parks, Historic Structures Reports of buildings in parks, and documentation for the Historic American Buildings Survey/Historic American Engineering Record of buildings both in and out of parks.

These site-specific studies were occasionally augmented by published local histories, a list of which follows. Additional research in both primary and secondary sources, informal interviews of knowledgeable people, and the buildings themselves provided additional information.

GENERAL SOURCES

Native American

Birket-Smith, Kaj, and Frederica de Laguna. *The Eyak Indians of the Copper River Delta, Alaska.* 1938. Reprint. New York: AMS Press, 1976.

Building Alaska. Alaska State Housing Authority. 1967–68.

Carpenter, Edmund. *Eskimo Realities.* New York: Holt, Rinehart, and Winston, 1973.

Cole, Douglas. *Captured Heritage: The Scramble for Northwest Coast Artifacts.* Seattle: University of Washington Press, 1985.

Curtis, Edward S. *The North American Indian.* Vol. 20. 1930. Reprint. New York: Johnson Reprint, 1970.

Damas, David, ed. *Handbook of North American Indians.* Volume 5, *Arctic.* Washington, D.C.: Smithsonian Institution Press, 1984.

de Laguna, Frederica. *The Archeology of Cook Inlet, Alaska.* 1934. Reprint. Anchorage: Alaska Historical Society, 1975.

———. *Under Mount Saint Elias: The History and*

Culture of the Yakutat Tlingit. Smithsonian Contributions to Anthropology, vol. 7. Washington, D.C.: Smithsonian Institution Press, 1972.

Drucker, Philip. *Cultures of the North Pacific Coast.* San Francisco: Chandler Publishing, 1965.

Emmons, George F. "The Whale House of the Chilkat." *Anthropological Papers of the American Museum of Natural History* 19 (1916): 1–33.

Fitzhugh, William W., and Aron Crowell. *Crossroads of Continents: Cultures of Siberia and Alaska.* Washington, D.C.: Smithsonian Institution Press, 1988.

Forrest, Linn A., Architects. *Angoon Clan House Restoration Project.* Angoon: Kootznoowoo Heritage Foundation, 1882.

Gagnon, Paul L. "The Beaver Report." Alaska Rural Development Board, 1959.

Garfield, Viola E., and Linn A. Forrest. *The Wolf and the Raven: Totem Poles of Southeastern Alaska.* 1948. Reprint. Seattle: University of Washington Press, 1961.

Helm, June, ed. *Handbook of North American Indians.* Volume 6, *Subarctic.* Washington, D.C.: Smithsonian Institution Press, 1981.

Jones, Livingston F. *A Study of the Thlingets of Alaska.* New York: Fleming H. Revell Co., 1914.

Krause, Aurel. *The Tlingit Indians.* 1885, in German. Translated by Erna Gunther, 1956. Reprint. Seattle: University of Washington Press, 1989.

Laughlin, William S. *Aleuts: Survivors of the Bering Land Bridge.* New York: Holt, Rinehart and Winston, 1980.

McClintock, Eva, ed. *Life in Alaska: Letters of Mrs. Eugene S. Willard.* Philadelphia: Presbyterian Board of Publication, 1884.

MacDonald, George F. *Haida Monumental Art: Villages of the Queen Charlotte Islands.* Vancouver: University of British Columbia Press, 1983.

Moore, Riley D. "Social Life of the Eskimo of St. Lawrence Island." *American Anthropologist* 23 (1923): 339–75.

Murdoch, John. *Ethnological Results of the Point Barrow Expedition.* 1892. Reprint. Washington, D.C.: Smithsonian Institution Press, 1988.

Nabokov, Peter, and Robert Easton. *Native American Architecture.* New York: Oxford University Press, 1989.

Nelson, Edward W. *The Eskimo about Bering Sea.* 1899. Reprint. New York: Johnson Reprint, 1971.

Nelson, Richard K. *Hunters of the Northern Forest: Designs for Survival among the Alaskan Kutchin.* Chicago: University of Chicago Press, 1973.

Niblack, Albert P. *The Coast Indians of Southern Alaska and Northern British Columbia.* 1888. Reprint. New York: Johnson Reprint, 1970.

Osgood, Cornelius. *The Han Indians: A Compilation*

of Ethnographic and Historical Data on the Alaska-Yukon Boundary Area. New Haven: Yale University, Department of Anthropology, 1971.

Oswalt, Wendell H. *Alaskan Eskimos.* San Francisco: Chandler Publishing, 1967.

———. *Bashful No Longer: An Alaskan Eskimo Ethnohistory, 1778–1988.* Norman: University of Oklahoma Press, 1990.

———. *Napaskiak: An Alaskan Eskimo Community.* Tucson: University of Arizona Press, 1963.

Panigeo, Mabel, trans. "North Slope Borough." Transcript of Elders Conference discussion of "Iglut." 1984.

Ray, Dorothy Jean. "The Eskimo Dwelling." *Alaska Sportsman* 26 (August 1960): 13.

———. *The Eskimos of Bering Strait, 1650–1898.* Seattle: University of Washington Press, 1975.

———. "Nineteenth Century Settlement and Subsistence Patterns in Bering Strait." *Arctic Anthropology* 2 (1964): 61–94.

Sackett, Russell. *The Chilkat Tlingit: A General Overview.* Fairbanks: University of Alaska, Anthropology and Historic Preservation, Cooperative Park Studies Unit, 1979.

Sczawinski, Timothy M. "The Little Diomede Kugeri." *The Northern Engineer* 13 (Winter 1981): 19–25.

Shotridge, Louis, and Florence Shotridge. "Chilkat Dwelling House." *University of Pennsylvania Museum Journal.* 4 (1913): 86–99.

Slaughter, Dale C. "The Point Barrow Type House: An Analysis of Archeological Examples from Siraagruk and Other Sites in Northern Alaska." *Anthropological Papers of the University of Alaska* 20 (1982): 141–58.

Spencer, Robert F. *The North Alaskan Eskimo: A Study in Ecology and Society.* 1959. Reprint. Washington, D.C.: Smithsonian Institution Press, 1969.

Stefansson, Vilhjalmur. *My Life with the Eskimo.* 1913. Reprint. New York: Macmillan, 1951.

Stuck, Hudson. *Ten Thousand Miles with a Dog Sled.* 1914. Reprint. Lincoln: University of Nebraska Press, 1988.

Suttles, Wayne, ed. *Handbook of North American Indians.* Volume 7, *Northwest Coast.* Washington, D.C.: Smithsonian Institution Press, 1990.

VanStone, James W. *Eskimos of the Nushagak River: An Ethnographic History.* Seattle: University of Washington Press, 1967.

———. *Point Hope, An Eskimo Community in Northwest Alaska.* Fort Wainwright, Alaska: Arctic Aeromedical Laboratory, 1961.

Vastokas, Joan. "Architecture of the Northwest Coast Indians of America." Ph.D. diss., Columbia University, 1966.

Whymper, Frederick. *Travel and Adventure in the Territory of Alaska.* New York: Harper and Brothers, 1869.

Wyatt, Victoria. *Images from the Inside Passage: An Alaskan Portrait by Winter & Pond.* Seattle: University of Washington Press, 1989.

Russian Alaskan

Afonsky, Bishop Gregory. "The Orthodox Church in Alaska." *Orthodox Alaska* 5, no. 5 (1975): 2–11; 5, no. 6 (1975): 3–22; 6, no. 1 (1977): 3–27; 6, no. 2 (1977): 7–21.

———. "The Church in Alaska after 200 Years." *Orthodox Alaska* 6/3 (1977): 5–11.

Alaskan Russian Church Archives, Manuscript Division, Library of Congress.

Bancroft, Hubert Howe. *History of Alaska, 1730–1885.* 1886. Reprint. New York: Antiquarian Press, 1960.

Bearne, Colin, trans., Richard A. Pierce, ed. *The Russian Orthodox Religious Mission in America, 1794–1837.* Kingston, Ontario: Limestone Press, 1978.

Bensin, Basil M. *The Russian Orthodox Church in Alaska, 1794–1967.* Russian Orthodox Greek Catholic Church of North America, 1967.

Brooke, John. "Sitka, Alaska." *A Report on the Hygiene of the United States Army with descriptions of military posts.* War Department, Surgeon-General's Office. Washington, D.C.: Government Printing Office, 1875.

Brooks, Alfred Hulse. *Blazing Alaska's Trails.* 1953. Reprint. Fairbanks: University of Alaska Press, 1973.

Brumfield, William Craft. *Gold in Azure: One Thousand Years of Russian Architecture.* Boston: David K. Godine, 1983.

"Concerning the Orthodox Mission in America." Translated by Sister Victoria. *Orthodox Alaska* 6/1 (1977): 36–46.

Dall, William H. *Alaska and Its Resources.* Boston: Lee and Shepard, 1870.

Davis, Nancy Yaw. "The Role of the Russian Orthodox Church in Five Pacific Eskimo Villages as Revealed by the Earthquake." In *The Great Alaska Earthquake of 1964: Human Ecology,* edited by the Committee on the Alaska Earthquake of the Division of Earth Sciences, National Research Council, 125–46. Washington, D.C.: National Academy of Sciences, 1970.

DeArmond, R. N., ed. *Lady Franklin Visits Sitka, Alaska 1870: The Journal of Sophia Cracroft, Sir John Franklin's Niece.* Anchorage: Alaska Historical Society, 1981.

Dmytryshyn, Basil, E.A.P. Crownhart-Vaughan, and Thomas Vaughan, eds. and trans. *The Russian American Colonies: A Documentary Record, 1798–1867.* Portland: Oregon Historical Society Press, 1989.

Documents Relative to the History of Alaska. Microfilm of typescript translation of Russian-language and other documents, including excerpts from the Alaska Church Collection in vols. 1 and 2; the Yudin Collection, vol. 3; the Russian-American Company, vol. 4; the *Russian Orthodox American Messenger,* vol. 5. Library of Congress, Washington, D.C. (Cited as DRHA.)

Fedorova, Svetlana. *Ethnic Processes in Russian Amer-*

ica. Anchorage: Anchorage Historical and Fine Arts Museum, 1975.

———. *The Russian Population in Alaska and California, Late 18th Century-1867.* Translated and edited by Richard A. Pierce and Alton S. Donnelly. Kingston, Ontario: Limestone Press, 1973.

Gibson, James R. *Imperial Russia in Frontier America: The Changing Geography of Supply of Russian America, 1784–1867.* New York: Oxford University Press, 1976.

Golovin, Pavel N. *Civil and Savage Encounters: The Worldly Travel Letters of an Imperial Russian Navy Officer, 1860–61.* Portland: Oregon Historical Society, 1983.

———. *The End of Russian America.* 1862. Reprint. Translated by Basil Dmytryshyn and E.A.P. Crownhart-Vaughan. Portland: Oregon Historical Society, 1979.

A History of Public Buildings Under the Control of the Treasury Department. Washington, D.C.: Government Printing Office, 1901.

Michael, Henry N., ed. *Lieutenant Zagoskin's Travels in Russian America, 1842–1844.* Toronto: University of Toronto Press for Arctic Institute of North America, 1967.

Okun, S. B. *The Russian-American Company.* Cambridge: Harvard University Press, 1951.

Oleska, Michael, ed. *Alaskan Missionary Spirituality.* New York: Paulist Press, 1987.

Opolovnikov, Alexander, and Yelena Opolovnikova. *The Wooden Architecture of Russia: Houses, Fortifications, Churches.* New York: Harry N. Abrams, 1989.

Oswalt, Wendell H. *Kolmakovskiy Redoubt: The Ethnoarcheology of a Russian Fort in Alaska.* Los Angeles: University of California, Institute of Archaeology, 1980.

Petroff, Ivan. *Report on the Population, Industries, and Resources of Alaska.* Washington, D.C.: Government Printing Office, 1884.

Pierce, Richard A. "Reconstructing 'Baranov's Castle.'" *Alaska History* 4 (Spring 1989): 27–44.

Records of the Russian-American Company, Correspondence of the Governors General, Communications Sent.

Shelikhov, Grigorii I. *A Voyage to America, 1783–1786.* Translated by Marina Ramsay; edited by Richard A. Pierce. Kingston, Ontario: Limestone Press, 1981.

Shenitz, Helen A. "The Vestiges of Old Russia in Alaska." *Russian Review* 14 (January 1955): 55–59.

Smith, Barbara Sweetland. "Cathedral on the Yukon." *Alaska Journal* 12 (Spring 1982): 4.

———. *Orthodoxy and Native Americans: The Alaskan Mission.* Syosset, N.Y.: Orthodox Church in America, 1980.

Smith, Barbara Sweetland, and Redmond J. Barnett, eds. *Russian America: The Forgotten Frontier.* Tacoma: Washington State Historical Society, 1990.

Starr, S. Frederick, ed. *Russia's American Colony.* Durham: Duke University Press, 1987.

Tikhmenev, P. A. *A History of the Russian-American Company.* Volume 1. 1861–1863. Reprint. Translated and edited Richard A. Pierce and Alton S. Donnelly. Seattle: University of Washington Press, 1978.

———. *A History of the Russian-American Company.* Volume 2, *Documents.* 1863. Reprint. Translated by Dmitri Krenov; edited by Richard A. Pierce and Alton S. Donnelly. Kingston: Limestone Press, 1979.

U.S. National Park Service. "Alaska History 1741–1910." The National Survey of Historic Sites and Buildings, 1961. National Park Service, History Division, Washington, D.C.

Veniaminov, Innokentii. "The Condition of the Orthodox Church in Russian America." *Pacific Northwest Quarterly* 63 (April 1972): 41–54. Translated and edited by Robert Nichols and Robert Croskey. (Originally published 1840.)

———. "The Russian Orthodox Church in Alaska." Translated by Robert Croskey. *Pacific Northwest Quarterly* 66 (January 975): 26–29. (Originally published 1858.)

Voyce, Arthur. "National Elements in Russian Architecture." *Journal of the Society of Architectural Historians* 16 (May 1957): 6–16.

Wrangell, Ferdinand Petrovich. *Russian America: Statistical and Ethnographic Information.* 1839. Reprint. Translated by Mary Sadouski; edited by Richard A. Pierce. Kingston, Ontario: Limestone Press, 1980.

American Alaskan

Aids to Navigation in Alaska History. Alaska Division of Parks, 1974.

The Alaska Almanac: Facts About Alaska—1990 Edition. Anchorage: Alaska Northwest Books, 1989.

Alaska Railroad, Office of the Territories Classified Files, 1907–1951, RG 126, National Archives and Records Service.

Antonson, Joan M., and William S. Hanable. "Administrative History of Sitka National Historical Park." Anchorage: National Park Service, Anchorage Region, 1987.

———. *Alaska's Heritage.* Anchorage: Alaska Historical Society for Alaska Historical Commission, Department of Education, State of Alaska, 1985.

Armstrong, Neal A. "Sheldon Jackson Scenes: A Documentary History of Sheldon Jackson Junior College, Sitka, Alaska, 1878–1967." M.A. thesis, George Peabody College for Teachers, 1967.

Bean, Tarleton H., U.S. Fish Commission. *Report on the Salmon and Salmon Rivers of Alaska.* Washington, D.C.: Government Printing Office, 1890.

Berton, Pierre. *The Klondike Fever: The Life and Death of the Last Great Gold Rush.* New York: Alfred A. Knopf, 1958.

Bowman, Phyllis. *Metlakahtla—The Holy City!* Privately printed, 1983.

Brooks, Alfred Hulse. *Blazing Alaska's Trails.* 1953. Fairbanks: University of Alaska Press, 1973.

Bryant, C. A. (Bert). "Another Man's Life." Alaska Historical Library, typescript, 1937.

Burton, G. Marion. "Automobiling on the Valdez Trail." *Collier's Outdoor America,* 16 July 1910, 21–22.

Bush, James D., Jr. "Narrative Report of Alaska Construction, 1941–1944." U.S. Army Corps of Engineers, 1944.

Carberry, Michael, and Donna Lane. *Patterns of the Past: An Inventory of Anchorage's Historic Resources.* Municipality of Anchorage, 1986.

Carlson, Axel. "Why Build a Log House?" *Alaska* 42 (August 1976): 16–18.

Cohen, Stan. *The Great Alaska Pipeline.* Missoula, Mont.: Pictorial Histories Publishing, 1988.

Colby, Merle, Federal Writers' Project. *A Guide to Alaska: Last American Frontier.* 1939. Reprint. New York: Macmillan, 1950.

Crittenden, Edwin B. "Cold Dry Climate Construction: Design and Construction under Arctic Conditions." In *Encyclopedia of Architecture: Design, Engineering and Construction,* edited by J. A. Wilkes and R. T. Packard, 642–59. New York: John Wiley and Sons, 1988.

Dean, David M. *Breaking Trail: Hudson Stuck of Texas and Alaska.* Athens: Ohio University Press, 1988.

DeLoach, Daniel B. *The Salmon Canning Industry.* Corvallis: Oregon State College, 1939.

Dunn, Stephen M. "Prebuilts and Conventional Construction: A Comparative Analysis of Single-Family Residential Development in Alaskan Metropolitan Areas." Typescript, 1972.

Frey, Martha. "Nuts About Huts." *Anchorage Historic Properties News* 2 (Summer 1989): 1–3.

Greeley, A. W. *Handbook of Alaska: Its Resources, Products, and Attractions.* New York: Charles Scribner's Sons, 1909.

Gruening, Ernest. *The State of Alaska.* New York: Random House, 1954.

Haigh, Jane G. *Alaska Pioneer Interiors: An Annotated Photographic File.* Fairbanks: Tanana-Yukon Historical Society, 1986.

Henderson, Alice Palmer. *The Rainbow's End: Alaska.* Chicago: Herbert S. Stone, 1898.

Hinckley, Ted C. *Alaskan John G. Brady: Missionary, Businessman, Judge, and Governor, 1878–1918.* Columbus: Ohio State University Press for Miami University, 1982.

———. "The Alaska Labors of Sheldon Jackson, 1877–1890." Ph.D. diss., Indiana University, 1961.

———. *The Americanization of Alaska, 1867–1897.* Palo Alto: Pacific Books, 1972.

Hulley, Clarence C. *Alaska: Past and Present.* Portland, Oreg.: Binfords and Mort, 1958.

Hunt, William R. *North of 53: The Wild Days of the Alaska-Yukon Mining Frontier, 1870–1914.* New York: Macmillan, 1974.

Johns, William Douglas. "The Early Yukon, Alaska, and the Klondike Discovery As They Were Before the Great Klondike Stampede Swept Away the Old Conditions Forever by One Who Was There." University of Washington Manuscript Collection. Typescript [1939].

Kieburtz, J. Richard. "Prefabrication in Alaska." *PF-The Magazine of Prefabrication* 2 (February 1954): 14–17.

Knik, Matanuska, Susitna: A Visual History of the Valleys. Matanuska-Susitna Borough, 1986.

McCarthy, Muriel Quest. *David R. Williams: Pioneer Architect.* Dallas: Southern Methodist University Press, 1984.

Mangusso, Mary Childers, and Stephen S. Haycox, eds. *Interpreting Alaska's History: An Anthology.* Anchorage: Alaska Pacific University Press, 1989.

Miller, Orlando W. *The Frontier in Alaska and the Matanuska Colony.* New Haven: Yale University Press, 1975.

Moore, William D. "From Peru to Alaska." University of Washington Manuscript Collection. Typescript [1923].

Moser, Jefferson F., U.S. Commission of Fish and Fisheries. *The Salmon and Salmon Fisheries of Alaska.* Washington, D.C.: Government Printing Office, 1899.

Murray, Peter. *The Devil and Mr. Duncan: A History of the Two Metlakatlas.* Victoria, B.C.: Sono Nis Press, 1985.

Naske, Claus-M. *Paving Alaska's Trails: The Work of the Alaska Road Commission.* Lanham, Md.: University Press of America, 1986.

Naske, Clause-M., and Herman E. Slotnick. 1979. 2d ed. *Alaska: A History of the 49th State.* Norman: University of Oklahoma Press, 1987.

Progress of Alaska Since Purchase: How Its Industries Began. Juneau: Alaska Bureau of Publicity, 1917.

Reports of the Governor of Alaska to the Secretary of the Interior, 1885–1903. Washington, D.C.: Government Printing Office, 1885–1903.

Selkregg, Lidia, Edwin B. Crittenden, and Norman Williams, Jr. "Urban Planning in the Reconstruction." In *The Great Alaska Earthquake of 1964: Human Ecology,* 186–242. Washington, D.C.: National Academy of Sciences, 1970.

Shortridge, James R. "The Alaskan Agricultural Empire: An American Agrarian Vision, 1898–1929." *Pacific Northwest Quarterly* 69 (October 1978): 145–58.

Spude, Robert L. S. *Skagway, District of Alaska, 1884–1912: Building the Gateway to the Klondike.* Fairbanks: University of Alaska Cooperative Park Studies Unit, 1983.

Spude, Robert L. S., and Sandra McDermott Faulkner, comps. *Kennecott, Alaska.* Anchorage: National Park Service, Alaska Region, 1987.

Stewart, Robert Laird. *Sheldon Jackson.* New York: Fleming H. Revell, 1908.

Stone, David, and Brenda Stone. *Hard Rock Gold: The Story of the Great Mines That Were the Heartbeat of Juneau.* Juneau: City and Borough of Juneau, Juneau Centennial Committee, 1980.

Stuck, Hudson. *The Alaskan Missions of the Episcopal Church.* New York: Domestic and Foreign Missionary Society, 1920.

———. *Ten Thousand Miles with a Dog Sled: A Narrative of Winter Travel in Interior Alaska.* 1914. Reprint. Lincoln: University of Nebraska Press, 1988.

Super, F. P. "The Men in the Wanigan," *Alaska Sportsman* 5 (November 1939): 10.

Tompkins, Stuart Ramsay. *Alaska: Promyshlennik and Sourdough.* Norman: University of Oklahoma Press, 1945.

"The Trans-Alaska Oil Pipeline: The Whole Story." *Alaska Construction and Oil.* Special Pipeline Report. September 1975.

U.S. Treasury Department, Bureau of Statistics. "Commercial Alaska in 1901." In *Summary of Commerce and Finance for May 1902.* Washington, D.C.: Government Printing Office, 1902.

Wharton, David. *The Alaska Gold Rush.* Bloomington: Indiana University Press, 1972.

Wickersham, James. *Old Yukon: Tales—Trails—and Trials.* Washington, D.C.: Washington Law Book Company, 1938.

———. Correspondence. University of Alaska Fairbanks, Archives.

———. Journal. Microfilm copy, University of Alaska Fairbanks, Archives.

Wilke, Steve, et al. "Cultural Resource Evaluation of the Old Kasaan Village Site and New Kasaan Community House and Totem Park, Alaska." Kasaan: Kavilco, 1982.

Wilson, William H. *Railroad in the Clouds: The Alaska Railroad in the Age of Steam, 1914–1945.* Boulder, Colo.: Pruett, 1977.

REGIONAL SOURCES

South-Central Region

ANCHORAGE

Evangeline Atwood. *Anchorage: All-American City.* Portland: Binfords and Mort, 1957.

Carberry, Michael, and Donna Lane. *Patterns of the Past: An Inventory of Anchorage's Historic Resources.* Anchorage: Municipality of Anchorage, 1986.

Municipality of Anchorage. *The Preservation and Reuse of the Potter Section House.* 1980.

Naske, Claus-M., and Ludwig J. Rowinski. *Anchorage: A Pictorial History.* Norfolk, Va.: The Donning Company, 1981.

CORDOVA

Arvidson, Rose C. *Cordova, The First 75 Years: A Photographic History.* Cordova: Fathom, 1984.

Nielsen, Nicki J. *From Fish and Copper: Cordova's Heritage and Buildings.* Cordova: Cordova Historical Society, 1984.

———. *The Red Dragon and St. George's: Glimpses into Cordova's Past.* 1983.

EKLUTNA

Ann Chandonnet. *On the Trail of Eklutna.* 1979. Reprint. Privately printed, 1985.

KENAI PENINSULA

Barry, Mary J. *A History of Mining on the Kenai Peninsula.* Anchorage: Alaska Northwest, 1973.

Klein, Janet. *A History of Kachemak Bay: The Country, the Communities.* Homer: Homer Society of Natural History, 1987.

Pederson, Elsa, ed. *A Larger History of the Kenai Peninsula.* Sterling: W. and E. Pederson, 1983.

KENNECOTT

Spude, Robert L. S., and Sandra McDermott Faulkner, comps. *Kennecott, Alaska.* Anchorage: National Park Service, 1987.

MAT-SU

Knik, Matanuska, Susitna: a Visual History of the Valleys. 1985. Reprint. Sutton, Alaska: Matanuska-Susitna Borough, 1986.

SEWARD

Barry, Mary J. *Seward, Alaska: A History of the Gateway City.* Part I: Prehistory to 1914. Anchorage, 1986.

Southeast Region

ANGOON

Frederica de Laguna. *The Story of a Tlingit Community: A Problem in the Relationship Between Archeological, Ethnological, and Historical Methods.* Smithsonian Institution, Bureau of American Ethnology, Bulletin 172, 1960. Reprint. Brighton, Mich.: Native American Book Publishers, 1980s.

HAINES

City of Haines: Survey of Historic Structures. *Building History.* 1983.

Hakkinen, Elisabeth S. *Haines—The First Century.* 1979.

JUNEAU

City and Borough of Juneau Planning Department. *Inventory of Historic Sites and Structures, City and Borough of Juneau, Alaska.* 1986.

Croft, Toni, and Phyllice Bradner. *Touring Juneau, or Backstreets, Byways, Bawdy-houses, Bars and Bodacious Biographies.* 1973

Stone, David, and Brenda Stone. *Hard Rock Gold . . . The Story of the Great Mines That Were the Heartbeat of Juneau, Alaska.* Juneau: City and Borough of Juneau, Juneau Centennial Committee, 1983.

KASAAN

Geo-Recon International. "Cultural Resource Evaluation of the Old Kasaan Village Site and New Kasaan Community House and Totem Park, Alaska." June 1982.

KETCHIKAN

Tucker, Phil. *Ketchikan: A City Historic Properties Survey.* Volume 2, *History and Preservation.* 1984.

METLAKATLA

Bowman, Phyllis. *Metlakahtla—The Holy City!* Privately printed, 1983.

Murray, Peter. *The Devil and Mr. Duncan: A History of the Two Metlakatlas.* Victoria, B.C.: Sono Nis Press, 1985.

SKAGWAY

Spude, Robert L. S. *Skagway, District of Alaska, 1884–1912: Building the Gateway to the Klondike.* Fairbanks: University of Alaska Cooperative Park Studies Unit, 1983.

———. *Chilkoot Trail.* Fairbanks: University of Alaska Cooperative Park Studies Unit,1980.

Interior

EAGLE

Shinkwin, Anne D., Elizabeth F. Andrews, Russell H. Sackett, and Mary V. Kroul. *Fort Egbert and the Eagle Historic District: Results of Archeological and Historic Research.* Anchorage: Bureau of Land Management, 1977.

FAIRBANKS

Boswell, John C. *History of Alaskan Operations of United States Smelting, Refining and Mining Company.* Mineral Industries Research Laboratory, UAF, 1979.

Cole, Terrence. *E. T. Barnette: The Strange Story of the Man Who Founded Fairbanks, Alaska.* 1981. Rev. ed. Anchorage: Alaska Northwest, 1984.

———. *Ghosts of the Gold Rush: A Walking Tour of Fairbanks.* 1977. Rev. ed. Tanana Yukon Historical Society, 1987.

Matheson, Janet. *Fairbanks: A City Historic Building Survey.* Fairbanks: City of Fairbanks, 1985.

Matheson, Janet, and F. Bruce Haldeman. *Historic Resources in the Fairbanks North Star Borough.* Fairbanks: Fairbanks North Star Planning Department, 1981.

Naske, Claus-M., and Ludwig J. Rowinski. *Fairbanks: A Pictorial History.* Norfolk, Va.: Donning Co., 1981.

Wold, Jo Anne. *This Old House: The Story of Clara Rust, Alaska Pioneer.* Anchorage: Alaska Northwest, 1976.

WISEMAN

Marshall, Robert. *Arctic Village.* New York: The Literary Guild, 1933.

Northern Region

ANAKTUVUK PASS

Spearman, Grant. "Land Use Values Through Time in the Anaktuvuk Pass Area." Fairbanks: University of Alaska Cooperative Park Studies Unit, 1978.

BARROW

Blackman, Margaret B. *Sadie Brower Neakok: An Inupiaq Woman.* Seattle: University of Washington Press, 1989.

Brower, Charles D. *Fifty Years Below Zero.* New York: Dodd, Mead and Co., 1942.

POINT HOPE

Shinkwin, Anne. *A Preservation Plan for Tigara Village.* North Slope Borough Commission on History and Culture, 1978.

PRUDHOE BAY

Crittenden, Edwin B. "ARCO Prudhoe Bay Operations Center." *The Northern Engineer* 9 (Spring 1977): 9–16.

Floyd, Peter. "The North Slope Center: How Was It Built?" *The Northern Engineer* 6 (Fall 1974): 22–36.

Western Region

BETHEL

Lenz, Mary, and James H. Barker. *Bethel: The First 100 Years.* Bethel: City of Bethel Centennial History Project, 1985.

IDITAROD TRAIL

Bureau of Land Management. *The Iditarod National Historic Trail: Seward to Nome Route.* Vol. 1, *A Comprehensive Management Plan.* Anchorage: 1981.

NOME

Cole, Terrence. *Nome: "City of the Golden Beaches."* Anchorage: Alaska Geographic, 1984.

PILGRIM HOT SPRINGS

Renner, Louis L., S.J. *Pioneer Missionary to the Bering Strait Eskimos: Bellarmine Lafortune, S.J.* Portland: Binford and Mort, 1979.

RUBY

Hart, Betsy. *The History of Ruby, Alaska, "The Gem of the Yukon."* National Bilingual Materials Development Center, Rural Education, University of Alaska, Anchorage, for Village History Project of U.S. Department of Interior, Anchorage, 1981.

Southwestern Region

DUTCH HARBOR

Denfeld, D. Colt. *The Defense of Dutch Harbor, Alaska, from Military Construction to Base Cleanup.* Anchorage: U.S. Army Corps of Engineers, 1987.

Faulkner, Sandra McDermott, and Robert L. S. Spude. *Naval Operating Base, Dutch Harbor and Fort Mears.* Anchorage: National Park Service, 1987.

Glossary

AIA See American Institute of Architects.

ambulatory A passageway around the apse of a church, allowing for circulation behind the sanctuary.

American Foursquare See foursquare house.

American Institute of Architects The national professional organization of architects, established in New York in 1857. The first national convention was held in New York in 1867, and at that meeting, provision was made for the creation of local chapters. In 1889, the American Institute of Architects absorbed the independent Chicago-based Western Association of Architects (established 1884). The headquarters of the national organization moved from New York to Washington in 1898. Abbreviated as AIA.

amvon In Russian Orthodox churches in Alaska, the dias in front of the iconostas. Derived from ambo or ambon.

antefix In classical architecture, a small upright decoration at the eaves of a roof, originally devised to hide the ends of the roof tiles. A similar ornament along the ridge of the roof.

antiquity The broad epoch of Western history preceding the Middle Ages and including such ancient civilizations as Egyptian, Greek, and Roman.

apse, apsidal A semicircular or polygonal feature projecting as a major element from an important interior space, especially at the chancel end of a church. Distinguished from an exedra, which is a semicircular or polygonal space, usually containing a bench, in the wall of a garden or nonreligious building. A substantial apse in a church, containing an ambulatory and radiating chapels, is called a chevet. The terms apse and chevet are used to describe the *form* of the end of the church containing the altar, while the terms chancel, choir, and sanctuary are used to describe the liturgical *function* of this end of the church and the spaces within it. Less substantial projections in nonreligious buildings are called bays if polygonal or bowfronts if curved.

arbor 1 An openwork structure covered with climbing plants. Distinguished from a trellis, which is generally a simpler, more two-dimensional structure, often attached to a wall. Distinguished from a pergola, which is an openwork structure supported by a colonnade, creating a shaded walk. **2** A grouping of closely planted trees or shrubs, trained together and self-supporting.

arcade 1 A series of arches, carried on columns or piers or other supports. **2** A covered walkway, one side of which is part of a building, while the other is open, as a series of arches, to the exterior. **3** In the nineteenth and early twentieth centuries, an interior street or other extensive space lined with shops and stores.

arch A curved construction that spans an opening. (Some arches may be flat or triangular, and many have a complex or compound curvature.) A masonry arch consists of a series of wedge-shaped parts (voussoirs) that press together toward the center while being restrained from spreading outward by the surrounding wall or the adjacent arch.

architrave 1 The lowest member of a classical entablature. **2** The moldings on the face of a wall around a doorway or other opening. Sometimes called the casing. Distinguished from the jambs, which are the vertical linings perpendicular to the wall planes at the sides of an opening. Distinguished from surround, a term usually applied to the entire door or window frame considered as a unit.

Art Deco A decorative style stimulated by the 1925 Exposition Internationale des Arts Décoratifs et Industriels Modernes, held in Paris. As the first phase of the Moderne, Art Deco is characterized by sharp angular and curvilinear forms, by a richness of materials (including polished metal, stone, and exotic woods), and by an overall sleekness of design. The style was often used in the commercial and residential architecture of the 1930s (e.g., skyscrapers, hotels, apartment buildings). Sometimes called Art Deco Moderne, Deco, Jazz Moderne, Zigzag Moderne, Zigzag Modernistic. See also the more general term Moderne and the related terms Mayan Revival, PWA Moderne, Streamline Moderne.

Art Moderne See Moderne.

Art Nouveau A style in architecture, interior design, and the decorative arts that flourished principally in France and Belgium in the 1890s. The Art Nouveau is characterized by undulating and whiplash lines and by sensuous organic forms. The Art Nouveau in Britain and the United States evolved from and overlapped with the Aesthetic movement.

Arts and Crafts A late nineteenth- and early twentieth-century movement in interior design and the decorative arts, emphasizing the importance of handcrafting for everyday objects. Arts and Crafts works are characterized by rectilinear geometries and high contrasts between figure and ground, and the furniture often features expressed construction. The term originated with the Arts and Crafts Exhibition Society, founded in England in 1888. Designers associated with the movement include C. F. A. Voysey (1857–1941) in England and the brothers Charles S. Greene

(1868–1957) and Henry M. Greene (1870–1954) in America. The Arts and Crafts movement evolved from and overlapped with the Aesthetic movement. For a more specific term, used in the United States after 1900, see also CRAFTSMAN.

ashlar Squared blocks of stone that fit tightly against one another.

atelier 1 A studio where the fine arts, including architecture, are taught. Applied particularly to the offices of prominent architects in Paris who provided design training to students enrolled in or informally attached to the Ecole des Beaux-Arts. By extension, any working office where some organized teaching is done. **2** A place where artworks or handicrafts are produced by skilled workers. **3** An artist's studio or workshop.

attic 1 The area beneath the roof and above the main stories (or story) of a building. Sometimes called a garret. **2** A low story above the entablature, often a blocklike mass that caps the building.

axis An imaginary center line to which are referred the parts of a building or the relations of a number of buildings to one another.

axonometric drawing A pictorial drawing using axonometric projection, in which horizontal lines that are perpendicular (usually at two 45-degree angles from the vertical, or at complementary angles of 30 and 60 degrees). Consequently, all angular and dimensional relationships in plan remain the same in the drawing as in the thing depicted. Sometimes called an axon or an axonometric. See also the relted terms ISOMETRIC DRAWING, PERSPECTIVE DRAWING.

baluster One of a series of short vertical members, often vase-shaped in profile, used to support a handrail for a stair or a railing. Balusters that are thinner and simpler in profile are sometimes called banisters.

balustrade A series of balusters or posts supporting a rail or coping across the top (and sometimes resting on a lower rail). Balustrades are often found on stairs, balconies, parapets, and terraces.

band course Ambiguous term. See instead BAND MOLDING or STRINGCOURSE.

band molding In masonry or frame construction, any horizontal flat member or molding or group of moldings projecting slightly from a wall and marking a division in the wall. Not properly a synonym for band course. Simpler horizontal bands in masonry are generally called stringcourses.

banister 1 Corrupted spelling of baluster, in use since about the seventeenth century. Now occasionally used for balusters that are thinner and simpler in profile than classical vase-shaped balusters. **2** Improperly used to mean the handrail of a stair.

barabara Russian term for the traditional Aleut semisubterranean, sod-covered dwelling.

bargeboard An ornate fascia board that is attached to the sloping edges (verges) of a roof, covering the ends of the horizontal roof timbers (purlins).

Bargeboards are usually ornamented with carved, turned, or jigsawn forms. Sometimes called gableboards, vergeboards. Less ornate boards along the verges of a roof are simply called fascia boards.

Baroque A style of art and architecture that flourished in Europe and colonial North America during the seventeenth and eighteenth centuries. Although based on the architecture of the Renaissance, Baroque architecture was more dynamic, with circles frequently giving way to ovals, flat walls to curved or undulating ones, and separate elements to interlocking forms. It was a monumental and richly three-dimensional style with elaborate systems of ornamental and figural sculpture. See also the related terms RENAISSANCE, ROCOCO.

Baroque Revival See NEO-BAROQUE.

barrel vault A vaulted roof or ceiling of semicircular or semielliptical cross section, forming a tunnellike enclosure over an apartment, corridor, or similar space.

basement 1 The lowest story of a building, either partly or entirely below grade. **2** The lower part of the walls of any building, usually articulated distinctly from the upper part of the walls.

batten 1 A narrow strip of wood applied to cover a joint along the edges of two parallel boards in the same plane. **2** A strip of wood fastened across two or more parallel boards to hold them together. Sometimes called a cross batten. See also the related term BOARD-AND-BATTEN SIDING.

battered (adjective). Inclined from the vertical. A wall is said to be battered or to have a batter when it recedes as it rises.

battlement, battlemented See CRENELLATION.

bay 1 The interval between two recurring members. A facade is frequently measured by window bays, a skeletal frame by structural bays. **2** A polygonal or curved unit of one or more stories, projecting from the wall and usually containing grouped windows (bay windows) on each story. See also the more specific term BOWFRONT.

bay window The horizontally grouped windows in a projecting bay (definition **2**), or the projecting bay itself, if it is not more than one story. Distinguished from an oriel, which does not rise from the foundation and has a suspended rather than rooted appearance. A semicircular or semielliptical bay window is called a bow window. A bay window with a central section of plate glass in a late nineteenth-century commercial building is called a Chicago window.

beam A structural spanning member of stone, wood, iron, steel, or reinforced concrete. See also the more specific terms GIRDER, I-BEAM, JOIST.

bearing wall A wall that is fully structural, carrying the load of the floors and roof all the way to the foundation. Sometimes called a supporting wall. Distinguished from curtain wall. See also the related term LOAD-BEARING.

Beaux-Arts Historicist design on a monumental

scale, as taught at the Ecole des Beaux-Arts in Paris throughout the nineteenth century and early twentieth century. The term Beaux-Arts is generally applied to an eclectic Roman-Renaissance-Baroque architecture of the 1850s through the 1920s, disseminated internationally by students and followers of the Ecole des Beaux-Arts. As a general style term Beaux-Arts connotes an academically grounded discipline for historical eclecticism, rather than one single style, as well as the disciplined development of a *parti* into a fully visualized design. More specific style terms include Neo-Grec (1840s-1870s) and Beaux-Arts Classicism (1870s–1930s). See also the related terms NEOCLASSICISM, for describing Ecole-related work from the 1790s to the 1840s, and SECOND EMPIRE, for describing the work from the 1850s to the 1880s.

Beaux-Arts Classicism, Beaux-Arts Classical Term applied to eclectic Roman-Renaissance-Baroque architecture and urbanism after the Neo-Grec and Second Empire phases, i.e., from the 1870s through the 1930s. Sometimes called Classic Revival, Classical Revival, McKim Classicism, Neoclassical Revival. See also the more general term BEAUX-ARTS and the related terms CITY BEAUTIFUL MOVEMENT, PWA MODERNE.

belfry A cupola, turret, or room in a tower where a bell is housed.

belt course See STRINGCOURSE.

belvedere 1 Any building, especially a pavilion or shelter, that is located to take advantage of a view. See also the related term GAZEBO. **2** See CUPOLA (definition 2).

beveled siding As used here, horizontal wood siding of boards with bevels at top and bottom edges, which when laid together create recessed V-joints.

blind (adjective). Term applied to the surface use of elements that would otherwise articulate an opening but where no opening exists. Used in such combinations as blind arcade, blind arch, blind door, blind window.

board-and-batten siding A type of siding for wood frame buildings, consisting of wide vertical boards with narrow strips of wood (battens) covering the joints. In rare instances, the battens may be fastened behind the joints. If the gaps between boards are wide and the back battens approach the width of the outer boards, the siding is called board-on-board.) See also the related term BATTEN.

board-on-board siding A type of siding for wood frame buildings, consisting of two layers of vertical boards, with the outer layer of boards covering the wide gaps between the boards of the inner layer.

bowfront A semicircular or semielliptical bay (definition 2).

bow window A semicircular or semielliptical bay window.

brace A single wooden or metal member placed diagonally within a framework or truss or beneath an overhang. Distinguished from a bracket, which is a more substantial triangular feature, and from a strut, which is essentially a post set in a diagonal position.

braced frame construction A combination of heavy and light timber frame construction, in which the principal vertical and horizontal framing members (posts and girts) are fastened by mortise and tenon joints, while the one-story-high studs are nailed to the heavy timber frame. The overall frame is made more rigid by diagonal braces. Sometimes called braced framing.

bracket Any solid, pierced, or built-up triangular feature projecting from the face of a wall to support a projecting element, like the top member of a cornice or the verges or eaves of a roof. Brackets are frequently used for ornamental as well as structural purposes. Distinguished from a brace, which is a simple barlike structural member. Distinguished from the more specific term console, which has a height greater than its projection from the wall. See also the related term CORBEL.

brick bonds, brickwork See the more specific terms COMMON BOND, ENGLISH BOND, FLEMISH BOND, RUNNING BOND.

British colonial A term applied to buildings, towns, landscapes, and other artifacts from the period of actual British colonial occupation of large parts of eastern North American (c. 1607–1781 for the United States; c. 1750s–1867 for much of Canada). The British colonial period saw the introduction into the New World of various regional strains of English and Scotch-Irish folk culture, as well as high-style Anglo-European Renaissance, Baroque, and Neoclassical design. Sometimes called English colonial. Loosely called colonial or Early American. See also the related term GEORGIAN PERIOD.

Brutalism An architectural style of the 1950s through 1970s, characterized by complex massing and by a frank expression of structural members, elements of building systems, and materials (especially concrete). Some of the work of Paul Rudolph (born 1918) is associated with this style. Sometimes called New Brutalism.

bungalow A low one- or one-and-a-half-story house of modest pretensions with a low-pitched gable or hipped roof, a conspicuous porch, and projecting eaves. This house type was a popular builders' type from around 1900 to 1930. The term bungalow was also loosely applied to any vernacular building of a semirustic nature, including vacation cottages and lodges.

buttress An exterior mass of masonry bonded into a wall that it strengthens or supports. Buttresses often absorb lateral thrusts from roofs or vaults.

Byzantine Term applied to the art and architecture of the Eastern Roman Empire centered at Byzantium (i.e., Constantinople, Istanbul) from the early 500s to the mid-1400s. Byzantine architecture is characterized by massive domes, round arches, richly carved capitals, and the extensive use of mosaic.

Byzantine Revival See NEO-BYZANTINE.

cache A storage building, usually raised on posts.

campanile In Italian, a bell tower. While usually freestanding in medieval and Renaissance architecture, it was often incorporated as a prominent unit in the massing of picturesque nineteenth-century buildings.

cantilever A beam, girder, slab, truss, or other structural member that projects beyond its supporting wall or column.

cap A canopy, ledge, molding, or pediment over a window. Sometimes called a window cap. Distinguished from a hood, which is a similar feature over a door. See also the related term HEAD MOLD-ING.

capital The moldings and carved enrichment at the top of a column, pilaster, pier, or pedestal.

Carpenter's Gothic. Term applied to a version of the Gothic Revival (c.1840–1870), in which Gothic motifs are adapted to the kind of wooden details that can be produced by lathes, jigsaws, and molding machines. Sometimes called Gingerbread style, Steamboat Gothic. See also the more general term GOTHIC REVIVAL.

carriage porch See PORTE-COCHÈRE.

casement window A window that opens from the side on hinges, like a door, out from the plane of the wall. Distinguished from a double-hung window.

casing See ARCHITRAVE (definition 2).

cast iron Iron shaped by a molding process, generally strong in compression but brittle in tension. Distinguished from wrought iron, which has been forged to increase its tensile properties.

cast-iron front An architectural facade made of prefabricated molded iron parts, often markedly skeletal in appearance with extensive glass infilling. Prevalent from the late 1840s to the early 1870s.

cement A mixture of burnt lime and clay with water, which hardens permanently when dry. When a fine aggregate of sand is added, the cement may be used as a mortar for masonry construction or as a plaster or stucco coating. When a coarser aggregate of gravel or crushed stone is added, along with sand, the mixture is called concrete.

chamfer The oblique surface formed by cutting off a square edge at an equal angle to each face.

chancel 1 The end of a Roman Catholic or High Episcopal church containing the altar and set apart for the clergy and choir by a screen, rail, or steps. Usually the entire east end of a church beyond the crossing. In churches that have a long chancel space, the part of the chancel between the crossing and the apse, where the singers participate in the service, is called the choir. The innermost part of the chancel, containing the principal altar, is called the sanctuary. **2** In less extensive Catholic and Episcopal churches, the terms chancel and choir are often used interchangeably to mean the entire eastern arm of the church.

choir 1 The part of a Roman Catholic or High Episcopal church where the singers participate in the service. Usually the space within the chancel arm of the church, situated between the crossing to the west and the sanctuary to the east. **2** In less extensive Catholic and Episcopal churches, the terms choir and chancel are often used interchangeably to mean the entire eastern arm of the church.

clapboard A tapered board that is thinner along the top edge and thicker along the bottom edge, applied horizontally with edges overlapping to provide weathertight siding on a building of wood construction. Early clapboards were split (rived, riven) and were used for barrel staves and for wainscoting. The term now applies to any beveled siding board, whether split or sawn, rabbeted or not, regardless of length or width. (The term is sometimes applied only to a form of bevel siding used in New England, about 4 feet long and quarter-sawn.) Sometimes called weatherboards.

classical orders See ORDER.

classical rectangle See GOLDEN SECTION.

Classical Revival Ambiguous term, suggesting **1** Neoclassical design of the late eighteenth and early nineteenth centuries, including the Greek Revival; or **2** Beaux-Arts Classical design of the late nineteenth and early twentieth centuries. Sometimes called Classic Revival. See instead BEAUX-ARTS CLASSICISM, GREEK REVIVAL, NEOCLASSICISM.

classicism, classical, classicizing Terms describing the application of principles or elements derived from the visual arts of the Greco-Roman era (seventh century B.C.E. through fourth century C.E.) at any subsequent period of Western civilization, but particularly since the Renaissance. More a descriptive term for an approach to design and for a general cultural sensibility than for any particular style. See also the related term NEOCLASSI-CISM.

clipped gable roof See JERKINHEAD ROOF.

coffer A recessed panel, usually square or octagonal, in a ceiling. Such panels are also found on the inner surfaces of domes and vaults.

colonial 1 Not strictly a style term, but a term for the entire period during which a particular European country held political dominion over a part of the Western Hemisphere, Africa, Asia, Australia, or Oceania. See also the more specific terms BRITISH COLONIAL, DUTCH COLONIAL, FRENCH CO-LONIAL, SPANISH COLONIAL. **2** Loosely used to mean the British colonial period in North America (c. 1607–1781 for the United States; c. 1750s–1867 for much of Canada).

Colonial Revival Generally understood to mean the revival of forms from British colonial design. The Colonial Revival began in New England in the 1860s and continues nationwide into the present. Sometimes called Neo-Colonial. See also the more specific term GEORGIAN REVIVAL and the related terms FEDERAL REVIVAL, SHINGLE STYLE.

colonnade A series of freestanding or engaged columns supporting an entablature or simple beam.

colonnette A diminutive, often attenuated, column.

colossal order See GIANT ORDER.

column 1 A vertical supporting element, usually cylindrical and slightly tapering, consisting of a base (except in the Greek Doric order), shaft, and capital. See also the related terms ENTABLATURE, ENTASIS, ORDER. **2** Any vertical supporting element in a skeletal frame.

concrete An artificial stone made by mixing cement, water, sand, and a coarse aggregate (such as gravel or crushed stone) in specified proportions. The mix is shaped in molds called forms. Distinguished from cement, which is the binder without the aggregate.

corbel A projecting stone that supports a superincumbent weight. In medieval architecture and its derivatives, a support for such major features as vaulting shafts, vaulting ribs, or oriels. See also the related term BRACKET.

corbeled construction Masonry that is built outward beyond the vertical by letting successive courses project beyond those below. Sometimes called corbeling.

corbeled cornice A cornice made up of courses of projecting masonry, each of which extends farther outward than the one below.

cornice The crowning member of a wall or entablature.

Corporate International style A term, not widely used, for curtain wall commercial, institutional, and governmental buildings since the Second World War, which represent a widespread adoption of selected International style ideas from the 1920s. See also the more general term INTERNATIONAL STYLE.

cottage 1 A relatively modest rural or suburban dwelling. Distinguished from a villa, which is a more substantial and often more elaborate dwelling. **2** A seasonal dwelling, regardless of size, especially one located in a resort community.

course A layer of building blocks, such as bricks or stones, extending the full length and thickness of a wall.

coved ceiling A ceiling in which the transition between wall and ceiling is formed by a large concave panel or molding. Sometimes called a cove ceiling.

coved cornice A cornice with a concave profile. Sometimes called a cavetto cornice.

Craftsman A style of furniture and interior design belonging to the Arts and Crafts movement in the United States, and specifically related to *The Craftsman* magazine (1901–1916), published by Gustav Stickley (1858–1942). Some entire houses known to be derived from this publication can be called Craftsman houses. See also the more general term ARTS AND CRAFTS.

crenellation, crenellated A form of embellishment on a parapet consisting of indentations (crenels or embrasures) alternating with solid blocks of wall (merlons). Virtually synonymous with battlement, battlemented; embattlement, embattled.

cresting An ornamental strip or fencelike feature, usually of metal or tile, along the ridgeline or summit of a roof.

cribbed roof Roof of logs or planks laid horizontally in alternate directions and closer together each round, so that the roof slopes.

crossing In a church with a cruciform plan, the area where the arms of the cross intersect; specifically, the space where the transept crosses the nave and chancel.

cross rib See LIERNE.

cross section See SECTION.

crown The central, or highest, part of an arch or vault.

crown molding The highest in a series of moldings.

cruciform In the shape of a cross. Usually used to describe the ground plans of buildings. See also the more specific terms GREEK CROSS, LATIN CROSS.

cupola 1 A small domed structure on top of a belfry, steeple, or tower. **2** A lantern, square or polygonal in plan, with windows or vents, which is located at the summit of a roof. Sometimes called a belvedere. Distinguished from a skylight, which is a lesser feature located on the slope of a roof. **3** In historic English usage, synonymous with dome. A dome is now understood to be a more substantial feature.

curtain wall In skeleton frame or reinforced concrete construction, a thin nonstructural cladding of stone, brick, terracotta, glass, or metal veneer. Distinguished from bearing wall. See also the related term LOAD-BEARING.

cusp The pointed, roughly triangular intersection of the arcs of lobes or foils in the tracery of windows, screens, or panels.

Deco See ART DECO.

dentil, denticulated A small ornamental block forming one of a series set in a row. A dentil molding is composed of such a series.

discharging arch See RELIEVING ARCH.

dome A major hemispherical or curved roof feature rising from a circular, polygonal, or square base. Distinguished from a cupola, which is a smaller, usually subordinate, domical element.

dormer A roof-sheltered window (or vent), usually with vertical sides and front, set into a sloping roof. Sometimes called a dormer window.

double-hung window A window consisting of a pair of frames, or sashes, one above the other, arranged to slide up and down. Their movement is sometimes stabilized by a system of cords and counterbalancing weights contained in narrow boxing at each side of the window frame. Sometimes called guillotine sash.

drum 1 A cylindrical or polygonal wall zone upon which a dome rests. **2** One of the cylinders of stone that form the shaft of a column.

Dutch colonial A term applied to buildings, towns, landscapes, and other artifacts from the period of actual Dutch colonial occupation of the Hudson River valley and adjacent areas (c. 1614–1664). Meaning has been extended to apply to the artifacts of Dutch ethnic groups and their descendants, even into the early nineteenth century.

Dutch Colonial Revival The revival of forms from design in the Dutch tradition.

Early Gothic Revival A term for the Gothic Revival work of the late eighteenth to the mid-nineteenth century. See also the related term LATE GOTHIC REVIVAL.

Eastlake A decorative arts and interior design term of the 1860s and 1880s sometimes applied to architecture. Named after Charles Locke Eastlake (1836–1906), an English advocate of the application of Gothic principles of construction and design, rather than mere Gothic elements. Characterized by simplicity and solidity of forms, which are sometimes embellished with chamfered, turned, or incised details. Sometimes called Eastlake Gothic, Modern Gothic. See also the related term QUEEN ANNE.

eaves The horizontal lower edges of a roof plane, usually projecting beyond the wall below. Distinguished from verges, which are the sloping edges of a roof plane.

eclecticism, eclectic A sensibility in design, prevalent since the eighteenth century, involving the selection of elements from a variety of sources, including historical periods of high-style design (Western and non-Western), vernacular design (Western and non-Western), and (in the twentieth century) contemporary industrial design. Distinguished from historicism and revivalism by drawing upon a wider range of sources than the historical periods of high-style design.

Ecole, Ecole des Beaux-Arts See BEAUX-ARTS.

Egyptian Revival Term applied to eclectic works or elements of those works that emulate forms in the visual arts of ancient Egyptian civilization.

elevation A drawing (in orthographic projection) of an upright, planar aspect of an object or building. The vertical complement of a plan. Sometimes loosely used in the sense of a facade view or any frontal representation of a wall, whether photograph or drawing, whether measured to scale or not.

Elizabethan Manor Style See NEO-TUDOR.

engaged column A half-round column attached to a wall. Distinguished from a freestanding column by seeming to be built into the wall. Distinguished from a pilaster, which is a flattened column. Distinguished from a recessed column, which is a fully round column set into a nichelike space.

English colonial See BRITISH COLONIAL.

entablature In a classical order, a richly detailed horizontal member resting on columns or pilasters. It is divided horizontally into three main parts. The lowest is the architrave (definition 1), the structural part, and is generally an unornamented continuous beam or series of beams. The middle part is the frieze (definition 1), which is

generally the most freely ornamented part. The uppermost is the cornice. Composed of a sequence of moldings, the cornice overhangs the frieze and architrave and serves as a crown to the whole. Each part has the moldings and decorative treatment that are characteristic of the particular order, but modern adaptations often alter canonical details. See also the related terms COLUMN, ORDER.

exotic revivals A term occasionally used to suggest a distinction between revivals of European styles (e.g., Greek, Gothic Revivals) and non-European styles (e.g., Egyptian, Moorish Revivals). See also the more specific terms EGYPTIAN REVIVAL, MAYAN REVIVAL, MOORISH REVIVAL.

eyebrow dormer A low dormer with a small segmental window or vent but no sides. The roofing warps or bows over the window or vent in a wavy line.

facade An exterior face of a building, especially the principal or entrance front. Distinguished from an elevation, which is an orthographic drawing of a building face.

false half-timbering A surface treatment that simulates half-timber construction, consisting of a lattice of broad boards and stucco applied as an exterior veneer on a building of masonry or wood frame construction. Most commonly seen in domestic architecture from the late nineteenth century onward.

fanlight A semicircular or semielliptical window over a door, with radiating mullions in the form of an open fan. Sometimes called a sunburst light. See also the more general term TRANSOM (definition 1) and the related term SIDELIGHT.

fan vault A type of Gothic vault in which the primary ribs all have the same curvature and radiate in a half circle around the springing point.

fascia 1 A plain, molded, or ornamented board that covers the horizontal edges (eaves) or sloping edges (verges) of a roof. Distinguished from the more specific term bargeboards, which are ornate fascia boards attached to the sloping edges of a roof. Distinguished from a frieze (definition 2), which is located at the top of a wall. **2** One of the broad continuous bands that make up the architrave of the IONIC, CORINTHIAN, or COMPOSITE ORDER.

Federal A version of Neoclassical architecture in the United States popular from New England to Virginia, and in other regions influenced by the Northeast. It flourished from the 1790s through the 1820s and is found in some regions as late as the 1840s. Sometimes called American Adam style. Not to be confused with FEDERALIST. See also the related term ROMAN REVIVAL.

festoon A motif representing entwined leaves, flowers, or fruits, hung in a catenary curve from two points. Distinguished from a swag, which is a motif representing a fold of drapery hung in a similar curve. See also the more general term GARLAND.

fireproofing In metal skeletal framing, the wrapping of structural members in terracotta tile or other fire-resistant material.

flashing A strip of metal, plastic, or various flexible compositional materials used at roof valleys and ridges and at chimney corners to keep water out. Any similar material used to protect door and window heads and sills.

Flemish gable A gable whose upper slopes ascend in steps rather than in a straight line. These steps may be rectilinear or curved, or a combination of both.

fluting, fluted A series of parallel grooves or channels (flutes), usually semicircular or semielliptical in plan, that accentuate the verticality of the shaft of a column or pilaster.

foliated (adjective). In the form of leaves or leaflike shapes.

folk Not a style term in itself, but a descriptive term, applicable to all the visual arts and all styles and periods. Applied to **1** a regional, often ethnic, tradition in which continuities through the years in the overall appearance of artifacts (including buildings) are more important than changes in stylistic embellishment; **2** the work of individual artists and artisans unexposed to or uninterested in prevailing or avant-garde ideals of form and technique. Approximate synonyms include anonymous, naive, primitive, traditional. For architecture, see also the more general term VERNACULAR and the related term POPULAR.

foursquare house A hipped-roof, two-story house with four principal rooms on each floor and a symmetrical facade. It usually has a front porch across the full width of the house and one or more large dormers on the roof. A common suburban house type from the 1890s to the 1920s. Sometimes called American Foursquare, Prairie Box.

frame construction, frame Ambiguous terms. See instead BRACED FRAME CONSTRUCTION, LIGHT FRAME CONSTRUCTION (PLATFORM FRAME CONSTRUCTION), SKELETON CONSTRUCTION, TIMBER FRAME CONSTRUCTION. Not properly synonymous with wood construction, wood-clad, or wooden.

frieze 1 The broad horizontal band that forms the central part of a classical entablature. **2** Any long horizontal band or zone, especially one that has a chiefly decorative purpose, located at the top of a wall. Distinguished from a fascia, which is attached to the horizontal edge of a roof.

front gabled Term applied to a building whose principal gable end faces the front of the lot or some feature like a street or open space. Sometimes called gable front. Distinguished from side gabled.

gable The wall area immediately below the end of a gable, gambrel, or jerkinhead roof.

gableboard See BARGEBOARD.

gable front See FRONT GABLED.

gable roof A roof in which the two planes slope equally toward each other to a common ridge. Sometimes called a pitched roof.

gambrel roof A roof that has a single ridgepole

but a double pitch. The lower plane, which rises from the eaves, is rather steep. The upper plane, which extends from the lower plane to the ridgeline, has a flatter pitch.

garland A motif representing a rope of entwined leaves, flowers, ribbons, or drapery, regardless of its shape or position. It may be formed into a wreath, festoon, or swag, or follow the outline of a rectilinear architectural element.

gauged brick A brick that has been cut or rubbed to a uniform size and shape.

gazebo A small pavilion, usually polygonal or circular in plan and serving as a garden or park shelter. Distinguished from a kiosk, which generally has some commercial or public function. See also the related terms BANDSTAND, BELVEDERE (definition 1).

Georgian period A term for a period in British and British colonial history, and not, in architecture or the other visual arts, a sufficiently specific style term. The Georgian period begins with the coronation of George I in 1714 and extends until about 1781 in the area that became the United States (and in Britain, until the death of George IV in 1830). See also the related terms ANGLO-PALLADIANISM, BRITISH COLONIAL.

Georgian Revival A revival of Georgian period forms—in England, from the 1860s to the present, and in the United States, from the 1880s to the present. Sometimes called Neo-Georgian. See also the more general term COLONIAL REVIVAL and the related term FEDERAL REVIVAL.

Gingerbread style See CARPENTER'S GOTHIC.

girder A major horizontal spanning member, comparable in function to a beam, but larger and often built up of a number of parts. It usually runs at right angles to the beams and serves as their principal means of support.

girt In timber-frame construction, a horizontal beam at intermediate (e.g., second-floor) level, spanning between posts.

glazing bar See MUNTIN.

Gothic An architectural style prevalent in Europe from the twelfth century into the fifteenth in Italy (and into the sixteenth century in the rest of Europe). It is characterized by pointed arches and ribbed vaults and by the dominance of openings over masonry mass in the wall. The Gothic was preceded by the Romanesque and followed by the Renaissance.

Gothic Revival A movement in Europe and North America devoted to reviving the forms and the spirit of Gothic architecture and the allied arts. It originated in the mid-eighteenth century. Sometimes called the Pointed style in the nineteenth century, and sometimes called Neo-Gothic. See also the more specific terms EARLY GOTHIC REVIVAL, HIGH VICTORIAN GOTHIC, LATE GOTHIC REVIVAL.

Grecian A nineteenth-century term for GREEK REVIVAL.

Greek cross A cross with four equal arms. Usually

used to describe the ground plan of a building. See also the more general term CRUCIFORM.

Greek Revival A movement in Europe and North America devoted to reviving the forms and the spirit of Classical Greek architecture, sculpture, and decorative arts. It originated in the mid-eighteenth century, culminated in the 1830s, and continued into the 1850s. Sometimes called Grecian in the nineteenth century. See also the more general term NEOCLASSICAL.

HABS See HISTORIC AMERICAN BUILDINGS SURVEY.

HAER See HISTORIC AMERICAN ENGINEERING RECORD.

half-timber construction A variety of timber frame construction in which the framing members are exposed on the exterior of the wall, with the spaces between timbers being filled with wattle-and-daub (i.e., woven lath and plaster) or masonry materials, such as brick or stone. These masonry materials may also be covered with stucco. Sometimes called half-timbered construction.

head molding A molding or set of moldings designed to shelter and embellish the top of a door or window. Sometimes called a drip molding. See also the related terms CAP (for windows) and HOOD (for doors).

heavy timber construction See TIMBER-FRAME CONSTRUCTION.

high style or high-style (adjective). Not a style term in itself, but a descriptive term, applicable to all the visual arts and all styles and periods. Applied to the works of the masters and their schools and disciples, usually reflecting a cosmopolitan awareness of traditions beyond a particular place or time. Usually contrasted with vernacular (including the folk and popular traditions).

high tech Term applied to architecture in which building materials and elements of building systems are used to celebrate contemporary technology. Elemental geometric forms, primary colors, and metallic finishes are used to heighten the technological imagery.

High Victorian Gothic A version of the Gothic Revival that originated in England in the 1850s and spread to North America in the 1860s. Characterized by polychromatic exteriors inspired by the medieval Gothic architecture of northern Italy. Sometimes called Ruskin Gothic, Ruskinian Gothic, Venetian Gothic, Victorian Gothic. See also the more general term GOTHIC REVIVAL.

hip gable roof See JERKINHEAD ROOF.

hip roof A roof that pitches inward from all four sides. The edge where any two planes meet is called the hip.

Historic American Buildings Survey A branch of the National Park Service of the United States Department of the Interior, established in 1933 to produce detailed documentation of American architecture. Such documentation typically includes historical and architectural data, photographs, and measured drawings, and is deposited in the Prints

and Photographs Division of the Library of Congress. Abbreviated as HABS. See also the related term HISTORIC AMERICAN ENGINEERING RECORD.

Historic American Engineering Record A branch of the National Park Service of the United States Department of the Interior, established in 1969 to produce detailed documentation of sites and structures associated with industry, transportation, and other areas of technology. Abbreviated as HAER. See also the related term HISTORIC AMERICAN BUILDINGS SURVEY.

historicism, historicist, historicizing A type of eclecticism prevalent since the eighteenth century, involving the use of forms from historical periods of high-style design (usually in the Western tradition) and, occasionally, from favored traditions of vernacular design (such as the various colonial traditions in the United States). Historicist influences are designated by the use of the prefix Neo- with a previous historical style (e.g., Neo-Baroque). Distinguished from the more general term eclecticism, which draws upon a wider range of sources in addition to the historical. See also the more specific term REVIVALISM.

hood A canopy, ledge, molding, or pediment over a door. Distinguished from a cap, which is a similar feature over a window. Sometimes called a hood molding. See also the related term HEAD MOLDING.

horizontal plank frame construction A system of wood construction in which horizontal planks are set or nailed into the corner posts of a timber frame building. There are, however, no studs or intermediate posts connecting the sill and the plate. See also the related term VERTICAL PLANK FRAME CONSTRUCTION.

hyphen A subsidiary building unit, often one story, connecting the central block and the wings or dependencies.

I-beam The most common profile in steel structural shapes (although it also appears in cast iron and in reinforced concrete). Used especially for spanning elements, it is shaped like the capital letter "I" to make the most efficient use of the material consistent with a shape that permits easy assemblage. The vertical face of the "I" is the web. The horizontal faces are the flanges. Other standard shapes for steel framing elements are Hs, Ts, Zs, Ls (known as angles), and square-cornered Us (channels).

iconostas Alaskan term from the Russian for the more usual iconostasis. The partition wall separating the sanctuary and nave, decorated with icons and with three doorways.

International style A style that originated in the 1920s and flourished into the 1970s, characterized by the expression of volume and surface and by the suppression of historicist ornament and axial symmetry. The term was originally applied by Henry-Russell Hitchcock and Philip Johnson to the new, nontraditional, mostly European, architecture of the 1920s in their 1932 exhibition at the Museum of Modern Art and in their accompanying book, *The International Style.* Also called International, International Modern. See also the related terms BAUHAUS, MIESIAN, SECOND CHICAGO SCHOOL.

Italianate 1 A general term for an eclectic Neo-Renaissance and Neo-Romanesque style, originating in England and Germany in the early nineteenth century and prevalent in the United States between the 1840s and 1880s, not only in houses but also in Main Street commercial buildings. The Italianate is characterized by prominent window heads and bracketed cornices. Called the Bracketed style in the nineteenth century. See also the more specific term ITALIAN VILLA STYLE and the related terms RENAISSANCE REVIVAL, ROUND ARCH MODE, SECOND EMPIRE. **2** A specific term for Italianate buildings that are predominantly symmetrical in plan and elevation. Distinguished from Barryesque, which is applied to more formal institutional and governmental buildings.

Jacobean period A term for a period in British history coinciding with the rule of James I (1603–1625). See also the related term ELIZABETHAN PERIOD for the immediately preceding period, which itself is part of the TUDOR PERIOD.

jamb The vertical side face of a door or window opening, amounting to the full thickness of the wall, and usually enriched with paneling, moldings, or jamb shafts (which are engaged columns set into a splayed, or angled, jamb). In an opening containing a door or window, the jamb is distinguished from the reveal, which is the portion of wall thickness between the door or window frame and the outer surface of the wall. (In an opening without a door or window, the terms jamb and reveal are used interchangeably.) Also distinguished from an architrave (definition 2), which consists of the moldings on the face of a wall around the opening.

jerkinhead roof A gable roof in which the upper portion of the gable end is hipped, or inclined inward along the ridgeline, forming a small triangle of roof surface. Sometimes called a clipped gable roof or hipped gable roof.

joist One of a series of small horizontal beams that support a floor or ceiling.

kashim Russian term for a large building used by male Eskimos for social or ritual gatherings. The word was *kazigi* or *kashgee* in Yupik, *karigi* in Inupiaq.

keystone The central wedge-shaped stone at the crown of an arch.

king post In a truss, the vertical suspension member that connects the tie beam with the apex of opposing principal rafters.

kiosk Originally, a Turkish summer palace. Since the nineteenth century, the term has been applied to any small pavilion or stand, usually found in public gardens, parks, streets, and malls, where it serves some commercial or public function. Distinguished from a gazebo, which may be found in public or private gardens or parks, but which

usually serves as a sheltered resting place. See also the related term BANDSTAND.

label 1 A drip molding, over a square-headed door or window, which extends for a short distance down each side of the opening. **2** A similar vertical downward extension of a drip molding over an arch of any form. Sometimes called a label molding.

Late Gothic Revival A term for the Gothic Revival work of the late nineteenth and early twentieth centuries. See also the more specific term COLLEGIATE GOTHIC (definition **2**) and the related term EARLY GOTHIC REVIVAL.

lath A latticelike, continuous surface of small wooden strips or metal mesh nailed to walls or partitions to hold plaster.

Latin cross A cross with one long and three short arms. Usually used to describe the ground plans of Roman Catholic and Protestant churches. See also the more general term CRUCIFORM.

leaded glass Panes of glass held in place by lead strips, or cames. The panes, clear or stained, may be of any shape.

lean-to roof See SHED ROOF.

lierne In a Gothic vault, a short ornamental rib connecting the major transverse ribs and the secondary tiercerons. Sometimes called a cross rib or tertiary rib.

lintel A horizontal structural member that supports the wall over an opening or spans between two adjacent piers or columns.

load-bearing Term applied to a wall, column, pier, or any vertical supporting member, constructed so that all loads are carried to the ground through the wall, column, or pier. See also the related terms BEARING WALL, CURTAIN WALL.

loggia 1 A porch or open-air room, particularly one set within the body of a building. **2** An arcaded or colonnaded structure, open on one or more sides, sometimes with an upper story. **3** An eighteenth- and nineteenth-century term for a porch or veranda.

mansard roof A hip roof with double pitch. The upper slope may approach flatness, while the lower slope has a very steep pitch, sometimes flaring in a concave curve (or swelling in a convex curve) as it comes to the eaves. This lower slope usually has windows, and the area under the roof often amounts to a full story. The name is a corruption of that of François Mansart (1598–1666), who designed roofs of this type, which was revived in Paris during the Second Empire period.

Mansard style, Mansardic See SECOND EMPIRE.

manufactured houses Houses that are built in a factory and mass produced. They are usually delivered in two long sections and assembled on site.

masonry Construction using stone, brick, block, or some other hard and durable material laid up in units and usually bonded by mortar.

massing The grouping or arrangement of the primary volumetric components of a building.

medieval Term applied to the Middle Ages in European civilization between the age of antiquity and the age of the Renaissance (i.e., mid-400s to mid-1400s in Italy; mid-400s to late 1500s in England). In architecture and the other visual arts, the medieval period included the end of the Early Christian period, then the Byzantine, the Romanesque, and the Gothic styles or periods.

Middle Ages See MEDIEVAL.

modern Ambiguous term, applied in various ways during the past century to the history of the visual arts and world history generally: **1** from the 1910s to the present (see also the more specific terms BAUHAUS, INTERNATIONAL STYLE); **2** from the 1860s, 1870s, 1880s, or 1890s to the present; **3** from the Enlightenment or the advent of Neoclassicism or the industrial revolution, c. 1750, to the present; **4** from the Renaissance in Italy, c. 1450, to the present.

Modern Gothic See EASTLAKE.

Moderne A term applied to a wide range of design work from the 1920s through the 1940s, in which aspects of traditionalism and modernism coexist and in which eclecticism (from a historical, exotic, or machine aesthetic) is inseparable from the urge for stylization. Sometimes called Art Moderne, Modernistic. See also the more specific terms ART DECO, PWA MODERNE, STREAMLINE MODERNE.

modillion One of a series of small, thin scroll brackets under the projecting crown molding of a classical cornice. It is found in the Corinthian and Composite orders. Distinguished from a console, which usually is larger and has a height greater than its projection from the wall.

molding A running surface composed of parallel and continuous sections of simple or compound curves and flat areas.

monitor An extensive shed-roofed feature on a roof, containing a band of windows or vents. It may be located along one of the roof slopes (a trapdoor monitor) or along the ridgeline (a clerestory monitor), and it usually runs the entire length of the roof. Distinguished from a skylight, which is a low-profile or flush-mounted feature in the plane of the roof.

mortar A mixture of cement or lime with water and a fine aggregate of sand used to secure bricks or stones in masonry construction.

mortise-and-tenon joint A timber framing joint that is made by one member having its end shaped into a projecting piece (tenon) that fits exactly into a hole (mortise) in the other member. Once joined, the pieces are held together by a peg that passes through the tenon.

mullion **1** A post or similar vertical member dividing a window into two or more units, or lights, each of which may be further subdivided (by muntins) into panes. **2** A post or similar vertical member dividing a wall opening into two or more contiguous windows.

National Register of Historic Places A branch of the National Park Service of the United States Department of the Interior, established by the National Historic Preservation Act of 1966, to maintain files of documentation on districts, sites, buildings, structures, and objects of national, state, or local significance. Properties listed on the National Register are afforded administrative—and, ultimately, judicial—review in instances where projects funded or assisted by federal agencies might have an impact on the historic property. Properties listed on the register may also be eligible for certain tax benefits.

nave **1** The entire body of a church between the entrance and the crossing. **2** The central space of a church, between the side aisles, extending from the entrance end to the crossing.

Neo-Colonial See COLONIAL REVIVAL.

Neo-Federal See FEDERAL REVIVAL.

Neo-Georgian See GEORGIAN REVIVAL.

Neo-Gothic Term applied to eclectic works or elements of those works that emulate forms in the visual arts of the Gothic style or period. The cultural movement that produced so many such works in the eighteenth, nineteenth, and twentieth centuries is called the Gothic Revival, though that term covers a wide range of work.

Neo-Tudor Term applied to eclectic works or elements of those works that emulate forms in the visual arts of the Tudor period. Sometimes called Elizabethan Manor style, English half-timber style, Jacobethan Revival, Tudor Revival.

New Brutalism See BRUTALISM.

New Formalism A style prevalent since the 1960s, characterized by symmetrical arrangements, rich materials (marble cladding, metal grillework), and stylized classical (even Gothic) detailing. Architects associated with this style include Philip Johnson (b. 1906), Edward Durell Stone (1902–1978), and Minoru Yamasaki (1912–1985).

newel post A post at the head or foot of a flight of stairs, to which the handrail is fastened. Newel posts occur in a variety of shapes, in profile and cross section, and are generally more substantial elements than the individual balusters that support the handrail.

niche A recess in a wall, usually designed to contain sculpture or an urn. A niche is often semicircular in plan and surmounted by a half dome or shell form. See also the related terms AEDICULE, TABERNACLE (definition **1**).

nogging Brickwork that fills the spaces between members of a timber frame wall or partition.

novelty siding Horizontal wood siding with curved recess along the upper edge.

ogee arch A pointed arch formed by a pair of opposing S-shaped curves.

order The most important constituents of classical architecture are the orders, first developed as a structural-aesthetic system by the ancient Greeks. An order has two major components. A column with its capital is the main vertical supporting member. The principal horizontal member is the entablature. The Greeks developed three different types of order, the Doric, Ionic, and Corinthian, each distinguishable by its own decorative system and proportions. All three were taken over and modified by the Romans, who added two orders of their own, the Tuscan, which is a simplified form of the Doric, and the Composite, which is made up of elements of both the Ionic and the Corinthian. The Romans often used the orders as a structural system in the same manner as the Greeks. Unlike the Greeks, however, they also applied them as decoration to the surfaces of walls that were supported by other means. Sometimes called classical orders. See also the related terms COLUMN, ENTABLATURE, GIANT ORDER, SUPERPOSITION (definition 1).

oriel A projecting polygonal or curved window unit of one or more stories, supported on brackets or corbels. Sometimes called an oriel window. Distinguished from a bay window, which rises from the foundation and has a rooted rather than a suspended appearance. However, a multistory projection in a tall building, whether cantilevered out or built from the foundation, is called a projecting bay or a unit of bay windows.

outbuilding A building subsidiary to and completely detached from another building. Distinguished from a dependency, which may be attached or detached.

overhang The projection of part of a structure beyond the portion below.

PWA Moderne A synthesis of the Moderne (i.e., Art Deco or Streamline Moderne) with an austere late type of Beaux-Arts Classicism, often associated with federal government buildings of the 1930s and 1940s during the Public Works Administration. See also the more general term MODERNE and the related terms ART DECO, BEAUX-ARTS CLASSICISM, STREAMLINE MODERNE.

Palladianism, Palladian Work influenced by the Italian Renaissance architect Andrea Palladio (1508–1580), particularly by means of his treatise, *I Quattro Libri dell'Architettura* (*The Four Books of Architecture,* originally published in 1570 and disseminated throughout Europe in numerous translations and editions until the mid-eighteenth century). The most significant flourishing of Palladianism was in England, from the 1710s to the 1760s, and in the British North American colonies, from the 1740s to the 1790s. Sometimes called Neo-Palladian, Palladian classical. See also the more specific term ANGLO-PALLADIANISM.

Palladian motif A three-part composition for a door or window, in which a round-headed opening is flanked by lower flat-headed openings and separated from them by columns, pilasters, or mullions. The flanking sections, and sometimes the entire unit, may be blind (i.e., not open).

Palladian window A window subdivided as in the Palladian motif.

parapet A low wall at the edge of a roof, balcony, or terrace, sometimes formed by the upward extension of the wall below.

parquet Inlaid wood flooring, usually set in simple geometric patterns.

pavilion 1 A central or corner unit that projects from a larger architectural mass and is usually accented by a special treatment of the wall or roof. **2** A detached or semidetached structure used for specialized activities, as at a hospital. **3** In a garden or fairground, a temporary structure or tent, usually ornamented.

pediment 1 In classical architecture, the low triangular gable end of the roof, framed by raking cornices along the inclined edges of the roof and by a horizontal cornice below. **2** In Renaissance and Baroque and later clasically derived architecture, the triangular or curvilinear culmination of a prominent part of a facade. **3** A similar but smaller-scale feature over a door or window. It may be triangular or curvilinear.

period house Term applied to suburban and country houses in which period revival styles are dominant.

period revival Term applied to eclectic works—particularly suburban and country houses—of the first three decades of the twentieth century, in which a particular historical or regional style is dominant. See also the more specific terms COLONIAL REVIVAL, DUTCH COLONIAL REVIVAL, GEORGIAN REVIVAL, NEO-TUDOR, SPANISH COLONIAL REVIVAL.

perspective drawing A pictorial drawing representing an object, building, or space, as if seen from a single vantage point. The illusion of three dimensions is created by using a system based on the optical laws of converging lines and vanishing points. See also the related terms AXONOMETRIC DRAWING, ISOMETRIC DRAWING.

picturesque An aesthetic category in architecture and landscape architecture in the late eighteenth and early nineteenth centuries. It is characterized by relationships among buildings and landscape features that evoke the qualities of landscape paintings, in which the eye is led past a variety of forms and spaces into the distance and the mind is led to contemplate a sense of age (by means of ruins, fallen trees, weathered rocks, and mossy surfaces on all of these). In actual settings, asymmetrical and eclectic buildings, indirect approaches, and contrasting clusters of plantings heighten the experience of the picturesque.

pier 1 A freestanding mass, supporting a concentrated load from an arch, a beam, a truss, or a girder. While generally rectilinear in plan, piers in buildings based upon medieval precedents are often curvilinear in plan. **2** An upright portion of a wall that performs a columnar function. The pier may be continuous with the plane of the wall, or it may be distinguished from the plane of the wall to give it a columnlike independence.

pier and spandrel A type of skeletal wall organization in which the vertical metal columns (and their square-cornered cladding) project in front of the plane of windows and their spandrel panels.

The spandrel panels may be exposed structural spanning members. More often they provide decorative covering for the structure.

pilaster **1** A flattened column, with or without fluting, that is attached to a wall. It is usually finished with the same capital and base as a freestanding column. **2** Any narrow, vertical strip attached to a wall. Distinguished from an engaged column, which has a convex curvature.

pitched roof See GABLE ROOF.

plan A drawing (in orthographic projection) representing all or part of an object, building, or space, as if viewed from directly above. A floor plan is a drawing of a horizontal cut through a building, usually at the level of the windows, showing the configuration of walls and openings. Other types of plans may illustrate ceilings, roofs, structural elements, and mechanical systems.

plank construction General term. See instead the more specific terms HORIZONTAL PLANK FRAME CONSTRUCTION, VERTICAL PLANK CONSTRUCTION.

plate **1** In timber frame construction, the topmost horizontal structural member of a wall, to which the roof rafters are fastened. **2** In platform and balloon frame construction, the horizontal members to which the tops and bottoms of studs are nailed. The bottom plate is sometimes called the sill plate or sole plate.

polychromy, polychromatic, polychrome A many-colored treatment, especially the combination of materials in various colors or the application of surface color, to articulate wall and roof planes and to highlight structure.

popular A term applied to vernacular architecture influenced by such publications as books of the orders, builders' guides, style books, pattern books, mail-order catalogs, architectural periodicals, and household magazines. Architecture in the popular tradition may be built according to commercially available plans or from widely distributed components; or it may be built by local practitioners (architects, builders, contractors) emulating buildings that are represented in publications. The distinction between popular architecture and high-style architecture by lesser-known architects depends on one's point of view with regard to the division between vernacular and high-style. See also the more general term VERNACULAR and the related term FOLK.

porch A structure attached to a building to shelter an entrance or to serve as a semienclosed sitting, working, or sleeping space. Distinguished from a portico, which is either a pedimented feature at least one story in height supported by classical columns or a more extensive colonnaded feature.

porte-cochère A porch projecting over a driveway and providing shelter to people leaving a vehicle and entering a building or vice versa. Also called a carriage porch.

portico **1** A porch at least one story in height consisting of a low-pitched roof supported on classical columns and finished in front with an entablature and pediment. **2** An extensive porch supported by a colonnade.

post A vertical supporting element, either square or circular in plan. Posts are the integral vertical members of a frame or truss, whether of wood or metal. Posts may also carry fences or gates, or may serve as freestanding markers (e.g., mileposts).

post-and-beam construction A structural system in which the main support is provided by vertical members (posts) carrying horizontal members (beams or lintels). Sometimes called post-and-girt construction, post and lintel construction, trabeation, trabeated construction.

Postmodernism, Postmodern A term applied to work that involves a reaction against the ideas and works of various twentieth-century modern movements, particularly the Bauhaus and the International style. Postmodern work makes use of historicism, yet the traditional elements are often merely applied to buildings that, in every other respect, are products of modern movement design. The term is also applied to works that are attempting to demonstrate an extension of the principles of various modern movements.

pressed metal Thin sheets of metal (usually galvanized or tin-plated iron) stamped into patterned panels for covering ceilings and exterior and interior walls or into molding profiles and other details for assembly into exterior and interior cornices. Loosely called pressed tin or stamped metal. Prevalent from the 1870s through the 1920s.

program The list of functional, spatial, and other requirements that guides an architect in developing a design.

proscenium In a recessed stage, the area between the orchestra and the curtain.

proscenium arch In a recessed stage, the enframement of the opening.

provincialism, provincial Term applied to work in an isolated area (such as a province of a cosmopolitan center or a colony of a mother country), where traditional practices persist, with some awareness of what is being done in the cosmopolitan center or the homeland.

purlin In roof construction, a structural member laid across the principal rafters and parallel to the wall plate and the ridge beam. The light common rafters to which the roofing surface is attached are fastened across the purlins. See also the related term RAFTER.

pylon **1** Originally, the gateway facade of an Egyptian temple complex, consisting of a truncated broad pyramidal form with battered (inclined) wall surfaces on all four sides, or two truncated pyramidal towers flanking an entrance portal. **2** Any towerlike structure from which bridge cables or utility lines are suspended.

quatrefoil A type of Gothic tracery having four parts (lobes or foils) separated by pointed elements (cusps).

Queen Anne Ambiguous but widely used term. **1**

In architecture, the Queen Anne style is an eclectic style of the 1860s through 1910s in England and the United States, characterized by the incorporation of forms from postmedieval vernacular architecture and the architecture of the Georgian period. Sometimes called Queen Anne Revival. See also the more specific term SHINGLE STYLE and the related terms EASTLAKE, STICK STYLE. **2** In architecture, the original Queen Anne period extends from the late seventeenth into the early eighteenth century. **3** In the decorative arts, the Queen Anne style and period properly refer to work of the early eighteenth century during the reign of Queen Anne (1702–1714, i.e., after William and Mary and before Georgian). **4** In the decorative arts, eclectic work of the 1860s to 1880s is properly referred to as Queen Anne Revival.

quoin One of the bricks or stones laid in alternating directions, which bond and form the exterior corner of a building. Sometimes simulated in wood or stucco.

rafter One of the inclined structural members of a roof. Principal rafters are primary supporting elements spanning between the walls and the apex of the roof and carrying the longitudinal purlins. Common rafters are secondary supporting elements fastened onto purlins to carry the roof surfacing. See also the related term PURLIN.

recessed column A fully round column set into a nichelike space only slightly larger than the column. Distinguished from an engaged column, which appears to be built into the wall.

reentrant angle An acute angle created by the juncture of two planes, such as walls.

regionalism 1 The sum of cultural characteristics (including material culture, language) that define a geographic region, usually extending beyond a single state or province, and coinciding with one or more large physiographic areas. **2** The conscious use, within a region, of forms and materials identified with that region, creating an architecture that is in keeping with the historical architecture of the region, and even a distinctive new regional style.

register A horizontal zone of a wall, altarpiece, or other vertical feature. Usually synonymous with story, but more inclusive, allowing for the description of zones with no corresponding interior spaces.

Renaissance Revival 1 In architecture, an ambiguous term, applied to (a) Italianate work of the 1840s through 1880s and (b) Beaux-Arts Classical work of the 1880s through 1920s. **2** In the decorative arts, an eclectic furniture style incorporating a variety of Renaissance, Baroque, and Neo-Grec architectural motifs and utilizing wood marquetry, incised lines (often gilded), and ormolu and porcelain ornaments. Sometimes called Neo-Renaissance.

rendering Any drawing, whether orthographic (plan, elevation, section) or pictorial (perspective), in which shades and shadows are represented.

reredos A screen or wall at the back of an altar, usually with architectural and figural decoration.

revival, revivalism A type of historicism prevalent since the eighteenth century, involving the adaptation of historical forms to contemporary functions. Distinguished from a more pervasive historicism by an ideological conviction that sought to rationalize the choice of a historical style according to the values of the historical period that produced it. (The Gothic Revival, for instance, was associated with the Christianity of the Middle Ages.) Revival works, therefore, tend to invoke a single historical style. More hybrid works are manifestations of a less dogmatic historicism or eclecticism. See also the more general terms HISTORICISM, ECLECTICISM.

Richardsonian Term applied to any work showing the influence of the American architect Henry Hobson Richardson (1838–1886). See the note under the more limiting term RICHARDSONIAN ROMANESQUE.

Richardsonian Romanesque Term applied to Neo-Romanesque work showing the influence of the American architect Henry Hobson Richardson (1838–1886). While many of Richardson's works make eclectic use of round arches and Romanesque details, many of his works show a creative eclecticism that transcends any particular historical style. The term Richardsonian, therefore, is a more inclusive term for the work of his followers than Richardsonian Romanesque—a term that continues to be widely used. Sometimes called Richardson Romanesque, Richardsonian Romanesque Revival.

ridgepole The horizontal beam or board at the apex of a roof, to which the upper ends of the rafters are fastened. Sometimes called a ridge beam, ridgeboard, ridge piece.

rock-faced Term applied to the rough, unfinished face of a stone used in building. Sometimes called quarry-faced.

rosette A circular floral ornament similar to an open rose.

rotunda 1 A circular hall in a large building, especially an area beneath a dome or cupola. **2** A building round both inside and outside, usually domed.

rubble masonry A type of masonry utilizing uncut or roughly shaped stone, such as fieldstone or boulders.

Rustic Decoration by means of rough woodwork, usually with large logs, sometimes with the bark left in place, and of heavy masonry with fieldstones or rough-cut stone. Typical of park lodges.

rustication, rusticated Masonry in which the joints are emphasized by narrow recessed channels or grooves outlining each block. Sometimes simulated in wood or stucco.

sacristy A room in a church where liturgical vessels and vestments are kept.

safety arch See RELIEVING ARCH.

sanctuary 1 The part of a church that contains the principal altar. Usually the innermost space within the chancel arm of the church, situated to the east of the choir. **2** Loosely used to mean a place of worship, a sacred place.

sash Any framework of a window. It may be movable or fixed. It may slide in a vertical plane (as in a double-hung window) or may be pivoted (as in a casement window).

sash bar See MUNTIN.

section A drawing (in orthographic projection) representing a vertical cut through an object, building, or space. An architectural section shows interior relationships of space and structure, and may also include mechanical systems. Sometimes called a cross section.

segmental arch An arch formed on a segmental curve. Its center lies below the springing line.

segmental curve A curve that is a segment (i.e., less than half the circumference) of a circle or an ellipse. The base line of the curve is a chord measuring less than the diameter of the larger circle from which the segment is taken.

segmental pediment A pediment whose top is a segmental curve.

segmental vault A vault whose cross section is a segmental curve. A dome built on segmental curves is called a saucer dome.

setback **1** In architecture, particularly in the design of tall buildings, a series of upper stories that are stepped back to allow more sunlight to reach the streets. **2** In planning, the amount of space between the lot line and the perimeter of a building.

shaft The tall part of a column between the base and the capital.

shed roof A roof having only one sloping plane. Sometimes called a lean-to roof.

Shingle style A term applied primarily to American domestic architecture of the 1870s through the 1890s, in which broad expanses of wood shingles dominate the exterior roof and wall planes. Rooms open widely into one another and to the outdoors, and the ample living hall or stair hall is often the dominant feature of the interior. The term was coined in the 1940s by Vincent Scully for a series of seaside and suburban houses of the northeastern United States. The Shingle style is a version of the Anglo-American Queen Anne style. See also the related terms COLONIAL REVIVAL, STICK STYLE.

side gabled Term applied to a building whose gable ends face the sides of a lot. Distinguished from front gabled.

side light A framed area of fixed glass alongside a door or window. See also the related term FAN-LIGHT.

sill course In masonry, a stringcourse set at windowsill level, usually differentiated from the wall by its greater projection, its finish, or its thickness. Not applicable to frame construction.

sill plate See PLATE (definition 2).

skeleton construction, skeleton frame A system of construction in which all loads are carried to the ground through a rigid framework of iron, steel, or reinforced concrete. The exterior walls are curtain walls (i.e., not load-bearing).

skylight A window in a roof, specifically one that is flush with the roof plane or only slightly protruding. Distinguished from a cupola (definition **2**), which is a major centralized feature at the summit of a roof. Distinguished from a monitor, which is an extensive roof feature containing a band of windows or vents.

soffit The exposed underside of any overhead component, such as an arch, beam, cornice, or lintel. See also the related term INTRADOS.

sole plate See PLATE (definition 2).

space frame A series of trusses placed side by side and joined to one another by triangulated rods, tubes, or beams, so that the individual planar trusses are united into a three-dimensional structural framework. Often used in roof structures requiring long spans.

spandrel **1** The quasi-triangular space between two adjoining arches and a line connecting their crowns, or between an arch and the columns and entablature that frame it. **2** In skeletal construction, the wall area between the top of a window and the sill of the window in the story above. Sometimes called a spandrel panel.

spire A slender pointed element surmounting a building. A tall, attenuated pyramidal form with any number of thin triangular faces that are unbroken or articulated only with crockets, pinnacles, or small dormers. Distinguished from a steeple, which is divided into stages and which may be topped with a spire.

splay The slanting surface formed by cutting off a right-angle corner at an oblique angle to one face. A reveal at an oblique angle to the exterior face of the wall.

stair A series of steps, or flights of steps connected by landings, which connects two or more levels or floors.

staircase The ensemble of a stair and its enclosing walls. Sometimes called a stairway.

stair tower A projecting tower or other building block that contains a stair.

stamped metal See PRESSED METAL.

Steamboat Gothic See CARPENTER'S GOTHIC.

steeple **1** A tall structure rising from a tower, consisting of a series of superimposed stages diminishing in plan, and usually topped by a spire or small cupola. Distinguished from a spire, which is not divided into stages. **2** Less commonly used to mean the whole of the tower, from the ground to the top of the spire or cupola.

stepped gable A gable in which the wall rises in a series of steps above the planes of the roof.

stereotomy The science of cutting three-dimensional shapes from stone, such as the units that make up a carefully fitted masonry vault.

Stick style A term applied primarily to American domestic architecture of the 1850s through the 1870s, in which exterior wall planes are subdivided into bays and stories outlined by narrow boards called "stickwork." The term was coined by Vincent Scully in the 1940s for a series of houses with clearly articulated wall panels and sticklike porch supports and eaves brackets. Sources include the English and German picturesque traditions, as well as the French rationalist tradition. See also the related terms QUEEN ANNE, SHINGLE STYLE.

story (plural: stories). The space in a building between floor levels. British spelling is storey, storeys. Sometimes called a register, a more inclusive term applied to horizontal on a vertical plane zones that do not correspond to actual floor levels.

string In a stair, an inclined board that supports the ends of the steps. Sometimes called a stringer.

stringcourse In masonry, a horizontal band, generally narrower than other courses, extending across the facade of a building and in some instances encircling such features as pillars or columns. It may be flush or projecting; of identical or contrasting material; flat, molded, or richly carved. Not applicable to frame construction. Sometimes called a band course or belt course. More elaborate horizontal bands in masonry or frame construction are generally called band moldings.

strut A column, post, or pole that is set in a diagonal position and thus serves as a stiffener by triangulation. Distinguished from a brace, which is usually a shorter bracketlike member.

stucco 1 An exterior plaster finish, usually textured, composed of portland cement, lime, and sand, which are mixed with water. **2** A fine plaster used for decorative work or moldings.

stud One of the vertical supporting elements in a wall, especially in balloon and platform frame construction. Studs are relatively lightweight members (usually two-by-fours).

sunburst light See FANLIGHT.

supercapital See IMPOST BLOCK.

supercolumniation See SUPERPOSITION (definition 1).

superimposition, superimposed See SUPERPOSITION.

superposition, superposed 1 The use of an ensemble of the classical orders, one above the other, as the major elements articulating a facade. When this is done, the Doric, considered the simplest order, is used on or near the ground story. The Ionic, considered more complex, comes next; and the Corinthian, considered the most complex, is used at the top. Sometimes the Tuscan order or rusticated masonry may be used for the ground story beneath the Doric order, and the Composite order may be used above the Corinthian order. Sometimes called supercolumniation, superimposition. See also the related term ORDER. **2** Less commonly, any vertical relationship of architectural elements (e.g., windows, piers, colonnettes) in any style or period.

superstructure A structure raised upon another structure, as a building upon a foundation, basement, or substructure.

Supervising Architect The Supervising Architect of the United States Treasury Department, whose office was responsible for the design and construction of all major federal government buildings (such as courthouses, customhouses, and post offices) from the 1850s through the 1930s. The Office of the Supervising Architect was formally established by Congress in 1864 and lasted until 1939, when its functions were absorbed into the Public Buildings Administration (and in 1949, into the General Services Administration).

supporting wall See BEARING WALL.

surround An encircling border or decorative frame around a door or window. Distinguished from architrave (definition **2**), a term usually applied to the frame around an opening when considered as a series of relatively flat face moldings.

suspended ceiling A ceiling suspended from rodlike hangers below the level of the floor above. The interval between the floor slab above and the suspended ceiling often serves as a space for ducts, utilities, and air circulation. Sometimes called a hung ceiling.

swag A motif representing a suspended fold of drapery hanging in a catenary curve from two points. Distinguished from a festoon, which is a motif representing entwined leaves, flowers, or fruits, hung in a similar curve. See also the more general term GARLAND.

tabernacle 1 A niche or recess, usually on an interior wall, framed by columns or pilasters and topped by an entablature and pediment. Distinguished from an aedicule, which more often occurs on an exterior wall. See also the related term NICHE. **2** In the Jewish religion, a portable sanctuary. **3** In Protestant denominations, a large auditorium church.

terracotta A hard ceramic material used for **1** fireproofing, especially as a fitted cladding around metal skeletal construction; or **2** an exterior or interior wall cladding, which is often glazed and multicolored.

tertiary rib See LIERNE.

three-hinged arch An arch in two major segments anchored with cylindrical "hinge" pins at either end and at the crown. Movement within the arch, caused by temperature changes, the torsion of wind movements, or other forces, can be absorbed by the movement of the arch around the pins, thereby avoiding stresses that would occur in the structural frame if the arches were fixed.

tie beam A horizontal tension member that ties together the opposing angular members of a truss and prevents them from spreading.

tier A group of stories or any zone of architectural

tie rod A metal rod that spans the distance between two structural members and, by its tensile strength, restrains them against tendencies to collapse outward.

timber-frame construction, timber framing A type of wood frame construction in which heavy timber posts and beams (six-by-sixes and larger) are fastened using mortise and tenon joints. Sometimes called heavy timber construction. Distinguished from light frame construction, in which relatively light structural members (two-by-fours to two-by-tens) are fastened with nails.

tracery Decoration within an arch or other opening, made up of narrow curvilinear bands or more elaborately molded strips. In Gothic architecture, the curved interlocking stone bars that contain the leaded stained glass.

transept The lateral arm of a cross-shaped church, usually between the nave (the area for the congregation) and the chancel (the area for the altar, clergy, and choir).

transom 1 A narrow horizontal window unit, either fixed or movable, over a door. Sometimes called a transom light. See also the more specific term FANLIGHT. 2 A horizontal bar, as distinguished from a vertical mullion, especially one crossing a door or window opening near the top.

trellis Any open latticework made of strips of wood or metal crossing one another, usually supporting climbing plants. Distinguished from an arbor, which is generally a more substantial yet compact three-dimensional structure, and from a pergola, which is a more extensive colonnaded structure.

truss A rigid triangular framework made up of beams, posts, braces, struts, and ties and used for the spanning of large spaces. The major horizontal or inclined members are called chords. The connecting vertical and diagonal elements are called the web members.

Tudor period A term for a period in English history coinciding with the rule of monarchs of the house of Tudor (1485–1603). Tudor period architecture is Late Gothic, with only hints of the Renaissance. See also the more specific term ELIZABETHAN PERIOD for the end of this period, and the related term JACOBEAN PERIOD for the succeeding period.

Tudor Revival See NEO-TUDOR.

turret A small towerlike structure, often circular in plan, built against the side or at an exterior or interior corner of a building.

vault An arched roof or ceiling, usually constructed in brick or stone, but also in tile, metal or concrete. A nonstructural plaster ceiling that simulates a masonry vault.

vernacular Not a style in itself, but a descriptive term, applicable primarily to architecture, covering the vast range of ordinary buildings that are produced outside the high-style tradition of well-known architects. The vernacular tradition includes the folk tradition of regional and ethnic buildings whose forms (plan and massing) remain relatively constant through the years, in spite of stylistic embellishments. The term vernacular architecture is often used as if it meant only folk architecture. However, the vernacular tradition in architecture also includes the popular tradition of buildings whose design was influenced by such publications as books of the orders, builders' guides, style books, pattern books, mail-order catalogs, architectural periodicals, and household magazines. Usually contrasted with high style. See also the more specific terms FOLK, POPULAR.

vestibule A small entry hall between the outer door and the main hallway of a building.

Victorian period A term for a period in British, British colonial, and Anglo-American history, and not, in architecture or the other visual arts, a sufficiently specific style term. The Victorian period extended across eight decades, from the coronation of Queen Victoria in 1837 to her death in 1901. See instead EASTLAKE, GOTHIC REVIVAL, GREEK REVIVAL, QUEEN ANNE, SHINGLE STYLE, STICK STYLE, and other specific style terms.

voussoir A wedge-shaped stone or brick used in the construction of an arch. Its tapering sides coincide with radii of the arch.

wainscot A decorative or protective facing, usually of wood paneling, applied to the lower portion of an interior partition or wall. Distinguished from a dado, which is the zone at the base of a wall, regardless of the material used to cover it. Wainscot properly connotes woodwork. Sometimes called wainscoting.

wanigan Small, wood-framed dwelling on sledlike runners, or skids, for easy transport.

water table 1 In masonry, a course of molded bricks or stones set forward several inches near the base of a wall and serving as the cap of the basement courses. 2 In frame construction, a ledge or projecting molding just above the foundation to protect it from rainwater. 3 In masonry or frame construction, any horizontal exterior ledge on a wall, pier, or buttress. Often sloped and provided with a drip molding to prevent water from running down the face of the wall below.

weatherboard See CLAPBOARD.

weathering The inclination given to the upper surface of any element so that it will shed water.

wrought iron Iron shaped by a hammering process, to improve the tensile properties of the metal. Distinguished from cast iron, a brittle material, which is formed in molds.

Yukon stove An oil drum laid horizontally and fitted with legs, stovepipe, and a patented door.

Illustration Credits

All photographs by Jet Lowe, Historic American Buildings Survey/Historic American Engineering Record (HABS/HAER), National Park Service, taken between 1981 and 1991, with the following exceptions:

INTRODUCTION

John Murdoch, "Ethnological Results of the Point Barrow Expedition," *Ninth Annual Report of the Bureau of Ethnology to the Smithsonian Institution, 1887–88* (Washington, D.C.: Government Printing Office, 1892): **pp. 7, 9, 10.** Alaska State Library: **pp. 8, 11,** Clarence Leroy Andrews Collection, PCA 45–38 and PCA 45–76; **pp. 22–23,** Winter and Pond Collection, PCA 87–1502; **p. 46,** A Summer on the *Thetis*, PCA 27–7; **p. 48,** Gray and Hereford, PCA 185–11; **p. 63,** Alaska Railroad, PCA 108–137; **p. 63,** Alaska Railroad, PCA 108–137; **p. 70,** Winter and Pond, PCA 87–148. Library of Congress, Prints and Photographs Division: **p. 10,** LC-USZ62–60824; **p. 11,** LC-USZ62–62721; **p. 15,** LC-USZ62–33027; **p. 18,** LC-USZ62–56183; **p. 18,** LC-USZ62–62790. Anchorage Museum of History and Art: **pp. 15, 35, 54.** Louis and Florence Shotridge, "Chilkat Houses," *University of Pennsylvania Museum Journal* 4 (1913): **pp. 17, 18.** University of Alaska Fairbanks, Alaska and Polar Regions Dept., Archives: **p. 21,** Alaska Excursion Album, 79–142–30; **p. 21,** Travel Album, 85–174–28; **p. 35,** Rare Book Collection, CO024; **p. 36,** Rare Book Collection, CO023; **p. 58,** Pope Albums, 66–15, 635; **pp. 59, 61,** Vertical File-Holy Cross, 83–209–30N, 83–209–29; **p. 67,** Vide Bartlett, 77–89–31; **p. 68,** Lanier McKee, 88–231–121N. U.S. Forest Service: **p. 30.** Library of Congress, Maps and Geographic Division: **pp. 36, 38,** 107159, 107159. William H. Dall, *Alaska and Its Resources* (Boston: Lee and Shepherd, 1870): **p. 46.** Library of Congress, Manuscript Division, Alaskan Russian Church Archives: **p. 46.** Bancroft Library: **p. 42,** 1971.055:473–STER. University of Alaska Anchorage, Consortium Library, Archives and Manuscripts Department: **pp. 54, 72.** *Seal and Salmon Fisheries and General Resources of Alaska* (Washington: GPO, 1898), 3: opp. p. 568: **p. 55.** Library of Congress, Prints and Photographs Division, Historic American Engineering Record Collection: **p. 61.**

SOUTH-CENTRAL REGION

SC019 Anchorage Museum of History and Art, Alison K. Hoagland; **SC035.3** Detail of Loxtave corner construction, delineated by Alfonso A. Narvaez, 1985, HABS; **SC053** Saint Peter's Episcopal Church, Walter Smalling, Jr., 1982, HABS; **SC054** Van Gilder Hotel, Walter Smalling, Jr., 1982, HABS; **SC063** Holy Assumption Russian Orthodox Church (both drawings), delineated by K. Martin, 1986, HABS; **SC064** Saint Nicholas Russian Orthodox Chapel (both drawings), delineated by Randall Skeirik, 1986, HABS; **SC065** Russian Orthodox Rectory (both drawings), delineated by K. Martin, 1986, HABS; **SC081** Alaska Railroad Depot, courtesy Alaska State Library, Alaska Railroad Collection PCA 108–112; **SC099** Leon Smith Igloo, Alison K. Hoagland; **SC119.1** Concentration Mill/Leaching Plant, delineated by David C. Anderson and Nanon Adair Anderson, 1985, HAER; **SC119.5** Bunkhouse, delineated by David C. Anderson and Nanon Adair Anderson, 1985, HAER

SOUTHEAST REGION

SE016 Alaska Governer's Mansion (historic view) courtesy Alaska State Library, Winter and Pond, PCA 87–892; **SE017** Alaska State Capitol, courtesy Alaska State Library, Winter and Pond, PCA 87–902; **SE040** Saint Michael the Archangel Russian Orthodox Church, delineated by Roger E. Pelissier, 1961, HABS; **SE041** Russian Bishop's House, floor plan, 1843–1844 drawings courtesy Sitka National Historical Park; **SE044** Saint Peter's-by-the-Sea Episcopal Church, courtesy Alaska State Library, Winter and Pond, PCA 87–1532; **SE064** Chief Son-i-hat House, U.S. Forest Service photo, National Archives; **SE073** Totem Bight Community House, photographer and date unknown, HABS; **SE075–SE079** Metlakatla, courtesy University of Alaska, Fairbanks, Alaska and Polar Regions Department Archives, Historical Photograph, 804–7N.

INTERIOR

IN008.2 Murphy Hall (Building 1045), James Stuhler, 1986, HABS; **IN008.4** Hangar No. 1 (Building 1557), James Stuhler, 1986, HABS; **IN029.2** Pearson Cabin (both drawings), delineated by Dave Snow, 1984, HABS; **IN031** (Episcoal) Church of our Saviour, photograph c. 1912–1917, courtesy Alaska State Library, P.C. Pittman 78–6; **IN038** Northern Commercial Company Store, delineated by Kate Solovjova and James E. Creech, 1991, HABS; **IN042** Wickersham House (historic view), courtesy Alaska State Library, Wickersham State Historic Site 277–42; **IN046** Ed Biederman Fish Camp (both drawings), delineated by Randall Skeirik, 1985, HABS; **IN048** George McGregor Cabin, delineated by Randall Skeirik, 1985, HABS; **IN049** Slaven Roadhouse, delineated by David C. Anderson, 1984, and Randall Skeirik, 1986, HABS; **IN060** Vincent Knorr Cabin, delineated by James Creech, 1985, HABS

WESTERN REGION

WE003 John Iyapana Kugeri, delineated by Timothy M. Sczawinski, 1978; **WE010.1** Saint Joseph's Roman

Catholic Church, delineated by L. Kinn, 1985, HABS; **WE014.2** Our Lady of Lourdes Church, Alison K. Hoagland

SOUTHWESTERN REGION

SW001 Russian-American Company Magazin (Baranof Museum, Erskine House), delineated by James Flath-mann, 1966, HABS; **SW014** Church of the Holy Ascension (plan), delineated by Andrew Feinberg, 1989, and Kate Solovjova, 1990, HABS; **SW014** Church of the Holy Ascension (section), delineated by Raymond Todd, 1989, and Kate Solovjova, 1990, HABS; **SW018** Saint Nicholas Russian Orthodox Church, delineated by Raymond Todd, 1989, Lidiya Velichko, 1989, and Kate Solvjova, 1990, HABS

Index

Pages with illustrations are indicated in bold.

331